A PAI

THE NEW WESSEX EDITION

General Editor P. N. Furbank

Desperate Remedies
Introduction by C. J. P. Beatty

Far from the Madding Crowd
Introduction by John Bayley

The Hand of Ethelberta
Introduction by Robert Gittings

Jude the Obscure
Introduction by Terry Eagleton

A Laodicean
Introduction by Barbara Hardy

The Mayor of Casterbridge
Introduction by Ian Gregor

A Pair of Blue Eyes
Introduction by Ronald Blythe

The Return of the Native
Introduction by Derwent May

Tess of the d'Urbervilles
Introduction by P. N. Furbank

The Trumpet-Major
Introduction by Barbara Hardy

Two on a Tower
Introduction by F. B. Pinion

Under the Greenwood Tree
Introduction by Geoffrey Grigson

The Well-Beloved
Introduction by J. Hillis Miller

The Woodlanders
Introduction by David Lodge

THE NEW WESSEX EDITION

A Pair of Blue Eyes

THOMAS HARDY

INTRODUCTION BY

Ronald Blythe

'A violet in the youth of primy nature,
Forward, not permanent, sweet, not lasting,
The perfume and suppliance of a minute;
No more.'

ISBN: 0 333 17758 4

First edition published elsewhere 1873
The New Wessex Edition first published 1975 by
MACMILLAN LONDON LIMITED
London and Basingstoke
Associated companies in Auckland, Dallas, Delhi, Dublin, Hong Kong, Johannesburg, Lagos, Manzini, Melbourne, Nairobi, New York, Singapore, Tokyo, Washington and Zaria
Reprinted 1981 (4th impression)

CO-ORDINATING EDITORS
Caroline Hobhouse
Edward Leeson

Published in the United States by
ST MARTIN'S PRESS INC.
175 Fifth Avenue, New York, N.Y. 10010
Library of Congress catalog card no. 7781875
ISBN: 0312 59466 6

Filmset in Photon Times 10 on 11 pt and printed in Great Britain by
RICHARD CLAY (THE CHAUCER PRESS) LTD
Bungay, Suffolk

Contents

BIOGRAPHY 7
ACKNOWLEDGEMENTS 11
INTRODUCTION BY RONALD BLYTHE 13
MAP OF HARDY'S WESSEX 34
PREFACE BY THOMAS HARDY 35
THE PERSONS 37

A PAIR OF BLUE EYES 39

NOTES 405
NOTE ON THE TEXT 419
HARDY'S GENERAL PREFACE TO THE WESSEX EDITION OF 1912 423
GLOSSARY OF PLACE-NAMES 429

Biography

1840 Hardy born at Higher Bockhampton, near Dorchester. His father and grandfather were master-stonemasons, also keen performers in the band or 'quire' of the local parish church.

1848 Attended school established by his local patroness Julia Augusta Martin. About this time his mother gave him Dryden's *Virgil*, *Rasselas* and *Paul and Virginia*.

1849 Transferred to school in Dorchester. Played fiddle at local weddings and dances.

1856–61 Articled to Dorchester architect John Hicks. Studied Latin and Greek from five to eight in the morning. Began writing verse. Was introduced to modern thought by his friend Horace Moule, son of the Vicar of Fordington.

1862–7 In London, working for the architect Arthur Blomfield. Read widely; studied paintings in National Gallery; became an agnostic.

1867–70 Returned to Dorset for health reasons and was employed by Hicks, and his successor Crickmay, on church restoration.

1868 Completed draft of first novel, 'The Poor Man and the Lady' (later destroyed).

1870 Sent by Crickmay to St Juliot in Cornwall and met future wife Emma Lavinia Gifford. Writing *Desperate Remedies*, his first published novel.

1873 Invited by Leslie Stephen to contribute serial (*Far from the Madding Crowd*) to *Cornhill*.

1874 Married and took rooms in Surbiton.

1876–8 Living at Sturminster Newton; writing *The Return of the Native*.

1878–81 Living in London. Was becoming well known in literary circles. Had serious illness while writing *A Laodicean*.

1881 Took house at Wimborne Minster.

1883 Went to live in Dorchester.

1885 Moved into the house, Max Gate, in Dorchester, which he had built for himself. He and his wife continued to make long annual visits to London.

1888–91 Writing many short stories. Publication of *Tess of the d'Urbervilles* in 1891 created furore.

1892 His father died.

1892–4 Worsening relations with his wife, the trouble being exacerbated by the writing of *Jude the Obscure*. In 1893 they visited Dublin and met Mrs Henniker, with whom he collaborated on a short story and perhaps fell in love.

1895–6	Publication of *Jude* causes scandal. He resolved to give up novel-writing.
1897–8	Writing and revising poems for his first collection, *Wessex Poems.*
1902	Began *The Dynasts.*
1904	His mother died.
1910	Received the Order of Merit.
1912	Making final revision of the Wessex novels. His wife died in November.
1913	In March made penitential pilgrimage to St Juliot and later to his wife's birthplace, Plymouth. Wrote flood of poems 'in expiation'.
1914	Married Florence Dugdale. At outbreak of war joined group of writers pledged to write for the Allied Cause.
1914–28	Wrote and revised the material for several more collections of verse.
1928	Died. His ashes were buried in Westminster Abbey and his heart in his first wife's grave in Stinsford churchyard.

Hardy's Major Works with year of book publication

1871 Desperate Remedies
1872 Under the Greenwood Tree
1873 A Pair of Blue Eyes
1874 Far from the Madding Crowd
1876 The Hand of Ethelberta
1878 The Return of the Native
1880 The Trumpet-Major
1881 A Laodicean
1882 Two on a Tower
1886 The Mayor of Casterbridge
1887 The Woodlanders
1888 Wessex Tales
1891 A Group of Noble Dames
1891 Tess of the d'Urbervilles
1894 Life's Little Ironies
1896 [1895] Jude the Obscure
1897 The Well-Beloved
1898 Wessex Poems
1902 Poems of the Past and the Present
1903 The Dynasts, pt 1
1905 The Dynasts, pt 2
1908 The Dynasts, pt 3
1909 Time's Laughingstocks
1913 A Changed Man and Other Tales
1914 Satires of Circumstance
1917 Moments of Vision
1922 Late Lyrics and Earlier
1923 The Famous Tragedy of the Queen of Cornwall
1925 Human Shows
1928 Winter Words
1952 Our Exploits at West Poley

Acknowledgements

THE General Editor thanks the following for their kind assistance in answering queries: the Librarian of the English Folk Dance and Song Society; Mr John S. Creasey of the Museum of English Rural Life; Anthony W. Shipps, Librarian for English, Indiana University; and the Editor of *Notes and Queries*. He would also like to express a general indebtedness to R. L. Purdy's *Thomas Hardy: a bibliographical study* (Oxford University Press, 1954; reissued 1968); F. B. Pinion's *A Hardy Companion* (Macmillan, 1968); and Denys Kay-Robinson's *Hardy's Wessex Re-appraised* (David & Charles, 1972).

P. N. FURBANK

Introduction

ON Monday, 7 March 1870 Thomas Hardy, who was then staying with his parents at Bockhampton, rose very early in the morning and set out while it was still starlight for Cornwall. It was to be the most significant journey he was ever to make. He was twenty-nine. A few days before he had finished his second novel *Desperate Remedies* and sent it off to Alexander Macmillan, who was to reject it. His first novel, 'The Poor Man and the Lady', also turned down, lay in a drawer. Apart from these creations his writings to date consisted of poems which would not be published until many years later and a light-hearted essay in *Chambers's Journal* entitled 'How I Built Myself a House'. Yet in spite of the tenuous nature of such a claim at such a time, and in spite of a common sense which resigned him to architecture as a livelihood, he had inwardly moved to a position which committed him to literature. Thus it was the manuscript of a poem, and not the plan for restoring the parish church, which was observed jutting from his pocket when he arrived at St Juliot Rectory, Boscastle, between six and seven that evening.

A woman of his own age dressed in brown welcomed him, and from that moment there proceeded emotions, events and imaginings which were to culminate in one of the major sequences of love poetry in the English language, and in *A Pair of Blue Eyes*, the first novel by Hardy to carry his name. It was a book whose autobiographical element was to provide much intrigue and speculation, and was greater than he cared to admit. Unlike the magnificent love-remembered poems of 1912, the transmuting forces of time are absent in this story. It was written while the experiences and thoughts which suggested it were happening to him in the most intimate personal sense. His method of artistically coping with his own courtship, his spiritual universe from which a benign creator had been deposed and the invasion of rural insularity by disturbing new elements belonged more to the sphere of the poet than to that of the novelist, and his early readers were swift to see it. Coventry Patmore, reading the newly published *A Pair of Blue Eyes*, 'regretted at almost every page that such unequalled beauty and power should not have assured themselves the immortality which would have been impressed upon them by the form of verse', and Tennyson was enthralled by its poetic conception and, later, confessed to Hardy that he liked it the best of all his novels.

In 1877 Hardy wrote in his notebook, 'The ultimate aim of the poet should be to touch our hearts by showing his own,' and this final personal intention pervades the sad story of Elfride. It is a fragile work but not a slight one. In many ways it is surprisingly advanced, for, although all its characters announce themselves in stereotyped 1860s fashion, they soon break through the convention of mid-Victorian fiction and emerge as moderns, with their uncomfortable semi-awareness of confused genders. A further fascination is felt when it is perceived that these characters and their landscape – one of 'those sequestered spots outside the Gates of the World' – both belong to the most important experiences of Hardy's youth. The novel attracted a special kind of attention and admiration from the start. Forty years later Hardy was still defensive about it. In 1913 he informed a correspondent, 'It is very strange that you should have been attracted by *A Pair of Blue Eyes*. The character of the heroine is somewhat – indeed, rather largely – that of my late wife, and the background of the tale the place where she lived. But of course the adventures, loves, etc., are fictitious entirely, though people used sometimes to ask her why she did this and that.'[1]

Proust, a great reader of Hardy, said of *A Pair of Blue Eyes* that it was 'of all books the one he would himself most gladly have written'. Its picture of individuals nervously exploring private emotional thresholds which they either cannot wholly comprehend or accept allows the reader an uncommon amount of personal interpretation. Although it is constructed with the characteristic mesh of plot and sub-plot which typifies all of Hardy's fiction, there is in this fresh morning work only a suggestion of the imperious tragic philosophy which was to dominate future novels. What occurs at Endelstow is poignant to an unforgettable degree, yet it is but a lead up to those 'dramas of grandeur and unity truly Sophoclean [which] are enacted in the real, by virtue of the concentrated passions and closely-knit interdependence on the lives there-

[1] Michael Millgate, *Thomas Hardy: his career as a novelist* (1971).

in', as Hardy described the subjects of his mature period. The celebrated irony, however, is immediately recognisable. Humanity as time's laughingstock has made its entrance. Human order is derisively measured against some hollow cosmic disorder. The fate of lovers is made infinitely more melancholy when its trivial connection with the vast unfeeling forces called Nature is exposed. These forces are given a precise geographical location in the shape of the immense, beautiful and frightening north Cornish seaboard, so that the heroine is seen on both an actual and a symbolic cliff-edge. The pounding Atlantic mocks her heartbeat. 'At Beeny Cliff...' wrote Hardy in his notebook in 1872,

> green towards the land, blue-black towards the sea. Every ledge has a little, starred, green grass upon it: all vertical parts bare.... The sea is full of motion internally, but still as a whole. Quiet and silent in the distance, noisy and restless close at hand.

Forty years later, after his wife's death, the cliff's edge balances an old happiness –

> The woman now is – elsewhere – whom the ambling pony bore,
> And nor knows nor cares for Beeny, and will laugh there nevermore.

Elfride and the boy architect who makes his descent upon her father's parish are a decade younger than Hardy and Emma Gifford when they first met at St Juliot. This immaturity is the key to the novel. Elfride knows little about herself and nothing about men, but she has no reason to think that intelligence and instinct will not tell her plenty about both in due time. She is not ambitious and she lacks the type of self-dramatisation which sees herself as a storm centre. Such fantasies are reserved for her pen, for, like Emma Gifford, she is writing a romance.[1] Elfride, in fact, is rather ordinary and a bit gauche, easily impressed and has 'special facilities for getting rid of trouble after a decent interval and is shocked when she finds out how many people cling to their misery'. Suitors besiege her. She expects them to know what they are about. But their movements are tentative and unsure, and they push her into making bad mistakes. In spite of their essential weakness, the egotism of

[1] See Emma Hardy, *Some Recollections*, ed. Evelyn Hardy and Robert Gittings (1961) p. 90, for details of Emma Hardy's unpublished novel 'The Maid on the Shore'.

these very different young men involves them in a great deal more action than the circumstances really warrant and none of them stops to ask himself if his violence or self-concern is endangering the girl.

Unsuspecting and entirely vulnerable, Elfride has gradually to learn that hers is not a happy destiny. She tells a friend that she asks very little of life and that she is 'content to build happiness on any accidental basis that may lie near at hand', but the irony remains that there is not one single accidental factor pointing to happiness connected with her existence. All things work together for ill. For what purpose? No one can say. She is 'unlucky', that is all. Some people are. Instead of her successes and mistakes merging into a tolerable if flawed entity, which is the common lot, bit by bit everything goes wrong for her and she is left with nothing to cling to. The stars are not to blame. They and the huge seas, rocks and winds among which she has always lived know nothing about her. It is vanity to imagine that she is even the lowly component of a vast creation which needs her and is aware of her. Others as well as Hardy had at this moment arrived at a state of black disbelief in the benign intentions of the cosmos. Richard Jefferies continued to worship terrestrial glory and to give himself up to the ecstasies of the physical world but, in *The Story of My Heart*, he admitted: 'there is nothing human in nature. The earth, though loved so dearly, would let me perish on the ground, and neither bring forth food nor water. Burning in the sky the great sun, of whose company I have been so fond, would merely burn on and make no motion to assist me.... The trees care nothing for us; the hill I visited so often in days gone by has not missed me.... If the entire human race perished at this hour, what difference would it make to the earth?' If a man falls from a cliff 'the air parts: the earth beneath dashes him to pieces'. Nature has no special concern for humanity. Worse. Science has destroyed the old protection. The safety-net of the Everlasting Arms is no longer trustworthy. Elfride Swancourt slips towards the abyss, her fate entirely unseen by those who insist that they love her.

These are Felix Jethway, Stephen Smith, Henry Knight and Spenser Luxellian. The first, after a single attempt to kiss her, dies because he seems to have convinced himself that Elfride is beyond his reach. The second is direct, attractive and able to delight her –

until the realities of life demonstrate that he is as much a child as she is and in no position to become her husband. The third, who is the eldest of the suitors by several years, has a problem where women are concerned. Elfride is dazzled by his intellectual qualities but is bothered by him in other respects and complains, 'I almost wish you were of a grosser nature, Harry.' The fourth lover, Lord Luxellian, her kinsman and a young widower still in his twenties, marries her and makes her pregnant. She dies of a miscarriage only five months after her wedding-day. The inexorable progress from the time when she was free as a bird and, like Emma Gifford, Hardy's own rectory girl, 'scampering up and down the hills on my beloved mare alone, wanting no protection, the rain going down my back often, and my hair floating on the wind,'[1] to her Shakespearian descent into the Luxellian family vault occupies less than five years. The four lovers – each in his own unwitting way – have driven her into the dark. Or have they?

The plot of *A Pair of Blue Eyes* is really the basis of a poem. It is composed of symbols and metaphor, and even where it is luridly invaded by melodrama it retains the power of poetry. Hardy has had to invent a special kind of story-telling to carry the multiplicity of his private experience which has not as yet provided the moral philosophy which he used to control his later novels. It is a book which contains many of the impulses and much of the emotion of a tragic ballad.

An exceedingly handsome boy arrives at a dull country rectory with instructions from his employer, a London architect, to draw up plans for 'restoring' the parish church. He stays at the rectory with the latitudinarian Mr Swancourt and falls in love with his daughter Elfride. The rector allows the friendship, believing that Stephen and Elfride are too young for seriousness, and then finds out that this person is not at all the well-bred, educated man which everything about him implies, but the son of one of his humble parishioners, Smith the mason. More nonplussed than angry, Mr Swancourt forbids further contact between the pair. Thrillingly caught up in first love, they elope to Plymouth, intending to get married, but an inefficiency on Stephen's part concerning the licence forces them to

[1] *Some Recollections*, pp. 50–1.

travel on to London for the ceremony. There they panic. 'I don't like it here – nor myself – nor you!' says Elfride on Paddington Station, her faith in Stephen as protector quite vanished. They scramble back to Cornwall on the very next train. The entire escapade has been muddled and innocent, but Elfride is terrified that somebody from Endelstow will have seen her and conclude otherwise. She has indeed been observed (village cognisance) and by none other than Mrs Jethway, the vengeance-seeking mother of her first admirer.

When Elfride reaches the rectory it is to find that her father has chosen that very time for his secret marriage to their neighbour, the rich Mrs Troyton. The new Mrs Swancourt launches the girl upon the London Season and for a few weeks the parochial matters of Endelstow seem of small account. When her stepmother's famous relative, the essayist and critic Henry Knight, accepts an invitation to Cornwall, life seems to be opening up for Elfride. Knight is in his early thirties and highly sophisticated. Elfride is first awed by him, then dazzled. He has had a long and influential friendship with a lad from the very village he is now visiting, but only once, in a generalised way, does he make reference to him. This is in striking contrast to the hero-worshipping outpourings which Elfride has had to endure when Stephen tells her about Knight, and which ironically lay the foundations of her own admiration for the writer. Class partly prevents Knight from discussing someone like Stephen with a lady. From the first, instinct tells Elfride that Knight will either despise or forsake her if she tells him about the youth. Knight, however, will not allow Elfride any kind of reticence and demands to know all about her life before he entered it. Profoundly in love with the writer by now, she is alerted to the danger of her situation. For she has learned an unpleasant but unalterable fact about Knight – that he must have, in his own morbid phrase, 'untried lips'. His questioning of her on her sexual experience exposes far more of his own pathology than Elfride's guilt. The only lull in this questioning occurs when the pair of them are involved in a life-or-death struggle on the Cliff without a Name, when Elfride strips herself in order to save this virgin male from destruction. The scene, one of Hardy's greatest, magnificently combines thought and action.

After the rescue it seems that Knight must accept Elfride for what she is, and not force her to measure up to the fantasy he has about women. But he cannot. Grateful though he is, he cannot even bring himself to kiss her after she has saved his life. His 'peculiarity of nature' prevents him from doing so. There is a curious justice in his not doing so because, unknown to him, Elfride had gone to the cliff in the first place to watch a ship arrive carrying Stephen back from India. After the elopement débâcle, the boy had fled abroad to become the man, and to prove himself capable of supporting a wife. Part of the proof, a banker's receipt for £200, is concealed in Elfride's dress. But it is all of no avail, for Stephen has shrunk into insignificance in comparison with Knight. And so, a few days later, the young architect discovers that the girl whom he has been addressing as 'wife' in confident letters, and for whose sake he has worked so hard, is deeply in love with none other than his adored friend.

Soon afterwards, the three meet during one of the funeral episodes which are strung out like dark pendants along the whole length of the story. Stephen's father is preparing the vault to receive Lady Luxellian, and Stephen himself is in the tomb writing in a notebook when Elfride and Knight suddenly appear. Knight is patronising and doesn't at first introduce 'a lady betrothed to himself' to the mason's son; and Stephen, though bewildered and hurt, tactfully says little. He is shortly returning to India, he informs them. 'The scene was remembered by all three as an indelible mark in their history.' Each has been privately lacerated because 'the deed of deception was complete'.

Immediately afterwards, Knight renews his probing into Elfride's history – 'You don't tell me anything but what I wring out of you.' She breaks under his interrogation, her strength undermined by threatening letters from Mrs Jethway. Elfride and Knight are actually resting on Felix Jethway's grave when the truth is dragged out of her. While the reader knows how essentially innocent she is, it is possible to understand something of both Mrs Jethway's and Knight's points of view. It is also plain that Knight rejects her more out of terror at having to cope, as he thinks, with an experienced woman than because she might be scandalous. Disturbed by her openly loving nature – it permeates the novel with an irresistible sweetness – and more scared than shocked that she can compare his response to it with that of previous lovers, he abandons her, though not before offering prim advice. Desperately in love, Elfride rushes to London after him and pours out her pent-up criticism of his sexual timidity – 'O, could *I* but be the man and *you* the woman. How I wish you could have run away with twenty women before you knew me....' Knight flees from such emotional involvement to the Continent. His 'was a robust intellect, which would escape outside the atmosphere of heart...'. The psychological insight into the nature of an intellectual is a memorable feature of the novel.

Some considerable time later Stephen and Knight accidentally run into each other in London. The former has done meteorically well in India and has become an architect of fame and promise. He is also no longer a boy but a man, and Knight's cool attitude towards him reflects the development. It is as if maturity puts an end to any type of relationship which he can accept. He only displays an unflattering relief upon hearing who was Elfride's earlier lover. It was 'only Stephen'. What kind of rival was that! Immediately, and with no sense of how he has insulted her, Knight sets off for Cornwall to make her his wife, the meeting with Stephen having revived his masculinity. The young architect catches the same train with the same intent. Master and pupil are now simply predatory males in competition, each with his self-esteem in ribbons and his desire heightened. Unbeknown to either of them, Elfride herself joins the train at Chippenham in a special dark, strange carriage – in her coffin, in fact.

The full story emerges when the two suitors take shelter from the thudding Cornish rain in an inn called The Welcome Home on the road to Endelstow. They learn that Elfride had wed Lord Luxellian, her widowed kinsman, and had perished soon after. 'False,' whispers Knight to Smith, though he withdraws this accusation later. But his prying interest in the girl persists. Was her husband 'very fond of her?' he asks her maid. '*Very* fond of her?' he repeats.

The tragedy is played out against a background of rural violation and resurgence. Throughout its telling the railway creeps nearer and nearer to the village, and will soon not only bring crowds of visitors to it, but also make it easier for bright countrymen like Stephen Smith to escape from it. Its church, bastion of its defunct mysteries, is actually made to crash down upon its local Vengeance – Mrs Jethway. Two kinds of old village power are destroyed at a stroke.

All the ancient certainties are in flux. New people are coming in, the old are dying out. Faith is the casualty of improvement. Neither Stephen nor his parents show much feeling for Endelstow, while the talk of their neighbours is marked with village cynicism. What energy the place still possesses is taking a new direction. Dissenters are active; Mr Swancourt would not have rebuilt his church had it not been for their enthusiasm. Stephen's mother reveals both her agnosticism and her unsentimentality in remarks about snapdragons, which 'are more like Christians than flowers' and Jacob's Ladders, whose persistence she despises – 'I don't care for things that neglect won't kill.' The Smiths, like the Hardys, are 'liviers', that part of the village work-force which has become superior and independent of the gentry and farmers. Mrs Smith is also proud, talkative and downright, and for these reasons alone Stephen's deception at the Rectory could not in the ordinary way have occurred, village gossip being what it is. Considering his looks and his career, and his being an only child, who would not have heard of him in this tiny place? Even the Swancourts, surely, although they had only been at the Rectory for a year. Yet Lickpan and Worm, his father's intimates, wait on him without recognition. Stephen, then, must be accorded some of the licence of romance. He is Elfride's girlish dream of a lover come true; his the arrival which a thousand clergymen's daughters, languishing behind the ivy, must have prayed for.

Hardy's apparent indifference to certain realities (he revised the book more than once) must have been deliberate. He doesn't even allow Stephen to show emotion when he has to preside over the destruction of a church with which his family has been associated for generations. There has been a funeral on the day of the young architect's arrival but Hardy does not mention it until Chapter 8, so that when Stephen goes to the churchyard early the following morning to begin work he sees 'nothing horrible . . . in the shape of tight mounds bonded with sticks . . . or wheelmarks'. He should have seen Felix Jethway's new grave and, the evening before, some sign from Elfride that someone she knew had just been buried. A funeral had taken place the day after Hardy himself had arrived to restore St Juliot Church. 'To Mr Holder's room,' states his diary. 'Returned downstairs. Music. . . . A funeral. . . . Staying there [at the church] drawing measuring all day, with intervals for meals at the rectory.' This is an exact synopsis of what happened when Stephen came to Endelstow, except that news of the funeral is deferred. Stephen talks to the rector in his bedroom, has high tea prepared for him by Elfride, who is noticeably excited, and hears her sing a setting of Shelley's 'When the lamp is shattered'. Originally, Hardy made her sing 'The Banks of Allen Water' because he intended to use one of its lines, 'A winning tongue had he', as the title for the novel.

His livier background and arrival in Cornwall apart, Stephen Smith is decidedly not the young Thomas Hardy. Many critics have tended to dismiss Stephen as a nebulous creation, attractive but hazy, forgetting that he exists to shed light on the far more important character of Henry Knight. While Hardy remains almost indifferent to the verisimilitude of Stephen's feelings for his native village he is precise about the boy's feelings for his guide and mentor. He had 'adored' Knight 'as a man is very rarely adored by another in modern times'. The adoration stemmed for the most part from a young man's recognition of a higher being, someone from the university and the recipient of real education and taste. It is in this aspect of Stephen that we discover references to Hardy, for Henry Knight is now generally accepted as a portrait of Horace Moule, the young novelist's confidant and teacher, and probably his greatest friend.

Eight years his senior, Moule was the central figure in Hardy's early literary development. As a Cambridge graduate and a poet-reviewer-essayist, his was a profound influence on the boy working in the Dorchester architect's office and, later, the young writer encountering London publishers. It was Moule who told Hardy what to read and who introduced him to the Greek dramatists who were to influence his outlook on life and authorship so tremendously. Moule also gave him the copy of Palgrave's *Golden Treasury*, which supplied so many of the quotations for *A Pair of Blue Eyes*, and provided the perfect kind of intellectual male companionship for early genius. On 21 June 1873, three weeks or so after the novel, which he was to review, had been published, Moule was with Hardy in Cambridge. On 'a never to be forgotten morning', wrote Hardy, the two of them stood on the roof of King's

College Chapel and watched 'Ely Cathedral gleaming in the distant sunlight'. A little later that year, while Hardy was working on *Far from the Madding Crowd* at his parents' Bockhampton home, he received the appalling news that Moule had killed himself at Cambridge by cutting his throat. Five days later Hardy attended the funeral and wrote against the passage in *In Memoriam* which describes a rare spirit at the university, 'Cambridge. H.M.M.' In a poem called 'Standing by the Mantelpiece' he attempted to enter Moule's mind just before the suicide and makes this clergyman's son say,

> ... all's lost, and nothing really lies
> Above but shade, and shadier shade below....

Elfride, the clergyman's daughter, is driven to the same conclusion. No small part of her disaster lay in the coincidence of her falling in love with two men whose long and considerable friendship carried the seeds of her destruction. It is they, and not she, who are guilty when circumstances force them to adopt crude postures of male rivalry for which the older man in particular is quite unsuited. Knight had become acquainted with Stephen when he was still a child, had helped him with books and eventually formed a sympathetic 'but no great intellectual fellowship' with the boy. 'He somehow was his friend. Circumstances, as usual, did it all.'

The gentleman is not democratic and tells the village lad that, 'much to his regret', he sees a time coming 'when every man will pronounce even the common words of his own tongue as seems right in his own ears, and be thought none the worse for it'. It may be relevant that the dialect poet William Barnes was living next door to the office in which Hardy served his architect's apprenticeship. Stephen not only learns to speak like a gentleman, but to lace his talk with the Latin tags which indicated a gentleman's education. Yet Knight's interest in him was not so as to change his class by superficial means but to admit him to taste and culture. The Swancourts smelled a rat almost from the start but, having made fools of themselves over Stephen's beauty – the rector reads breeding into it and his daughter is simply dazzled – they are obliged to bite back a great many questions. Now and then a remark slips out, making the amiable impostor quake. 'Fancy a man not being able to ride,' says Elfride. Hardy goes to extreme lengths to give Stephen the kind of looks which disturb the judgement. He was, he said, the idealisation of a pupil who had followed him as a trainee in the office of his Dorchester employer John Hicks. Stephen's looks, like Tess's, were a kind of blood challenge. Fallen blue blood now having to make a professional living is how the snobbish rector sums it up. Had not his own family 'been coming to nothing for centuries'? We learn that Stephen looked 'patrician' and that he had a 'mouth like Pitt's'. And, 'though gentle, ambition was visible in his kindling eyes'. His complexion was 'as fine as Elfride's own' but because he has reversed the fairy-tale convention by arriving as prince and departing as peasant he is never permitted to be entirely satisfactory even before this bewildering transformation. 'His face is – well – *pretty*, just like mine,' Elfride complains.

Stephen's quandary in the country is all about roots. His roots should claim him but they do not. His friend Knight has grafted him on to a broader culture which he rightly believes supersedes Endelstow's claims to him. But, at twenty, everything is still formative and village pressures on one side and London freedom on the other make him feel like an impostor. 'I have a trouble,' he tells Elfride, 'though some might think it less a trouble than a dilemma.' He confides it to her and she, unlike her father, takes it in her stride. 'That sort of origin is getting so respected that it is acquiring some of the odour of Norman ancestry.' But the rector, about to marry a widow whose ancestral claims he knows are as 'raked-up' as the Indian provenance of Birmingham brass, treats Stephen like a confidence trickster. Marrying for money outside Society's magic circle is respectable, marrying for love is not. Stephen's mother is more realistic. She tells Stephen, 'You might go higher than a bankrupt Pa'son's girl.'

Hardy, who was to remain enthralled by the psychology of class throughout his life, takes stock of Stephen's situation at this point: 'his brain had extraordinary receptive powers, and no great creativeness. Quickly acquiring any kind of knowledge he saw around him, and having a plastic adaptability more common in woman than in man, he changed colour like a chameleon as the society he found himself in assumed a higher and more artificial tone. . . . Yet to a dispassionate observer his pretensions to Elfride, though rather premature, were far from absurd as marriages go, unless the proximity of simple but honest parents could be said to make them so.' Stephen's dilemma, a common one at the time, was how to pick up an education and the improved circumstances which went with it without looking like an adventurer. Hardy is not concerned with his morality in the sense with which Jane Austen is concerned with that of Frank Churchill in *Emma.* What fascinates him is the effect of opportunity on innocence.

Elfride's poise both attracts and upsets Stephen. She always comments when his standards differ from her own. His occasional odd ways of talking and behaving are among the things which make him so attractive to her. She knows, too, how to get under his skin, although sometimes her little digs are evidence of how certain aspects of his existence worry and irritate her. One of these is his obsessive talk and praise of someone who changed his life. When Elfride begins to call this man 'Mr Clever' the reader knows that she is referring to a rival. Ironically, she will only destroy Stephen's love for Knight by attempting to destroy Stephen's love for herself. This is galling for Stephen but lethal for Elfride. She has made a huge mistake. Unconscious of the fact that Stephen's worship of Knight could indicate that the latter 'was not shaped by Nature for a marrying man' or that 'his lifelong constraint towards women, which he had attributed to accident, was not chance after all, but the natural result of instinctive acts so minute as to be indiscernible even by himself', she forsakes Stephen for a different type of immaturity. Stephen's greenness at twenty is temporary; Knight's virginity at thirty-two is permanent. Stephen's love feeds on absence, whereas Elfride's is starved by it, so there can be no waiting game. Knight can never know what love is yet he attracts adoration. In the ordinary way he should have benefited by the excited girl which Stephen has left behind, but the truth is this aspect of her is repellent to him.

In what strikes one as a direct reference to his own experience in Cornwall, Hardy wrote of Elfride, 'Every woman who makes a permanent impression on a man is usually recalled in his mind's eye as she appeared in one particular scene, which seems ordained to be her special form of manifestation throughout the pages of his memory.' This is certainly how the reader thinks of the parson's daughter. Reminded by her father that, whatever the outsider might think of their provincialism, 'It is all the world to us', we see Elfride cheerfully enduring 'the monotony of life we associate with people of small incomes in districts out of the sound of the railway whistle', scribbling romances as she rides through the valley on her pony, or 'running with a boy's velocity'. When she says that she is 'content to build happiness on any accidental basis that may lie near at hand', she doesn't imply a dull contentment but an inner gaiety. The lopping-off of this gaiety, piecemeal and apparently without reason, is very shocking. Elfride cannot avoid this pointless destruction, nor can others recognise what is happening to her. When Knight was alone on the cliff-face she could restore him to the advanced, intellectual creation (staring at fossils in the black rock, he was humiliated to think that he was to be 'with the small in his death'). When the Luxellian children became motherless she could provide a loving substitution. When Stephen looked like being forsaken as an impostor, she never left his side. She even sees the pathetic solitary aspects of her father's situation, absurd though they are to her way of thinking, and supports his *amour propre.* But no one independently observes *her* desperate need for help, and Knight, the person who owes her most, turns away in distaste when she pleads for his assistance. Yet it is a vanity in any one of them to believe that it was their selfishness or evil which destroyed her, and their final remorse is as futile as their initial hope. A few months after his first visit to St Juliot, the geographic centre of his own heart and of *A Pair of Blue Eyes* –

Why go to Saint-Juliot? What's Juliot to me?
Some strange necromancy
But charmed me to fancy
That much of my life claims the spot as its key.

– Hardy wrote in his notebook, 'Mother's notion (and also mine) – that a figure stands in our van with an arm uplifted, to knock us back from any pleasant prospect we indulge in as probable.' Why me? Elfride in effect cries as the arm descends. Why anyone?

Elfride is the first of Hardy's lost women, pliant, suggestible and at her most enchanting when an arbitrary fate moves in and casually obliterates her joy. Except for Felix, the non-starter, she tries to please the love-led men who pursue her by trying to be the kind of girl they have in mind, while at the same time not quite comprehending to what extent these various emotional friendships are hastening her maturity. Because hers is all the movement in a vast, static landscape, she at first believes that hers is all the life too. Then comes the chastening truth: she is no more and no less than the rocks or the momentary spray. Hardy said that a later novel would explore this theme more fully. He meant *Tess*.

Much has been written about Hardy's fatalism. It stemmed partly from his direct contact with what was still a brutal countryside whose customs were more Georgian than mid-nineteenth-century, and in which was rooted his strong interest in pain; and partly from the scientific upheaval of the 1860s, which overturned all the old certainties. Divine caring – and vengeance – gave way to natural causality. For Hardy, as for others, there was a new view of life but no new order. Man had become simply another facet of matter and not the pinnacle of a creation which existed for his comfort and honour. As if this were not sad enough, Hardy has to inject this fresh situation with the personal morbidity which is so notable an aspect of his genius. He dramatically exploits the randomness of things, and when some mindless force checks Elfride's average expectations of happiness and spins her into the dark Hardy makes sure that Nature is sufficiently ruthless and thorough. What does it all mean? It *means* nothing. It is. It was. As Guildenstern told Hamlet, 'On fortune's cap we are not the very button.' The most intriguing thing about *A Pair of Blue Eyes*, however, is not its picture of a delightful girl receiving no more consideration from Nature than a blade of grass on the headland, but of a heroine being harried along to oblivion by her creator. She is even confined to a limited field like a coursed hare, and her escape made impossible. For, although she appears occasionally in London and three of her lovers, Stephen, Knight and Lord Luxellian, travel extensively, the pursuit takes place within the boundaries of a village and, in spite of its moor and ocean, Endelstow, like all villages, can close in without mercy upon those who belong to it. Visiting the same rocks, lanes, meadows and scenes with different men fills Elfride's mind with guilt and comparisons, and the reader's with a strong sense of her treachery. Hardy evokes the humus-like aspect of rural life by letting both Stephen and Knight hear of the existence of poor young Felix Jethway while sitting on his grave. The hyper-sensitive Knight has no doubt at all that someone else has accompanied Elfride along these paths before him and he questions her as though she were in the dock. She is evasive, muddled, angry and frightened. But she is also thrilled. Knight's raised voice soon becomes preferable to Stephen's soft talk. Mr Swancourt had disliked the latter – 'Uniform pleasantness is rather a defect than a faculty. It shows that a man hasn't sense enough to know whom to despise.' Knight often comes close to despising Elfride. He is smart and epigrammatic at her expense, and he insults her by making literary notes about her character. She gets her own back with her clumsy little references to his sexual timidity. Eventually, excited by his depths and contrasts, and awed by the way in which he dominates her, she begins to love him. She was to discover that 'It was infinitely more to be even the slave of the greater than the queen of the less.' She even attempts to rejoice in Knight's 'spare love-making' and his 'piquant snubbings', associating these with 'somebody further on in manhood' than Stephen. Male and female concepts, manhood, friendship, reliability, maturity, etc., all form part of the misunderstanding. Every now and then Hardy sets off down still-uncharted psychological paths and points to feelings and behaviour which are decades away from popular recognition. We learn, for example, that 'the emotional side of [Stephen's] constitution was built rather after a feminine than a male model', which illuminates why both Knight and Elfride were so successful in their friendships with him. But to the girl 'Stephen was hardly enough of a man'.

. . . Stephen's failure to make his hold on her heart a permanent one was his too timid habit of dispraising himself to her – a peculiarity which, exercised towards sensible men, stirs a kindly chord of attachment that a marked assertiveness would leave untouched, but inevitably leads the most sensible woman in the world to undervalue him who practises it. Directly domineering ceases in the man, snubbing begins in the woman. . . . [ch. 27]

While Elfride shows some astuteness where Stephen is concerned – though this doesn't excuse her for treating him so treacherously – she is quite mistaken about Knight's chilly, abrasive manner. She thinks it is male purposefulness when, in fact, it is the armour-plating which covers a fear of women. Hardy, brilliantly and melodramatically, puts Knight to the ordeal so that Elfride – and the reader – can see him stripped of every guard and protection. He stays brave and intelligent, but imminent death itself cannot make him declare much heart.

The literal cliff-hanger in which intellectual pride is questioned and humbled, and physical courage extolled, is a wonderful piece of descriptive writing, and one of the first indications of Hardy's genius. In it, the metaphorical and the actual are perfectly fused. Even the double sensations of physical and spiritual vertigo are made to reel against each other in sickening succession. The man-of-letters clings feebly to existence by his finger-tips, his whole ethos challenged, while the steamship *Puffin* with the 'fortune's favourite' Stephen aboard, casually passes by. Before the accident the two men had actually been staring at one another through telescopes, but without recognition. Each lens registered the basic outline of a male, no more. Then the shale gives way, and one figure, who has never been 'inconveniently in love', slips out of focus. Hanging there above the boiling sea, Knight should have changed, should have given love its pre-eminence over mind, but he doesn't. He cannot. It is Elfride's love which saves him. Knight knows it and is more astonished than grateful. Eventually, the lengths to which she went to rescue him do no more than stimulate his conjectures about what sort of lengths such a loving nature might have gone to before he arrived on the scene. Her capability to love upsets him; it was something which he believes that he should have taught her. If he did not, who did? Cruelly and remorselessly, he prises some of the past out of her, driving her foot by foot towards an abyss from which there can be no salvation. Oblivion.

Although *A Pair of Blue Eyes* appraises some of the claustrophobic pressures of village life, the ordinary village people are treated with small affection and considerable detachment. At best, they are poetically quaint, and talk and act like Shakespeare's bucolic mechanicals. They never approach the far more real picture of 'Endelstow' and its neighbourhood which Emma Hardy drew in her little memoir *Some Recollections.* She writes of the sullen congregation at Lanivet and the superstition and evil-speaking of St Juliot, 'where hard labour upon the stony soil made a cold mostly ill-natured working class, yet with some good traits and fine exceptions'. And although she never liked 'the Cornish working orders' and found 'their so-called independence of character ... most disagreeable to live with' she did occasionally discover 'a dear heart-whole person' among a populace of 'dull, aggressive workers'. The same account also reveals that, as with Elfride, Emma's love for the young architect who penetrated this not entirely happy scene was preceded by her being aware that she had attracted the interest of a farmer, 'a man gentle of nature, musical, christlike in guilelessness, handsome of face and figure, David-like farming his own land: he never married, and told after I had left of his disappointment, and attraction on first seeing me on the stairs'.

A Pair of Blue Eyes is, among much else, the story of escapes from a social class in the English countryside which perfectly understood its position between that of the brutalised field-workers and their gentry or yeoman employers. It was a position of unique village independence and Hardy himself derived from it. A lady such as Elfride would know little or nothing about this, and even as she was waiting, somewhat fatalistically, for Stephen to marry her she faced the prospect of her future in-laws with something verging on horror. Their 'deflecting influence' itself was almost enough to make her change her mind. Was not Mr Smith 'a decidedly common man' and his wife 'vulgar'? The novel's concentration on this particular social gap, that between the liviers and the aristocracy (for the parson and his daughter were connections of the local peer), puts everyone below it – virtually the entire community – out of court, so to speak. When the ordinary village men, mocked with names like Lickpan and Worm, make their entrance, it is mainly a comically picturesque one. It is the place and not its people which receives Hardy's most profound attention. It surges wildly and overwhelmingly across the tentative passions of the characters, providing great imagery and metaphor, symbolism and yardstick.

There a rather ordinary, conventional female innocence is made to shatter under the blows of male ambivalence, vanity and ignorance; and humanity in general is shown as temporary scratchers on the covering soil which thinly hides the barren rock.

RONALD BLYTHE

A star in the text indicates that an explanatory note is to be found at the end of the book, while superior numbers refer to footnotes.

A PAIR OF BLUE EYES

Thomas Hardy's WESSEX
Fictitious names as Exonbury
Real names as Portsmouth
0 5 10 15 Miles
Cliff without name
Targan Bay
Dundagel
Pallenty Vale
St. Launce's
Plymouth
OFF WESSEX
Trufal
Penzephyr
Lands End
Bristol Channel
Stancy Castle
Exon Moor
Dunkery Beacon
Downstaple
Quantock Hills
Mendip Hills
Bristol
Bath
Fountall
Glaston
Sedgemoor
OUTER WESSEX
Toneborough
LOWER WESSEX
Tivworthy
Exonbury
Ivell
River Axe
Emminster
Pilsdon
Kings Hintock
High Stoy
Chalk Newton
SOUTH WESSEX
Port Bredy
Idmouth
Deadmans Bay
Casterbridge
Blackon
Egdon Heath
Talbothays
Frome
Overcombe
Budmouth
Isle of Slingers
The Beal
The Race
Lightship
Tor-upon-Sea
The Channel
Wellbridge
Anglebury
Knollsea
Sandbourne
Havenpool
Flintcomb-Ash
Bulbarrow
Vale of Blackmore
Sherton Abbas
Stourcastle
Shaston
Shottsford Forum
Warborne
Stour Head
The Chase
Wingreen
Trantridge Cross
Chaseborough
Lornton Inn
The Great Forest
Melchester
The Great Plain
Stonehenge
WESSEX
MID WESSEX
Marlbury Downs
Batton Castle
Kennetbridge
Inkpen Beacon
NORTH WESSEX
Christminster
Lumsdon
Alfredston
Marygreen
Castle Royal
Aldbrickham
Stoke Barehills
Quartershot
Weydon Priors
Icenway House
UPPER WESSEX
Wintoncester
Deansleigh
Southampton
The Island
Solentsea
Portsmouth
Septentrio
Oriens
Meridies
Occidens
0 5 10 15 Miles

Preface

THE following chapters were written at a time when the craze for indiscriminate church-restoration* had just reached the remotest nooks of western England, where the wild and tragic features of the coast had long combined in perfect harmony with the crude Gothic Art of the ecclesiastical buildings scattered along it, throwing into extraordinary discord all architectural attempts at newness there. To restore the grey carcases of a mediævalism whose spirit had fled seemed a not less incongruous act than to set about renovating the adjoining crags themselves.

Hence it happened that an imaginary history of three human hearts, whose emotions were not without correspondence with these material circumstances, found in the ordinary incidents of such church-renovations a fitting frame for its presentation.

The shore and country about 'Castle Boterel' is now getting well known, and will be readily recognized. The spot, I may add, is among the furthest westward of all those convenient corners wherein I have ventured to erect my theatre for these imperfect dramas of country life and passions; and it lies near to, or no great way beyond, the vague border of the Wessex kingdom on that side, which, like the westering verge of modern American settlements, was progressive and uncertain.

This, however, is of little importance. The place is pre-eminently (for one person at least) the region of dream and mystery. The ghostly birds, the pall-like sea, the frothy wind, the eternal soliloquy of the waters, the bloom of dark purple cast that seems to exhale from the shoreward precipices, in themselves lend to the scene an atmosphere like the twilight of a night vision.

One enormous sea-bord cliff in particular figures in the narrative; and for some forgotten reason or other this cliff was described in the story as being without a name. Accuracy would require the statement to be that a remarkable cliff which resembles in many points the cliff of the description bears a name that no event has made famous.

March 1895

P.S. – The first edition of this tale, in three volumes, was issued in the early summer of 1873. In its action it exhibits the romantic stage of an idea which was further developed in a later book.* To the ripe-minded critic of the present one an immaturity in its views of life and in its workmanship will of course be apparent. But to correct these by the judgment of later years, even had correction been possible, would have resulted, as with all such attempts, in the disappearance of whatever freshness and spontaneity the pages may have as they stand.

To add a word on the topography of the romance in answer to queries, unimportant as the point may be. The mansion called 'Endelstow House' is to a large degree really existent, though it has to be looked for at a spot several miles south of its supposed site. The church, too, of the story was made to be more open to the ocean than is its original.

June 1912 T.H.

The Persons

Elfride Swancourt	*a young Lady*
Christopher Swancourt	*a Clergyman*
Stephen Smith	*an Architect*
Henry Knight	*a Reviewer and Essayist*
Charlotte Troyton	*a rich Widow*
Gertrude Jethway	*a poor Widow*
Spenser Hugo Luxellian	*a Peer*
Lady Luxellian	*his Wife*
Mary and Kate	*two little Girls*
William Worm	*a dazed Factotum*
John Smith	*a Master-mason*
Jane Smith	*his Wife*
Martin Cannister	*a Sexton*
Unity	*a Maid-servant*

Other servants, masons, labourers, grooms, nondescripts, etc., etc.

THE SCENE

Off-Wessex, or Lyonnesse, on the outskirts of Lower Wessex*

CHAPTER ONE

'A fair vestal, throned in the west'*

ELFRIDE SWANCOURT was a girl whose emotions lay very near the surface. Their nature more precisely, and as modified by the creeping hours of time, was known only to those who watched the circumstances of her history.

Personally she was the combination of very interesting particulars, whose rarity, however, lay in the combination itself rather than in the individual elements combined. As a matter of fact you did not see the form and substance of her features when conversing with her; and this charming power of preventing a material study of her lineaments by an interlocutor, originated not in the cloaking effect of a well-formed manner (for her manner was childish and scarcely formed), but in the attractive crudeness of the remarks themselves. She had lived all her life in retirement – the *monstrari digito** of idle men had not flattered her, and at the age of nineteen or twenty she was no further on in social consciousness than an urban young lady of fifteen.

One point in her, however, you did notice: that was her eyes. In them was seen a sublimation of all of her; it was not necessary to look further: there she lived.

These eyes were blue; blue as autumn distance – blue as the blue we see between the retreating mouldings of hills and woody slopes on a sunny September morning. A misty and shady blue, that had no beginning or surface, and was looked *into* rather than *at*.

As to her presence, it was not powerful; it was weak. Some women can make their personality pervade the atmosphere of a whole banqueting hall; Elfride's was no more pervasive than that of a kitten.

Elfride had as her own the thoughtfulness which appears in the face of the Madonna della Sedia,* without its rapture: the warmth and spirit of the type of woman's feature most common to the beauties – mortal and immortal – of Rubens, without their insistent fleshiness. The characteristic expression of the female faces of Correggio* – that of the yearning human thoughts that lie too deep for tears* – was hers sometimes, but seldom under ordinary conditions.

The point in Elfride Swancourt's life at which a deeper current may be said to have permanently set in, was one winter afternoon when she found herself standing, in the character of hostess, face to face with a man she had never seen before – moreover, looking at him with a Miranda-like curiosity* and interest that she had never yet bestowed on a mortal.

On this particular day her father, the rector of a parish on the sea-swept outskirts of Lower Wessex, and a widower, was suffering from an attack of gout. After finishing her household supervisions Elfride became restless, and several times left the room, ascended the staircase, and knocked at her father's chamber-door.

'Come in!' was always answered in a hearty out-of-door voice from the inside.

'Papa,' she said on one occasion to the genial-faced, handsome man of fifty,* who, puffing and fizzing like a bursting bottle, lay on the bed wrapped in a dressing-gown, and every now and then enunciating, in spite of himself, a letter or two of some word or words that were almost oaths; 'papa, will you not come downstairs this evening?' She spoke distinctly, he was rather deaf.

'Afraid not – eh-h-h! – very much afraid I shall not, Elfride. Piph-ph-ph! I can't bear even a handkerchief upon this deuced toe of mine, much less a stocking or slipper – piph-ph-ph! There 'tis again! No, I shan't get up till to-morrow.'

'Then I hope this London man won't come; for I don't know what I should do, papa.'

'Well, it would be awkward, certainly.'

'I should hardly think he would come to-day.'

'Why?'

'Because the wind blows so.'

'Wind! What ideas you have, Elfride! Who ever heard of wind stopping a man from doing his business? The idea of this toe of mine coming on so suddenly! . . . If he should arrive, you must send him up to me, I suppose, and then give him some food and put him to bed in some way. Dear me, what a nuisance all this is!'

'Must he have dinner?'

'Too heavy for a tired man at the end of a tedious journey.'

'Tea, then?'

'Not substantial enough.'

'High tea,* then? There is cold fowl, rabbit-pie, some pasties, and things of that kind.'

'Yes, high tea.'

'Must I pour out his tea, papa?'

'Of course; you are the mistress of the house.'

'What! sit there all the time with a stranger, just as if I knew him, and not anybody to introduce us?'

'Nonsense, child, about introducing; you know better than that. A practical professional man, tired and hungry, who has been travelling ever since daylight this morning, will hardly be inclined to talk and air courtesies to-night. He wants food and shelter, and you must see that he has it, simply because I am suddenly laid up and cannot. There is nothing so dreadful in that, I hope? You get all kinds of stuff into your head from reading so many of those novels.'

'O no; there is nothing dreadful in it when it becomes plainly a case of necessity like this. But, you see, you are always there when people come to dinner, even if we know them; and this is some strange London man of the world, who will think it odd, perhaps.'

'Very well; let him.'

'Is he Mr Hewby's partner?'

'I should scarcely think so: he may be.'

'How old is he, I wonder?'

'That I cannot tell. You will find the copy of my letter to Mr Hewby, and his answer, upon the table in the study. You may read them, and then you'll know as much as I do about our visitor.'

'I have read them.'

'Well, what's the use of asking questions, then? They contain all I know. Ugh-h-h! . . . Od* plague you, you young scamp! don't put anything there! I can't bear the weight of a fly.'

'O, I am sorry, papa. I forgot; I thought you might be cold,' she said, hastily removing the rug she had thrown upon the feet of the sufferer; and waiting till she saw that consciousness of her offence had passed from his face, she withdrew from the room, and retired again downstairs.

CHAPTER TWO

'Twas on the evening of a winter's day.'

WHEN two or three additional hours had merged the same afternoon in evening, some moving outlines might have been observed against the sky on the summit of a wild lone hill in that district. They circumscribed two men, having at present the aspect of silhouettes, sitting in a dog-cart* and pushing along in the teeth of the wind. Scarcely a solitary house or man had been visible along the whole dreary distance of open country they were traversing; and now that night had begun to fall, the faint twilight, which still gave an idea of the landscape to their observation, was enlivened by the quiet appearance of the planet Jupiter, momentarily gleaming in intenser brilliancy in front of them, and by Sirius shedding his rays in rivalry from his position over their shoulders. The only lights apparent on earth were some spots of dull red glowing here and there upon the distant hills, which, as the driver of the vehicle gratuitously remarked to the hirer, were smouldering fires for the consumption of peat and gorse-roots, where the common was being broken up for agricultural purposes. The wind prevailed with but little abatement from its daytime boisterousness, three or four small clouds, delicate and pale, creeping along under the sky southward to the Channel.

Thirteen of the fifteen miles intervening between the railway terminus and the end of their journey had been gone over, when they began to pass along the brink of a valley some miles in extent, wherein the wintry skeletons of a more luxuriant vegetation than had hitherto surrounded them proclaimed an increased richness of soil, which showed signs of far more careful enclosure and management than had any slopes they had yet passed. A little further, and an opening in the elms stretching up from this fertile valley revealed a mansion.

'That's Endelstow House, Lord Luxellian's,'* said the driver.

'Endelstow House, Lord Luxellian's,' repeated the other mechanically. He then turned himself sideways, and keenly scrutinized the almost invisible house with an interest which the indistinct picture itself seemed far from adequate to create. 'Yes, that's Lord Luxellian's,' he said yet again after a while, as he still looked in the same direction.

'What, be we going there?'

'No; Endelstow Rectory, as I have told you.'

'I thought you m't have altered your mind, sir, as ye have stared that way at nothing so long.'

'O no; I am interested in the house, that's all.'

'Most people be, as the saying is.'

'Not in the sense that I am.'

'Ah! . . . Well, his family is no better than my own, 'a b'lieve.'

'How is that?'

'Hedgers and ditchers by rights. But once in ancient times one of 'em, when he was at work, changed clothes with King Charles the Second, and saved the king's life. King Charles came up to him like a common man, and said off-hand, "Man in the smock-frock,* my name is Charles the Second; will you lend me your clothes?" "I don't mind if I do," said Hedger Luxellian; and they changed there and then. "Now mind ye," King Charles the Second said, like a common man, as he rode away, "if ever I come to the crown, you come to court, knock at the door, and say out bold, 'Is King Charles the Second at home?' Tell your name, and they shall let you in, and you shall be made a lord." Now, that was very nice of Master Charley?'

'Very nice indeed.'

'Well, as the story is, the king came to the throne; and some years after that, away went Hedger Luxellian, knocked at the king's door, and asked if King Charles the Second was in. "No, he isn't," they said. "Then, is Charles the Third?" said Hedger Luxellian. "Yes," said a young feller standing by like a common man, only he had a crown on, "my name is Charles the Third." And—'

'I really fancy that must be a mistake. I don't recollect anything in English history about Charles the Third,' said the other in a tone of mild remonstrance.

'O that's right history enough, only 'twasn't prented;* he was rather a queer-tempered man, if you remember.'

'Very well; go on.'

'And, by hook or by crook, Hedger Luxellian was made a lord, and everything went on well till some time after, when he got into a most terrible row with King Charles the Fourth—'

'I can't stand Charles the Fourth. Upon my word, that's too much.'

'Why? There was a George the Fourth, wasn't there?'

'Certainly.'

'Well, Charleses be as common as Georges. However I'll say no more about it. . . . Ah, well! 'tis the funniest world ever I lived in—upon my life 'tis. Ah, that such should be!'

The dusk had thickened into darkness while they thus conversed, and the outline and surface of the mansion gradually disappeared. The windows, which had before been as black blots on a lighter expanse of wall, became illuminated, and were transfigured to squares of light on the general dark body of the night landscape as it absorbed the outlines of the edifice into its gloomy monochrome.

Not another word was spoken for some time, and they climbed a hill, then another hill piled on the summit of the first. An additional mile of plateau followed, from which could be discerned two lighthouses on the coast they were nearing, reposing on the horizon with a calm lustre of benignity. The parish of their destination seemed to lie not far inshore, and somewhere between Cam Beak and Tintagel. Another oasis was reached; a little dell lay like a nest at their feet, towards which the driver pulled the horse at a sharp angle, and descended a steep slope which dived under the trees like a rabbit's burrow. They sank lower and lower.

'Endelstow Rectory is inside here,' continued the man with the reins. 'This part about here is West Endelstow; Lord Luxellian's is East Endelstow, and has a church to itself. Pa'son Swancourt is the pa'son of both, and bobs backward and forward. Ah, well! 'tis a funny world. 'A b'lieve there was once a quarry where this house stands. The man who built it in past time scraped all the glebe* for earth to put round the rectory, and laid out a little paradise of flowers and trees in the soil he had got together in this way, whilst the fields he scraped have been good for nothing ever since.'

'How long has the present incumbent been here?'

'Maybe about a year, or a year and half: 'tisn't two years; for they don't scandalize him yet; and, as a rule, a parish begins to scandalize the pa'son at the end of two years among 'em familiar. But he's a very nice party. Ay, Pa'son Swancourt knows me pretty well from often driving over; and I know Pa'son Swancourt.'

They emerged from the bower, swept round in a curve, and the chimneys and gables of the rectory became darkly visible. Not a light showed anywhere. They alighted; the man felt his way into the porch, and rang the bell.

At the end of three or four minutes, spent in patient waiting without hearing any sounds of a response, the stranger advanced and repeated the call in a more decided manner. He then fancied he heard footsteps in the hall, and sundry movements of the door-knob, but nobody appeared.

'Perhaps they bean't at home,' sighed the driver. 'And I promised myself a bit of supper in Pa'son Swancourt's kitchen. Sich lovely meat-pies and figged keakes,* and cider, and drops o' cordial that they do keep here!'

'All right, naibours! Be ye rich men or be ye poor men, that ye must needs come to the world's end at this time o' night?' exclaimed a voice at this instant; and, turning their heads, they saw a rickety individual shambling round from the back door with a horn lantern* dangling from his hand.

'Time o' night, 'a b'lieve! and the clock only gone seven of 'em. Show a light, and let us in, William Worm.'

'Oh, that you, Robert Lickpan?'

'Nobody else, William Worm.'

'And is the visiting man a-come?'

'Yes,' said the stranger. 'Is Mr Swancourt at home?'

'That 'a is, sir. And would ye mind coming round by the back way? The front door is got stuck wi' the wet, as he will do sometimes; and the Turk* can't open en. I know I am only a poor wambling* man that 'ill never pay the Lord for my making, sir; but I can show the way in, sir.'

The new arrival followed his guide through a little door in a wall, and then promenaded a scullery and a kitchen, along which he passed with eyes rigidly fixed in advance, an inbred horror of prying forbidding him to gaze around apartments that formed the back side of the household tapestry. Entering the hall, he was about to be shown to his room, when from the inner lobby of the front entrance, whither she had gone to learn the cause of the delay, sailed forth the form of Elfride. Her start of amazement at the sight of the visitor coming forth from under the stairs proved that she had not been expecting this surprising flank movement,* which had been originated entirely by the ingenuity of William Worm.

She appeared in the prettiest of all feminine guises, that is to say, in demi-toilette,* with plenty of loose curly hair tumbling down about her shoulders. An expression of uneasiness pervaded her countenance; and altogether she scarcely appeared woman enough for the situation. The visitor removed his hat, and the first words were spoken; Elfride prelusively* looking with a deal of interest, not unmixed with surprise, at the person towards whom she was to do the duties of hospitality.

'I am Mr Smith,' said the stranger in a musical voice.

'I am Miss Swancourt,' said Elfride.

Her constraint was over. The great contrast between the reality she beheld before her, and the dark, taciturn, sharp, elderly man of business who had lurked in her imagination – a man with clothes smelling of city smoke, skin sallow from want of sun, and talk flavoured with epigram – was such a relief to her that Elfride smiled, almost laughed, in the new-comer's face.

Stephen Smith, who has hitherto been hidden from us by the darkness, was at this time of his life but a youth in appearance, and not yet a man in years. Judging from his look, London was the last place in the world that one would have imagined to be the scene of his activities: such a face surely could not be nourished amid smoke and mud and fog and dust; such an open countenance could never even have seen anything of 'the weariness, the fever, and the fret'* of Babylon the Second.*

His complexion was as fine as Elfride's own; the pink of his cheeks almost as delicate. His mouth as perfect as Cupid's bow in form, and as cherry-red in colour as hers. Bright curly hair; bright sparkling blue-gray eyes; a boy's blush and manner; neither whisker nor moustache, unless a little light-brown fur on his upper lip deserved the latter title: this composed the London professional man, the prospect of whose advent had so troubled Elfride.

Elfride hastened to say she was sorry to tell him that Mr

Swancourt was not able to receive him that evening, and gave the reason why. Mr Smith replied, in a voice boyish by nature and manly by art, that he was very sorry to hear this news; but that as far as his reception was concerned, it did not matter in the least.

Stephen was shown up to his room. In his absence Elfride stealthily glided into her father's.

'He's come, papa. Such a young man for a business man!'

'O, indeed!'

'His face is – well – *pretty*; just like mine.'

'H'm! what next?'

'Nothing; that's all I know of him yet. It is rather nice, is it not?'

'Well, we shall see that when we know him better. Go down and give the poor fellow something to eat and drink, for Heaven's sake. And when he has done eating, say I should like to have a few words with him, if he doesn't mind coming up here.'

The young lady glided downstairs again, and whilst she awaits young Smith's entry, the letters referring to his visit had better be given.

1. – Mr Swancourt to Mr Hewby

Endelstow Rectory, *Feb. 18, 18–*

Sir, – We are thinking of restoring the tower and aisle of the church in this parish; and Lord Luxellian, the patron of the living, has mentioned your name as that of a trustworthy architect whom it would be desirable to ask to superintend the work.

I am exceedingly ignorant of the necessary preliminary steps. Probably, however, the first is that (should you be, as Lord Luxellian says you are, disposed to assist us) yourself or some member of your staff come and see the building, and report thereupon for the satisfaction of parishioners and others.

The spot is a very remote one: we have no railway within fifteen miles; and the nearest place for putting up at – called a town, though merely a large village – is Castle Boterel, two miles further on; so that it would be most convenient for you to stay at the rectory – which I am glad to place at your disposal – instead of pushing on to the hotel at Castle Boterel, and coming back again in the morning.

Any day of the next week that you like to name for the visit will find us quite ready to receive you. – Yours very truly,

Christopher Swancourt

2. – MR HEWBY TO MR SWANCOURT

PERCY PLACE, CHARING CROSS, *Feb. 20, 18–*

DEAR SIR, – Agreeably to your request of the 18th instant I have arranged to survey and make drawings of the aisle and tower of your parish church, and of the dilapidations which have been suffered to accrue thereto, with a view to its restoration.

My assistant, Mr Stephen Smith, will leave London by the early train to-morrow morning for the purpose. Many thanks for your proposal to accommodate him. He will take advantage of your offer, and will probably reach your house at some hour of the evening. You may put every confidence in him, and may rely upon his discernment in the matter of church architecture.

Trusting that the plans for the restoration, which I shall prepare from the details of his survey, will prove satisfactory to yourself and Lord Luxellian, I am, dear sir, yours faithfully,

WALTER HEWBY

CHAPTER THREE

'Melodious birds sing madrigals.'*

THAT first repast in Endelstow Rectory was a very agreeable one to young Stephen Smith. The table was spread, as Elfride had suggested to her father, with the materials for the heterogeneous meal called high tea – a class of refection* welcome to all when away from men and towns, and particularly attractive to youthful palates. The table was prettily decked with winter flowers and leaves, amid which the eye was greeted by chops, chicken, pie, etc., and two huge pasties overhanging the sides of the dish with a cheerful aspect of abundance.

At the end, towards the fireplace, appeared the tea-service, of old-fashioned Worcester porcelain, and behind this arose the slight form of Elfride, attempting to add matronly dignity to the movement of pouring out tea, and to have a weighty and concerned look in matters of marmalade, honey, and clotted cream. Having made her own meal before he arrived she found to her embarrassment that there was nothing left for her to do but talk when not assisting him. She asked him if he would excuse her finishing a letter she had been writing at a side-table, and, after sitting down to it, tingled with a sense of being grossly rude. However, seeing that he noticed nothing personally wrong in her, and that he too was embarrassed when she attentively watched his cup to refill it, Elfride became better at ease; and when furthermore he accidentally kicked the leg of the table, and then nearly upset his tea-cup, just as schoolboys did, she felt herself mistress of the situation, and could talk very well. In a few minutes ingenuousness and a common term of years obliterated all recollection that they were strangers just met. Stephen began to wax eloquent on extremely slight experiences connected with his professional pursuits; and she, having no experiences to fall back upon, recounted with much animation stories that had been related to her by her father, which would have astonished him had he heard with what fidelity of action and tone they were rendered. Upon the whole, a very interesting picture of Sweet-and-Twenty* was on view that evening in Mr Swancourt's house.

Ultimately Stephen had to go upstairs and talk loud to the rector, receiving from him between his puffs a great many apologies for calling him so unceremoniously to a stranger's bedroom. 'But,' continued Mr Swancourt, 'I felt that I wanted to say a few words to you before the morning, on the business of your visit. One's patience gets exhausted by staying a prisoner in bed all day through a sudden freak of one's enemy – new to me, though – for I have known very little of gout as yet. However, he's gone to my other toe in a very mild manner, and I expect he'll slink off altogether by the morning. I hope you have been well attended to downstairs?'

'Perfectly. And though it is unfortunate, and I am sorry to see you laid up, I beg you will not take the slightest notice of my being in the house the while.'

'I will not. But I shall be down to-morrow. My daughter is an excellent doctor. A dose or two of her mild mixtures will fetch me round quicker than all the drug stuff in the world. Well, now about the church business. Take a seat, do. We can't afford to stand upon ceremony in these parts as you see, and for this reason, that a civilized human being seldom stays long with us; and so we cannot waste time in approaching him, or he will be gone before we have had the pleasure of close acquaintance. This tower of ours is, as you will notice, entirely gone beyond the possibility of restoration; but the church itself is well enough. You should see some of the churches in this county. Floors rotten: ivy lining the walls.'

'Dear me!'

'Oh, that's nothing. The congregation of a neighbour of mine, whenever a storm of rain comes on during service, open their umbrellas and hold them up till the dripping ceases from the roof. Now, if you will kindly bring me those papers and letters you see lying on the table, I will show you how far we have got.'

Stephen crossed the room to fetch them, and the rector seemed to notice more particularly the slim figure of his visitor.

'I suppose you are quite competent?' he said.

'Quite,' said the young man, colouring slightly.

'You are very young, I fancy – I should say you are not more than nineteen?'

'I am just over twenty.'

'Not half my age; I am past fifty.'

'By the way,' said Mr Swancourt, after some conversation, 'you said your whole name was Stephen Fitzmaurice, and that your grandfather came originally from Caxbury. Since I have been speaking, it has occurred to me that I know something of you. You belong to a well-known ancient county family – not ordinary Smiths in the least.'

'I don't think we have any of their blood in our veins.'

'Nonsense! you must. Hand me the "Landed Gentry".* Now, let me see. There, Stephen Fitzmaurice Smith – he lies in St Mary's Church, doesn't he? Well, out of that family sprang the Leaseworthy Smiths, and collaterally came General Sir Stephen Fitzmaurice Smith of Caxbury—'

'Yes; I have seen his monument there,' shouted Stephen. 'But there is no connection between his family and mine: there cannot be.'

'There is none, possibly to your knowledge. But look at this, my dear sir,' said the rector, striking his fist upon the bedpost for emphasis. 'Here are you, Stephen Fitzmaurice Smith, living in London, but springing from Caxbury. Here in this book is a genealogical tree of the Stephen Fitzmaurice Smiths of Caxbury Manor. You may be only a family of professional men now – I am not inquisitive: I don't ask questions of that kind; it is not in me to do so – but it is as plain as the nose in your face that there's your origin! And, Mr Smith, I congratulate you upon your blood; blue blood, sir; and, upon my life, a very desirable colour, as the world goes.'

'I wish you could congratulate me upon some more tangible quality,' said the younger man, sadly no less than modestly.

'Nonsense! that will come with time. You are young: all your life is before you. Now look – see how far back in the mists of antiquity my own family of Swancourt have a root. Here, you see,' he continued, turning to the page, 'is Geoffrey, the one among my ancestors who lost a barony because he would cut his joke.* Ah, it's the sort of us! But the story is too long to tell now. Ay, I'm a poor man – a poor gentleman, in fact: those I would be friends with, won't be friends with me; those who are willing to be friends with me, I am above being friends with. Beyond dining with a neighbouring incumbent or two, and an occasional chat – sometimes dinner – with Lord Luxellian, a connection of mine, I am in absolute solitude – absolute.'

'You have your studies, your books, and your – daughter.'

'O yes, yes; and I don't complain of poverty. *Canto coram latrone*.* Well, Mr Smith, don't let me detain you any longer in a sick room. Ha! that reminds me of a story I once heard in my younger days.' Here the rector began a series of small private laughs, and Stephen looked inquiry. 'O no, no! it is too bad – too bad to tell!' continued Mr Swancourt in undertones of grim mirth. 'Well, go downstairs; my daughter must do the best she can with you this evening. Ask her to sing to you – she plays and sings very nicely. Good-night; I feel as if I had known you for five or six years. I'll ring for somebody to show you down.'

'Never mind,' said Stephen, 'I can find the way.' And he went downstairs, thinking of the delightful freedom of manner in the remoter counties by comparison with the reserve of London.

'I forgot to tell you that my father was rather deaf,' said Elfride anxiously, when Stephen entered the little drawing-room.

'Never mind; I know all about it, and we are great friends,' the man of business replied enthusiastically. 'And, Miss Swancourt, will you kindly sing to me?'

To Miss Swancourt this request seemed, what in fact it was, exceptionally point-blank; though she guessed that her father had some hand in framing it, knowing, rather to her cost, of his unceremonious way of utilizing her for the benefit of dull sojourners. At the same time, as Mr Smith's manner was too frank to provoke criticism, and his age too little to inspire fear, she was ready – not to say pleased – to accede. Selecting from the canterbury* some old family ditties, that in years gone by had been played and sung by her mother, Elfride sat down to the pianoforte, and began ''Twas on the evening of a winter's day', in a pretty contralto voice. Next she took 'Should he upbraid',* which suited her exquisitely both in voice and mien.

'Do you like that old thing, Mr Smith?' she said at the end.

'Yes, I do much,' said Stephen, words he would have uttered, and sincerely, to anything on earth, from glee to requiem, that she might have chosen.

'You shall have a little one by de Leyre,* that was given me by a young French lady who was staying at Endelstow House:

> '"Je l'ai planté, je l'ai vu naître,
> Ce beau rosier où les oiseaux," &c.;

and then I shall want to give you my own favourite for the very last, Shelley's "When the lamp is shattered",* as set to music by my poor mother. I so much like singing to anybody who *really* cares to hear me.'

Every woman who makes a permanent impression on a man is usually recalled to his mind's eye as she appeared in one particular scene, which seems ordained to be her special form of manifestation throughout the pages of his memory. As the patron Saint has her attitude and accessories in mediæval illumination, so the sweetheart may be said to have hers upon the table of her true Love's fancy, without which she is rarely introduced there except by effort; and this though she may, on further acquaintance, have been observed in many other phases which one would imagine to be far more appropriate to Love's young dream.

Miss Elfride's image chose the form in which she was beheld during these minutes of singing, for her permanent attitude of visitation to Stephen's eyes during his sleeping and waking hours in after days. The profile is seen of a young woman in a pale gray silk dress with trimmings of swan's-down, and opening up from a point in front, like a waistcoat without a shirt; the cool colour contrasting admirably with the warm bloom of her neck and face. The furthermost candle on the piano comes immediately in a line with her head, and half invisible itself, forms the accidentally frizzled hair into a nebulous haze of light, surrounding her crown like an aureola.* Her hands are in their place on the keys, her lips parted, and trilling forth, in a tender *diminuendo*,* the closing words of the sad apostrophe:

> 'O Love, who bewailest
> The frailty of all things here,
> Why choose you the frailest
> For your cradle, your home, and your bier!'*

Her head is forward a little, and her eyes directed keenly upward to the top of the page of music confronting her. Then comes a rapid look into Stephen's face, and a still more rapid look back again to her business, her face having dropped its sadness, and acquired a certain expression of mischievous archness the while; which lingered there for some time, but was never developed into a positive smile of flirtation.

Stephen suddenly shifted his position from her right hand to her left, where there was just space enough for a small ottoman to stand between the piano and the corner of the room. Into this nook he squeezed himself, and gazed wistfully up into Elfride's face. So long and so earnestly gazed he, that her cheek deepened to a more and more crimson tint as each line was added to her song. Concluding, and pausing motionless after the last word for a minute or two, she ventured to look at him again. His features wore an expression of unutterable heaviness.

'You don't hear many songs, do you, Mr Smith, to take so much notice of these of mine?'

'Perhaps it was the means and vehicle of the song that I was noticing: I mean yourself,' he answered gently.

'Now, Mr Smith!'

'It is perfectly true; I don't hear much singing. You mistake what I am, I fancy. Because I come as a stranger to a secluded spot, you think I must needs come from a life of bustle, and know the latest movements of the day. But I don't. My life is as quiet as yours, and more solitary; solitary as death.'

'The death which comes from a plethora of life? But seriously, I can quite see that you are not the least what I thought you would be before I saw you. You are not critical, or experienced, or – much to mind. That's why I don't mind singing airs to you that I only half know.' Finding that by this confession she had vexed him in a way she did not intend, she added naïvely, 'I mean, Mr Smith, that you are better, not worse, for being only young and not very experienced. You don't think my life here so very tame and dull, I know.'

'I do not, indeed,' he said with fervour. 'It must be delightfully poetical, and sparkling, and fresh, and—'

'There you go, Mr Smith! Well, men of another kind, when I get them to be honest enough to own the truth, think just the reverse:

that my life must be a dreadful bore in its normal state, though pleasant for the exceptional few days they pass here.'

'I could live here always!' he said, and with such a tone and look of unconscious revelation that Elfride was startled to find that her harmonies had fired a small Troy,* in the shape of Stephen's heart. She said quickly:

'But you can't live here always.'

'O no.' And he drew himself in with the sensitiveness of a snail.

Elfride's emotions were sudden as his in kindling, but the least of woman's lesser infirmities – love of admiration – caused an inflammable disposition on his part, so exactly similar to her own, to appear as meritorious in him as modesty made her own seem culpable in her.

CHAPTER FOUR

'Where heaves the turf in many a mould'ring heap.'*

FOR reasons of his own, Stephen Smith was stirring a short time after dawn the next morning. From the window of his room he could see, first, two bold escarpments sloping down together like the letter V. Towards the bottom, like liquid in a funnel, appeared the sea, gray and small. On the slant of one hill, of rather greater altitude than its neighbour, stood the church which was to be the scene of his operations. The lonely edifice was black and bare, cutting up into the sky from the profile of the hill. It had a square mouldering tower, owning neither battlement nor pinnacle, and seemed a monolithic termination, of one substance with the ridge, rather than a structure raised thereon. Round the church ran a low wall; over-topping the wall in general level was the graveyard; not as a graveyard usually is, a fragment of landscape with its due variety of chiaro-oscuro, but a mere margin against the sky, serrated with the outlines of graves and a very few memorial stones. Not a tree could exist up there: nothing but the monotonous gray-green grass.

Five minutes after this casual survey was made his bedroom was empty, and its occupant had vanished quietly from the house.

At the end of two hours he was again in the room, looking warm and glowing. He now pursued the artistic details of dressing, which on his first rising had been entirely omitted. And a very blooming boy he looked, after that mysterious morning scamper. His mouth was a triumph of its class. It was the cleanly-cut, piquantly pursed-up mouth of William Pitt,* as represented in the well or little known bust by Nollekens* – a mouth which is in itself a young man's fortune, if properly exercised. His round chin, where its upper part turned inward, still continued its perfect and full curve, seeming to press in to a point the bottom of his nether lip at their place of junction.

Once he murmured the name of Elfride. Ah, there she was! On the lawn in a plain dress, without hat or bonnet, running with a boy's velocity, superadded to a girl's lightness, after a tame rabbit she was endeavouring to capture, her strategic intonations of coaxing words alternating with desperate rushes so much out of keeping with them that the hollowness of such expressions was but too evident to her pet, who darted and dodged in carefully timed counterpart.

The scene down there was altogether different from that of the hills. A thicket of shrubs and trees enclosed the favoured spot from the wilderness without; even at this time of the year the grass was luxuriant there. No wind blew inside the protecting belt of evergreens, wasting its force upon the higher and stronger trees forming the outer margin of the grove.

Then he heard a heavy person shuffling about in slippers, and calling 'Mr Smith!' Smith proceeded to the study, and found Mr Swancourt. The young man expressed his gladness to see his host downstairs.

'O yes; I knew I should soon be right again. I have not made the acquaintance of gout for more than two years, and it generally goes off the second night. Well, where have you been this morning? I saw you come in just now, I think?'

'Yes; I have been for a walk.'

'Start early?'

'Yes.'

'Very early, I think?'

'Yes, it was rather early.'

'Which way did you go? To the sea, I suppose. Everybody goes seaward.'

'No; I followed up the river as far as the park wall.'

'You are different from your kind. Well, I suppose such a wild place is a novelty, and so tempted you out of bed?'

'Not altogether a novelty. I like it.'

The youth seemed averse to explanation.

'You must, you must; to go cock-watching* the morning after a journey of fourteen or sixteen hours. But there's no accounting for tastes, and I am glad to see that yours are no meaner. After breakfast, but not before, I shall be good for a ten miles' walk, Master Smith.'

Certainly there seemed nothing exaggerated in that assertion. Mr Swancourt by daylight showed himself to be a man who, in common with the other two people under his roof, had really strong claims to be considered handsome, – handsome, that is, in the sense in which the moon is bright: the ravines and valleys which, on a close inspection, are seen to diversify its surface, being left out of the argument. His face was of a tint that never deepened upon his cheeks nor lightened upon his forehead, but remained uniform throughout; the usual neutral salmon-colour of a man who feeds well – not to say too well – and does not think hard; every pore being in visible working order. His *ensemble** was that of a highly improved class of farmer dressed up in the wrong clothes; that of a firm-standing perpendicular man, whose fall would have been backwards in direction if he had ever lost his balance.

The rector's background was at present what a rector's background should be, his study. Here the consistency ends. All along the chimneypiece were ranged bottles of horse, pig, and cow medicines, and against the wall was a high table, made up of the fragments of an old oak lych-gate.* Upon this stood stuffed specimens of owls, divers, and gulls, and over them bunches of wheat and barley ears, labelled with the date of the year that produced them. Some cases and shelves, more or less laden with books, the prominent titles of which were Dr Brown's 'Notes on the Romans', Dr Smith's 'Notes on the Corinthians', and Dr Robinson's 'Notes on the Galatians, Ephesians, and Philippians', just saved the character of the place, in spite of a girl's doll's-house standing above them, a marine aquarium in the window, and Elfride's hat hanging on its corner.

'Business, business!' said Mr Swancourt after breakfast. He began to find it necessary to act the part of a fly-wheel* towards the somewhat irregular forces of his visitor.

They prepared to go to the church; the rector, on second thoughts, mounting his coal-black mare to avoid exerting his foot too much at starting. Stephen said he should want a man to assist him. 'Worm!' the rector shouted.

A minute or two after a voice was heard round the corner of the building, mumbling, 'Ah, I used to be strong enough, but 'tis altered now! Well, there, I'm as independent as one here and there, even if they do write 'squire after their names.'

'What's the matter?' said the rector, as William Worm appeared;

when the remarks were repeated to him.

'Worm says some very true things sometimes,' Mr Swancourt said, turning to Stephen. 'Now, as regards that word "esquire". Why, Mr Smith, that word "esquire" is gone to the dogs, – used on the letters of every jackanapes who has a black coat. Anything else, Worm?'

'Ay, the folk have begun frying again!'

'Dear me! I'm sorry to hear that.'

'Yes,' Worm groaned to Stephen, 'I've got such a noise in my head that there's no living night nor day. 'Tis just for all the world like people frying fish: fry, fry, fry, all day long in my poor head, till I don't know whe'r I'm here or yonder. There, God A'mighty will find it out sooner or later, I hope, and relieve me.'

'Now, my deafness,' said Mr Swancourt impressively, 'is a dead silence; but William Worm's is that of people frying fish in his head. Very remarkable, isn't it?'

'I can hear the frying-pan a-fizzing as naterel* as life,' said Worm corroboratively.

'Yes, it is remarkable,' said Mr Smith.

'Very peculiar, very peculiar,' echoed the rector; and they all then followed the track along the hill-slope, fenced on each side by a little stone wall from which gleamed fragments of quartz and blood-red marbles, apparently of inestimable value, in their setting of brown alluvium. Stephen walked with the dignity of a man close to the horse's head, Worm stumbled along a stone's throw in the rear, and Elfride was nowhere in particular, yet everywhere; sometimes in front, sometimes behind, sometimes at the sides, hovering about the procession like a butterfly; not definitely engaged in travelling, yet somehow chiming in at points with the general progress.

The rector explained things as he went on: 'The fact is, Mr Smith, I didn't want this bother of church restoration at all, but it was necessary to do something in self-defence, on account of those d—dissenters:* I use the word in its scriptural meaning, of course, not as an expletive.'

'How very sad!' said Stephen, with the concern demanded of serious friendliness.

'Sad? That's nothing to how it is in the parish of Twinkley. Both the churchwardens are—; there, I won't say what they are; and the clerk and the sexton as well.'

'How very strange!' said Stephen.

'Strange? My dear sir, that's nothing to how it is in the parish of Sinnerton. However, as to our own parish, I hope we shall make some progress soon.'

'You must trust to circumstances.'

'There are no circumstances to trust to. We may as well trust in Providence if we trust at all. But here we are. A wild place, isn't it? But I like it on such days as these.'

The churchyard was entered on this side by a stone stile, over which having clambered, you remained still on the wild hill, the within not being so divided from the without as to obliterate the sense of open freedom. A delightful place to be buried in, postulating that delight can accompany a man to his tomb under any circumstances. There was nothing horrible in this churchyard, in the shape of tight mounds bonded with sticks, which shout imprisonment in the ears rather than whisper rest; or trim garden-flowers, which only raise images of people in new black crape and white handkerchiefs coming to tend them; or wheel-marks, which remind us of hearses and mourning coaches; or cypress-bushes, which make a parade of sorrow; or coffin-boards and bones lying behind trees, showing that we are only leaseholders of our graves. No; nothing but long, wild, untutored grass, diversifying the forms of the mounds it covered, – themselves irregularly shaped, with no eye to effect; the impressive presence of the old mountain that all this was a part of being nowhere excluded by disguising art. Outside were similar slopes and similar grass; and then the serene impassive sea, visible to a width of half the horizon, and meeting the eye with the effect of a vast concave, like the interior of a blue vessel. Detached rocks stood upright afar, a collar of foam girding their bases, and repeating in its whiteness the plumage of a countless multitude of gulls that restlessly hovered about.

'Now, Worm!' said Mr Swancourt sharply; and Worm started into an attitude of attention at once to receive orders. Stephen and himself were then left in possession, and the work went on till early in the afternoon, when dinner was announced by Unity of the rectory kitchen running to the church without a bonnet.

*

Elfride did not make her appearance inside the building till late in the afternoon, and came then by special invitation from Stephen during dinner. She looked so intensely *living* and full of movement as she came into the old silent place that young Smith's world began to be lit by 'the purple light'* in all its definiteness. Worm was got rid of by sending him to measure the height of the tower.

What could she do but come close – so close that a minute arc of her skirt touched his foot – and ask him how he was getting on with his sketches, and set herself to learn the principles of practical mensuration as applied to irregular buildings? Then she must ascend the pulpit to re-imagine for the hundredth time how it would seem to be a preacher.*

Presently she leant over the front of the pulpit.

'Don't you tell papa, will you, Mr Smith, if I tell you something?' she said with a sudden impulse to make a confidence.

'O no, that I won't,' said he, staring up.

'Well, I write papa's sermons for him very often, and he preaches them better than he does his own; and then afterwards he talks to people and to me about what he said in his sermon to-day, and forgets that I wrote it for him. Isn't it absurd?'

'How clever you must be!' said Stephen. 'I couldn't write a sermon for the world.'

'O, it's easy enough,' she said, descending from the pulpit and coming close to him to explain more vividly. 'You do it like this. Did you ever play a game of forfeits* called "When is it? where is it? what is it?"'

'No, never.'

'Ah, that's a pity, because writing a sermon is very much like playing that game. You take the text. You think, why is it? what is it? and so on. You put that down under "Generally". Then you proceed to the First, Secondly, and Thirdly. Papa won't have Fourthlys – says they are all my eye. Then you have a final Collectively, several pages of this being put in great black brackets, writing opposite, "*Leave this out if the farmers are falling asleep.*" Then comes your In Conclusion, then A Few Words And I Have Done. Well, all this time you have put on the back of each page, "*Keep your voice down*" – I mean,' she added, correcting herself, 'that's how I do in papa's sermon-book, because otherwise he gets louder and louder, till at last he shouts like a farmer up a-field. O, papa is so funny in some things!'

Then, after this childish burst of confidence, she was frightened, as if warned by womanly instinct, which for the moment her ardour had outrun, that she had been too forward to a comparative stranger.

Elfride saw her father then, and went away into the wind, being caught by a gust as she ascended the churchyard slope, in which gust she had the motions, without the motives, of a hoiden;* the grace, without the self-consciousness, of a pirouetter. She conversed for a minute or two with her father, and proceeded homeward, Mr Swancourt coming on to the church to Stephen. The wind had freshened his warm complexion as it freshens the glow of a brand. He was in a mood of jollity, and watched Elfride homeward with a smile.

'You little flyaway! you look wild enough now,' he said, and turned to Stephen. 'But she's not a wild child at all, Mr Smith. As steady as you; and that you are steady I see from your diligence here.'

'I think Miss Swancourt very clever,' Stephen observed.

'Yes, she is; certainly, she is,' said her father, adopting as much as possible the neutral tone of disinterested criticism. 'Now, Smith, I'll tell you something; but she mustn't know it for the world – not for the world, mind, for she insists upon keeping it a dead secret. Why, *she writes my sermons for me often*, and a very good job she makes of them!'

'She can do anything.'

'She can do that. The little rascal has the very trick of the trade. But, mind you, Smith, not a word about it to her, not a single word!'

'Not a word,' said Smith.

'Look there,' said Mr Swancourt. 'What do you think of my roofing?' He pointed with his walking-stick at the chancel roof.

'Did you do that, sir?'

'Yes, I worked in shirt-sleeves all the time that was going on. I pulled down the old rafters, fixed the new ones, put on the battens, slated the roof, all with my own hands, Worm being my assistant. We worked like slaves, didn't we, Worm?'

'Ay, sure, we did; harder than some here and there – hee, hee!'

said William Worm, cropping up from somewhere. 'Like slaves, 'a b'lieve – hee, hee! And weren't ye foaming mad, sir, when the nails wouldn't go straight? Mighty I!* There, 'tisn't so bad to cuss and keep it in as to cuss and let it out, is it, sir?'

'Well – why?'

'Because you, sir, when ye were a-putting on the roof, only used to cuss in your mind, which is, I suppose, no harm at all.'

'I don't think you know what goes on in my mind, Worm.'

'O doan't I, sir – hee, hee! Maybe I'm but a poor wambling thing, sir, and can't read much; but I can spell as well as some here and there. Doan't ye mind, sir, that blustrous night when ye asked me to hold the candle to ye in yer workshop, when you were making a new chair for the chancel?'

'Yes; what of that?'

'I stood with the candle, and you said you liked company, if 'twas only a dog or cat – maning me; and the chair wouldn't do nohow.'

'Ah, I remember.'

'No; the chair wouldn't do nohow. 'A was very well to look at; but, Lord! –'

'Worm, how often have I corrected you for irreverent speaking!'

'– 'A was very well to look at, but you couldn't sit in the chair nohow. 'Twas all a-twist wi' the chair, like the letter Z, directly you sat down upon the chair. "Get up, Worm," says you, when you seed the chair go all a-sway wi' me. Up you took the chair, and flung en like fire and brimstone to t'other end of your shop – all in a passion. "Damn the chair!" says I. "Just what I was thinking," says you, sir. "I could see it in your face, sir," says I, "and I hope you and God will forgi'e me for saying what you wouldn't." To save your life you couldn't help laughing, sir, at a poor wambler reading your thoughts so plain. Ay, I'm as wise as one here and there.'

'I thought you had better have a practical man to go over the church and tower with you,' Mr Swancourt said to Stephen the following morning, 'so I got Lord Luxellian's permission to send for one when you came. I told him to be there at ten o'clock. He's a very intelligent man, and he will tell you all you want to know about the state of the walls. His name is John Smith.'

Elfride did not like to be seen again at the church with Stephen. 'I will watch here for your appearance at the top of the tower,' she said laughingly. 'I shall see your figure against the sky.'

'And when I am up there I'll wave my handkerchief to you, Miss Swancourt,' said Stephen. 'In twelve minutes from this present moment,' he added, looking at his watch, 'I'll be at the summit and look out for you.'

She went round to the corner of the shrubbery, whence she could watch him up the slope leading to the side of the hill on which the church stood. There she saw waiting for him a white spot – a mason in his working clothes. Stephen met this man and stopped.

To her surprise, instead of their moving on to the churchyard, they both leisurely sat down upon a stone close by their meeting-place, and remained as if in deep conversation. Elfride looked at the time; nine of the twelve minutes had passed, and Stephen showed no signs of moving. More minutes passed – she grew cold with waiting, and shivered. It was not till the end of a quarter of an hour that they began to wend to the church at a snail's pace.

'Rude and unmannerly!' she said to herself, colouring with pique. 'Anybody would think he was in love with that horrid mason instead of with—'

The sentence remained unspoken, though not unthought.

She returned to the porch.

'Is the man you sent for a lazy, sit-still, do-nothing kind of man?' she inquired of her father.

'No,' he said surprised; 'quite the reverse. He is Lord Luxellian's master-mason.'

'Oh,' said Elfride indifferently, and returned towards her bleak station, and waited and shivered again. It was a trifle, after all – a childish thing – looking out from a tower and waving a handkerchief. But her new friend had promised, and why should he tease her so? The effect of a blow is as proportionate to the texture of the object struck as to its own momentum; and she had such a superlative capacity for being wounded that little hits struck her hard.

It was not till the end of half an hour that two figures were seen above the parapet of the dreary old pile, motionless as bitterns on a ruined mosque. Even then Stephen was not true enough to perform what he was so courteous to promise, and he vanished without making a sign.

He returned at midday. Elfride looked vexed when unconscious that his eyes were upon her; when conscious, severe. However, her attitude of coldness had long outlived the coldness itself, and she could no longer utter feigned words of indifference.

'Ah, you weren't kind to keep me waiting in the cold, and break your promise,' she said at last reproachfully, in tones too low for her father's powers of hearing.

'Forgive, forgive me!' said Stephen with dismay. 'I had forgotten – quite forgotten! Something prevented my remembering.'

'Any further explanation?' said Miss Capricious, pouting.

He was silent for a few minutes, and looked askance.

'None,' he said, with the accent of one who concealed a sin.

CHAPTER FIVE

'Bosom'd high in tufted trees'*

It was breakfast time.

As seen from the rectory dining-room, which took a warm tone of light from the fire, the weather and scene outside seemed to have stereotyped themselves in unrelieved shades of gray. The long-armed trees and shrubs of juniper, cedar, and pine varieties, were grayish-black; those of the broad-leaved sort, together with the herbage, were grayish-green; the eternal hills and tower behind them were grayish-brown; the sky, dropping behind all, gray of the purest melancholy.

Yet in spite of this sombre artistic effect the morning was not one which tended to lower the spirits. It was even cheering. For it did not rain, nor was rain likely to fall for many days to come.

Elfride had turned from the table towards the fire and was idly elevating a hand-screen before her face, when she heard the click of a little gate outside.

'Ah, here's the postman!' she said, as a shuffling, active man came through an opening in the shrubbery and across the lawn. She vanished, and met him in the porch, afterwards coming in with her hands behind her back.

'How many are there? Three for papa, one for Mr Smith, none for Miss Swancourt. And, papa, look here, one of yours is from – whom do you think? – Lord Luxellian. And it has something *hard* in it – a lump of something. I've been feeling it through the envelope, and can't think what it is.'

'What does Luxellian write for, I wonder?' Mr Swancourt had said simultaneously with her words. He handed Stephen his letter, and took his own, putting on his countenance a higher class of look than was customary, as became a poor gentleman who was going to read a letter from a peer connected with his family.

Stephen read his missive with a countenance quite the reverse of the rector's.

PERCY PLACE, *Thursday Evening*

DEAR SMITH, – Old H. is in a towering rage with you for being so long about the church sketches. Swears you are more trouble than you are worth. He says I am to write and say you are to stay no longer on any consideration – that he would have done it all in three hours very easily. I told him that you were not like an experienced hand, which he seemed to forget, but it did not make much difference. However, between you and me privately, if I were you I would not alarm myself for a day or so, if I were not inclined to return. I would make out the week and finish my spree. He will blow up just as much if you appear here on Saturday as if you keep away till Monday morning. – Yours very truly,

SIMPKINS JENKINS

'Dear me – very awkward!' said Stephen, rather *en l'air*,* and confused with the kind of confusion that assails an understrapper when he has been enlarged by accident to the dimensions of a superior, and is somewhat rudely pared down to his original size.

'What is awkward?' said Miss Swancourt.

Smith by this time recovered his equanimity, and with it the professional dignity of an experienced architect.

'Important business demands my immediate presence in London, I regret to say,' he replied.

'What! Must you go at once?' said Mr Swancourt, looking over the edge of his letter. 'Important business? A young fellow like you to have important business!'

'The truth is,' said Stephen blushing, and rather ashamed of having pretended even so slightly to a consequence which did not belong to him, – 'the truth is, Mr Hewby has sent to say I am to come home; and I must obey him.'

'I see; I see. It is politic to do so, you mean. Now I can see more than you think. You are to be his partner. I booked you for that directly I read his letter to me the other day, and the way he spoke of you. He thinks a great deal of you, Mr Smith, or he wouldn't be so anxious for your return.'

Unpleasant to Stephen such remarks as these could not sound; to have the expectancy of partnership with one of the largest-practising architects in London thrust upon him was cheering, however untenable he felt the idea to be. He saw that, whatever Mr Hewby might think, Mr Swancourt certainly thought much of him to entertain such an idea on such slender ground as to be absolutely no ground at all. And then, unaccountably, his speaking face exhibited a cloud of sadness, which a reflection on the remoteness of any such contingency could hardly have sufficed to cause.

Elfride was struck with that look of his; even Mr Swancourt noticed it.

'Well,' he said cheerfully, 'never mind that now. You must come again on your own account; not on business. Come to see me as a visitor, you know – say, in your holidays – all you town men have holidays like schoolboys. When are they?'

'In August, I believe.'

'Very well; come in August; and then you need not hurry away so. I am glad to get somebody decent to talk to, or at, in this outlandish *ultima Thule*.* But, by the bye, I have something to say – you won't go to-day?'

'No; I need not,' said Stephen hesitatingly. 'I am not obliged to get back before Monday morning.'

'Very well, then, that brings me to what I am going to propose. This is a letter from Lord Luxellian. I think you heard me speak of him as the resident landowner in this district, and patron of this living?'*

'I – know of him.'

'He is in London now. It seems that he has run up on business for a day or two, and taken Lady Luxellian with him. He has written to ask me to go to his house, and search for a paper among his private memoranda, which he forgot to take with him.'

'What did he send in the letter?' inquired Elfride.

'The key of a private desk in which the papers are. He doesn't like to trust such a matter to anybody else. I have done such things for him before. And what I propose is, that we make an afternoon of it – all three of us. Go for a drive to Targan Bay, come home by way of Endelstow House; and whilst I am looking over the documents you can ramble about the rooms where you like. I have the run of the house at any time, you know. The building, though nothing but a mass of gables outside, has a splendid hall, staircase, and gallery within; and there are a few good pictures.'

'Yes, there are,' said Stephen.

'Have you seen the place, then?'

'I saw it as I came by,' he said hastily.

'O yes; but I was alluding to the interior. And the church – St Eval's – is much older than our St Agnes' here. I do duty in that and this alternately, you know. The fact is, I ought to have some help; riding across that park for two miles on a wet morning is not at all the thing. If my constitution were not well seasoned, as thank God it is,' – here Mr Swancourt looked down his front, as if his constitution were visible there, – 'I should be coughing and barking all the year round. And when the family goes away there are only about three servants to preach to when I get there. Well, that shall be the arrangement, then. Elfride, you will like to come too?'

Elfride assented; and the little breakfast-party separated. Stephen rose to go and take a few final measurements at the church, the rector following him to the door with a mysterious expression of inquiry on his face.

'You'll put up with our not having family prayer this morning, I hope?' he whispered.

'Yes; quite so,' said Stephen.

'To tell you the truth,' he continued in the same undertone, 'we don't make a regular thing of it; but when we have strangers visiting us, I am strongly of opinion that it is the proper thing to do, and I always do it. I am very strict on that point. But you, Smith, there is something in your face which makes me feel quite at home; no nonsense about you, in short. Ah, it reminds me of a splendid story I used to hear when I was a helter-skelter young fellow – such a story! But' – here the rector shook his head self-forbiddingly, and grimly laughed.

'Was it an interesting story?' said young Smith, smiling too.

'O yes; but 'tis too bad – too bad! Couldn't tell it to you for the world!'

Stephen went across the lawn, hearing the parson chuckling privately at the recollection as he withdrew.

They started at three o'clock. The grey morning had resolved itself into an afternoon bright with a pale pervasive sunlight, without the sun itself being visible. Lightly they trotted along – first to Parrett Down – the horse's hoofs clapping, almost ringing, upon the hard, white, turnpike road* as it followed the level ridge in a perfectly straight line, seeming to be absorbed ultimately by the white of the sky.

Targan Bay – which had the merit of being easily got at – was next visited. They then swept round by innumerable lanes, in which not twenty consecutive yards were either straight or level, to the domain of Lord Luxellian. A woman with a double chin and thick neck, like the Queen Anne portrait by Dahl,* threw open the lodge gate, a little boy standing behind her.

'I'll give him something, poor little fellow,' said Elfride, pulling out her purse and hastily opening it. From the band of her purse a host of bits of paper, like a flock of white birds, floated into the air, and were blown about in all directions.

'Well, to be sure!' said Stephen with a slight laugh.

'What the dickens is all that?' said Mr Swancourt. 'Not halves of bank-notes, Elfride?'

Elfride looked annoyed and guilty. 'They are only something of mine, papa,' she faltered, whilst Stephen leapt out, and, assisted by the lodge-keeper's little boy, crept about round the wheels and horse's hoofs till the papers were all gathered together again. He handed them back to her, and remounted.

'I suppose you are wondering what those scraps were?' she said, as they bowled along up the sycamore avenue. 'And so I may as well tell you. They are notes for a romance I am writing.'

She could not help colouring at the confession, much as she tried to avoid it.

'A story, do you mean?' said Stephen, Mr Swancourt half listening, and catching a word of the conversation now and then.

'Yes; *The Court of King Arthur's Castle: a Romance of Lyonnesse.* Such writing is out of date now, I know; but I like doing it.'

'A romance tucked into a purse! If a highwayman were to rob you, he would be taken in.'

'Yes; that's my way of carrying manuscript. The real reason is, that I mostly write bits of it on scraps of paper when I am on horseback; and I put them there for convenience.'

'What are you going to do with your romance when you have

written it?' said Stephen.

'I don't know,' she replied, and turned her head to look at the prospect.

For by this time they had reached the precincts of Endelstow House. Driving through an ancient gateway of dun-coloured stone, spanned by the high-shouldered Tudor arch,* they found themselves in a spacious court, closed by a façade on each of its three sides. The substantial portions of the existing building dated from the reign of Henry VIII; but the picturesque and sheltered spot had been the site of an erection of a much earlier date. A licence to crenellate *mansum infra manerium suum** was granted by Edward II to 'Hugo Luxellen chivaler';* but though the faint outline of the ditch and mound was visible at points, no sign of the original building remained.

The windows on all sides were long and many-mullioned; the roof lines broken up by dormer lights* of the same pattern. The apex stones* of these dormers, together with those of the gables, were surmounted by grotesque figures in rampant, passant, and couchant* variety. Tall octagonal and twisted chimneys thrust themselves high up into the sky, surpassed in height, however, by some poplars and sycamores at the back, which showed their gently rocking summits over ridge and parapet. In the corners of the court polygonal bays, whose surfaces were entirely occupied by buttresses and windows, broke into the squareness of the enclosure; and a far-projecting oriel,* springing from a fantastic series of mouldings, overhung the archway of the chief entrance to the house.

As Mr Swancourt had remarked, he had the freedom of the mansion in the absence of its owner. Upon a statement of his errand they were all admitted to the library, and left entirely to themselves. Mr Swancourt was soon up to his eyes in the examination of a heap of papers he had taken from the cabinet described by his correspondent. Stephen and Elfride had nothing to do but to wander about till her father was ready.

Elfride entered the gallery, and Stephen followed her without seeming to do so. It was a long sombre apartment, enriched with fittings a century or so later in style than the walls of the mansion. Pilasters* of Renaissance workmanship supported a cornice from which sprang a curved ceiling, panelled in the awkward twists and curls of the period. The old Gothic quarries* still remained in the upper portion of the large window at the end, though they had made way for a more modern form of glazing elsewhere.

Stephen was at one end of the gallery looking towards Elfride, who stood in the midst beginning to feel somewhat depressed by the society of Luxellian shades of cadaverous complexion fixed by Holbein, Kneller, and Lely,* and seeming to gaze at and through her in a moralizing mood. The silence, which cast almost a spell upon them, was broken by the sudden opening of a door at the far end.

Out bounded a pair of little girls, lightly yet warmly dressed. Their eyes were sparkling; their hair swinging about and around; their red mouths laughing with unalloyed gladness.

'Ah, Miss Swancourt: dearest Elfie! we heard you. Are you going to stay here? You are our little mamma, are you not – our big mamma is gone to London,' said one.

'Let me tiss you,' said the other, in appearance very much like the first, but to a smaller pattern.

Their pink cheeks and yellow hair were speedily intermingled with the folds of Elfride's dress; she then stooped and tenderly embraced them both.

'Such an odd thing,' said Elfride smiling, and turning to Stephen. 'They have taken it into their heads lately to call me "little mamma", because I am very fond of them, and wore a dress the other day something like one of Lady Luxellian's.'

These two young creatures were the Honourable Mary and the Honourable Kate – scarcely appearing large enough as yet to bear the weight of such ponderous prefixes. They were the only two children of Lord and Lady Luxellian, and, as it proved, had been left at home during their parents' temporary absence, in the custody of nurse and governess. Lord Luxellian was dotingly fond of the children; rather indifferent towards his wife, since she had begun to show an inclination not to please him by giving him a boy.

All children instinctively ran after Elfride, looking upon her more as an unusually nice large specimen of their own tribe than as a grown-up elder. It had now become an established rule that whenever she met them – indoors or out-of-doors, weekdays or Sundays – they were to be severally pressed against her face and bosom for the space of a quarter of a minute, and otherwise made much of on the delightful system of cumulative epithet and caress to which unpractised girls will occasionally abandon themselves.

A look of misgiving by the youngsters towards the door by which they had entered directed attention to a maid-servant appearing from the same quarter, to put an end to this sweet freedom of the poor Honourables Mary and Kate.

'I wish you lived here, Miss Swancourt,' piped one like a melancholy bullfinch.

'So do I,' piped the other like a rather more melancholy bullfinch. 'Mamma can't play with us so nicely as you do. I don't think she ever learnt playing when she was little. When shall we come to see you?'

'As soon as you like, dears.'

'And sleep at your house all night? That's what I mean by coming to see you. I don't care to see people with hats and bonnets on, and all standing up and walking about.'

'As soon as we can get mamma's permission you shall come and stay as long as ever you like. Good-bye!'

The prisoners were then led off, Elfride again turning her attention to her guest, whom she had left standing at the remote end of the gallery. On looking around for him he was nowhere to be seen. Elfride stepped down to the library, thinking he might have rejoined her father there. But Mr Swancourt, now cheerfully illuminated by a pair of candles, was still alone, untying packets of letters and papers, and tying them up again.

As Elfride did not stand on a sufficiently intimate footing with the object of her interest to justify her, as a proper young lady, to commence the active search for him that youthful impulsiveness prompted, and as, nevertheless, for a nascent reason connected with those divinely cut lips of his, she did not like him to be absent from her side, she wandered desultorily back to the oak staircase, pouting and casting her eyes about in hope of discerning his boyish figure.

Though daylight still prevailed in the rooms, the corridors were in a depth of shadow – chill, sad, and silent; and it was only by looking along them towards light spaces beyond that anything or anybody could be discerned therein. One of these light spots she found to be caused by a side-door with glass panels in the upper part. Elfride opened it, and found herself confronting a secondary or inner lawn, separated from the principal lawn front by a shrubbery.

And now she saw a perplexing sight. At right angles to the face of the wing she had emerged from, and within a few feet of the door, jutted out another wing of the mansion, lower and with less architectural character. Immediately opposite to her, in the wall of this wing, was a large broad window, having its blind drawn down, and illuminated by a light in the room it screened.

On the blind was a shadow from somebody close inside it – a person in profile. The profile was unmistakably that of Stephen. It was just possible to see that his arms were uplifted, and that his hands held an article of some kind. Then another shadow appeared – also in profile – and came close to him. This was the shadow of a woman. She turned her back towards Stephen: he lifted and held out what now proved to be a shawl or mantle – placed it carefully – *so* carefully – round the lady; disappeared; reappeared in her front – fastened the mantle. Did he then kiss her? Surely not. Yet the motion *might* have been a kiss. Then both shadows swelled to colossal dimensions – grew distorted – vanished.

Two minutes elapsed.

'Ah, Miss Swancourt! I am so glad to find you. I was looking for you,' said a voice at her elbow – Stephen's voice. She stepped into the passage.

'Do you know any of the members of this establishment?' said she.

'Not a single one: how should I?' he replied.

CHAPTER SIX

'Fare thee weel awhile!'*

SIMULTANEOUSLY with the conclusion of Stephen's remark, the sound of the closing of an external door in their immediate neighbourhood reached Elfride's ears. It came from the further side of the wing containing the illuminated room. She then discerned, by the aid of the dusky departing light, a figure, whose sex was undistinguishable, walking down the gravelled path by the parterre* towards the river. The figure grew fainter, and vanished under the trees.

Mr Swancourt's voice was heard calling out their names from a distant corridor in the body of the building. They retraced their steps and found him with his coat buttoned up and his hat on, awaiting their advent in a mood of self-satisfaction at having brought his search to a successful close. The carriage was brought round, and without further delay the trio drove away from the mansion, under the echoing gateway arch and along by the leafless sycamores, as the stars began to kindle their trembling lights behind the maze of branches and twigs.

No words were spoken either by youth or maiden. Her unpractised mind was completely occupied in fathoming its recent acquisition. The young man who had inspired her with such novelty of feeling, who had come directly from London on business to her father, having been brought by chance to Endelstow House had, by some means or other, acquired the privilege of approaching some lady he had found therein, and of honouring her by *petits soins** of a marked kind, – all in the space of half an hour.

What room were they standing in? thought Elfride. As nearly as she could guess, it was Lord Luxellian's business-room, or office. What people were in the house? None but the governess and servants, as far as she knew, and of these he had professed a total ignorance. Had the person she had indistinctly seen leaving the house anything to do with the performance? It was impossible to say without appealing to the culprit himself, and that she would never do. The more Elfride reflected, the more certain did it appear that the meeting was a chance rencounter,* and not an appointment. On the ultimate inquiry as to the individuality of the woman, Elfride at once assumed that she could not be an inferior. Stephen Smith was not the man to care about passages-at-love with women beneath him. Though gentle, ambition was visible in his kindling eyes; he evidently hoped for much; hoped indefinitely, but extensively. Elfride was puzzled, and being puzzled, was, by a natural sequence of girlish sensations, vexed with him. No more pleasure came in recognizing that from liking to attract him she was getting on to love him, boyish as he was and innocent as he had seemed.

They reached the bridge which formed a link between the eastern and western halves of the parish. Situated in a valley that was bounded outwardly by the sea, it formed a point of depression from which the road ascended with great steepness to West Endelstow and the rectory. There was no absolute necessity for either of them to alight, but as it was the rector's custom after a long journey to humour the horse in making this winding ascent, Elfride, moved by an imitative instinct, suddenly jumped out when Pleasant had just begun to adopt the deliberate stalk he associated with this portion of the road.

The young man seemed glad of any excuse for breaking the silence. 'Why, Miss Swancourt, what a risky thing to do!' he exclaimed, immediately following her example by jumping down on the other side.

'O no, not at all,' replied she coldly; the shadow phenomenon at Endelstow House still paramount within her.

Stephen walked along by himself for two or three minutes, wrapped in the rigid reserve dictated by her tone. Then apparently thinking that it was only for girls to pout he came serenely round to her side, and offered his arm with Castilian gallantry,* to assist her in ascending the remaining three-quarters of the steep.

Here was a temptation: it was the first time in her life that Elfride had been treated as a grown-up woman in this way – offered an arm in a manner implying that she had a right to refuse it. Till to-night she had never received masculine attentions beyond those which might be contained in such homely remarks as 'Elfride, give me your hand'; 'Elfride, take hold of my arm', from her father. Her callow heart made an epoch of the incident; she considered her array of feelings, for and against. Collectively they were for taking this offered arm; the single one of pique determined her to punish Stephen by refusing.

'No, thank you, Mr Smith; I can get along better by myself.'

It was Elfride's first fragile attempt at browbeating a lover. Fearing more the issue of such an undertaking than what a gentle young man might think of her waywardness, she immediately afterwards determined to please herself by reversing her statement.

'On second thoughts I will take it,' she said.

They slowly went their way up the hill, a few yards behind the carriage.

'How silent you are, Miss Swancourt!' Stephen observed.

'Perhaps I think you silent too,' she returned.

'I may have reason to be.'

'Scarcely; it is sadness that makes people silent, and you can have none.'

'You don't know: I have a trouble; though some might think it less a trouble than a dilemma.'

'What is it?' she asked impulsively.

Stephen hesitated. 'I might tell,' he said; 'at the same time, perhaps, it is as well—'

She let go his arm and imperatively pushed it from her, tossing her head. She had just learnt that a good deal of dignity is lost by asking a question to which an answer is refused, even ever so politely; for though politeness does good service in cases of requisition and compromise, it but little helps a direct refusal. 'I don't wish to know anything of it; I don't wish it,' she went on. 'The carriage is waiting for us at the top of the hill; we must get in'; and Elfride flitted to the front. 'Papa, here is your Elfride!' she exclaimed to the dusky figure of the old gentleman, as she sprang up and sank by his side without deigning to accept aid from Stephen.

'Ah, yes!' uttered the parson in artificially alert tones, awaking from a most profound sleep, and suddenly preparing to alight.

'Why, what *are* you doing, papa? We are not home yet.'

'O no, no; of course not; we are not at home yet,' Mr Swancourt said very hastily, endeavouring to dodge back to his original position with the air of a man who had not moved at all. 'The fact is I was so lost in deep meditation that I forgot whereabouts we were.' And in a minute the rector was snoring again.

That evening, being the last, seemed to throw an exceptional shade of sadness over Stephen Smith, and the repeated injunctions of the rector that he was to come and revisit them in the summer, apparently tended less to raise his spirits than to unearth some misgiving.

He left them in the gray light of dawn, whilst the colours of earth were sombre, and the sun was yet hidden in the east. Elfride had fidgeted all night in her little bed lest none of the household should be awake soon enough to start him, and also lest she might miss seeing again the bright eyes and curly hair to which their owner's possession of a hidden mystery added a deeper tinge of romance. To some extent – so soon does womanly interest take a solicitous turn – she felt herself responsible for his safe conduct. They breakfasted before daylight; Mr Swancourt, being more and more taken with his guest's ingenuous appearance, having determined to rise early and bid him a friendly farewell. It was, however, rather to the rector's astonishment that he saw Elfride walk in to the breakfast-table, candle in hand.

Whilst William Worm performed his toilet (during which performance the inmates of the rectory were always in the habit of waiting with exemplary patience), Elfride wandered desultorily to the summer house. Stephen followed her thither. The copse-covered valley was visible from this position, a mist now lying all along its length, hiding the stream which trickled through it, though the observers themselves were in clear air.

They stood close together, leaning over the rustic balustrading which bounded the arbour on the outward side, and formed the crest of a steep slope beneath. Elfride constrainedly pointed out some features of the distant uplands rising irregularly opposite. But the artistic eye was, either from nature or circumstance, very faint in Stephen now, and he only half attended to her description, as if he spared time from some other thought going on within him.

'Well, good-bye,' he said suddenly; 'I must never see you again, I suppose, Miss Swancourt, in spite of invitations.'

His genuine tribulation played directly upon the delicate chords of her nature. She could afford to forgive him for a concealment or two. Moreover, the shyness which would not allow him to look her in the face lent bravery to her own eyes and tongue.

'Oh, *do* come again, Mr Smith!' she said prettily.

'I should delight in it; but it will be better if I do not.'

'Why?'

'Certain circumstances in connection with me make it undesirable. Not on my account; on yours.'

'Goodness! As if anything in connection with you could hurt me,' she said with serene supremacy; but seeing that this plan of treatment was inappropriate she tuned a smaller note. 'Ah, I know why you will not come. You don't want to. You'll go home to London and to all the stirring people there, and will never want to see us any more!'

'You know I have no such reason.'

'And go on writing letters to the lady you are engaged to, just as before.'

'What does that mean? I am not engaged.'

'You wrote a letter to a Miss Somebody; I saw it in the letter-rack.'

'Pooh! an elderly woman who keeps a stationer's shop; and it was to tell her to keep my newspapers till I get back.'

'You needn't have explained: it was not my business at all.' Miss Elfride was rather relieved to hear that statement, nevertheless. 'And you won't come again to see my father?' she insisted.

'I should like to – and to see you again, but—'

'Will you reveal to me that matter you hide?' she interrupted petulantly.

'No; not now.'

She could not but go on, graceless as it might seem.

'Tell me this,' she importuned with a trembling mouth. 'Does any meeting of yours with a lady at Endelstow House clash with – any interest you may take in me?'

He started a little. 'It does not,' he said emphatically; and looked into the pupils of her eyes with the confidence that only honesty can give, and even that to youth alone.

The explanation had not come, but a gloom left her. She could not but believe that utterance. Whatever enigma might lie in the shadow on the blind, it was not an enigma of underhand passion.

She turned towards the house, entering it through the conservatory. Stephen went round to the front door. Mr Swancourt was standing on the step in his slippers. Worm was adjusting a buckle in the harness, and murmuring about his poor head; and everything was ready for Stephen's departure.

'You named August for your visit. August it shall be; that is, if you care for the society of such a fossilized Tory,' said Mr Swancourt.

Mr Smith only responded hesitatingly that he should like to come again.

'You said you would, and you must,' insisted Elfride, coming to the door and speaking under her father's arm.

Whatever reason the youth may have had for not wishing to enter the house as a guest, it no longer predominated. He promised, and bade them adieu, and got into the pony-carriage, which crept up the slope, and bore him out of their sight.

'I never was so much taken with anybody in my life as I am with that young fellow – never! I cannot understand it – can't understand it anyhow,' said Mr Swancourt quite energetically to himself; and went indoors.

CHAPTER SEVEN

'No more of me you knew, my love!'*

STEPHEN SMITH revisited Endelstow Rectory, agreeably to his promise. He had a genuine artistic reason for coming, though no such reason seemed to be required. Six-and-thirty old seat-ends,* of exquisite fifteenth-century workmanship, were rapidly decaying in an aisle of the church; and it became politic to make drawings of their worm-eaten contours ere they were battered past recognition in the turmoil of the so-called restoration.

He entered the house at sunset, and the world was pleasant again to the two fair-haired ones. A momentary pang of disappointment had, nevertheless, passed through Elfride when she casually discovered that he had not come that minute post-haste from London, but had reached the neighbourhood the previous evening. Surprise would have accompanied the feeling had she not remembered that several tourists were haunting the coast at this season, and that Stephen might have chosen to do likewise.

They did little besides chat that evening, Mr Swancourt beginning to question his visitor, closely yet paternally, and in good part, on his hopes and prospects from the profession he had embraced. Stephen gave vague answers. The next day it rained. In the evening, when twenty-four hours of Elfride had completely rekindled her admirer's ardour, a game of chess was proposed between them.

The game had its value in helping on the developments of their future.

Elfride soon perceived that her opponent was but a learner. She next noticed that he had a very odd way of handling the pieces when castling or taking a man. Antecedently she would have supposed that the same performance must be gone through by all players in the same manner; she was taught by his differing action that all ordinary players, who learn the game by sight, unconsciously touch the men in a stereotyped way. This impression of indescribable oddness in Stephen's touch culminated in speech when she saw him, at the taking of one of her bishops, push it aside with the taking man instead of lifting it as a preliminary to the move.

'How strangely you handle the men, Mr Smith!'

'Do I? I am sorry for that.'

'O no – don't be sorry; it is not a matter great enough for sorrow. But who taught you to play?'

'Nobody, Miss Swancourt,' he said. 'I learnt from a book lent me by my friend Mr Knight, the noblest man in the world.'

'But you have seen people play?'

'I have never seen the playing of a single game. This is the first time I ever had the opportunity of playing with a living opponent. I have worked out many games from books, and studied the reasons of the different moves, but that is all.'

This was a full explanation of his mannerism; but the fact that a man with the desire for chess should have grown up without being able to see or engage in a game astonished her not a little. She pondered on the circumstance for some time, looking into vacancy and hindering the play.

Mr Swancourt was sitting with his eyes fixed on the board, but apparently thinking of other things. Half to himself he said, pending the move of Elfride:

'"Quæ finis aut quod me manet stipendium?"'

Stephen replied instantly:

'"Effare: jussas cum fide pœnas luam."'*

'Excellent – prompt – gratifying!' said Mr Swancourt with feeling, bringing down his hand upon the table, and making three pawns and a knight dance over their borders by the shaking. 'I was musing on those words as applicable to a strange course I am steering – but enough of that. I am delighted with you, Mr Smith, for it is so seldom in this desert that I meet with a man who is gentleman and scholar enough to continue a quotation, however trite it may be.'

'I also apply the words to myself,' said Stephen quietly.

'You? The last man in the world to do that, I should have thought.'

'Come,' murmured Elfride poutingly, and insinuating herself between them, 'tell me all about it. Come, construe, construe!'

Stephen looked steadfastly into her face, and said slowly, and in a voice full of a far-off meaning that seemed quaintly premature in one so young:

'Quæ finis *What will be the end*, aut *or*, quod stipendium *what fine*, manet me *awaits me*? Effare *Speak out*; luam *I will pay*, cum fide *with faith*, jussas pœnas *the penalty required*.'

The rector, who had listened with a critical compression of the lips to this school-boy recitation, and by reason of his imperfect hearing had missed the marked realism of Stephen's tone in the English words, now said hesitatingly: 'By the bye, Mr Smith (I know you'll excuse my curiosity), though your translation was unexceptionably correct and close, you have a way of pronouncing your Latin which to me seems most peculiar. Not that the pronunciation of a dead language is of much importance; yet your accents and quantities have a grotesque sound to my ears. I thought first that you had acquired your way of breathing the vowels from some of the northern colleges; but it cannot be so with the quantities. What I was going to ask was, if your instructor in the classics could possibly have been an Oxford or Cambridge man?'

'Yes; he was an Oxford man – Fellow of St Cyprian's.'

'Really?'

'O yes; there's no doubt about it.'

'The oddest thing ever I heard of!' said Mr Swancourt, starting with astonishment. 'That the pupil of such a man –'

'The best and cleverest man in England!' cried Stephen enthusiastically.

'– That the pupil of such a man should pronounce Latin in the way you pronounce it beats all I ever heard. How long did he instruct you?'

'Four years.'

'Four years!'

'It is not so strange when I explain,' Stephen hastened to say. 'It was done in this way – by letter. I sent him exercises and construing twice a week, and twice a week he sent them back to me corrected, with marginal notes of instruction. That is how I learnt my Latin and Greek, such as it is. He is not responsible for my scanning. He has never heard me scan a line.'

'A novel case, and a singular instance of patience!' cried the parson.

'On his part, not on mine. Ah, Henry Knight is one in a thousand! I remember his speaking to me on this very subject of pronunciation. He says that, much to his regret, he sees a time coming when every man will pronounce even the common words of his own tongue as seems right in his own ears, and be thought none the worse for it; that the speaking age is passing away, to make room for the writing age.'

Both Elfride and her father had waited attentively to hear Stephen go on to what would have been the most interesting part of the story, namely, what circumstances could have necessitated such an unusual method of education. But no further explanation was volunteered; and they saw, by the young man's manner of concentrating himself upon the chess-board, that he was anxious to drop the subject.

The game proceeded. Elfride played by rote; Stephen by thought. It was the cruellest thing to checkmate him after so much labour, she considered. What was she dishonest enough to do in her compassion? To let him checkmate her. A second game followed; and being herself absolutely indifferent as to the result (her playing was above the average among women, and she knew it), she allowed him to give checkmate again. A final game, in which she adopted the Muzio gambit* as her opening, was terminated by Elfride's victory at the twelfth move.

Stephen looked up suspiciously. His heart was throbbing even more excitedly than was hers, which itself had quickened when she seriously set to work on this last occasion. Mr Swancourt had left the room.

'You have been trifling with me till now!' he exclaimed, his face flushing. 'You did not play your best in the first two games?'

Elfride's guilt showed in her face. Stephen became the picture of vexation and sadness, which, relishable for a moment, caused her the next instant to regret the mistake she had made.

'Mr Smith, forgive me!' she said sweetly. 'I see now, though I did not at first, that what I have done seems like contempt for your skill. But, indeed, I did not mean it in that sense. I could not, upon my conscience, win a victory in those first and second games over one who fought at such a disadvantage and so manfully.'

He drew a long breath, and murmured bitterly, 'Ah, you are

cleverer than I. You can do everything – I can do nothing! O Miss Swancourt!' he burst out wildly, his heart swelling in his throat, 'I must tell you how I love you! All these months of my absence I have worshipped you.'

He leapt from his seat like the impulsive lad that he was, slid round to her side, and almost before she suspected it his arm was round her waist, and the two sets of curls intermingled.

So entirely new was full-blown love to Elfride that she trembled as much from the novelty of the emotion as from the emotion itself. Then she suddenly withdrew herself and stood upright, vexed that she had submitted unresistingly even to his momentary pressure. She resolved to consider this demonstration as premature.

'You must not begin such things as those,' she said with coquettish hauteur of a very transparent nature. 'And – you must not do so again – and papa is coming.'

'Let me kiss you – only a little one,' he said with his usual delicacy, and without reading the factitiousness of her manner.

'No; not one.'

'Only on your cheek?'

'No.'

'Forehead?'

'Certainly not.'

'You care for somebody else, then? Ah, I thought so!'

'I am sure I do not.'

'Nor for me either?'

'How can I tell?' she said simply, the simplicity lying merely in the broad outlines of her manner and speech. There were the semitone of voice and half-hidden expression of eyes which tell the initiated how very fragile is the ice of reserve at these times.

Footsteps were heard. Mr Swancourt then entered the room, and their private colloquy ended.

The day after this partial revelation Mr Swancourt proposed a drive to the cliffs beyond Targan Bay, a distance of three or four miles.

Half an hour before the time of departure a crash was heard in the back yard, and presently Worm came in, saying partly to the world in general, partly to himself, and slightly to his auditors:

'Ay, ay, sure! That frying of fish will be the end of William

Worm. They be at it again this morning – same as ever – fizz, fizz, fizz!'

'Your head bad again, Worm?' said Mr Swancourt. 'What was that noise we heard in the yard?'

'Ay, sir, a weak wambling man am I; and the frying have been going on in my poor head all through the long night and this morning as usual; and I was so dazed wi' it that down fell a piece of leg-wood* across the shaft of the pony-shay,* and splintered it off. "Ay," says I, "I feel it as if 'twas my own shay; and though I've done it, and parish pay* is my lot if I go from here, perhaps I am as independent as one here and there."'

'Dear me, the shaft of the carriage broken!' cried Elfride. She was disappointed: Stephen doubly so. The rector showed more warmth of temper than the accident seemed to demand, much to Stephen's uneasiness and rather to his surprise. He had not supposed so much latent sternness could co-exist with Mr Swancourt's frankness and good-nature.

'You shall not be disappointed,' said the latter at length. 'It is almost too long a distance for you to walk. Elfride can trot down on her pony, and you shall have my old nag, Smith.'

Elfride exclaimed triumphantly, 'You have never seen me on horseback – O, you must!' She looked at Stephen and read his thoughts immediately. 'Ah, you don't ride, Mr Smith?'

'I am sorry to say I don't.'

'Fancy a man not able to ride!' said she rather pertly.

The rector came to his rescue. 'That's common enough; he has had other lessons to learn. Now, I recommend this plan: let Elfride ride on horseback, and you, Mr Smith, walk beside her.'

The arrangement was welcomed with secret delight by Stephen. It seemed to combine in itself all the advantages of a long slow ramble with Elfride, without the contingent possibility of the enjoyment being spoilt by her becoming weary. The pony was saddled and brought round.

'Now, Mr Smith,' said the lady imperatively, coming downstairs, and appearing in her riding-habit, as she always did in a change of dress, like a new edition of a delightful volume, 'you have a task to perform to-day. These earrings are my very favourite darling ones; but the worst of it is that they have such short hooks that they are liable to be dropped if I toss my head about much, and when I am riding I can't give my mind to them. It would be doing me knight service if you keep your eyes fixed upon them, and remember them every minute of the day, and tell me directly I drop one. They have had such hair-breadth escapes, haven't they, Unity?' she continued to the parlour-maid who was standing at the door.

'Yes, miss, that they have!' said Unity with round-eyed commiseration.

'Once 'twas in the lane that I found one of them,' pursued Elfride reflectively:

'And then 'twas by the gate into Eighteen Acres,' Unity chimed in.

'And then 'twas on the carpet in my own room,' rejoined Elfride merrily.

'And then 'twas dangling on the embroidery of your petticoat, miss; and then 'twas down your back, miss, wasn't it? And O, what a way you was in, miss, wasn't you? my! until you found it!'

Stephen took Elfride's slight foot upon his hand: 'One, two, three, and up!' she said.

Unfortunately not so. He staggered and lifted, and the horse edged round; and Elfride was ultimately deposited upon the ground rather more forcibly than was pleasant. Smith looked all contrition.

'Never mind,' said the rector encouragingly; 'try again! 'Tis a little accomplishment that requires some practice, although it looks so easy. Stand closer to the horse's head, Mr Smith.'

'Indeed, I shan't let him try again,' said she with a microscopic look of indignation. 'Worm, come here, and help me to mount.' Worm stepped forward, and she was in the saddle in a trice.

Then they moved on, going for some distance in silence, the hot air of the valley being occasionally brushed from their faces by a cool breeze, which wound its way along ravines leading up from the sea.

'I suppose,' said Stephen, 'that a man who can neither sit in a saddle himself nor help another person into one seems a useless incumbrance; but, Miss Swancourt, I'll learn to do it all for your sake; I will, indeed.'

'What is so unusual in you,' she said, in a didactic tone justifiable in a horsewoman's address to a benighted walker, 'is that your knowledge of certain things should be combined with your ignorance of certain other things.'

Stephen lifted his eyes to hers.

'You know,' he said, 'it is simply because there are so many other things to be learnt in this wide world that I didn't trouble about that particular bit of knowledge. I thought it would be useless to me; but I don't think so now. I will learn riding, and all connected with it, because then you would like me better. Do you like me much less for this?'

She looked sideways at him with critical meditation tenderly rendered.

'Do I seem like *La Belle Dame sans merci*?'* she began suddenly, without replying to his question. 'Fancy yourself saying, Mr Smith:

"I set her on my pacing steed,
    And nothing else saw all day long,
For sidelong would she bend, and sing
        A faery's song....
She found me roots of relish sweet,
    And honey wild, and manna dew";

and that's all she did.'

'No, no,' said the young man stilly, and with a rising colour:

'"And sure in language strange she said.
        I love thee true."'

'Not at all,' she rejoined quickly. 'See how I can gallop. Now, Pansy, off!' And Elfride started; and Stephen beheld her light figure contracting to the dimensions of a bird as she sank into the distance – her hair flowing.

He walked on in the same direction, and for a considerable time could see no signs of her returning. Dull as a flower without the sun he sat down upon a stone, and not for fifteen minutes was any sound of horse or rider to be heard. Then Elfride and Pansy appeared on the hill in a round trot.

'Such a delightful scamper as we have had!' she said, her face flushed and her eyes sparkling. She turned the horse's head, Stephen arose, and they went on again.

'Well, what have you to say to me, Mr Smith, after my long absence?'

'Do you remember a question you could not exactly answer last night – whether I was more to you than anybody else?' said he.

'I cannot exactly answer now, either.'

'Why can't you?'

'Because I don't know if *I* am more to *you* than any one else.'

'Yes, indeed, you are!' he exclaimed in a voice of intensest appreciation, at the same time gliding round and looking into her face.

'Eyes in eyes,' he murmured playfully; and she blushingly obeyed, looking back into his.

'And why not lips on lips?' continued Stephen daringly.

'No, certainly not. Anybody might look; and it would be the death of me. You may kiss my hand if you like.'

He expressed by a look that to kiss a hand through a glove, and that a riding-glove, was not a great treat in the circumstances.

'There, then; I'll take my glove off. Isn't it a pretty white hand? Ah, you don't want to kiss it, and you shall not now!'

'If I do not, may I never kiss again, you severe Elfride! You know I think more of you than I can tell; that you are my queen. I would die for you, Elfride!'

A rapid red again filled her cheeks, and she looked at him meditatively. What a proud moment it was for Elfride then! She was ruling a heart with absolute despotism for the first time in her life.

Stephen stealthily pounced upon her hand.

'No; I won't, I won't!' she said intractably; 'and you shouldn't take me by surprise.'

There ensued a mild form of tussle for absolute possession of the much-coveted hand, in which the boisterousness of boy and girl was far more prominent than the dignity of man and woman. Then Pansy became restless. Elfride recovered her position and remembered herself.

'You make me behave in not a nice way at all!' she exclaimed, in a tone neither of pleasure nor reproof, but partaking of both. 'I ought not to have allowed such a romp! We are too old now for that sort of thing.'

'I hope you don't think me too – too much of a creeping-round sort of man,' said he in a penitent tone, conscious that he too had lost a little dignity by the proceeding.

'You are too familiar; and I can't have it! Considering the shortness of the time we have known each other, Mr Smith, you take too much upon you. You, a town man, think I am a country girl, and it doesn't matter how you behave to me!'

'I assure you, Miss Swancourt, that I had no idea of freak* in my mind. I wanted to imprint a sweet serious kiss upon your hand; and that's all.'

'Now, that's creeping round again! And you mustn't look into my eyes so,' she said, shaking her head at him, and trotting on a few paces in advance. Thus she led the way out of the lane and across some fields in the direction of the cliffs. At the boundary of the fields nearest the sea she expressed a wish to dismount. The horse was tied to a post, and they both followed an irregular path, which ultimately terminated upon a flat ledge passing round the face of the huge blue-black rock at a height about midway between the sea and the topmost verge. There, far beneath and before them, lay the everlasting stretch of ocean; there, upon detached rocks, were the white screaming gulls, seeming ever intending to settle and yet always passing on. Right and left ranked the toothed and zigzag line of storm-torn heights, forming the series which culminated in the one beneath their feet.

Behind the youth and maiden was a tempting alcove and seat, formed naturally in the beetling* mass, and wide enough to admit two or three persons. Elfride sat down, and Stephen sat beside her.

'I am afraid it is hardly proper of us to be here, either,' she said half inquiringly. 'We have not known each other long enough for this kind of thing, have we!'

'O yes,' he replied judicially; 'quite long enough.'

'How do you know?'

'It is not length of time, but the manner in which our minutes beat, that makes enough or not enough in our acquaintanceship.'

'Yes, I see that. But I wish papa suspected or knew what a *very new thing* I am doing. He does not think of it at all.'

'Darling Elfie, I wish we could be married! It is wrong for me to say it – I know it is – before you know more; but I wish we might be, all the same. Do you love me deeply, deeply?'

'No!' she said in a fluster.

At this point-blank denial Stephen turned his face away decisively, and preserved an ominous silence; the only objects of interest on earth for him being apparently the three or four-score sea-birds circling in the air afar off.

'I didn't mean to stop you quite,' she faltered with some alarm; and seeing that he still remained silent she added more anxiously, 'If you say that again, perhaps, I will not be quite – quite so obstinate – if – if you don't like me to be.'

'O my Elfride!' he exclaimed, and kissed her.

It was Elfride's first kiss. And so awkward and unused was she; full of striving – no relenting. There was none of those apparent struggles to get out of the trap which only result in getting further in: no final attitude of receptivity: no easy close of shoulder to shoulder, hand upon hand, face upon face, and, in spite of coyness, the lips in the right place at the supreme moment. That graceful though apparently accidental falling into position, which many have noticed as precipitating the end and making sweethearts the sweeter, was not here. Why? Because experience was absent. A woman must have had many kisses before she kisses well.

In fact, the art of tendering feminine lips for these amatory salutes follows the principles laid down in treatises on legerdemain* for performing the trick called Forcing a Card. The card is to be shifted nimbly, withdrawn, edged under, and withal not to be offered till the moment the unsuspecting person's hand reaches the pack; this forcing to be done so modestly and yet so coaxingly that the person trifled with imagines he is really choosing what is in fact thrust into his hand.

Well, there were no such facilities now; and Stephen was conscious of it – first with a momentary regret that his kiss should be spoilt by her confused receipt of it, and then with the pleasant perception that her awkwardness was her charm.

'And you do care for me and love me?' said he.

'Yes.'

'Very much?'

'Yes.'

'And I mustn't ask you if you'll wait for me, and be my wife some day?'

'Why not?' she said naïvely.

'There is a reason why, my Elfride.'

'Not any one that I know of.'

'Suppose there is something connected with me which makes it almost impossible for you to agree to be my wife, or for your father to countenance such an idea?'

'Nothing shall make me cease to love you: no blemish can be found upon your personal nature. That is pure and generous, I know; and having that, how can I be cold to you?'

'And shall nothing else affect us – shall nothing beyond my nature be a part of my quality in your eyes, Elfie?'

'Nothing whatever,' she said with a breath of relief. 'Is that all? Some outside circumstance? What do I care?'

'You can hardly judge, dear, till you know what has to be judged. For that, we will stop till we get home. I believe in you, but I cannot feel bright.'

'Love is new, and fresh to us as the dew; and we are together. As the lover's world goes, this is a great deal. Stephen, I fancy I see the difference between me and you – between men and women generally, perhaps. I am content to build happiness on any accidental basis that may lie near at hand; you are for making a world to suit your happiness.'

'Elfride, you sometimes say things which make you seem suddenly to become five years older than you are, or than I am; and that remark is one. I couldn't think so *old* as that, try how I might. . . . And no lover has ever kissed you before?'

'Never.'

'I knew that; you were so unused. You ride well, but you don't kiss nicely at all; and I was told once, by my friend Knight, that that is an excellent fault in woman.'

'Now, come; I must mount again, or we shall not be home by dinner-time.' And they returned to where Pansy stood tethered. 'Instead of entrusting my weight to a young man's unstable palm,' she continued gaily, 'I prefer a surer "upping-stock"* (as the villagers call it), in the form of a gate. There – now I am myself again.'

They proceeded homeward at the same walking pace.

Her blitheness won Stephen out of his thoughtfulness, and each forgot everything but the tone of the moment.

'What did you love me for?' she said, after a long musing look at a flying bird.

'I don't know,' he replied idly.

'O yes, you do,' insisted Elfride.

'Perhaps for your eyes.'

'What of them? – now, don't vex me by a light answer. What of my eyes?'

'Oh, nothing to be mentioned. They are indifferently good.'

'Come, Stephen, I won't have that. What did you love me for?'

'It might have been for your mouth?'

'Well, what about my mouth?'

'I thought it was a passable mouth enough—'

'That's not very comforting.'

'With a pretty pout and sweet lips; but actually, nothing more than what everybody has.'

'Don't make up things out of your head as you go on, there's a dear Stephen. Now – what – did – you – love – me – for?'

'Perhaps, 'twas for your neck and hair; though I am not sure: or for your idle blood, that did nothing but wander away from your cheeks and back again; but I am not sure. Or your hands and arms, that they eclipsed all other hands and arms; or your feet, that they played about under your dress like little mice;* or your tongue, that it was of a dear delicate tone. But I am not altogether sure.'

'Ah, that's pretty to say; but I don't care for your love, if it made a mere flat picture of me in that way, and not being sure, and such cold reasoning; but what you *felt* I was, you know, Stephen' (at this a stealthy laugh and frisky look into his face), 'when you said to yourself, "I'll certainly love that young lady."'

'I never said it.'

'When you said to yourself, then, "I never will love that young lady."'

'I didn't say that, either.'

'Then was it, "I suppose, I must love that young lady"?'

'No.'

'What, then?'

‘’Twas much more fluctuating – not so definite.’

‘Tell me; do, do.’

‘It was that I ought not to think about you if I loved you truly.’

‘Ah, that I don’t understand. There’s no getting it out of you. And I’ll not ask you ever any more – never more – to say out of the deep reality of your heart what you loved me for.’

‘Sweet tantalizer, what’s the use? It comes to this sole simple thing: That at one time I had never seen you, and I didn’t love you; that then I saw you, and I did love you. Is that enough?’

‘Yes; I will make it do. . . . I know, I think, what I love you for. You are nice-looking, of course; but I didn’t mean for that. It is because you are so docile and gentle.’

‘Those are not quite the correct qualities for a man to be loved for,’ said Stephen, in rather a dissatisfied tone of self-criticism. ‘Well, never mind. I must ask your father to allow us to be engaged directly we get indoors. It will be for a long time.’

‘I like it the better. . . . Stephen, don’t mention it till to-morrow.’

‘Why?’

‘Because, if he should object – I don’t think he will; but if he should – we shall have a day longer of happiness from our ignorance. . . . Well, what are you thinking of so deeply?’

‘I was thinking how my dear friend Knight would enjoy this scene. I wish he could come here.’

‘You seem very much engrossed with him,’ she answered, with a jealous little toss. ‘He must be an interesting man to take up so much of your attention.’

‘Interesting!’ said Stephen, his face glowing with his fervour; ‘noble, you ought to say.’

‘O yes, yes; I forgot,’ she said half satirically. ‘The noblest man in England, as you told us last night.’

‘He is a fine fellow, laugh as you will, Miss Elfie.’

‘I know he is your hero. But what does he do? anything?’

‘He writes.’

‘What does he write? I have never heard of his name.’

‘Because his personality, and that of several others like him, is absorbed into a huge WE, namely, the impalpable entity called THE PRESENT – a social and literary Review.’

‘Is he only a reviewer?’

'*Only*, Elfie! Why, I can tell you it is a fine thing to be on the staff of *The Present*. Finer than being a novelist considerably.'

'That's a hit at me, and my poor *Court of King Arthur's Castle*.'

'No, Elfride,' he whispered; 'I didn't mean that. I mean that he is really a literary man of some eminence, and not altogether a reviewer. He writes things of a higher class than reviews, though he reviews a book occasionally. His ordinary productions are social and ethical essays – all that *The Present* contains which is not literary reviewing.'

'I admit he must be talented if he writes for *The Present*. We have it sent to us irregularly. I want papa to be a subscriber, but he's so conservative. Now the next point in this Mr Knight – I suppose he is a very good man?'

'An excellent man. I shall try to be his intimate friend some day.'

'But aren't you now?'

'No; not so much as that,' replied Stephen, as if such a supposition were extravagant. 'You see, it was in this way – he came originally from the same place as I, and taught me things; but I am not intimate with him. Shan't I be glad when I get richer and better known, and hob and nob* with him!' Stephen's eyes sparkled.

A pout began to shape itself upon Elfride's soft lips. 'You think always of him, and like him better than you do me!'

'No, indeed, Elfride. The feeling is different quite. But I do like him, and he deserves even more affection from me than I give.'

'You are not nice now, and you make me as jealous as possible!' she exclaimed perversely. 'I know you will never speak to any third person of me so warmly as you do to me of him.'

'But you don't understand, Elfride,' he said with an anxious movement. 'You shall know him some day. He is so brilliant – no, it isn't exactly brilliant; so thoughtful – nor does thoughtful express him – that it would charm you to talk to him. He's a most desirable friend, and that isn't half I could say.'

'I don't care how good he is; I don't want to know him, because he comes between me and you. You think of him night and day, ever so much more than of anybody else; and when you are thinking of him I am shut out of your mind.'

'No, dear Elfride; I love you dearly.'

'And I don't like you to tell me so warmly about him when you are in the middle of loving me. Stephen, suppose that I and this man Knight of yours were both drowning, and you could only save one of us—'

'Yes – the stupid old proposition – which would I save?'

'Well, which? Not me.'

'Both of you,' he said, pressing her pendent hand.

'No, that won't do; only one of us.'

'I cannot say; I don't know. It is disagreeable – quite a horrid idea to have to handle.'

'A-ha, I know. You would save him, and let me drown, drown, drown; and I don't care about your love!'

She had endeavoured to give a playful tone to her words, but the latter speech was rather forced in its gaiety.

At this point in the discussion she trotted off to turn a corner which was avoided by the footpath, the road and the path reuniting at a point a little further on. On again making her appearance she continually managed to look in a direction away from him, and left him in the cool shade of her displeasure. Stephen was soon beaten at this game of indifference. He went round and entered the range of her vision.

'Are you offended, Elfie? Why don't you talk?'

'Save me, then, and let that Mr Clever of yours drown. I hate him. Now, which would you?'

'Really, Elfride, you should not press such a hard question. It is ridiculous.'

'Then I won't be alone with you any more. Unkind, to wound me so!' She laughed at her own absurdity but persisted.

'Come, Elfie, let's make it up and be friends.'

'Say you would save me, then, and let him drown.'

'I would save you – and him too.'

'And let him drown. Come, or you don't love me!' she teasingly went on.

'And let him drown,' he ejaculated despairingly.

'There; now I am yours!' she said, and a woman's flush of triumph lit her eyes.

'Only one earring, miss, as I'm alive,' said Unity on their entering the hall.

With a face expressive of wretched misgiving, Elfride's hand flew like an arrow to her ear.

'There!' she exclaimed to Stephen, looking at him with eyes full of reproach.

'I quite forgot, indeed. If I had only remembered!' he answered, with a conscience-stricken face.

She wheeled herself round, and turned into the shrubbery. Stephen followed.

'If you had told *me* to watch anything, Stephen, I should have religiously done it,' she capriciously went on, as soon as she heard him behind her.

'Forgetting is forgivable.'

'Well, you will find it, if you want me to respect you and be engaged to you when we have asked papa.' She considered a moment, and added more seriously, 'I know now where I dropped it, Stephen. It was on the cliff. I remember a faint sensation of some change about me, but I was too absent to think of it then. And that's where it is now, and you must go and look there.'

'I'll go at once.'

And he strode away up the valley, under a broiling sun and amid the deathlike silence of early afternoon. He ascended, with giddy-paced haste, the windy range of rocks to where they had sat, felt and peered about the stones and crannies, but Elfride's stray jewel was nowhere to be seen. Next Stephen slowly retraced his steps, and, pausing at a cross-road to reflect a while, he left the plateau and struck downwards across some fields in the direction of Endelstow House.

He walked along the path by the river without the slightest hesitation as to its bearing, apparently quite familiar with every inch of the ground. As the shadows began to lengthen and the sunlight to mellow he passed through two wicket-gates,* and drew near the outskirts of Endelstow Park. The river now ran along under the park fence, previous to entering the grove itself, a little further on.

Here stood a cottage, between the fence and the stream, on a slightly elevated spot of ground, round which the river took a turn. The characteristic feature of this snug habitation was its one chimney in the gable end, its squareness of form disguised by a huge cloak of ivy, which had grown so luxuriantly and extended so far from its base as to increase the apparent bulk of the chimney to the dimensions of a tower. Some little distance from the back of the house rose the park boundary, and over this were to be seen the sycamores of the grove, making slow inclinations to the just-awakening air.

Stephen crossed the little wood bridge in front, went up to the cottage door, and opened it without knock or signal of any kind.

Exclamations of welcome burst from some person or persons when the door was thrust ajar, followed by the scrape of chairs on a stone floor, as if pushed back by their occupiers in rising from a table. The door was closed again, and nothing could now be heard from within, save a lively chatter and the rattle of plates.

CHAPTER EIGHT

'Allen-a-Dale is no baron or lord.'*

THE mists were creeping out of pools and swamps for their pilgrimages of the night when Stephen came up to the front door of the rectory. Elfride was standing on the step illuminated by a lemon-hued expanse of western sky.

'You never have been all this time looking for that earring?' she said anxiously.

'O no; and I have not found it.'

'Never mind. Though I am much vexed; they are my prettiest. But, Stephen, whatever have you been doing – where have you been? I have been so uneasy. I feared for you, knowing not an inch of the country. I thought, suppose he has fallen over the cliff! But now I am inclined to scold you for frightening me so.'

'I must speak to your father now,' he said rather abruptly; 'I have so much to say to him – and to you, Elfride.'

'Will what you have to say endanger this nice time of ours, and is it that same shadowy secret you allude to so frequently, and will it make me unhappy?'

'Possibly.'

She breathed heavily, and looked around as if for a prompter.

'Put it off till to-morrow,' she said.

He involuntarily sighed too.

'No; it must come to-night. Where is your father, Elfride?'

'Somewhere in the kitchen garden, I think,' she replied. 'That is his favourite evening retreat. I will leave you now. Say all that's to be said – do all there is to be done. Think of me waiting anxiously for the end.' And she re-entered the house.

She waited in the drawing-room, watching the lights sink to shadows, the shadows sink to darkness, until her impatience to know what had occurred in the garden could no longer be controlled. She passed round the shrubbery, unlatched the garden door, and skimmed with her keen eyes the whole twilighted space that the four walls enclosed and sheltered: they were not there. She mounted a little ladder which had been used for gathering fruit, and looked over the wall into the field. This field extended to the limits of the glebe, which was enclosed on that side by a privet-hedge. Under the hedge was Mr Swancourt, walking up and down, and talking aloud – to himself, as it sounded at first. No: another voice shouted occasional replies; and this interlocutor seemed to be on the other side of the hedge. The voice, though soft in quality, was not Stephen's.

The second speaker must have been in the long-neglected garden of an old manor-house hard by, which, together with a small estate attached, had lately been purchased by a person named Troyton, whom Elfride had never seen. Her father might have struck up an acquaintanceship with some member of that family through the privet-hedge, or a stranger to the neighbourhood might have wandered thither.

Well, there was no necessity for disturbing him. And it seemed that, after all, Stephen had not yet made his desired communication to her father. Again she went indoors, wondering where Stephen could be. For want of something better to do she went upstairs to her own little room. Here she sat down at the open window, and, leaning with her elbow on the table and her cheek upon her hand, she fell into meditation.

It was a hot and still August night. Every disturbance of the silence which rose to the dignity of a noise could be heard for miles, and the merest sound for a long distance. So she remained, thinking of Stephen, and wishing he had not deprived her of his company to no purpose, as it appeared. How delicate and sensitive he was, she reflected; and yet he was man enough to have a private mystery, which considerably elevated him in her eyes. Thus, looking at things with an inward vision, she lost consciousness of the flight of time.

Strange conjunctions of phenomena, particularly those of a trivial everyday kind, are so frequent in an ordinary life that we grow used to their unaccountableness, and forget the question whether the very long odds against such juxtaposition is not almost a disproof of it being a matter of chance at all. What occurred to Elfride at this moment was a case in point. She was vividly imagining, for the twentieth time, the kiss of the morning, and putting her lips together in the position another such a one would demand, when she heard the identical operation performed on the lawn, immediately beneath her window.

A kiss – not of the quiet and stealthy kind, but decisive, loud, and smart.

Her face flushed and she looked out, but to no purpose. The dark rim of the upland drew a keen sad line against the pale glow of the sky, unbroken except where a young cedar on the lawn, that had outgrown its fellow trees, shot its pointed head across the horizon, piercing the firmamental lustre like a sting.

It was just possible that, had any persons been standing on the grassy portions of the lawn, Elfride might have seen their dusky forms. But the shrubs, which once had merely dotted the glade, had now grown bushy and large, till they hid at least half the enclosure containing them. The kissing pair might have been behind some of these; at any rate, nobody was in sight.

Had no enigma ever been connected with her lover by his hints and absences, Elfride would never have thought of admitting into her mind a suspicion that he might be concerned in the foregoing enactment. But the reservations he at present insisted on, while they added to the mystery without which perhaps she would never have seriously loved him at all, were calculated to nourish doubts of all kinds, and with a slow flush of jealousy she asked herself, might he not be the culprit?

Elfride glided downstairs on tiptoe, and out to the precise spot on which she had parted from Stephen to enable him to speak privately to her father. Thence she wandered into all the nooks around the place from which the sound had seemed to proceed – among the huge laurestines, about the tufts of pampas grasses, amid the variegated hollies, under the weeping wych-elm* – nobody was there. Returning indoors she called 'Unity!'

'She is gone to her aunt's, to spend the evening,' said Mr Swancourt, thrusting his head out of his study door, and letting the light of his candles stream upon Elfride's face – less revealing than, as it seemed to herself, creating the blush of uneasy perplexity that was burning upon her cheek.

'I didn't know you were indoors, papa,' she said with surprise. 'Surely no light was shining from the window when I was on the lawn?' and she looked and saw that the shutters were still open.

'O yes, I am in,' he said indifferently. 'What did you want Unity for? I think she laid supper before she went out.'

'Did she? – I have not been to see – I didn't want her for that.'

Elfride scarcely knew, now that a definite reason was required, what that reason was. Her mind for a moment strayed to another subject, unimportant as it seemed. The red ember of a match was lying inside the fender, which explained that why she had seen no rays from the window was because the candles had only just been lighted.

'I'll come directly,' said the rector. 'I thought you were out somewhere with Mr Smith.'

Even the inexperienced Elfride could not help thinking that her father must be wonderfully blind if he failed to perceive what was the nascent consequence of herself and Stephen being so unceremoniously left together; wonderfully careless, if he saw it and did not think about it; wonderfully good, if, as seemed to her by far the most probable supposition, he saw it and thought about it and approved of it. These reflections were cut short by the appearance of Stephen just outside the porch, silvered about the head and shoulders with touches of moonlight that had begun to creep through the trees.

'Has your trouble anything to do with a kiss on the lawn?' she asked abruptly, almost passionately.

'Kiss on the lawn?'

'Yes!' she said, imperiously now.

'I didn't comprehend your meaning, nor do I now exactly. I certainly have kissed nobody on the lawn, if that is really what you want to know, Elfride.'

'You know nothing about such a performance?'

'Nothing whatever. What makes you ask?'

'Don't press me to tell; it is nothing of importance. And, Stephen, you have not yet spoken to papa about our engagement?'

'No,' he said regretfully, 'I could not find him directly; and then I went on thinking so much of what you said about objections, refusals – bitter words possibly – ending our happiness, that I resolved to put it off till to-morrow; that gives us one more day of delight – delight of a tremulous kind.'

'Yes; but it would be improper to be silent too long, I think,' she said in a delicate voice. 'I want him to know we love, Stephen. Why did you adopt my thought of delay as your own?'

'I will explain; but I want to tell you of my secret first – to tell you now. It is two or three hours yet to bedtime. Let us walk up the hill to the church.'

Elfride passively assented, and they went from the lawn by a side wicket, and ascended into the open expanse of moonlight which streamed around the lonely edifice on the slope of the hill.

The door was locked. They turned from the porch, and walked hand in hand to find a resting-place in the churchyard. Stephen chose a flat tomb, showing itself to be newer and whiter than those around it, and sitting down himself gently drew her hand towards him.

'No, not there,' she said.

'Why not here?'

'A mere fancy; but never mind.' And she sat down.

'Elfie, will you love me, in spite of everything that may be said against me?'

'O Stephen, what makes you repeat that so continually and so sadly? You know I will. Yes, indeed,' she said, drawing closer, 'whatever may be said of you – and nothing bad can be – I will cling to you just the same. Your ways shall be my ways until I die.'

'Did you ever think what my parents might be, or what society I originally moved in?'

'No, not particularly. I have observed one or two little points in your manners which are rather quaint – no more. I suppose you have moved in the ordinary society of professional people.'

'Supposing I have not – that none of my family have a profession except me?'

'I don't mind. What you are only concerns me.'

'Where do you think I went to school – I mean, to what kind of school?'

'Dr Somebody's academy,' she said simply.

'No. To a dame school* originally, then to a national school.'*

'Only to those! Well, I love you just as much, Stephen, dear Stephen,' she murmured tenderly, 'I do indeed. And why should you tell me these things so impressively? What do they matter to me?'

He held her closer and proceeded:

'What do you think my father is – does for his living, that is to say?'

'He practises some profession or calling, I suppose.'

'No; he is a mason.'

'A Freemason?'

'No; a cottager and working master-mason.'

Elfride said nothing at first. After a while she whispered:

'That is a strange idea to me. But never mind; what does it matter?'

'But aren't you angry with me for not telling you before?'

'No, not at all. Is your mother alive?'

'Yes.'

'Is she a nice lady?'

'Very – the best mother in the world. Her people had been well-to-do yeomen for centuries, but she was only a dairy-woman, having been left an orphan.'

'O Stephen!' came from her in whispered exclamation.

'She continued to manage a dairy long after my father married her,' pursued Stephen, without further hesitation. 'And I remember very well how, when I was very young, I used to go to the milking, look on at the skimming, sleep through the churning, and make believe I helped her. Ah, that was a happy time enough!'

'No, never – not happy.'

'Yes, it was.'

'I don't see how happiness could be where the drudgery of dairy-work had to be done for a living – the hands red and chapped, and the shoes clogged.... Stephen, I do own that it seems odd to regard you in the light of – of – having been so rough in your youth, and done menial things of that kind.' (Stephen withdrew an inch or two from her side.) 'But I *do love you* just the same,' she continued, getting closer under his shoulder again, 'and I don't care anything about the past; and I see that you are all the worthier for having pushed on in the world in such a way.'

'It is not my worthiness; it is Knight's, who pushed me.'

'Ah, always he – always he!'

'Yes, and properly so. Now, Elfride, you see the reason of his teaching me by letter. I knew him years before he went to Oxford, but I had not got far enough in my reading for him to entertain the idea of helping me in classics till he left home. Then I was sent away from the village, and we very seldom met; but he kept up this system of tuition by correspondence with the greatest regularity. I will tell you all the story, but not now. There is nothing more to say now, beyond giving places, persons, and dates.' His voice became timidly slow at this point.

'No; don't take trouble to say more. You are a dear honest fellow to say so much as you have; and it is not so dreadful either. It has become a normal thing that millionaires commence by going up to London with their tools at their back, and half-a-crown in their pockets. That sort of origin is getting so respected,' she continued cheerfully, 'that it is acquiring some of the odour of Norman ancestry.'

'Ah, if I had *made* my fortune, I shouldn't mind. But I am only a possible maker of it as yet.'

'It is quite enough. And so *this* is what your trouble was?'

'I thought I was doing wrong in letting you love me without telling you my story; and yet I feared to do so, Elfie. I dreaded to lose you, and I was cowardly on that account.'

'How plain everything about you seems after this explanation! Your peculiarities in chess-playing, the pronunciation papa noticed in your Latin, your odd mixture of book-knowledge with ignorance of ordinary social accomplishments, are accounted for in a moment. And has this anything to do with what I saw at Lord Luxellian's?'

'What did you see?'

'I saw the shadow of yourself putting a cloak round a lady. I was at the side door; you two were in a room with the window towards me. You came to me a moment later.'

'She was my mother.'

'Your mother *there*!' She withdrew herself to look at him silently in her interest.

'Elfride,' said Stephen, 'I was going to tell you the remainder to-morrow – I have been keeping it back – I must tell it now, after all. The remainder of my revelation refers to where my parents are. Where do you think they live? You know them – by sight at any rate.'

'*I* know them!' she said in suspended amazement.

'Yes. My father is John Smith, Lord Luxellian's master-mason, who lives under the park wall by the river.'

'O Stephen! can it be?'

'He built – or assisted at the building of the house you live in, years ago. He put up those stone gate piers at the lodge entrance to Lord Luxellian's park. My grandfather planted the trees that belt in your lawn; my grandmother – who worked in the fields with him – held each tree upright whilst he filled in the earth: they told me so when I was a child. He was the sexton, too, and dug many of the graves around us.'

'And was your unaccountable vanishing on the first morning of your arrival, and again this afternoon, a run to see your father and mother? . . . I understand now; no wonder you seemed to know your way about the village!'

'No wonder. But remember, I have not lived here since I was nine years old. I then went to live with my uncle, a builder, near Exonbury, in order to be able to attend a national school as a day scholar; there was none on this remote coast then. It was there I met with my friend Knight. And when I was fifteen and had been fairly educated by the schoolmaster – and more particularly by Knight – I was put as a pupil in an architect's office in that town, because I was skilful in the use of the pencil. A full premium* was paid by the efforts of my mother and father, rather against the wishes of Lord Luxellian, who likes my father, however, and thinks a great deal of him. There I stayed till six months ago, when I obtained a situation as improver,* as it is called, in a London office. That's all of me.'

'To think *you*, the London visitor, the town man, should have been born here, and have known this village so many years before I did. How strange – how very strange it seems to me!' she murmured.

'My mother curtseyed to you and your father last Sunday,' said Stephen, with a pained smile at the thought of the incongruity. 'And your papa said to her, "I am glad to see you so regular at church, *Jane.*"'

'I remember it, but I have never spoken to her. We have only been here eighteen months, and the parish is so large.'

'Contrast with this,' said Stephen, with a miserable laugh, 'your father's belief in my "blue blood", which is still prevalent in his mind. The first night I came he insisted upon proving my descent from one of the most ancient west-county families, on account of my second Christian name; when the truth is, it was given me because my grandfather was assistant gardener in the Fitzmaurice-Smith family for thirty years. Having seen your face, my darling, I had not heart to contradict him, and tell him what would have cut me off from a friendly knowledge of you.'

She sighed deeply. 'Yes, I see now how this inequality may be made to trouble us,' she murmured, and continued in a low, sad whisper, 'I wouldn't have minded if they had lived far away. Papa might have consented to an engagement between us if your connection had been with villagers a hundred miles off; remoteness softens family contrasts. But he will not like – O Stephen, Stephen! what can I do?'

'Do?' he said tentatively, yet with heaviness. 'Give me up; let me go back to London, and think no more of me.'

'No, no; I cannot give you up! This hopelessness in our affairs makes me care more for you. . . . I see what did not strike me at first. Stephen, why do we trouble? Why should papa object? An architect in London is an architect in London. Who inquires there? Nobody. We shall live there, shall we not? Why need we be so alarmed?'

'And Elfie,' said Stephen, his hopes kindling with hers, 'Knight thinks nothing of my being only a cottager's son; he says I am as worthy of his friendship as if I were a lord's; and if I am worthy of his friendship I am worthy of you, am I not, Elfride?'

'I not only have never loved anybody but you,' she said, instead of giving an answer, 'but I have not even formed a strong friendship, such as you have for Knight. I wish you hadn't. It diminishes me.'

'Now, Elfride, you know better,' he said wooingly. 'And had you really never any sweetheart at all?'

'None that was ever recognized by me as such.'

'But did nobody ever love you?'

'Yes – a man did once; very much, he said.'

'How long ago?'

'Oh, a long time.'

'How long, dearest?'

'A twelvemonth.'

'That's not *very* long' (rather disappointedly).

'I said long, not very long.'

'And he did want to marry you?'

'I believe he did. But I didn't see anything in him. He was not good enough, even if I had loved him.'

'May I ask what he was?'

'A large farmer.'

'A large farmer not good enough – how much richer than my family!' Stephen murmured.

'Where is he now?' he continued to Elfride.

'*Here.*'

'Here! what do you mean by that?'

'I mean that he is here.'

'Where here?'

'Under us. He is under this tomb. He is dead, and we are sitting on his grave.'

'Elfie,' said the young man, standing up and looking at the tomb, 'how odd and sad that revelation seems! It quite depresses me for the moment.'

'Stephen, I didn't wish to sit here; but you would do so.'

'You never encouraged him?'

'Never by look, word, or sign,' she said solemnly. 'He died of consumption, and was buried the day you first came.'

'Let us go away. I don't like standing by *him*, even if you never loved him. He was *before* me.'

'Worries make you unreasonable,' she half pouted, following Stephen at the distance of a few steps. 'Perhaps I ought to have told you before we sat down. Yes; let us go.'

CHAPTER NINE

'Her father did fume.'*

OPPRESSED, in spite of themselves, by a foresight of impending complications, Elfride and Stephen returned along the lane hand in hand. At the door they paused wistfully, like children late at school.

Women accept their destiny more readily than men. Elfride had now resigned herself to the overwhelming idea of her lover's antecedents; Stephen had not forgotten the trifling grievance that Elfride had known earlier admiration than his own.

'What was that young man's name?' he inquired.

'Felix Jethway; a widow's only son.'

'I remember the family.'

'She hates me now. She says I killed him.'

Stephen mused, and they entered the porch.

'Stephen, I love only you,' she tremulously whispered.

He pressed her fingers, and the trifling shadow passed away, to admit again the mutual and more tangible trouble.

The study appeared to be the only room lighted up. They entered, each with a demeanour intended to conceal the inconcealable fact that reciprocal love was their dominant chord. Elfride perceived a man, sitting with his back towards herself, talking to her father. She would have retired, but Mr Swancourt had seen her.

'Come in,' he said; 'it is only Martin Cannister, come for a copy of the register for poor Mrs Jethway.'

Martin Cannister, the sexton, was rather a favourite with Elfride. He used to absorb her attention by telling her of his strange experiences in digging up after long years the bodies of persons he had known, and recognizing them by some little sign (though in reality he had never recognized any). He had shrewd small eyes and a great wealth of double chin, which compensated in some measure for considerable poverty of nose.

The appearance of a slip of paper in Cannister's hand, and a few shillings lying on the table in front of him, denoted that the business had been transacted, and the tenor of their conversation went to show that a summary of village news was now engaging the attention of parishioner and parson.

Mr Cannister stood up and touched his forehead over his eye with his finger, in respectful salutation of Elfride, gave half as much salute to Stephen (whom he, in common with other villagers, had never for a moment recognized), then sat down again and resumed his discourse.

'Where had I got on to, sir?'

'To driving the pile,'* said Mr Swancourt.

'The pile 'twas. So, as I was saying, Nat was driving the pile in this manner, as I might say.' Here Mr Cannister held his walking-stick scrupulously vertical with his left hand, and struck a blow with great force on the knob of the stick with his right. 'John was steadying the pile so, as I might say.' Here he gave the stick a slight shake, and looked firmly in the various eyes around to see that before proceeding further his listeners well grasped the subject at that stage. 'Well, when Nat had struck some half-dozen blows more upon the pile, 'a stopped for a second or two. John, thinking he had done striking, put his hand upon the top o' the pile to gie en a pull, and see if 'a were firm in the ground.' Mr Cannister spread his hand over the top of the stick, completely covering it with his palm. 'Well, so to speak, Nat hadn't maned to stop striking, and when John had put his hand upon the pile, the beetle—'*

'O dreadful!' said Elfride.

'The beetle was already coming down, you see, sir. Nat just caught sight of his hand, but couldn't stop the blow in time. Down came the beetle upon poor John Smith's hand, and squashed en to a pummy.'*

'Dear me, dear me! poor fellow!' said the rector, with an intonation like the groans of the wounded in a pianoforte performance of the 'Battle of Prague'.*

'John Smith, the master-mason?' cried Stephen hurriedly.

'Ay, no other; and a better-hearted man God A'mighty never made.'

'Is he so much hurt?'

'I have heard,' said Mr Swancourt, not noticing Stephen, 'that he has a son in London, a very promising young fellow.'

'O, how he must be hurt!' repeated Stephen.

'A beetle couldn't hurt very little. Well, sir, good-night t'ye; and ye, sir; and you, miss, I'm sure.'

Mr Cannister had been making unnoticeable motions of withdrawal, and by the time this farewell remark came from his lips he was just outside the door of the room. He tramped along the hall, stayed more than a minute endeavouring to close the door properly, and then was lost to their hearing.

Stephen had meanwhile turned and said to the rector:

'Please excuse me this evening! I must leave. John Smith is my father.'

The rector did not comprehend at first.

'What did you say?' he inquired.

'John Smith is my father,' said Stephen deliberately.

A surplus tinge of redness rose from Mr Swancourt's neck, and came round over his face, the lines of his features became more firmly defined, and his lips seemed to get thinner. It was evident that a series of little circumstances, hitherto unheeded, were now fitting themselves together, and forming a lucid picture in Mr Swancourt's mind in such a manner as to render useless further explanation on Stephen's part.

'Indeed,' the rector said, in a voice dry and without inflection.

This being a word which depends entirely upon its tone for its meaning, Mr Swancourt's enunciation was equivalent to no expression at all.

'I have to go now,' said Stephen, with an agitated bearing, and a movement as if he scarcely knew whether he ought to run off or stay longer. 'On my return, sir, will you kindly grant me a few minutes' private conversation?'

'Certainly. Though antecedently it does not seem possible that there can be anything of the nature of private business between us.'

Mr Swancourt put on his straw hat, crossed the drawing-room, into which the moonlight was shining, and stepped out of the French window into the verandah. It required no further effort to perceive what, indeed, reasoning might have foretold as the natural colour of a mind whose pleasures were taken amid genealogies, good dinners, and patrician reminiscences, that Mr Swancourt's prejudices were too strong for his generosity, and that Stephen's moments as his friend and equal were numbered, or had even now ceased.

Stephen moved forward as if he would follow the rector, then as if he would not, and in absolute perplexity whither to turn himself, went awkwardly to the door. Elfride followed lingeringly behind him. Before he had receded two yards from the doorstep, Unity and Ann the housemaid came home from their visit to the village.

'Have you heard anything about John Smith? The accident is not so bad as was reported, is it?' said Elfride intuitively.

'O no; the doctor says it is only a bad bruise.'

'I thought so!' cried Elfride gladly.

'He says that, although Nat believes he did not check the beetle as it came down, he must have done so without knowing it – checked it very considerably too; for the full blow would have knocked his hand abroad, and in reality it is only made black-and-blue like.'

'How thankful I am!' said Stephen.

The perplexed Unity looked at him with her mouth rather than with her eyes.

'That will do, Unity,' said Elfride magisterially; and the two maids passed on.

'Elfride, do you forgive me?' said Stephen with a faint smile. 'No man is fair in love'; and he took her fingers lightly in his own.

With her head thrown sideways in the Greuze attitude* she looked a tender reproach at his doubt and pressed his hand. Stephen returned the pressure threefold, then hastily went off to his father's cottage by the wall of Endelstow Park.

'Elfride, what have you to say to this?' inquired her father, coming up immediately Stephen had retired.

With feminine quickness she grasped at any straw that would enable her to plead his cause. 'He had told me of it,' she faltered; 'so that it is not a discovery in spite of him. He was just coming in to tell you.'

'*Coming* to tell! Why hadn't he already told? I object as much, if not more, to his underhand concealment of this, than I do to the fact itself. It looks very much like his making a fool of me, and of you too. You and he have been about together, and corresponding together, in a way I don't at all approve of – in a most unseemly way. You should have known how improper such conduct is. A woman can't be too careful not to be seen alone with I-don't-know-whom.'

'You saw us, papa, and have never said a word.'

'My fault, of course; my fault. What the deuce could I be thinking of! He, a villager's son; and we, Swancourts, connections of the Luxellians. We have been coming to nothing for centuries, and now I believe we have got there. What shall I next invite here, I wonder!'

Elfride began to cry at this very unpropitious aspect of affairs. 'O papa, papa, forgive me and him! We care so much for one another, papa – O, so much! And what he was going to ask you is, if you will allow of an engagement between us till he is a gentleman as good as you. We are not in a hurry, dear papa; we don't want in the least to marry now; not until he is richer. Only will you let us be engaged, because I love him so, and he loves me?'

Mr Swancourt's feelings were a little touched by this appeal, and he was annoyed that such should be the case. 'Certainly not!' he replied. He pronounced the inhibition lengthily and sonorously, so that the 'not' sounded like 'n-o-o-o-t!'

'No, no, no; don't say it!'

'Foh! A fine story. It is not enough that I have been deluded by having him here, – the son of one of my village peasants, – but now I am to make him my son-in-law! Heavens above us, are you mad, Elfride?'

'You have seen his letters come to me ever since his first visit, papa, and you knew they were a sort of – love-letters; and since he has been here you have let him be alone with me almost entirely; and you guessed, you must have guessed, what we were thinking of, and doing, and you didn't stop him. Next to love-making comes love-winning, and you knew it would come to that, papa.'

The rector parried this common-sense thrust. 'I know – since you press me so – I know I did guess some childish attachment might arise between you; I own I did not take much trouble to prevent it; but I have not particularly countenanced it; and, Elfride, how can you expect that I should now? It is impossible; no father in England would hear of such a thing.'

'But he is the same man, papa; the same in every particular; and how can he be less fit for me than he was before?'

'He appeared a young man with well-to-do friends, and a little property; but having neither, he is another man.'

'You inquired nothing about him?'

'I went by Hewby's introduction. He should have told me. So should the young man himself; of course he should. I consider it a most dishonourable thing to come into a man's house like a treacherous I-don't-know-what.'

'But he was afraid to tell you, and so should I have been. He loved me too well to like to run the risk. And as to speaking of his friends on his first visit, I don't see why he should have done so at all. He came here on business: it was no affair of ours who his parents were. And then he knew that if he told you he would never be asked here, and would perhaps never see me again. And he wanted to see me. Who can blame him for trying, by any means, to stay near me – the girl he loves? All is fair in love. I have heard you say so yourself, papa; and you yourself would have done just as he has – so would any man!'

'And any man, on discovering what I have discovered, would also do as I do, and mend my mistake; that is, get shot of him again, as soon as the laws of hospitality will allow.' But Mr Swancourt then remembered that he was a Christian. 'I would not, for the world, seem to turn him out of doors,' he added; 'but I think he will have the tact to see that he cannot stay long after this, with good taste.'

'He will, because he's a gentleman. See how graceful his manners are,' Elfride went on; though perhaps Stephen's manners, like the feats of Euryalus,* owed their attractiveness in her eyes rather to the attractiveness of his person than to their own excellence.

'Ay; anybody can be what you call graceful, if he lives a little time in a city, and keeps his eyes open. And he might have picked up his gentlemanliness by going to the galleries of theatres, and watching stage drawing-room manners. He reminds me of one of the worst stories I ever heard in my life.'

'What story was that?'

'O no, thank you! I wouldn't tell you such an improper matter for the world!'

'If his father and mother had lived in the north or east of England,' gallantly persisted Elfride, though her sobs began to interrupt her articulation, 'anywhere but here – you – would have – only regarded – *him*, and not *them*! His station – would have – been what – his profession makes it, – and not fixed by – his father's humble position – at all; whom he never lives with – now. Though John Smith has saved lots of money, and is better off than we are, they say, or he couldn't have put his son to such an expensive profession. And it is clever and – honourable – of Stephen, to be the best of his family.'

'Yes. "Let a beast be lord of beasts, and his crib shall stand at the king's mess."'*

'You insult me, papa!' she burst out. 'You do, you do! He is my own Stephen, he is!'

'That may or may not be true, Elfride,' returned her father, again uncomfortably agitated in spite of himself. 'You confuse future probabilities with present facts, – what the young man may be with what he is. We must look at what he is, not what an improbable degree of success in his profession may make him. The case is this: the son of a working-man in my parish who may or may not be able to buy me up – a youth who has not yet advanced so far into life as to have any income of his own deserving the name, and therefore of his father's degree as regards station – wants to be engaged to you. His family are living in precisely the same spot in England as yours, so throughout this county – which is the world to us – you would always be known as the wife of Jack Smith the mason's son, and not under any circumstances as the wife of a London professional man. It is the drawback, not the compensating fact, that is talked of always. There, say no more. You may argue all night, and prove what you will; I'll stick to my words.'

Elfride looked silently and hopelessly out of the window with large heavy eyes and wet cheeks.

'I call it great temerity – and long to call it audacity – in Hewby,' resumed her father. 'I never heard such a thing – giving such a hobbledehoy* native of this place such an introduction to me as he did. Naturally you were deceived as well as I was. I don't blame you at all, so far.' He went and searched for Mr Hewby's original letter. 'Here's what he said to me: "Dear Sir, – Agreeably to your request of the 18th instant, I have arranged to survey and make drawings," *et cætera*. "My assistant, Mr Stephen Smith" – assistant, you see he called him, and naturally I understood him to mean a sort of partner. Why didn't he say "clerk"?'

'They never call them clerks in that profession, because they do not write. Stephen – Mr Smith – told me so. So that Mr Hewby simply used the accepted word.'

'Let me speak, please, Elfride! "My assistant, Mr Stephen Smith, will leave London by the early train to-morrow morning ... *many thanks for your proposal to accommodate him ... you may put every confidence in him*, and may rely upon his discernment in the matter of church architecture." Well, I repeat that Hewby ought to be ashamed of himself for making so much of a poor lad of that sort.'

'Professional men in London,' Elfride argued, 'don't know anything about their clerks' fathers and mothers. They have assistants who come to their offices and shops for years, and hardly even know where they live. What they can do – what profits they can bring the firm – that's all London men care about. And that is helped in him by his faculty of being uniformly pleasant.'

'Uniform pleasantness is rather a defect than a faculty. It shows that a man hasn't sense enough to know whom to despise.'

'It shows that he acts by faith and not by sight, as those you claim succession from directed.'

'That's some more of what he's been telling you, I suppose! Yes, I was inclined to suspect him, because he didn't care about sauces of any kind. I always did doubt a man's being a gentleman if his palate had no acquired tastes. An unedified palate is the irrepressible cloven foot* of the upstart. The idea of my bringing out a bottle of my '40 Martinez* – only eleven of them left now – to a man who didn't know it from eighteenpenny! Then the Latin line he gave to my quotation; it was very cut-and-dried, very; or I, who haven't looked into a classical author for the last eighteen years, shouldn't have remembered it. Well, Elfride, you had better go to your room; you'll get over this bit of tomfoolery in time.'

'No, no, no, papa,' she moaned. For of all the miseries attaching to miserable love, the worst is the misery of thinking that the passion which is the cause of them all may cease.

'Elfride,' said her father with rough friendliness, 'I have an excellent scheme on hand, which I cannot tell you of now. A scheme to benefit you and me. It has been thrust upon me for some little time –

yes, thrust upon me – but I didn't dream of its value till this afternoon, when the revelation came. I should be most unwise to refuse to entertain it.'

'I don't like that word,' she returned wearily. 'You have lost so much already by schemes. Is it those wretched mines again?'

'No; not a mining scheme.'

'Railways?'

'Nor railways. It is like those mysterious offers we see advertised, by which any gentleman with no brains at all may make so much a week without risk, trouble, or soiling his fingers. However, I am intending to say nothing till it is settled, though I will just say this much, that you soon may have other fish to fry than to think of Stephen Smith. Remember, I wish not to be angry, but friendly, to the young man; for your sake I'll regard him as a friend in a certain sense. But this is enough; in a few days you will be quite my way of thinking. There, now, go to your bedroom. Unity shall bring you up some supper. I wish you not to be here when he comes back.'

CHAPTER TEN

'Beneath the shelter of an aged tree'*

STEPHEN retraced his steps towards the cottage he had visited only two or three hours previously. He drew near and under the rich foliage growing about the outskirts of Endelstow Park, the spotty lights and shades from the shining moon maintaining a race over his head and down his back in an endless gambol. When he crossed the plank bridge and entered the garden-gate, he saw an illuminated figure coming from the enclosed plot towards the house on the other side. It was his father, with his hand in a sling, taking a general moonlight view of the garden, and particularly of a plot of the youngest of young turnips, previous to closing the cottage for the night.

He saluted his son with customary force. 'Hallo, Stephen! We should ha' been in bed in another ten minutes. Come to see what's the matter wi' me, I suppose, my lad?'

The doctor had come and gone, and the hand had been pronounced as injured but slightly, though it might possibly have been considered a far more serious case if Mr Smith had been a more important man. Stephen's anxious inquiry drew from his father words of regret at the inconvenience to the world of his doing nothing for the next two days, rather than of concern for the pain of the accident. Together they entered the house.

John Smith – brown as autumn as to skin, white as winter as to clothes – was a satisfactory specimen of the village artificer in stone. In common with most rural mechanics, he had too much individuality to be a typical 'working-man' – a resultant of that beach-pebble attrition with his kind only to be experienced in large towns, which metamorphoses the unit Self into a fraction of the unit Class.

There was not the speciality in his labour which distinguishes the handicraftsmen of towns. Though only a mason, strictly speaking, he was not above handling a brick, if bricks were the order of the day; or a slate or tile, if a roof had to be covered before the wet weather set in, and nobody was near who could do it better. Indeed, on one or two occasions in the depth of winter, when frost peremptorily forbids all use of the trowel, making foundations to settle, stones to fly, and mortar to crumble, he had taken to felling and sawing trees. Moreover, he had practised gardening in his own plot for so many years that, on an emergency, he might have made a living by that calling.

Probably our countryman was not such an accomplished artificer in a particular direction as his town brethren in the trades. But he was, in truth, like that clumsy pin-maker* who made the whole pin, and who was despised by Adam Smith on that account and respected by Macaulay, much more the artist nevertheless.

Appearing now, indoors, by the light of the candle, his stalwart healthiness was a sight to see. His beard was close and knotted as that of a chiselled Hercules; his shirt sleeves were partly rolled up, his waistcoat unbuttoned; the difference in hue between the snowy linen and the ruddy arms and face contrasting like the white of an egg and its yolk. Mrs Smith, on hearing them enter, advanced from the pantry.

Mrs Smith was a matron whose countenance addressed itself to the mind rather than to the eye, though not exclusively. She retained her personal freshness even now, in the prosy afternoon-time of her life; but what her features primarily indicated was a sound common sense behind them; as a whole, appearing to carry with them an argumentative commentary on the world in general.

The details of the accident were then rehearsed by Stephen's father in the dramatic manner common to Martin Cannister, other individuals of the neighbourhood, and the rural world generally. Mrs Smith threw in her sentiments between the acts, as Coryphæus* of the tragedy, to make the description complete. The story at last came to an end, as the longest will, and Stephen directed the conversation into another channel.

'Well, mother, they know everything about me now,' he said quietly.

'Well done!' replied his father; 'now my mind's at peace.'

'I blame myself – I never shall forgive myself – for not telling them before,' continued the young man.

Mrs Smith at this point abstracted her mind from the former subject. 'I don't see what you have to grieve about, Stephen,' she said. 'People who accidentally get friends don't, as a first stroke, tell the history of their families.'

'Ye've done no wrong, certainly,' said his father.

'No; but I should have spoken sooner. There's more in this visit of mine than you think – a good deal more.'

'Not more than *I* think,' Mrs Smith replied, looking contemplatively at him. Stephen blushed; and his father looked from one to the other in a state of utter incomprehension.

'She's a pretty piece enough,' Mrs Smith continued, 'and very lady-like and clever too. But though she's very well fit for you as far as that is, why, mercy 'pon me, what ever do you want any woman at all for yet?'

John made his naturally short mouth a long one, and wrinkled his forehead. 'That's the way the wind d'blow, is it?' he said.

'Mother,' exclaimed Stephen, 'how absurdly you speak! Criticizing whether she's fit for me or no, as if there were room for doubt on the matter! Why, to marry her would be the great blessing of my life – socially and practically, as well as in other respects. No such good fortune as that, I'm afraid; she's too far above me. Her family doesn't want such country lads as I in it.'

'Then if they don't want you, I'd see them dead corpses before I'd want them, and go to families who do want you.'

'Ah, yes; but I could never put up with the distaste of being welcomed among such people as you mean, whilst I could get indifference among such people as hers.'

'What crazy twist of thinking will enter your head next?' said his mother. 'And come to that, she's not a bit too high for you, or you too low for her. See how careful I am to keep myself up. I'm sure I never stop for more than a minute together to talk to any journeymen people; and I never invite anybody to our party o' Christmases who are not in business for themselves. And I talk to several carriage people that come to my lord's without saying ma'am or sir to 'em, and they take it as quiet as lambs.'

'You curtseyed to the rector, mother; and I wish you hadn't.'

'But it was before he called me by my Christian name, or he would have got very little curtseying from me!' said Mrs Smith, bridling and sparkling with vexation. 'You go on at me, Stephen, as if I were your worst enemy! What else could I do with the man to get rid of him, banging it into me and your father by side and by seam about his greatness, and what happened when he was a young fellow at college, and I don't know what-all; the tongue o' en flopping round his mouth like a mop-rag round a dairy, didn't it, John?'

'That's about the size o't,' replied her husband.

'Every woman now-a-days,' resumed Mrs Smith, 'if she marry at all, must expect a father-in-law of a rank lower than her father. The men have gone up so, and the women have stood still. Every man you meet is more the dand* than his father; and you are just level with her.'

'That's what she thinks herself.'

'It only shows her sense. I knew she was after 'ee, Stephen – I knew it.'

'After me! Good Lord, what next!'

'And I really must say again that you ought not to be in such a hurry, and wait for a few years. You might go higher than a bankrupt pa'son's girl then.'

'The fact is, mother,' said Stephen impatiently, 'you don't know anything about it. I shall never go higher, because I don't want to, nor should I if I lived to be a hundred. As to you saying that she's after me, I don't like such a remark about her, for it implies a scheming woman, and a man worth scheming for, both of which are not only untrue, but ludicrously untrue, of this case. Isn't it so, father?'

'I'm afraid I don't understand the matter well enough to gie my opinion,' said his father, in the tone of the fox who had a cold and could not smell.

'She couldn't have been very backward anyhow, considering the short time you have known her,' said his mother. 'Well I think that five years hence you'll be plenty young enough to think of such things. And really she can very well afford to wait, and will too, take my word. Living down in an out-step* place like this, I am sure she ought to be very thankful that you took notice of her. She'd most likely have died an old maid if you hadn't turned up.'

'All nonsense,' said Stephen, but not aloud.

'A nice little thing she is,' Mrs Smith went on in a more complacent tone now that Stephen had been talked down; 'there's not a word to say against her, I'll own. I see her sometimes decked out like a horse going to fair, and I admire her for't. A perfect little lady. But people can't help their thoughts, and if she'd learnt to make figures instead of letters when she was at school 'twould have been better for her pocket; for as I said, there never were worse times for such as she than now.'

'Now, now, mother!' said Stephen with smiling deprecation.

'But I will!' said his mother with asperity. 'I don't read the papers for nothing, and I know men all move up a stage by marriage. Men of her class, that is, parsons, marry squires' daughters; squires marry lords' daughters; lords marry dukes' daughters; dukes marry queens' daughters. All stages of gentlemen mate a stage higher; and the lowest stage of gentlewomen are left single, or marry out of their class.'

'But you said just now, dear mother—' retorted Stephen, unable to resist the temptation of showing his mother her inconsistency. Then he paused.

'Well, what did I say?' And Mrs Smith prepared her lips for a new campaign.

Stephen, regretting that he had begun, since a volcano might be the consequence, was obliged to go on.

'You said I wasn't out of her class just before.'

'Yes, there, there! That's you; that's my own flesh and blood. I'll warrant that you'll pick holes in everything your mother says if you can, Stephen. You are just like your father for that; take anybody's part but mine. Whilst I am speaking and talking and trying and slaving away for your good, you are waiting to catch me out in that way. So you are in her class, but 'tis what *her* people would *call* marrying out of her class. Don't be so quarrelsome, Stephen!'

Stephen preserved a discreet silence, in which he was imitated by his father, and for several minutes nothing was heard but the ticking of the green-faced case-clock* against the wall.

'I'm sure,' added Mrs Smith in a more philosophic tone, and as a terminative speech, 'if there'd been so much trouble to get a husband in my time as there is in these days – when you must make a god-almighty of a man to get him to hae ye – I'd have trod clay for bricks* before I'd ever have lowered my dignity to marry, or there's no bread in nine loaves.'*

The discussion now dropped, and as it was getting late Stephen bade his parents farewell for the evening, his mother none the less warmly for their sparring; for although Mrs Smith and Stephen were always contending, they were never at enmity.

'And possibly,' said Stephen, 'I may leave here altogether to-morrow; I don't know. So that if I shouldn't call again before returning to London, don't be alarmed, will you?'

'But didn't you come for a fortnight?' said his mother. 'And haven't you a month's holiday altogether? They are going to turn you out, then?'

'Not at all. I may stay longer; I may go. If I go, you had better say nothing about my having been here, for her sake. At what time of the morning does the carrier* pass Endelstow lane?'

'Seven o'clock.'

And then he left them. His thoughts were, that should the rector permit him to become engaged, to hope for an engagement, or in any way to think of his beloved Elfride, he might stay longer. Should he be forbidden to think of any such thing he resolved to go at once. And the latter, even to young hopefulness, seemed the more probable alternative.

Stephen walked back to the rectory through the meadows, as he had come, surrounded by the soft musical purl of the water through little weirs, the modest light of the moon, the freshening smell of the dews outspread around. It was a time when mere seeing is meditation, and meditation peace. Stephen was hardly philosopher enough to avail himself of Nature's offer. His constitution was made up of very simple particulars; was one which, rare in the springtime of civilizations, seems to grow abundant as a nation gets older, individuality fades, and education spreads; that is, his brain had extraordinary receptive powers, and no great creativeness. Quickly acquiring any kind of knowledge he saw around him, and having a plastic adaptability more common in woman than in man, he changed colour like a chameleon as the society he found himself in assumed a higher and more artificial tone. He had not many original ideas, and yet there was scarcely an idea to which, under proper training, he could not have added a respectable co-ordinate.

He saw nothing outside himself to-night; and what he saw within was a weariness to his flesh. Yet to a dispassionate observer his pretensions to Elfride, though rather premature, were far from absurd as marriages go, unless the accidental proximity of simple but honest parents could be said to make them so.

The clock struck eleven when he entered the house. Elfride had been waiting with scarcely a movement since he departed. Before he had spoken to her she caught sight of him passing into the study with her father. She saw that he had by some means obtained the private interview he desired.

A nervous headache had been growing on the excitable girl during the absence of Stephen, and now she could do nothing beyond going up again to her room as she had done before. Instead of lying down she sat again in the darkness without closing the door, and listened with a beating heart to every sound from downstairs. The servants had gone to bed. She ultimately heard the two men come from the study and cross to the dining-room, where supper had been lingering for more than an hour. The door was left open, and she found that the meal, such as it was, passed off between her father and her lover without any remark, save commonplaces as to cucumbers and melons, their wholesomeness and culture, uttered in a stiff and formal way. It seemed to prefigure failure.

Shortly afterwards Stephen came upstairs to his bedroom, and was almost immediately followed by her father, who also retired for the night. Not inclined to get a light she partly undressed and sat on the bed, where she remained in pained thought for some time, possibly an hour. Then rising to close her door previously to fully unrobing she saw a streak of light shining across the landing. Her father's door was shut, and he could be heard snoring regularly. The light came from Stephen's room, and the slight sounds also coming thence emphatically denoted what he was doing. In the perfect silence she could hear the closing of a lid and the clicking of a lock, – he was fastening his hat-box. Then the buckling of straps and the click of another key, – he was securing his portmanteau. With trebled foreboding she opened her door softly, and went towards his. One sensation pervaded her to distraction. Stephen, her handsome youth and darling, was going away, and she might never see him again except in secret and in sadness – perhaps never more. At any rate she could no longer wait till the morning to hear the result of the interview, as she had intended. She flung her dressing-gown round her, tapped lightly at his door, and whispered 'Stephen!' He came instantly, opened the door, and stepped out.

'Tell me; are we to hope?'

He replied in a disturbed whisper, and a tear approached its outlet though none fell.

'I am not to think of such a preposterous thing – that's what he said. And I am going to-morrow. I should have called you up to bid you good-bye.'

'But he didn't say you were to go – O Stephen, he didn't say that?'

'No; not in words. But I cannot stay.'

'O, don't, don't go! Do come and let us talk. Let us come down to the drawing-room for a few minutes; he will hear us here.'

She preceded him down the staircase with the taper light in her hand, looking unnaturally tall and thin in the long dove-coloured dressing-gown she wore. She did not stop to think of the propriety or otherwise of this midnight interview under such circumstances. She thought that the tragedy of her life was beginning, and, for the first time almost, felt that her existence might have a grave side, the shade of which enveloped and rendered invisible the delicate gradations of custom and punctilio. Elfride softly opened the drawing-room door and they both went in. When she had placed the candle on the table he enclosed her with his arms, dried her eyes with his handkerchief, and kissed their lids.

'Stephen, it is over – happy love is over; and there is no more sunshine now!'

'I will make a fortune, and come to you, and have you. Yes, I will!'

'Papa will never hear of it – never – never! You don't know him. I do. He is either biassed in favour of a thing, or prejudiced against it. Argument is powerless against either feeling.'

'No; I won't think of him so,' said Stephen. 'If I appear before him some time hence as a man of established name, he will accept me – I know he will. He is not a wicked man.'

'No, he is not wicked. But you say "some time hence", as if it were no time. To you, among bustle and excitement, it will be comparatively a short time, perhaps; O, to me, it will be its real length trebled! Every summer will be a year – autumn a year – winter a year! O Stephen! and you may forget me!'

Forget: that was, and is, the real sting of waiting to fond-hearted woman. The remark awoke in Stephen the converse fear. 'You, too, may be persuaded to give me up, when time has made me fainter in your memory. For, remember, your love for me must be nourished in secret; there will be no long visits from me to support you. Circumstances will always tend to obliterate me.'

'Stephen,' she said, filled with her own misgivings, and unheeding his last words, 'there are beautiful women where you live – of course I know there are – and they may win you away from me.' Her tears came visibly as she drew a mental picture of his faithlessness. 'And it won't be your fault,' she continued, looking into the candle with doleful eyes. 'No! You will think that our family don't want you, and get to include me with them. And there will be a vacancy in your heart, and some others will be let in.'

'I could not, I would not. Elfie, do not be so full of forebodings.'

'O yes, they will,' she replied. 'And you will look at them, not caring at first, and then you will look and be interested, and after a while you will think, "Ah, they know all about city life, and assemblies, and coteries, and the manners of the titled, and poor little Elfie, with all the fuss that's made about her having me, doesn't know about anything but a little house and a few cliffs and a space of sea, far away." And then you'll be more interested in them, and they'll make you have them instead of me, on purpose to be cruel to me because I am silly, and they are clever and hate me. And I hate them, too; yes, I do!'

Her impulsive words had power to impress him at any rate with the recognition of the uncertainty of all that is not accomplished. And, worse than that general feeling, there of course remained the sadness which arose from the special features of his own case. However remote a desired issue may be, the mere fact of having entered the groove which leads to it, cheers to some extent with a sense of accomplishment. Had Mr Swancourt consented to an engagement of no less length than ten years, Stephen would have been comparatively cheerful in waiting; they would have felt that they were somewhere on the road to Cupid's garden. But, with a possibility of a shorter probation, they had not as yet any prospect of the beginning; the zero of hope had yet to be reached. Mr Swancourt would have to revoke his formidable words before the waiting for marriage could even set in. And this was despair.

'I wish we could marry now,' murmured Stephen, as an impossible fancy.

'So do I,' said she also, as if regarding an idle dream. ''Tis the only thing that ever does sweethearts good!'

'Secretly would do, would it not, Elfie?'

'Yes, secretly would do; secretly would indeed be best,' she said, and went on reflectively: 'All we want is to render it absolutely impossible for any future circumstance to upset our future intention of being happy together; not to begin being happy now.'

'Exactly,' he murmured in a voice and manner the counterpart of hers. 'To marry and part secretly, and live on as we are living now; merely to put it out of anybody's power to force you away from me, darling.'

'Or you away from me, dearest.'

'Or me from you. It is possible to conceive a force of circumstance strong enough to make any woman in the world marry against her will: no conceivable pressure, up to torture or starvation, can make a woman once married to her lover anybody else's wife.'

Now up to this point the idea of an immediate secret marriage had been held by both as an untenable hypothesis, wherewith simply to beguile a miserable moment. During a pause which followed Stephen's last remark, a fascinating perception, then an alluring conviction, flashed along the brain of both. The perception was that an immediate marriage *could* be contrived; the conviction that such an act, in spite of its daring, its fathomless results, its deceptiveness, would be preferred by each to the life they must lead under any other conditions.

The youth spoke first, and his voice trembled with the magnitude of the conception he was cherishing. 'How strong we should feel, Elfride! going on our separate courses as before, without the fear of ultimate separation! O Elfride! think of it; think of it!'

It is certain that the young girl's love for Stephen received a fanning from her father's opposition which made it blaze with a dozen times the intensity it would have exhibited if left alone. Never were conditions more favourable for developing a girl's first passing fancy for a handsome boyish face – a fancy rooted in inexperience and nourished by seclusion – into a wild unreflecting passion fervid enough for anything. All the elements of such a development were there, the chief one being hopelessness – a necessary ingredient always to perfect the mixture of feelings united under the name of loving to distraction.

'We would tell papa soon, would we not?' she inquired timidly. 'Nobody else need know. He would then be convinced that hearts cannot be played with; love encouraged be ready to grow, love discouraged be ready to die, at a moment's notice. Stephen, do you not think that if marriages against a parent's consent are ever justifiable, they are when young people have been favoured up to a point, as we have, and then have had that favour suddenly withdrawn?'

'Yes. It is not as if we had from the beginning acted in opposition to your papa's wishes. Only think, Elfie, how pleasant he was towards me but six hours ago! He liked me, praised me, never objected to my being alone with you.'

'I believe he *must* like you now,' she cried. 'And if he found that you irremediably belonged to me, he would own it and help you. O Stephen, Stephen,' she burst out again, as the remembrance of his packing came afresh to her mind, 'I cannot bear your going away like this! It is too dreadful. All I have been expecting miserably killed within me like this!'

Stephen flushed hot with impulse. 'I will not be a doubt to you – thought of you shall not be a misery to me!' he said. 'We will be wife and husband before we part for long!'

She hid her face on his shoulder. 'Anything to make *sure*!' she whispered.

'I did not like to propose it immediately,' continued Stephen. 'It seemed to me – it seems to me now – like trying to catch you – a girl better in the world than I.'

'Not that, indeed! And am I better in worldly station? What's the use of have beens? We may have been something once; we are nothing now.'

Then they whispered long and earnestly together; Stephen

hesitatingly proposing this and that plan, Elfride modifying them, with quick breathings, hectic flush, and unnaturally bright eyes. It was two o'clock before an arrangement was finally concluded.

She then told him to leave her, giving him his light to go up to his own room. They parted with an agreement not to meet again in the morning. After his door had been some time closed he heard her softly gliding into her chamber.

CHAPTER ELEVEN

'Journeys end in lovers meeting.'*

STEPHEN lay watching the Great Bear;* Elfride was regarding a monotonous parallelogram of window blind. Neither slept that night.

Early the next morning – that is to say, four hours after their stolen interview, and just as the earliest servant was heard moving about – Stephen Smith went downstairs, portmanteau in hand. Throughout the night he had intended to see Mr Swancourt again, but the sharp rebuff of the previous evening rendered such an interview particularly distasteful. Perhaps there was another and less honest reason. He decided to put it off. Whatever of moral timidity or obliquity may have lain in such a decision, no perception of it was strong enough to detain him. He wrote a note in his room, which stated simply that he did not feel happy in the house after Mr Swancourt's sudden veto on what he had favoured a few hours before; but that he hoped a time would come, and that soon, when his original feelings of pleasure as Mr Swancourt's guest might be recovered.

He expected to find the downstairs rooms wearing the gray and cheerless aspect that early morning gives to everything out of the sun. He found in the dining-room a breakfast laid, of which somebody had just partaken.

Stephen gave the maid-servant his note of adieu. She stated that Mr Swancourt had risen early that morning, and made an early breakfast. He was not going away that she knew of.

Stephen took a cup of coffee, left the house of his love, and turned into the lane. It was so early that the shaded places still smelt like night time, and the sunny spots had hardly felt the sun. The horizontal rays made every shallow dip in the ground to show as a well-marked hollow. Even the channel of the path was enough to throw shade, and the very stones of the road cast tapering dashes of darkness westward, as long as Jael's tent-nail.*

At a spot not more than a hundred yards from the parson's residence the lane leading thence crossed the high road. Stephen reached the point of intersection, stood still and listened. Nothing could be heard save the lengthy, murmuring line of the sea upon the adjacent shore. He looked at his watch, and then mounted a gate upon which he seated himself, to await the arrival of the carrier. Whilst he sat he heard wheels coming in two directions.

The vehicle approaching on his right he soon recognized as the carrier's. There were the accompanying sounds of the owner's voice and the smack of his whip, distinct in the still morning air, by which he encouraged his horses up the hill.

The other set of wheels sounded from the lane Stephen had just traversed. On closer observation, he perceived that they were moving from the precincts of the ancient manor-house adjoining the rectory grounds. A carriage then left the entrance gates of the house, and wheeling round came fully in sight. It was a plain travelling carriage, with a small quantity of luggage, apparently a lady's. The vehicle came to the junction of the four ways half-a-minute before the carrier reached the same spot, and crossed directly in his front, proceeding by the lane on the other side.

Inside the carriage Stephen could just discern an elderly lady with a younger woman, who seemed to be her maid. The road they had taken led to Stratleigh, a small watering-place* fourteen miles north.

He heard the manor-house gates swing again, and looking up saw another person leaving them, and walking off in the direction of the parsonage. 'Ah, how much I wish I were moving that way!' felt he parenthetically. The gentleman was tall, and resembled Mr Swancourt in outline and attire. He opened the rectory gate and went in. Mr Swancourt, then, it certainly was. Instead of remaining in bed that morning Mr Swancourt must have taken it into his head to see his new neighbour off on a journey. He must have been greatly interested in that neighbour to do such an unusual thing.

The carrier's conveyance had pulled up, and Stephen now handed in his portmanteau and mounted the shafts. 'Who is that lady in the carriage?' he inquired indifferently of Lickpan the carrier.

'That, sir, is Mrs Troyton, a widder wi' a mint o' money. She's the owner of all that part of Endelstow that is not Lord Luxellian's.

Only been here a short time; she came into it by law. The owner formerly was a terrible mysterious party – never lived here – hardly ever was seen here except in the month of September, as I might say.'

The horses were started again, and noise rendered further discourse a matter of too great exertion. Stephen crept inside under the tilt,* and was soon lost in reverie.

Three hours and a half of straining up hills and jogging down brought them to St Launce's, the market town and railway station nearest to Endelstow, and the place from which Stephen Smith had journeyed over the downs on the, to him, memorable winter evening at the beginning of the same year. The carrier's van was so timed as to meet a starting up-train, which Stephen entered. Two or three hours' railway travel through vertical cuttings in metamorphic rock,* through oak copses rich and green, stretching over slopes and down delightful valleys, glens, and ravines, sparkling with water like many-rilled Ida,* and he plunged amid the hundred and fifty thousand people composing the town of Plymouth.

There being some time upon his hands he left his luggage at the cloak-room, and went on foot along Bedford Street* to St Andrew's church.* Here Stephen wandered among the multifarious tombstones and looked in at the chancel window, dreaming of something that was likely to happen by the altar there in the course of the coming month. He turned away and ascended the Hoe, viewed the magnificent stretch of sea and massive promontories of land, but without particularly discerning one feature of the varied perspective. He still saw that inner prospect – the event he hoped for in yonder church. The wide Sound, the Breakwater, the lighthouse on far-off Eddystone, the dark steam-vessels, brigs, barques, and schooners, either floating stilly, or gliding with tiniest motion, were as the dream, then; the dreamed-of event was as the reality.

Soon Stephen went down from the Hoe, and returned to the railway station. He took his ticket, and entered the London train.

That day was an irksome time at Endelstow rectory. Neither father nor daughter alluded to the departure of Stephen. Mr Swancourt's manner towards her partook of the compunctious kindness that arises from a misgiving as to the justice of some previous act.

Either from lack of the capacity to grasp the whole *coup d'œil*,* or from a natural endowment for certain kinds of stoicism, women are cooler than men in critical situations of the passive form. Probably, in Elfride's case at least, it was blindness to the greater contingencies of the future she was preparing for herself, which enabled her to ask her father in a quiet voice if he could give her a holiday soon, to ride to St Launce's and go on to Plymouth.

Now, she had only once before gone alone to Plymouth, and that was in consequence of some unavoidable difficulty. Being a country girl, and a good, not to say a wild, horsewoman, it had been her delight to canter, without the ghost of an attendant, over the fourteen or sixteen miles of hard road intervening between their home and the station at St Launce's, put up the horse, and go on the remainder of the distance by train, returning in the same manner in the evening. It was then resolved that, though she had successfully accomplished this journey once, it was not to be repeated without some attendance.

But Elfride must not be confounded with ordinary young feminine equestrians. The circumstances of her lonely and narrow life made it imperative that in trotting about the neighbourhood she must trot alone or else not at all. Usage soon rendered this perfectly natural to herself. Her father, who had had other experiences, did not much like the idea of a Swancourt, whose pedigree could be as distinctly traced as a thread in a skein of silk, scampering over the hills like a farmer's daughter, even though he could habitually neglect her. But what with his not being able to afford her a regular attendant, and his inveterate habit of letting anything be to save himself trouble, the circumstance grew customary. And so there arose a chronic notion in the villagers' minds that all ladies rode without an attendant, like Miss Swancourt, except a few who were sometimes visiting at Lord Luxellian's.

'I don't like your going to Plymouth alone, particularly going to St Launce's on horseback. Why not drive, and take the man?'

'It is not nice to be so overlooked.' Worm's company would not seriously have interfered with her plans, but it was her humour to go without him.

'When do you want to go?' said her father.

She only answered, 'Soon.'

'I will consider,' he said.

Only a few days elapsed before she asked again. A letter had reached her from Stephen. It had been timed to come on that day by special arrangement between them. In it he named the earliest morning on which he could meet her at Plymouth. Her father had been on a journey to Stratleigh, and returned in unusual buoyancy of spirit. It was a good opportunity; and since the dismissal of Stephen the parson had been generally in a mood to make small concessions, that he might steer clear of large ones connected with that outcast lover of hers.

'Next Thursday week I am going from home in a different direction,' said her father. 'In fact, I shall leave home the night before. You might choose the same day, for they wish to take up the carpets, or some such thing, I think. As I said, I don't like you to be seen in a town on horseback alone; but go if you will.'

Thursday week. Her father had named the very day that Stephen also had named that morning as the earliest on which it would be of any use to meet her; that was, about fifteen days from the day on which he had left Endelstow. Fifteen days – that fragment of duration which has acquired such an interesting individuality from its connection with the English marriage law.*

She involuntarily looked at her father so strangely that on becoming conscious of the look she paled with embarrassment. The parson, too, looked confused. What was he thinking of?

There seemed to be a special facility offered her by a power external to herself in the circumstance that Mr Swancourt had proposed to leave home the night previous to her wished-for day. Her father seldom took long journeys; seldom slept from home except perhaps on the night following a remote Visitation.* Well, she would not inquire too curiously into the reason of the opportunity, nor did he, as would have been natural, proceed to explain it of his own accord. In matters of fact there had hitherto been no reserve between them, though they were not usually confidential in its full sense. But the divergence of their emotions on Stephen's account had produced an estrangement which just at present went even to the extent of reticence on the most ordinary household topics.

Elfride was almost unconsciously relieved, persuading herself that her father's reserve on his business justified her in secrecy as regarded her own – secrecy which was necessarily a foregone decision with her. So anxious is a young conscience to discover a palliative that the *ex post facto** nature of a reason is of no account in excluding it.

The intervening fortnight was spent by her mostly in walking by herself among the shrubs and trees, indulging sometimes in sanguine anticipations; more, far more frequently, in misgivings. All her flowers seemed dull of hue; her pets seemed to look wistfully into her eyes, as if they no longer stood in the same friendly relation to her as formerly. She wore melancholy jewellery, gazed at sunsets, and talked to old men and women. It was the first time that she had had an inner and private world apart from the visible one about her. She wished that her father, instead of neglecting her even more than usual, would make some advance – just one word; she would then tell all, and risk Stephen's displeasure. Thus brought round to the youth again, she saw him in her fancy, standing, touching her, his eyes full of sad affection, hopelessly renouncing his attempt because she had renounced hers; and she could not recede.

On the Wednesday she was to receive another letter. She had resolved to let her father see the arrival of this one, be the consequences what they might: the dread of losing her lover by this deed of honesty prevented her acting upon the resolve. Five minutes before the postman's expected arrival she slipped out, and down the lane to meet him. She met him immediately upon turning a sharp angle, which hid her from view in the direction of the rectory. The man smilingly handed one missive, and was going on to hand another, a circular from some tradesman.

'No,' she said; 'take that on to the house.'

'Why, miss, you are doing what your father has done for the last fortnight.'

She did not comprehend.

'Why, come to this corner, and take a letter of me every morning, all writ in the same handwriting, and letting any others for him go on to the house.' And on the postman went.

No sooner had he turned the corner behind her back than she heard her father meet and address the man. She had saved her letter by two minutes. Her father audibly went through precisely the same performance as she had just been guilty of herself.

This stealthy conduct of his was, to say the least, peculiar.

Given an impulsive inconsequent girl, neglected as to her inner life by her only parent, and the following forces alive within her; to determine a resultant:

First love acted upon by a deadly fear of separation from its object: inexperience, guiding onward a frantic wish to prevent the above-named issue: misgivings as to propriety, met by hope of ultimate exoneration: indignation at parental inconsistency in first encouraging, then forbidding: a chilling sense of disobedience, overpowered by a conscientious inability to brook a breaking of plighted faith with a man who, in essentials, had remained unaltered from the beginning: a blessed hope that opposition would turn an erroneous judgment: a bright faith that things would mend thereby, and wind up well.

Probably the result would, after all, have been nil, had not the following few remarks been made one day at breakfast.

Her father was in his old hearty spirits. He smiled to himself at stories too bad to tell, and called Elfride a little scamp for surreptitiously preserving some blind kittens that ought to have been drowned. After this expression she said to him suddenly:

'If Mr Smith had been already in the family, you would not have been made wretched by discovering he had poor relations?'

'Do you mean in the family by marriage?' he replied inattentively, and continuing to peel his egg.

The accumulating scarlet told that was her meaning, as much as the affirmative reply.

'I should have put up with it, no doubt,' Mr Swancourt observed.

'So that you would not have been driven into hopeless melancholy, but have made the best of him?'

Elfride's erratic mind had from her youth upwards been constantly in the habit of perplexing her father by hypothetical questions, based on absurd conditions. The present seemed to be cast so precisely in the mould of previous ones that, not being given to syntheses of circumstances, he answered it with customary complacency.

'If he were allied to us irretrievably, of course I, or any sensible man, should accept conditions that could not be altered; certainly not be hopelessly melancholy about it. I don't believe anything in the world would make me hopelessly melancholy. And don't let anything make you so, either.'

'I won't, papa,' she cried, with a serene brightness that pleased him.

Certainly Mr Swancourt must have been far from thinking that the brightness came from an exhilarating intention to hold back no longer from the mad action she had planned.

In the evening he drove away towards Stratleigh, quite alone. It was an unusual course for him. At the door Elfride had been again almost impelled by her feelings to pour out all.

'Why are you going to Stratleigh, papa?' she said, and looked at him longingly.

'I will tell you to-morrow when I come back,' he said cheerily; 'not before then, Elfride. Thou wilt not utter what thou dost not know, and so far will I trust thee, gentle Elfride.'*

She was repressed and hurt.

'I will tell you my errand to Plymouth, too, when I come back,' she murmured.

He went away. His jocularity made her intention seem the lighter, as his indifference made her more resolved to do as she liked.

It was a familiar September sunset, dark-blue fragments of cloud upon an orange-yellow sky. These sunsets used to tempt her to walk towards them, as any beautiful thing tempts a near approach. She went through the field to the privet hedge, clambered into the middle of it, and reclined upon the thick boughs. After looking westward for a considerable time she blamed herself for not looking eastward to where Stephen was, and turned round. Ultimately her eyes fell upon the ground.

A peculiarity was observable beneath her. A green field spread itself on each side of the hedge, one belonging to the glebe, the other being a part of the land attached to the manor-house adjoining. On the rectory side she saw a little footpath, the distinctive and altogether exceptional feature of which consisted in its being only about ten yards long; it terminated abruptly at each end.

A footpath, suddenly beginning and suddenly ending, coming from nowhere and leading nowhere, she had never seen before.

Yes, she had, on second thoughts. She had seen exactly such a path trodden in the front of barracks by the sentry.

And this recollection explained the origin of the path here. Her father had trodden it by pacing up and down, as she had once seen him doing.

Sitting on the hedge as she sat now, her eyes commanded a view of both sides of it. And a few minutes later, Elfride looked over to the manor side.

Here was another sentry path. It was like the first in length, and it began and ended exactly opposite the beginning and ending of its neighbour, but it was thinner, and less distinct.

Two reasons existed for the difference. This one might have been trodden by a similar weight of tread to the other, exercised a less number of times; or it might have been walked just as frequently, but by lighter feet.

Probably a gentleman from Scotland-yard,* had he been passing at the time, might have considered the latter alternative as the more probable. Elfride thought otherwise, so far as she thought at all. But her own great To-Morrow was now imminent; all thoughts inspired by casual sights of the eye were only allowed to exercise themselves in inferior corners of her brain, previously to being banished altogether.

Elfride was at length compelled to reason practically upon her undertaking. All her definite perceptions thereon, when the emotion accompanying them was abstracted, amounted to no more than these:

'Say an hour and three-quarters to ride to St Launce's.

'Say half an hour at the Falcon to change my dress.

'Say two hours waiting for some train and getting to Plymouth.

'Say an hour to spare before twelve o'clock.

'Total time from leaving Endelstow till twelve o'clock, five hours.

'Therefore I shall have to start at seven.'

No surprise or sense of unwontedness entered the minds of the servants at her early ride. The monotony of life we associate with people of small incomes in districts out of the sound of the railway whistle, has one exception, which puts into shade the experience of dwellers about the great centres of population – that is, in travelling. Every journey there is more or less an adventure; adventurous hours are necessarily chosen for the most commonplace outing. Miss Elfride had to leave early – that was all.

Elfride never went out on horseback but she brought home something – something found, or something bought. If she trotted to town or village, her burden was books. If to hills, woods, or the seashore, it was wonderful mosses, abnormal twigs, a handkerchief of wet shells or seaweed.

Once, in muddy weather, when Pansy was walking with her down the street of Castle Boterel, on a fair-day, a packet in front of her and a packet under her arm, an accident befell the packets, and they slipped down. On one side of her, three volumes of fiction lay kissing the mud; on the other numerous skeins of polychromatic wools lay absorbing it. Unpleasant women smiled through windows at the mishap, the men all looked round, and a boy, who was minding a gingerbread stall whilst the owner had gone to get drunk, laughed loudly. The blue eyes turned to sapphires, and the cheeks crimsoned with vexation.

After that misadventure she set her wits to work, and was ingenious enough to invent an arrangement of small straps about the saddle, by which a great deal could be safely carried thereon, in a small compass. Here she now spread out and fastened a plain dark walking-dress and a few other trifles of apparel. Worm opened the gate for her, and she vanished away.

One of the brightest mornings of late summer shone upon her. The heather was at its purplest, the furze at its yellowest, the grasshoppers chirped loud enough for birds, the snakes hissed like little engines, and Elfride at first felt lively. Sitting at ease upon Pansy, in her orthodox riding-habit and nondescript hat, she looked what she felt. But the mercury of those days had a trick of falling unexpectedly. First, only for one minute in ten had she a sense of depression. Then a large cloud, that had been hanging in the north like a black fleece, came and placed itself between her and the sun. It helped on what was already inevitable, and she sank into a uniformity of sadness.

She turned in the saddle and looked back. They were now on an open table-land, whose altitude still gave her a view of the sea by Endelstow. She looked longingly at that spot.

During this slight revulsion of feeling Pansy had been still advancing, and Elfride felt it would be absurd to turn her little mare's head the other way. 'Still,' she thought, 'if I had a mamma at home I *would* go back!'

And making one of those stealthy movements by which women let their hearts juggle with their brains, she did put the horse's head about, as if unconsciously, and went at a hand-gallop towards home for more than a mile. By this time, from the inveterate habit of valuing what we have renounced directly the alternative is chosen, the thought of her forsaken Stephen recalled her, and she turned about, and cantered on to St Launce's again.

This miserable strife of thought now began to rage in all its wildness. Overwrought and trembling, she dropped the rein upon Pansy's shoulders, and vowed she would be led whither the horse would take her.

Pansy slackened her pace to a walk, and walked on with her agitated burden for three or four minutes. At the expiration of this time they had come to a little by-way on the right, leading down a slope to a pool of water. The pony stopped, looked towards the pool, and then advanced and stooped to drink.

Elfride looked at her watch and discovered that if she were going to reach St Launce's soon enough to change her dress at the Falcon, and get a chance of some early train to Plymouth – there were only two available – it was necessary to proceed at once.

She was impatient. It seemed as if Pansy would never stop drinking; and the repose of the pool, the idle motions of the insects and flies upon it, the placid waving of the flags, the leaf-skeletons, like Genoese filigree,* placidly sleeping at the bottom, by their contrast with her own turmoil made her impatience greater.

Pansy did turn at last, and went up the slope again to the high-road. The pony came upon it, and stood crosswise, looking up and down. Elfride's heart throbbed erratically, and she thought, 'Horses, if left to themselves, make for where they are best fed. Pansy will go home.'

Pansy turned and walked on towards St Launce's.

Pansy at home, during summer, had little but grass to live on. After a run to St Launce's she always had a feed of corn to support her on the return journey. Therefore, being now more than half way, she preferred St Launce's.

But Elfride did not remember this now. All she cared to recognize was a dreamy fancy that to-day's rash action was not her own. She was disabled by her moods, and it seemed indispensable to adhere to the programme. So strangely involved are motives that, more than by her promise to Stephen, more even than by her love, she was forced on by a sense of the necessity of keeping faith with herself, as promised in the inane vow of ten minutes ago.

She hesitated no longer. Pansy went, like the steed of Adonis,* as if she told the steps. Presently the quaint gables and jumbled roofs of St Launce's were spread beneath her; and going down the hill she entered the courtyard of the Falcon. Mrs Buckle, the landlady, came to the door to meet her.

The Swancourts were well known here. The transition from equestrian to the ordinary guise of railway travellers had been more than once performed by father and daughter in this establishment.

In less than a quarter of an hour Elfride emerged from the door in her walking-dress, and went to the railway. She had not told Mrs Buckle anything as to her intentions, and was supposed to have gone out shopping.

An hour and forty minutes later, and she was in Stephen's arms at the Plymouth station. Not upon the platform – in the secret retreat of a deserted waiting-room.

Stephen's face boded ill. He was pale and despondent.

'What is the matter?' she asked.

'We cannot be married here to-day, my Elfie! I ought to have known it and stayed here. In my ignorance I did not. I have the licence, but it can only be used in my parish in London. I only came down last night, as you know.'

'What shall we do?' she said blankly.

'There's only one thing we can do, darling.'

'What's that?'

'Go on to London by a train just starting, and be married there to-morrow.'

'Passengers for the 11.5 up-train take their seats!' said a guard's voice on the platform.

'Will you go, Elfride?'

'I will.'

In three minutes the train had moved off,* bearing away with it Stephen and Elfride.

CHAPTER TWELVE

'Adieu! she cries, and waved her lily hand.'*

THE few tattered clouds of the morning enlarged and united, the sun withdrew behind them to emerge no more that day, and the evening came to a close in drifts of rain. The water-drops beat like duck shot against the window of the railway-carriage containing Stephen and Elfride.

The journey from Plymouth to Paddington, by even the most headlong express, allows quite enough leisure for passion of any sort to cool. Elfride's excitement had passed off, and she sat in a kind of stupor during the latter half of the journey. She was aroused by the clanging of the maze of rails over which they traced their way at the entrance to the station.

'Is this London?' she said.

'Yes, darling,' said Stephen in a tone of assurance he was far from feeling. To him, no less than to her, the reality so greatly differed from the prefiguring.

She peered out as well as the window, beaded with drops, would allow her, and saw only the lamps, which had just been lit, blinking in the wet atmosphere, and rows of hideous zinc chimney-pipes in dim relief against the sky. She writhed uneasily, as when a thought is swelling in the mind which must cause much pain at its deliverance in words. Elfride had known no more about the stings of evil report than the native wild-fowl knew of the effects of Crusoe's first shot.* Now she saw a little further, and a little further still.

The train stopped. Stephen relinquished the soft hand he had held all the day, and proceeded to assist her on to the platform.

This act of alighting upon strange ground seemed all that was wanted to complete a resolution within her.

She looked at her betrothed with despairing eyes.

'O Stephen,' she exclaimed, 'I am so miserable! I must go home again – I must – I must! Forgive my wretched vacillation. I don't like it here – nor myself – nor you!'

Stephen looked bewildered, and did not speak.

'Will you allow me to go home?' she implored. 'I won't trouble you to go with me. I will not be any weight upon you; only say you will agree to my returning; that you will not hate me for it, Stephen! It is better that I should return again; indeed it is, Stephen.'

'But we can't return now,' he said in a deprecatory tone.

'I must! I will!'

'How? When do you want to go?'

'Now. Can we go at once?'

The lad looked hopelessly along the platform.

'If you must go, and think it wrong to remain, dearest,' said he sadly, 'you shall. You shall do whatever you like, my Elfride. But would you in reality rather go now than stay till to-morrow, and go as my wife?'

'Yes, yes – much – anything to go now. I must; I must!' she cried.

'We ought to have done one of two things,' he answered gloomily. 'Never to have started, or not to have returned without being married. I don't like to say it, Elfride – indeed I don't; but you must be told this, that going back unmarried may compromise your good name in the eyes of people who may hear of it.'

'They will not; and I must go.'

'O Elfride! I am to blame for bringing you away.'

'Not at all. I am the elder.'

'By a month; and what's that? But never mind that now.' He looked around. 'Is there a train for Plymouth to-night?' he inquired of a guard. The guard passed on and did not speak.

'Is there a train for Plymouth to-night?' said Elfride to another.

'Yes, miss; the 8.10 – leaves in ten minutes. You have come to the wrong platform; it is the other side. Change at Bristol into the night mail. Down that staircase, and under the line.'

They run down the staircase – Elfride first – to the booking-office, and into a carriage with an official standing beside the door. 'Show your tickets, please.' They are locked in – men about the platform accelerate their velocities till they fly up and down like shuttles in a loom – a whistle – the waving of a flag – a human cry – a steam groan – and away they go to Plymouth again, just catching these words as they glide off:

'Those two youngsters had a near run for it, and no mistake!'

Elfride found her breath.

'And have you come too, Stephen? Why did you?'

'I shall not leave you till I see you safe at St Launce's. Do not think worse of me than I am, Elfride.'

And then they rattled along through the night, back again by the way they had come. The weather cleared, and the stars shone in upon them. Their two or three fellow-passengers sat for most of the time with closed eyes. Stephen sometimes slept; Elfride alone was wakeful and palpitating hour after hour.

The day began to break, and revealed that they were by the sea. Red rocks overhung them, and, receding into distance, grew livid in the blue grey atmosphere. The sun rose, and sent penetrating shafts of light in upon their weary faces. Another hour, and the world began to be busy. They waited yet a little, and the train slackened its speed in view of the platform at St Launce's.

She shivered, and mused sadly.

'I did not see all the consequences,' she said. 'Appearances are wofully against me. If anybody finds me out, I am, I suppose, disgraced.'

'Then appearances will speak falsely; and how can that matter, even if they do? I shall be your husband sooner or later, for certain, and so prove your purity.'

'Stephen, once in London I ought to have married you,' she said firmly. 'It was my only safe defence. I see more things now than I did yesterday. My only remaining chance is not to be discovered; and that we must fight for most desperately.'

They stepped out. Elfride pulled a thick veil over her face.

A woman with red and scaly eyelids and glistening eyes was sitting on a bench just inside the office-door. She fixed her eyes upon Elfride with an expression whose force it was impossible to doubt, but the meaning of which was not clear; then upon the carriage they had left. She seemed to read a sinister story in the scene.

Elfride shrank back, and turned the other way.

'Who is that woman?' said Stephen. 'She looked hard at you.'

'Mrs Jethway – a widow, and mother of that young man whose tomb we sat on the other night. Stephen, she is my enemy. Would that God had had mercy enough upon me to have hidden this from *her*!'

'Do not talk so hopelessly,' he remonstrated. 'I don't think she recognized us.'

'I pray that she did not.'

He put on a more vigorous mood.

'Now, we will go and get some breakfast.'

'No, no!' she begged. 'I cannot eat. I *must* get back to Endelstow.'

Elfride was as if she had grown years older than Stephen now.

'But you have had nothing since last night but that cup of tea at Bristol.'

'I can't eat, Stephen.'

'Wine and biscuit?'

'No.'

'Nor tea, nor coffee?'

'No.'

'A glass of water?'

'No. I want something that makes people strong and energetic for the present, that borrows the strength of to-morrow for use to-day – leaving to-morrow without any at all for that matter; or even that would take all life away to-morrow, so long as it enabled me to get home again now. Brandy, that's what I want. That woman's eyes have eaten my heart away!'

'You are wild; and you grieve me, darling. Must it be brandy?'

'Yes, if you please.'

'How much?'

'I don't know. I have never drunk more than a teaspoonful at once. All I know is that I want it. Don't get it at the Falcon.'

He left her in the fields, and went to the nearest inn in that direction. Presently he returned with a small flask nearly full, and some slices of bread-and-butter, thin as wafers, in a paper-bag. Elfride took a sip or two.

'It goes into my eyes,' she said wearily. 'I can't take any more. Yes, I will; I will close my eyes. Ah, it goes to them by an inside route. I don't want it; throw it away.'

However, she could eat, and did eat. Her chief attention was concentrated upon how to get the horse from the Falcon stables without suspicion. Stephen was not allowed to accompany her into the town. She acted now upon conclusions reached without any aid from him: his power over her seemed to have departed.

'You had better not be seen with me, even here where I am so little known. We have begun stealthily as thieves, and we must end stealthily as thieves, at all hazards. Until papa has been told by me myself, a discovery would be terrible.'

Walking and gloomily talking thus they waited till nearly nine o'clock, at which time Elfride thought she might call at the Falcon without creating much surprise. Behind the railway-station was the river, spanned by an old Tudor bridge,* whence the road diverged in two directions, one skirting the suburbs of the town, and winding round again into ,the high-road to Endelstow. Beside this road Stephen sat, and awaited her return from the Falcon.

He sat as one sitting for a portrait, motionless, watching the chequered lights and shades on the tree-trunks, the children playing opposite the school previous to entering for the morning lesson, the reapers in a field afar off. The certainty of possession had not come, and there was nothing to mitigate the youth's gloom, that increased with the thought of the parting now so near.

At length she came trotting round to him, in appearance much as on the romantic morning of their visit to the cliff, but shorn of the radiance which glistened about her then. However, her comparative immunity from further risk and trouble had considerably composed her. Elfride's capacity for being wounded was only surpassed by her capacity for healing, which rightly or wrongly is by some considered an index of transientness of feeling in general.

'Elfride, what did they-say at the Falcon?'

'Nothing. Nobody seemed curious about me. They knew I went to Plymouth, and I have stayed there a night now and then with Miss Bicknell. I rather calculated upon that.'

And now parting arose like a death to these children, for it was imperative that she should start at once. Stephen walked beside her for nearly a mile. During the walk he said sadly:

'Elfride, four-and-twenty hours have passed, and the thing is not done.'

'But you have insured that it shall be done.'

'How have I?'

'O Stephen, you ask how! Do you think I could marry another man on earth after having gone thus far with you? Have I not shown beyond possibility of doubt that I can be nobody else's? Have I not irretrievably committed myself? – pride has stood for nothing in the face of my great love. You misunderstood my turning back, and I cannot explain it. It was wrong to go with you at all; and though it would have been worse to go further, it would have been better policy, perhaps. Be assured of this, that whenever you have a home for me – however poor and humble – and come and claim me, I am ready.' She added bitterly, 'When my father knows of this day's work, he may be only too glad to let me go.'

'Perhaps he may, then, insist upon our marriage at once!' Stephen answered, seeing a ray of hope in the very focus of her remorse. 'I hope he may, even if we had still to part till I am ready for you, as we intended.'

Elfride did not reply.

'You don't seem the same woman, Elfie, that you were yesterday.'

'Nor am I. But good-bye. Go back now.' And she reined the horse for parting. 'O Stephen,' she cried, 'I feel so weak! I don't know how to meet him. Cannot you, after all, come back with me?'

'Shall I come?'

Elfride paused to think.

'No; it will not do. It is my utter foolishness that makes me say such words. But he will send for you.'

'Say to him,' continued Stephen, 'that we did this in the absolute despair of our minds. Tell him we don't wish him to favour us – only to deal justly with us. If he says, marry now, so much the better. If not, say that all may be put right by his promise to allow me to have you when I am good enough for you – which may be soon. Say I have nothing to offer him in exchange for his treasure – the more sorry I; but all the love, and all the life, and all the labour of an honest man shall be yours. As to when this had better be told, I leave you to judge.'

His words made her cheerful enough to toy with her position.

'And if ill report should come, Stephen,' she said, smiling, 'why, the orange-tree must save me,* as it saved virgins in St George's time from the poisonous breath of the dragon. There, forgive me for forwardness: I am going.'

Then the boy and girl beguiled themselves with words of half-parting only.

'Own wifie, God bless you till we meet again!'

'Till we meet again, good-bye!'

And the pony went on, and she spoke to him no more. He saw her figure diminish and her blue veil grow gray – saw it with the agonizing sensations of a slow death.

After thus parting from a man than whom she had known none greater as yet, Elfride rode rapidly onwards, a tear being occasionally shaken from her eyes into the road. What yesterday had seemed so desirable, so promising, even trifling, had now acquired the complexion of a tragedy.

She saw the rocks and sea in the neighbourhood of Endelstow, and heaved a sigh of relief.

When she passed a field behind the vicarage she heard the voices of Unity and William Worm. They were hanging a carpet upon a line. Unity was uttering a sentence that concluded with 'when Miss Elfride comes'.

'When d'ye expect her?'

'Not till evening now. She's safe enough at Miss Bicknell's, bless ye.'

Elfride went round to the door. She did not knock or ring; and seeing nobody to take the horse Elfride led her round to the yard, slipped off the bridle and saddle, drove her towards the paddock, and turned her in. Then Elfride crept indoors, and looked into all the ground-floor rooms. Her father was not there.

On the mantelpiece of the drawing-room stood a letter addressed to her in his handwriting. She took it and read it as she went upstairs to change her habit.

STRATLEIGH, *Thursday*

DEAR ELFRIDE, – On second thoughts I will not return to-day, but only come as far as Wadcombe. I shall be at home by to-morrow afternoon, and bring a friend with me. – Yours, in haste,

C.S.

After making a quick toilet she felt more revived, though still suffering from a headache. On going out of the door she met Unity at the top of the stair.

'O Miss Elfride! I said to myself 'tis her sperrit! We didn't dream o' you not coming home last night. You didn't say anything about staying.'

'I intended to come home the same evening, but altered my plan. I wished I hadn't afterwards. Papa will be angry, I suppose?'

'Better not tell him, miss,' said Unity.

'I do fear to,' she murmured. 'Unity, would you just begin telling him when he comes home?'

'What! and get you into trouble?'

'I deserve it.'

'No, indeed, I won't,' said Unity. 'It is not such a mighty matter, Miss Elfride. I says to myself, master's taking a hollerday, and because he's not been kind lately to Miss Elfride, she—'

'Is imitating him. Well, do as you like. And will you now bring me some luncheon?'

After satisfying an appetite which the fresh marine air had given her in its victory over an agitated mind, she put on her hat and went to the garden and summer-house. She sat down, and leant with her head in a corner. Here she fell asleep.

Half-awake, she hurriedly looked at the time. She had been there three hours. At the same moment she heard the outer gate swing together, and wheels sweep round the entrance; some prior noise from the same source having probably been the cause of her awaking. Next her father's voice was heard calling to Worm.

Elfride passed along a walk towards the house behind a belt of shrubs. She heard a tongue holding converse with her father, which was not that of either of the servants. Her father and the stranger were laughing together. Then there was a rustling of silk, and Mr Swancourt and his companion, or companions, to all seeming entered the door of the house, for nothing more of them was audible. Elfride had turned back to meditate on what friends these could be, when she heard footsteps, and her father exclaiming behind her:

'O Elfride, here you are! I hope you got on well?'

Elfride's heart smote her, and she did not speak.

'Come back to the summer-house a minute,' continued Mr Swancourt; 'I have to tell you of that I promised to.'

They entered the summer-house, and stood leaning over the knotty woodwork of the balustrade.

'Now,' said her father radiantly, 'guess what I have to say.' He seemed to be regarding his own existence so intently that he took no interest in nor even saw the complexion of hers.

'I cannot, papa,' she said sadly.

'Try, dear.'

'I would rather not, indeed.'

'You are tired. You look worn. The ride was too much for you. Well, this is what I went away for. I went to be married!'

'Married!' she faltered, and could hardly check an involuntary 'So did I.' A moment after and her resolve to confess perished like a bubble.

'Yes; to whom do you think? Mrs Troyton, the new owner of the estate over the hedge, and of the old manor-house. It was only finally settled between us when I went to Stratleigh a few days ago.' He lowered his voice to a sly tone of merriment. 'Now, as to your stepmother, you'll find she is not much to look at, though a good deal to listen to. She is half-a-dozen years older than myself, for one thing.'

'You forget that I know her. She called here once, after we had been to her, and found her away from home.'

'Of course, of course. Well, whatever her looks are, she's as excellent a woman as ever breathed. She has had lately left her as absolute property three thousand five hundred a year, besides the devise of this estate* – and, by the way, a large legacy came to her in satisfaction of dower,* as it is called.'

'Three thousand five hundred a year!'

'And a large – well, a fair-sized – mansion in town, and a pedigree as long as my walking-stick; though that bears evidence of being rather a raked-up affair – done since the family got rich – people do those things now as they build ruins on maiden estates and cast antiques at Birmingham.'

Elfride merely listened and said nothing.

He continued more quietly and impressively. 'Yes, Elfride, she is wealthy in comparison with us, though with few connections. However, she will introduce you to the world a little. We are going to exchange her house in Baker Street for one at Kensington, for your sake. Everybody is going there now, she says. At Easters we shall fly to town for the usual three months – I shall have a curate of course by that time. Elfride, I am past love, you know, and I honestly confess that I married her for your sake. Why a woman of her standing should have thrown herself away upon me, God knows.

But I suppose her age and plainness were too pronounced for a town man. With your good looks, if you now play your cards well, you may marry anybody. Of course, a little contrivance will be necessary; but there's nothing to stand between you and a husband with a title, that I can see. Lady Luxellian was only a squire's daughter. Now, don't you see how foolish the old fancy was? But come, she is indoors waiting to see you. It is as good as a play, too,' continued the rector, as they walked towards the house. 'I courted her through the privet hedge yonder: not entirely, you know, but we used to walk there of an evening – nearly every evening at last. But I needn't tell you details now; everything was terribly matter-of-fact, I assure you. At last, that day I saw her at Stratleigh, we determined to settle it off-hand.'

'And you never said a word to me,' replied Elfride, not reproachfully either in tone or thought. Indeed, her feeling was the very reverse of reproachful. She felt relieved and even thankful. Where confidence had not been given, how could confidence be expected?

Her father mistook her dispassionateness for a veil of politeness over a sense of ill-usage. 'I am not altogether to blame,' he said. 'There were two or three reasons for secrecy. One was the recent death of her relative the testator, though that did not apply to you. But remember, Elfride,' he continued in a stiffer tone, 'you had mixed yourself up so foolishly with those low people, the Smiths – and it was just, too, when Mrs Troyton and myself were beginning to understand each other – that I resolved to say nothing even to you. How did I know how far you had gone with them and their son? You might have made a point of taking tea with them every day, for all that I knew.'

Elfride swallowed her feelings as she best could, and languidly though flatly asked a question.

'Did you kiss Mrs Troyton on the lawn about three weeks ago? That evening I came into the study and found you had just had candles in?'

Mr Swancourt looked rather red and abashed, as middle-aged lovers are apt to do when caught in the tricks of younger ones.

'Well, yes; I think I did,' he stammered; 'just to please her, you know.' And then recovering himself he laughed heartily.

'And was this what your Horatian quotation referred to?'*

'It was, Elfride.'

They stepped into the drawing-room from the verandah. At that moment Mrs Swancourt came downstairs, and entered the same room by the door.

'Here, Charlotte, is my little Elfride,' said Mr Swancourt, with the increased affection of tone often adopted towards relations when newly produced.

Poor Elfride, not knowing what to do, did nothing at all; but stood receptive of all that came to her by sight, hearing, and touch.

Mrs Swancourt moved forward, took her stepdaughter's hand, then kissed her.

'Ah, darling!' she exclaimed good-humouredly, 'you didn't think when you showed a strange old woman over the conservatory a month or two ago, and explained the flowers to her so prettily, that she would so soon be here in new colours. Nor did she, I am sure.'

The new mother had been truthfully enough described by Mr Swancourt. She was not physically attractive. She was dark – very dark – in complexion, portly in figure, and with a plentiful residuum of hair in the proportion of half a dozen white ones to half a dozen black ones, though the latter were black indeed. No further observed, she was not a woman to like. But there was more to see. To the most superficial critic it was apparent that she made no attempt to disguise her age. She looked five-and-fifty at the first glance, and close acquaintanceship never proved her older.

Another and still more winning trait was one attaching to the corners of her mouth. Before she made a remark these often twitched gently: not backwards and forwards, the index of nervousness; not down upon the jaw, the sign of determination; but palpably upwards, in precisely the curve adopted to represent mirth in the broad caricatures of schoolboys. Only this element in her face was expressive of anything within the woman, but it was unmistakable. It expressed humour subjective as well as objective – which could survey the peculiarities of self in as whimsical a light as those of other people.

This is not all of Mrs Swancourt. She had held out to Elfride hands whose fingers were literally stiff with rings, *signis auroque rigentes*,* like Helen's robe. These rows of rings were not worn in vanity apparently. They were mostly antique and dull, though a few were the reverse.

RIGHT HAND

1st. Plainly set oval onyx, representing a devil's head. 2nd. Green jasper intaglio, with red veins. 3rd. Entirely gold, bearing figure of a hideous griffin. 4th. A sea-green monster diamond, with small diamonds round it. 5th. Antique cornelian intaglio of dancing figure of a satyr. 6th. An angular band chased with dragons' heads. 7th. A faceted carbuncle accompanied by ten little twinkling emeralds.

LEFT HAND

1st. A reddish-yellow toadstone.* 2nd. A heavy ring enamelled in colours, and bearing a jacynth. 3rd. An amethystine sapphire. 4th. A polished ruby, surrounded by diamonds. 5th. The engraved ring of an abbess. 6th. A gloomy intaglio.

Beyond this rather quaint array of stone and metal Mrs Swancourt wore no ornament whatever.

Elfride had been favourably impressed with Mrs Troyton at their meeting about two months earlier; but to be pleased with a woman as a momentary acquaintance was different from being taken with her as a stepmother. However, the suspension of feeling was but for a moment. Elfride decided to like her still.

Mrs Swancourt was a woman of the world as to knowledge, the reverse as to action, as her marriage suggested. Elfride and the lady were soon inextricably involved in conversation, and Mr Swancourt left them to themselves.

'And what do you find to do with yourself here?' Mrs Swancourt said, after a few remarks about the wedding. 'You ride, I know.'

'Yes, I ride. But not much, because papa doesn't like my going alone.'

'You must have somebody to look after you.'

'And I read, and write a little.'

'You should write a novel. The regular resource of people who don't go enough into the world to live a novel is to write one.'

'I have done it,' said Elfride, looking dubiously at Mrs

Swancourt, as if in doubt whether she would meet with ridicule there.

'That's right. Now, then, what is it about, dear?'

'About – well, it is a romance of the Early Ages.'

'Knowing nothing of the present age, which everybody knows about, for safety you chose an age known neither to you nor other people. That's it, eh? No, no; I don't mean it, dear.'

'Well, I have had some opportunities of studying mediæval art and manners in the library and private museum at Endelstow House, and I thought I should like to try my hand upon a fiction. I know the time for these tales is past; but I was interested in it, very much interested.'

'When is it to appear?'

'Oh, never, I suppose.'

'Nonsense, my dear girl. Publish it, by all means. All ladies do that sort of thing now; not for profit, you know, but as a guarantee of mental respectability to their future husbands.'

'An excellent idea of us ladies.'

'Though I am afraid it rather resembles the melancholy ruse of throwing loaves over castle-walls at besiegers, and suggests desperation rather than plenty inside.'

'Did you ever try it?'

'No; I was too far gone even for that.'

'Papa says no publisher will take my book.'

'That remains to be proved. I'll give my word, my dear, that by this time next year it shall be printed.'

'Will you, indeed?' said Elfride, partially brightening with pleasure, though she was sad enough in her depths. 'I thought brains were the indispensable, even if the only, qualification for admission to the republic of letters. A mere commonplace creature like me will soon be turned out again.'

'O no; once you are there you'll be like a drop of water in a piece of rock-crystal – your medium will dignify your commonness.'

'It will be a great satisfaction,' Elfride murmured, and thought of Stephen, and wished she could make a great fortune by writing romances, and marry him and live happily.

'And then we'll go to London, and then to Paris,' said Mrs Swancourt. 'I have been talking to your father about it. But we have first to move into the manor-house, and we think of staying at Torquay whilst that is going on. Meanwhile, instead of going on a honeymoon scamper by ourselves, we have come home to fetch you, and go all together to Bath for two or three weeks.'

Elfride assented pleasantly, even gladly; but she saw that, by this marriage, her father and herself had ceased for ever to be the close relations they had been up to a few weeks ago. It was impossible now to tell him the tale of her wild elopement with Stephen Smith.

He was still snugly housed in her heart. His absence had regained for him much of that aureola of saintship which had been nearly abstracted during her reproachful mood on that miserable journey from London. Rapture is often cooled by contact with its cause, especially if under awkward conditions. And that last experience with Stephen had done anything but make him shine in her eyes. His very kindness in letting her return was his offence. Elfride had her sex's love of sheer force in a man, however ill-directed; and at that critical juncture in London Stephen's only chance of retaining the ascendancy over her that his face and not his parts had acquired for him, would have been by doing what, for one thing, he was too youthful to undertake – that was, dragging her by the wrist to the rails of some altar, and peremptorily marrying her. Decisive action is seen by appreciative minds to be frequently objectless, and sometimes fatal; but decision, however suicidal, has more charm for a woman than the most unequivocal Fabian success.*

However, some of the unpleasant accessories of that occasion were now out of sight again, and Stephen had resumed not a few of his fancy colours.

CHAPTER THIRTEEN

'He set in order many proverbs.'*

It is London in October – two months further on in the story.

Bede's Inn* has this peculiarity, that it faces, receives from, and discharges into a bustling thoroughfare speaking only of wealth and respectability, whilst its postern* abuts on as crowded and poverty-stricken a network of alleys as are to be found anywhere in the metropolis. The moral consequences are, first, that those who occupy chambers in the Inn may see a great deal of shirtless humanity's habits and enjoyments without doing more than look down from a back window; and second, they may hear wholesome though unpleasant social reminders through the medium of a harsh voice, an unequal footstep, the echo of a blow or a fall, which originates in the person of some drunkard or wife-beater, as he crosses and interferes with the quiet of the square. Characters of this kind frequently pass through the Inn from a little foxhole of an alley at the back, but they never loiter there.

It is hardly necessary to state that all the sights and movements proper to the Inn are most orderly. On the fine October evening on which we follow Stephen Smith to this place, a placid porter is sitting on a stool under a sycamore-tree in the midst, with a little cane in his hand. We notice the thick coat of soot upon the branches, hanging underneath them in flakes, as in a chimney. The blackness of these boughs does not at present improve the tree – nearly forsaken by its leaves as it is – but in the spring their green fresh beauty is made doubly beautiful by the contrast. Within the railings is a flower-garden of respectable dahlias and chrysanthemums, where a man is sweeping the leaves from the grass.

Stephen selects a doorway, and ascends an old though wide wooden staircase, with moulded balusters and handrail, which in a country manor-house would be considered a noteworthy specimen of Renaissance workmanship. He reaches a door on the first floor, over which is painted, in black letters, 'Mr Henry Knight' –

'Barrister-at-law' being understood but not expressed. The wall is thick, and there is a door at its outer and inner face. The outer one happens to be ajar: Stephen goes to the other, and taps.

'Come in!' from distant penetralia.*

First was a small anteroom, divided from the inner apartment by a wainscoted archway two or three yards wide. Across this archway hung a pair of dark-green curtains, making a mystery of all within the arch except the spasmodic scratching of a quill pen. Here was grouped a chaotic assemblage of articles – mainly old framed prints and paintings – leaning edgewise against the wall, like roofing slates in a builder's yard. All the books visible here were folios too big to be stolen – some lying on a heavy oak table in one corner, some on the floor among the pictures, the whole intermingled with old coats, hats, umbrellas, and walking-sticks.

Stephen pushed aside the curtain, and before him sat a man writing away as if his life depended upon it – which it did.

A man of thirty in a speckled coat, with dark brown hair, curly beard, and crisp moustache: the latter running into the beard on each side of the mouth, and, as usual, hiding the real expression of that organ under a chronic aspect of impassivity.

'Ah, my dear fellow, I knew 'twas you,' said Knight, looking up with a smile, and holding out his hand.

Knight's mouth and eyes came to view now. Both features were good, and had the peculiarity of appearing younger and fresher than the brow and face they belonged to, which were getting sicklied o'er by the unmistakable pale cast.* The mouth had not quite relinquished rotundity of curve for the firm angularities of middle life; and the eyes, though keen, permeated rather than penetrated: what they had lost of their boy-time brightness by a dozen years of hard reading lending a quietness to their gaze which suited them well.

A lady would have said there was a smell of tobacco in the room: a man that there was not.

Knight did not rise. He looked at a timepiece on the mantelshelf, then turned again to his letters, pointing to a chair.

'Well, I am glad you have come. I only returned to town yesterday; now, don't speak, Stephen, for ten minutes; I have just that time to the late post. At the eleventh minute, I'm your man.'

Stephen sat down as if this kind of reception was by no means new, and away went Knight's pen, beating up and down like a ship in a storm.

Cicero called the library the soul of the house; here the house was all soul. Portions of the floor, and half the wall-space, were taken up by book-shelves ordinary and extraordinary; the remaining parts, together with brackets, side-tables, &c., being occupied by casts, statuettes, medallions, and plaques of various descriptions, picked up by the owner in his wanderings through France and Italy.

One stream only of evening sunlight came into the room from a window quite in the corner, overlooking a court. An aquarium stood in the window. It was a dull parallelepipedon* enough for living creatures at most hours of the day; but for a few minutes in the evening, as now, an errant, kindly ray lighted up and warmed the little world therein, when the many-coloured zoophytes* opened and put forth their arms, the weeds acquired a rich transparency, the shells gleamed of a more golden yellow, and the timid community expressed gladness more plainly than in words.

Within the prescribed ten minutes Knight flung down his pen, rang for the boy to take the letters to the post, and at the closing of the door exclaimed, 'There; thank God, that's done. Now, Stephen, pull your chair round, and tell me what you have been doing all this time. Have you kept up your Greek?'

'No.'

'How's that?'

'I haven't enough spare time.'

'That's nonsense.'

'Well, I have done a great many things, if not that. And I have done one extraordinary thing.'

Knight turned full upon Stephen. 'Ah-ha! Now, then, let me look into your face, put two and two together, and make a shrewd guess.'

Stephen changed to a redder colour.

'Why, Smith,' said Knight, after holding him rigidly by the shoulders, and keenly scrutinising his countenance for a minute in silence, 'you have fallen in love.'

'Well – the fact is—'

'Now, out with it.' But seeing that Stephen looked rather distressed he changed to a kindly tone. 'Now, Smith, my lad, you know me well enough by this time, or you ought to; and you know very well that if you choose to give me a detailed account of the phenomenon within you, I shall listen; if you don't, I am the last man in the world to care to hear it.'

'I'll tell this much: I *have* fallen in love, and I want to be *married*.'

Knight looked ominous as this passed Stephen's lips.

'Don't judge me before you have heard more,' cried Stephen anxiously, seeing the change in his friend's countenance.

'I don't judge. Does your mother know about it?'

'Nothing definite.'

'Father?'

'No. But I'll tell you. The young person—'

'Come, that's dreadfully ungallant. But perhaps I understand the frame of mind a little, so go on. Your sweetheart—'

'She is rather higher in the world than I am.'

'As it should be.'

'And her father won't hear of it, as I now stand.'

'Not an uncommon case.'

'And now comes what I want your advice upon. Something has happened at her house which makes it out of the question for us to ask her father again now. So we are keeping silent. In the meantime an architect in India has just written to Mr Hewby to ask whether he can find for him a young assistant willing to go over to Bombay to prepare drawings for work formerly done by the engineers. The salary he offers is 350 rupees a month, or about £35. Hewby has mentioned it to me, and I have been to Dr Wray, who says I shall acclimatize without much illness. Now, would you go?'

'You mean to say, because it is a possible road to the young lady.'

'Yes; I was thinking I could go over and make a little money, and then come back and ask for her. I have the option of practising for myself after a year.'

'Would she be staunch?'

'O yes! For ever – to the end of her life!'

'How do you know?'

'Why, how do people know? Of course she will.'

Knight leant back in his chair. 'Now, though I know her thoroughly as she exists in your heart, Stephen, I don't know her in the flesh. All I want to ask is, is this idea of going to India based entirely upon a belief in her fidelity?'

'Yes; I should not go if it were not for her.'

'Well, my boy, you have put me in rather an awkward position. If I give my true sentiments, I shall hurt your feelings; if I don't, I shall hurt my own judgment. And remember, I don't know much about women.'

'But you have had attachments, although you tell me very little about them.'

'And I only hope you'll continue to prosper till I tell you more.'

Stephen winced at this rap. 'I have never formed a deep attachment,' continued Knight. 'I never have found a woman worth it. Nor have I been once engaged to be married.'

'You write as if you had been engaged a hundred times, if I may be allowed to say so,' said Stephen in an injured tone.

'Yes, that may be. But, my dear Stephen, it is only those who half know a thing that write about it. Those who know it thoroughly don't take the trouble. All I know about women, or men either, is a mass of generalities. I plod along, and occasionally lift my eyes and skim the weltering surface of mankind lying between me and the horizon, as a crow might; no more.'

Knight stopped as if he had fallen into a train of thought, and Stephen looked with affectionate awe at a master whose mind, he believed, could swallow up at one meal all that his own head contained.

There was affective sympathy, but no great intellectual fellowship, between Knight and Stephen Smith. Knight had seen his young friend when the latter was a cherry-cheeked happy boy, had been interested in him, had kept his eye upon him, and generously helped the lad to books, till the mere connection of patronage grew to acquaintance, and that ripened to friendship. And so, though Smith was not quite the man Knight would have deliberately chosen as a friend – or even for one of a group of a dozen friends – he somehow was his friend. Circumstance, as usual, did it all. How many of us can say of our intimate *alter ego*,* leaving alone friends of the outer circle, that he is the man we should have finally chosen, as embodying the net result after adding up all the points in human nature that we love, and principles we hold, and subtracting all that we hate? The man is really somebody we got to know by mere physical juxtaposition long maintained, and was taken into our confidence, and even heart, as a makeshift.

'And what do you think of her?' Stephen ventured to say, after a silence.

'Taking her merits on trust from you,' said Knight, 'as we do those of the Roman poets of whom we know nothing but that they lived, I still think she will not stick to you through, say, three years of absence in India.'

'But she will!' cried Stephen desperately. 'She is a girl all delicacy and honour. And no woman of that kind, who has committed herself so into a man's hands as she has into mine, could possibly marry another.'

'How has she committed herself?' asked Knight curiously.

Stephen did not answer. Knight had looked on his love so sceptically that it would not do to say all that he had intended to say by any means.

'Well, don't tell,' said Knight. 'But you are begging the question, which is, I suppose, inevitable in love.'

'And I'll tell you another thing,' the younger man pleaded. 'You remember what you said to me once about women receiving a kiss. Don't you? Why, that instead of our being charmed by the fascination of their bearing at such a time, we should immediately doubt them if their confusion has any *grace* in it – that awkward bungling was the true charm of the occasion, implying that we are the first who has played such a part with them.'

'It is true, quite, though I didn't know I had said it,' murmured Knight musingly.

It often happened that the disciple thus remembered the lessons of the master long after the master himself had forgotten them.

'Well, that was like her!' cried Stephen triumphantly. 'She was in such a flurry that she didn't know what she was doing.'

'Splendid, splendid!' said Knight soothingly. 'So that all I have to say is, that if you see a good opening in Bombay there's no reason why you should not go without troubling to draw fine distinctions as to reasons. No man fully realizes what opinions he acts upon, or what his actions mean.'

'Yes; I go to Bombay. I'll write a note here, if you don't mind.'

'Sleep over it – it is the best plan – and write to-morrow. Meantime, go there to that window and sit down, and look at my

Humanity Show. I am going to dine out this evening, and have to dress here out of my portmanteau. I bring up my things like this to save the trouble of going down to my place at Richmond and back again.'

Knight then went to the middle of the room and flung open his portmanteau, and Stephen drew near the window. The streak of sunlight had crept upward, edged away, and vanished; the zoophytes slept: a dusky gloom pervaded the room. And now another volume of light shone over the panes.

'There!' said Knight, 'where is there in England a spectacle to equal that? I sit there and watch them every night before I go home. Softly open the sash.'

Beneath them was an alley running up to the wall, and thence turning sideways and passing under an arch, so that Knight's back window was immediately over the angle, and commanded a view of the alley lengthwise. Crowds – mostly of women – were surging, bustling, and pacing up and down. Gaslights glared from butchers' stalls, illuminating the lumps of flesh to splotches of orange and vermilion, like the wild colouring of Turner's later pictures,* whilst the purl and babble of tongues of every pitch and mood was to this human wild-wood what the ripple of a brook is to the natural forest.

Nearly ten minutes passed. Then Knight also came to the window.

'Well, now, I call a cab and vanish down the street in the direction of Berkeley Square,' he said, buttoning his waistcoat and kicking his morning suit into a corner. Stephen rose to leave.

'What a heap of literature!' remarked the young man, taking a final longing survey round the room, as if to abide there for ever would be the great pleasure of his life, yet feeling that he had almost outstayed his welcome-while. His eyes rested upon an arm-chair piled full of newspapers, magazines, and bright new volumes in green and red.

'Yes,' said Knight, also looking at them and breathing a sigh of weariness; 'something must be done with several of them soon, I suppose. My dear fellow, you needn't hurry away for a few minutes, you know, if you want to stay; I am not quite ready. Overhaul those volumes whilst I put on my coat, and I'll walk a little way with you.'

Stephen sat down beside the arm-chair and began to tumble the books about. Among the rest he found a novelette* in one volume, *The Court of King Arthur's Castle. By Ernest Field.*

'Are you going to review this?' inquired Stephen with apparent unconcern, and holding up Elfride's effusion.

'Which? Oh, that! I may – though I don't do much light reviewing now. But it is reviewable.'

'How do you mean?'

Knight never liked to be asked what he meant. 'Mean! I mean that the majority of books published are neither good enough nor bad enough to provoke criticism, and that that book does provoke it.'

'By its goodness or its badness?' Stephen said with some anxiety on poor little Elfride's score.

'Its badness. It seems to be written by some girl in her teens.'

Stephen said not another word. He did not care to speak plainly of Elfride after the unfortunate slip his tongue had made in respect of her having committed herself; and, apart from that, Knight's severe – almost dogged and self-willed – honesty in criticizing was unassailable by the humble wish of a youthful friend like Stephen.

Knight was now ready. Turning off the gas, and slamming together the door, they went downstairs and into the street.

CHAPTER FOURTEEN

'We frolic while 'tis May.'*

IT has now to be realized that nearly three-quarters of a year have passed away. In place of the autumnal scenery which formed a setting to the previous enactments, we have the culminating blooms of summer in the year following.

Stephen is in India, slaving away at an office in Bombay; occasionally going up the country on professional errands, and wondering why people who had been there longer than he complained so much of the effect of the climate upon their constitutions. Never had a young man a finer start than seemed now to present itself to Stephen. It was just in that exceptional heyday of prosperity which shone over Bombay some few years ago, that he arrived on the scene. Building and engineering partook of the general impetus. Speculation moved with an accelerated velocity every successive day, the only disagreeable contingency connected with it being the possibility of a collapse.

Elfride had never told her father of the four-and-twenty-hours' escapade with Stephen, nor had it, to her knowledge, come to his ears by any other route. It was a secret trouble and grief to the girl for a short time, and Stephen's departure was another ingredient in her sorrow. But Elfride possessed special facilities for getting rid of trouble after a decent interval. Whilst a slow nature was imbibing a misfortune little by little, she had swallowed the whole agony of it at a draught and was brightening again. She could slough off a sadness and replace it by a hope as easily as a lizard renews a diseased limb.

And two such excellent distractions had presented themselves. One was bringing out the romance and looking for notices in the papers, which, though they had been significantly short so far, had served to divert her thoughts. The other was migrating from the rectory to the more commodious old house of Mrs Swancourt's, overlooking the same valley. Mr Swancourt at first disliked the idea of being transplanted to feminine soil, but the obvious advantages of such an accession of dignity reconciled him to the change. So there was a radical 'move'; the two ladies staying at Torquay as had been arranged, the rector going to and fro.

Mrs Swancourt considerably enlarged Elfride's ideas in an aristocratic direction, and she began to forgive her father for his politic marriage. Certainly, in a worldly sense, a handsome face at fifty had never served a man in better stead.

The new house at Kensington was ready, and they were all in town.

The Hyde Park shrubs had been transplanted as usual, the chairs ranked in line, the grass edgings trimmed, the roads made to look as if they were suffering from a heavy thunderstorm; carriages had been called for by the easeful, horses by the brisk, and the Drive and Row* were again the groove of gaiety for an hour. We gaze upon the spectacle at six o'clock on this midsummer afternoon, in a melon-frame atmosphere and beneath a violet sky. The Swancourt equipage formed one in the stream.

Mrs Swancourt was a talker of talk of the incisive kind, which her low musical voice – the only beautiful point in the old woman – prevented from being wearisome.

'Now,' she said to Elfride, who, like Æneas at Carthage,* was full of admiration for the brilliant scene, 'you will find that our companionless state will give us, as it does everybody, an extraordinary power in reading the features of our fellow-creatures here. I always am a listener in such places as these – not to the narratives told by my neighbours' tongues, but by their faces – the advantage of which is, that whether I am in Row, Boulevard, Rialto, or Prado,* they all speak the same language. I may have acquired some skill in this practice through having been an ugly lonely woman for so many years, with nobody to give me information; a thing you will not consider strange when the parallel case is borne in mind, – how truly people who have no clocks will tell the time of day.'

'Ay, that they will,' said Mr Swancourt corroboratively. 'I have known labouring men at Endelstow and other farms who had framed complete systems of observation for that purpose. By means of shadows, winds, clouds, the movements of sheep and oxen, the singing of birds, the crowing of cocks, and a hundred other sights and sounds which people with watches in their pockets never know the existence of, they are able to pronounce within ten minutes of the hour almost at any required instant. That reminds me of an old story which I'm afraid is too bad – too bad to repeat.' Here the rector shook his head and laughed inwardly.

'Tell it – do!' said the ladies.

'I mustn't quite tell it.'

'That's absurd,' said Mrs Swancourt.

'It was only about a man who, by the same careful system of observation, was known to deceive persons for more than two years into the belief that he kept a barometer by stealth, so exactly did he foretell all changes in the weather by the braying of his ass and the temper of his wife.'

This might have been the story or not. Elfride laughed.

'Exactly,' said Mrs Swancourt. 'And in just the way that those learnt the signs of nature, I have learnt the language of her illegitimate sister – artificiality; and the fibbing of eyes, the contempt of nose-tips, the indignation of back hair, the laughter of clothes, the cynicism of footsteps, and the various emotions lying in walking-stick twirls, hat-liftings, the elevation of parasols, the carriage of umbrellas, become as A B C to me.

'Just look at that daughter's-sister class of mamma in the carriage across there,' she continued to Elfride, pointing with merely a turn of her eye. 'The absorbing self-consciousness of her position that is shown by her countenance is most humiliating to a lover of one's country. You would hardly believe, would you, that members of a Fashionable World, whose professed zero is far above the highest degree of the humble, could be so ignorant of the elementary instincts of reticence.'

'How?'

'Why, to bear on their faces, as plainly as on a phylactery,* the inscription, "Do, pray, look at the coronet on my panels."'

'Really, Charlotte,' said the rector, 'you see as much in faces as Mr Puff saw in Lord Burleigh's nod.'*

Elfride could not but admire the beauty of her fellow country-women, especially since herself and her own few acquaintances had always been slightly sunburnt or marked on the back of the hands by a bramble-scratch at this time of the year.

'And what lovely flowers and leaves they wear in their bonnets!' she exclaimed.

'O yes,' returned Mrs Swancourt. 'Some of them are even more striking in colour than any real ones. Look at that beautiful rose worn by the lady inside the rails. Elegant vine-tendrils introduced upon the stem as an improvement upon prickles, and all growing so naturally just over her ear – I say *growing* advisedly, for the pink of the petals and the pink of her handsome cheeks are equally from Nature's hand to the eyes of the most casual observer.'

'But praise them a little, they do deserve it!' said generous Elfride.

'Well, I do. See how the Duchess of —— waves to and fro in her seat, utilizing the sway of her landau* by looking around only when her head is swung forward, with a passive pride which forbids a resistance to the force of circumstance. Look at the pretty pout on the mouths of that family there, retaining no traces of being arranged beforehand, so well is it done. Look at the demure close of the little fists holding the parasols; the tiny alert thumb, sticking up erect against the ivory stem as knowing as can be, the satin of the parasol invariably matching the complexion of the face beneath it, yet seemingly by an accident, which makes the thing so attractive. There's the red book lying on the opposite seat, bespeaking the vast numbers of their acquaintance. And I particularly admire the aspect of that abundantly daughtered woman on the other side – I mean her look of unconsciousness that the girls are stared at by the walkers, and above all the look of the girls themselves – losing their gaze in the depths of handsome men's eyes without appearing to notice whether they are observing masculine eyes or the leaves of the trees. There's praise for you. But I am only jesting, child – you know that.'

'Piph-ph-ph – how warm it is, to be sure!' said Mr Swancourt, as if his mind were a long distance from all he saw. 'I declare that my watch is so hot that I can scarcely bear to touch it to see what the time is, and all the world smells like the inside of a hat.'

'How the men stare at you, Elfride!' said the elder lady. 'You will kill me quite, I am afraid.'

'Kill you?'

'As a diamond kills an opal in the same setting.'

'I have noticed several ladies and gentlemen looking at me,' said Elfride artlessly, showing her pleasure at being observed.

'My dear, you mustn't say "gentlemen" nowadays,' her stepmother answered in the tones of arch concern that so well became her ugliness. 'We have handed over "gentlemen" to the lower middle class, where the word is still to be heard at tradesmen's balls and provincial tea-parties, I believe. It is done with here.'

'What must I say, then?'

'"Ladies and *men*," always.'

At this moment appeared in the stream of vehicles moving in the contrary direction a chariot* presenting in its general surface the rich indigo hue of a midnight sky, the wheels and margins being picked out in delicate lines of ultramarine; the servants' liveries were dark-blue coats and silver lace, and breeches of neutral Indian red. The whole concern formed an organic whole, and moved along behind a pair of dark chestnut geldings, who advanced in an indifferently zealous trot, very daintily performed, and occasionally shrugged divers points of their veiny surface as if they were rather above the business.

In this sat a gentleman with no decided characteristics more than that he somewhat resembled a good-natured commercial traveller of the superior class. Beside him was a lady with skim-milky eyes and complexion, belonging to the 'interesting' class of women, where that class merges in the sickly, her greatest pleasure being apparently to enjoy nothing. Opposite this pair sat two little girls in white hats and blue feathers.

The lady saw Elfride, smiled and bowed, and touched her husband's elbow, who turned and received Elfride's movement of recognition with a gallant elevation of his hat. Then the two children held up their arms to Elfride, and laughed gleefully.

'Who is that?'

'Why, Lord Luxellian, isn't it?' said Mrs Swancourt, who with the rector had been seated with her back towards them.

'Yes,' replied Elfride. 'He is the one man of those I have seen here whom I consider handsomer than papa.'

'Thank you, dear,' said Mr Swancourt.

'Yes; but your father is so much older. When Lord Luxellian gets a little further on in life, he won't be half so good-looking as our man.'

'Thank you, dear, likewise,' said Mr Swancourt.

'See,' exclaimed Elfride, still looking towards them, 'how those little dears want me! Actually one of them is crying for me to come.'

'We were talking of bracelets just now. Look at Lady Luxellian's,' said Mrs Swancourt, as that baroness lifted up her hand to support one of the children. 'It is slipping up her arm – too large by half. I hate to see daylight between a bracelet and a wrist; I wonder women haven't better taste.'

'It is not on that account, indeed,' Elfride expostulated. 'It is that her arm has got thin, poor thing. You cannot think how much she has altered in this last twelvemonth.'

The carriages were now nearer together, and there was an exchange of more familiar greetings between the two families. Then the Luxellians crossed over and drew up under the plane-trees, just in the rear of the Swancourts. Lord Luxellian alighted, and came forward with a musical laugh.

It was his attraction as a man. People liked him for those tones, and forgot that he had no talents. Acquaintances remembered Mr Swancourt by his manner; they remembered Stephen Smith by his face, Lord Luxellian by his laugh.

Mr Swancourt made some friendly remarks – among other things upon the heat.

'Yes,' said Lord Luxellian, 'we were driving by a furrier's window this afternoon, and the sight filled us all with such a sense of suffocation that we were glad to get away. Ha-ha!' He turned to Elfride. 'Miss Swancourt, I have hardly seen or spoken to you since your literary feat was made public. I had no idea a chiel* was taking notes down at quiet Endelstow, or I should certainly have put myself and friends upon our best behaviour. Swancourt, why didn't you give me a hint!'

Elfride fluttered, blushed, laughed, said it was nothing to speak of, &c. &c.

'Well, I think you were rather unfairly treated by *The Present*; I certainly do. Writing a heavy review like that upon an elegant trifle like the *Court of King Arthur's Castle* was absurd.'

'What?' said Elfride, opening her eyes. 'Was I reviewed in *The Present*?'

'O yes; didn't you see it? Why, it was four or five months ago!'

'No, I never saw it. How sorry I am! What a shame of my publishers! They promised to send me every notice that appeared.'

'Ah, then, I am almost afraid I have been giving you disagreeable information, intentionally withheld out of courtesy. Depend upon it they thought no good would come of sending it, and so would not pain you unnecessarily.'

'O no; I am indeed glad you have told me, Lord Luxellian. It is quite a mistaken kindness on their part. Is the review so much against me?' she inquired tremulously.

'No, no; not that exactly – though I almost forget its exact purport now. It was merely – merely sharp, you know – ungenerous, I might say. But really my memory does not enable me to speak decidedly.'

'We'll drive to *The Present* office, and get one directly; shall we, papa?'

'If you are so anxious, dear, we will, or send. But to-morrow will do.'

'And do oblige me in a little matter now, Elfride,' said Lord Luxellian warmly, and looking as if he were sorry he had brought news that disturbed her. 'I am in reality sent here as a special messenger by my little Polly and Katie to ask you to come into our carriage with them for a short time. I am just going to walk across into Piccadilly, and my wife is left alone with them. I am afraid they are rather spoilt children; but I have half promised them you shall come.'

The steps were let down, and Elfride was transferred – to the intense delight of the little girls, and to the mild interest of loungers with red skins and long necks, who cursorily eyed the performance with their walking-sticks to their lips, occasionally laughing from far down their throats and with their eyes, their mouths not being concerned in the operation at all. Lord Luxellian then told the coachman to drive on, lifted his hat, smiled a smile that missed its mark and alighted on a total stranger, who bowed in bewilderment. Lord Luxellian looked long at Elfride.

The look was a manly, open, and genuine look of admiration; a momentary tribute of a kind which any honest Englishman might have paid to fairness without being ashamed of the feeling, or permitting it to encroach in the slightest degree upon his emotional obligations as a husband and head of a family. Then Lord Luxellian turned away, and walked musingly to the upper end of the promenade.

Mr Swancourt had alighted at the same time with Elfride, crossing over to the Row for a few minutes to speak to a friend he recognized there; and his wife was thus left sole tenant of the carriage.

Now, whilst this little act had been in course of performance, there stood among the promenading spectators a man of somewhat different description from the rest. Behind the general throng, in the rear of the chairs, and leaning against the trunk of a tree, he looked at Elfride with quiet and critical interest.

Three points about this unobtrusive person showed promptly to the exercised eye that he was not a Row man *pur sang*.* First, an irrepressible wrinkle or two in the waist of his frock-coat – denoting that he had not damned his tailor sufficiently to drive that tradesman up to the orthodox high pressure of cunning workmanship. Second, a slight slovenliness of umbrella, occasioned by its owner's habit of resting heavily upon it, and using it as a veritable walking-stick, instead of letting its point touch the ground in the most coquettish of kisses, as is the proper Row manner to do. Third, and chief reason, that try how you might, you could scarcely help supposing, on looking at his face, that your eyes were not far from a well-finished mind, instead of the well-finished skin *et prœterea nihil** which is by rights the Mark of the Row.

The probability is that, had not Mrs Swancourt been left alone in her carriage under the tree, this man would have remained in his unobserved seclusion. But seeing her thus he came round to the front, stooped under the rail, and stood beside the carriage-door.

Mrs Swancourt looked reflectively at him for a quarter of a minute, then held out her hand laughingly:

'Why, Henry Knight – of course it is! My – second – third – fourth cousin – what shall I say? At any rate, my kinsman.'

'Yes, one of a remnant not yet cut off. I scarcely was certain of you, either, from where I was standing.'

'I have not seen you since you first went to Oxford; consider the number of years! You know, I suppose, of my marriage?'

And there sprang up a dialogue concerning family matters of birth, death, and alliances, which it is not necessary to detail. Knight presently inquired:

'The young lady who changed into the other carriage is, then, your stepdaughter?'

'Yes, Elfride. You must know her.'

'And who was the lady in the carriage Elfride entered; who had an ill-defined and watery look, as if she were only the reflection of herself in a pool?'

'Lady Luxellian; very weakly, Elfride says. My husband is remotely connected with them; but there is not much intimacy on account of— However, Henry, you'll come and see us, of course. 24 Chevron Square. Come this week. We shall only be in town a week or two longer.'

'Let me see. I've got to run up to Oxford to-morrow, where I shall be for several days; so that I must, I fear, lose the pleasure of seeing you in London this year.'

'Then come to Endelstow; why not return with us?'

'I am afraid if I were to come before August I should have to leave again in a day or two. I should be delighted to be with you at the beginning of that month; and I could stay a nice long time. I have thought of going westward all the summer.'

'Very well. Now remember that's a compact. And won't you wait now and see Mr Swancourt? He will not be away ten minutes longer.'

'No; I'll beg to be excused; for I must get to my chambers again this evening before I go home; indeed, I ought to have been there now – I have such a press of matters to attend to just at present. You will explain to him, please? Good-bye.'

'And let us know the day of your appearance as soon as you can.'

'I will.'

CHAPTER FIFTEEN

'A wandering voice'*

THOUGH sheer and intelligible griefs are not charmed away by being confided to mere acquaintances, the process is a palliative to certain ill-humours. Among these, perplexed vexation is one – a species of trouble which, like a stream, gets shallower by the simple operation of widening it in any quarter.

On the evening of the day succeeding that of the meeting in the Park, Elfride and Mrs Swancourt were engaged in conversation in the dressing-room of the latter. Such a treatment of such a case was in course of adoption here.

Elfride had just before received an affectionate letter from Stephen Smith in Bombay, which had been forwarded to her from Endelstow. But since this is not the case referred to, it is not worth while to pry further into the contents of the letter than to discover that, with rash though pardonable confidence in coming times, he addressed her in high spirits as his darling future wife.

Probably there cannot be instanced a briefer and surer rule-of-thumb test of a man's temperament – sanguine or cautious – than this: did he or does he ante-date the word wife in corresponding with a betrothed he honestly loves?

She had taken this epistle into her own room, read a little of it, then *saved* the rest for to-morrow, not wishing to be so extravagant as to consume the pleasure all at once. Nevertheless, she could not resist the wish to enjoy yet a little more, so out came the letter again, and in spite of misgivings as to prodigality the whole was devoured. The letter was finally reperused and placed in her pocket.

What was this? Also a newspaper for Elfride, which she had overlooked in her hurry to open the letter. It was the old number of *The Present*, containing the article upon her book, forwarded as had been requested.

Elfride had hastily read it through, shrunk perceptibly smaller, and had then gone with the paper in her hand to Mrs Swancourt's dressing-room, to lighten or at least modify her vexation by a discriminating estimate from her stepmother.

She was now looking disconsolately out of the window.

'Never mind, my child,' said Mrs Swancourt after a careful perusal of the matter indicated. 'I don't see that the review is such a terrible one, after all. Besides, everybody has forgotten about it by this time. I'm sure the opening is good enough for any book ever written. Just listen – it sounds better read aloud than when you pore over it silently: "*The Court of King Arthur's Castle. A Romance of Lyonnesse. By Ernest Field.* In the belief that we were for a while escaping the monotonous repetition of wearisome details in modern social scenery, analyses of uninteresting character, or the unnatural unfoldings of a sensational plot, we took this volume into our hands with a feeling of pleasure. We were disposed to beguile ourselves with the fancy that some new change might possibly be rung upon donjon keeps, chain and plate armour, deeply scarred cheeks, tender maidens disguised as pages, to which we had not listened long ago." Now, that's a very good beginning, in my opinion, and one to be proud of having brought out of a man who has never seen you.'

'Ah, yes,' murmured Elfride wofully. 'But, then, see further on!'

'Well, the next bit is rather unkind, I must own,' said Mrs Swancourt, and read on. '"Instead of this we found ourselves in the hands of some young lady, hardly arrived at years of discretion, to judge by the silly device it has been thought worth while to adopt on the title-page, with the idea of disguising her sex."'

'I am not "silly"!' said Elfride indignantly. 'He might have called me anything but that.'

'You are not, indeed. Well: – "Hands of a young lady . . . whose chapters are simply devoted to impossible tournaments, towers, and escapades, which read like flat copies of like scenes in the stories of Mr G. P. R. James,* and the most unreal portions of *Ivanhoe.** The bait is so palpably artificial that the most credulous gudgeon turns away." Now, my dear, I don't see overmuch to complain of in that. It proves that you were clever enough to make him think of Sir Walter Scott, which is a great deal.'

'O yes; though I cannot romance myself, I am able to remind him of those who can!' Elfride intended to hurl these words sarcastically at her invisible enemy, but as she had no more satirical power than a wood-pigeon they merely fell in a pretty murmur from lips shaped to a pout.

'Certainly: and that's something. Your book is good enough to be bad in an ordinary literary manner, and doesn't stand by itself in a melancholy position altogether worse than assailable. – "That interest in an historical romance may nowadays have any chance of being sustained, it is indispensable that the reader find himself under the guidance of some nearly extinct species of legendary, who, in addition to an impulse towards antiquarian research and an unweakened faith in the mediæval halo, shall possess an inventive faculty in which delicacy of sentiment is far overtopped by a power of welding to stirring incident a spirited variety of the elementary human passions." Well, that long-winded effusion doesn't refer to you at all, Elfride, merely something put in to fill up. Let me see, when does he come to you again; . . . not till the very end, actually. Here you are finally polished off:

'"But to return to the little work we have used as the text of this article. We are far from altogether disparaging the author's powers. She has a certain versatility that enables her to use with effect a style of narration peculiar to herself, which may be called a murmuring of delicate emotional trifles, the particular gift of those to whom the social sympathies of a peaceful time are as daily food. Hence, where matters of domestic experience, and the natural touches which make people real, can be introduced without anachronisms too striking, she is occasionally felicitous; and upon the whole we feel justified in saying that the book will bear looking into for the sake of those portions which have nothing whatever to do with the story."

'Well, I suppose it is intended for satire; but don't think anything more of it now, my dear. It is seven o'clock.' And Mrs Swancourt rang for her maid.

Attack is more piquant than concord. Stephen's letter was concerning nothing but oneness with her: the review was the very reverse. And a stranger with neither name nor shape, age nor appearance, but a mighty voice, is naturally rather an interesting novelty to a lady he chooses to address. When Elfride fell asleep that night she was loving the writer of the letter, but thinking of the writer of that article.

CHAPTER SIXTEEN

'Then fancy shapes – as fancy can.'*

ON a day about three weeks later the Swancourt trio were sitting quietly in the drawing-room of The Crags, Mrs Swancourt's house at Endelstow, chatting, and taking easeful survey of their previous month or two of town – a tangible weariness to people whose acquaintances there might be counted on the fingers.

A mere season in London with her practised stepmother had so advanced Elfride's perceptions, that her courtship by Stephen seemed emotionally meagre, and to have drifted back several years into a childish past. In regarding our mental experiences, as in visual observation, our own progress reads like a dwindling of that we progress from.

She was seated on a low chair, looking over her romance with melancholy interest for the first time since she had become acquainted with the remarks of *The Present* thereupon.

'Still thinking of that reviewer, Elfie?'

'Not of him personally; but I am thinking of his opinion. Really, on looking into the volume after this long time has elapsed, he seems to have estimated one part of it fairly enough.'

'No, no; I wouldn't show the white feather* now! Fancy that of all people in the world the writer herself should go over to the enemy. How shall Monmouth's men fight when Monmouth runs away?'*

'I don't do that. But I think he is right in some of his arguments, though wrong in others. And because he has some claim to my respect I regret all the more that he should think so mistakenly of my motives in one or two instances. It is more vexing to be misunderstood than to be misrepresented; and he misunderstands me. I cannot be easy whilst a person goes to rest night after night attributing to me intentions I never had.'

'He doesn't know your name, or anything about you. And he has doubtless forgotten there is such a book in existence by this time.'

'I myself should certainly like him to be put right upon one or two matters,' said the rector, who had hitherto been silent. 'You see, critics go on writing, and are never corrected or argued with, and therefore are never improved.'

'Papa,' said Elfride brightening, 'write to him!'

'I would as soon write to him as look at him, for the matter of that,' said Mr Swancourt.

'Do! And say, the young person who wrote the book did not adopt a masculine pseudonym in vanity or conceit, but because she was afraid it would be thought presumptuous to publish her name, and that she did not mean the story for such as he, but as a sweetener of history for young people, who might thereby acquire a taste for what went on in their own country hundreds of years ago, and be tempted to dive deeper into the subject. O, there is so much to explain; I wish I might write myself!'

'Now, Elfie, I'll tell you what we will do,' answered Mr Swancourt, tickled with a sort of bucolic humour at the idea of criticizing the critic. 'You shall write a clear account of what he is wrong in, and I will copy it and send it as mine.'

'Yes, now, directly!' said Elfride, jumping up. 'When will you send it, papa?'

'O, in a day or two, I suppose,' he returned. Then the rector paused and slightly yawned, and in the manner of elderly people began to cool from his ardour for the undertaking now that it came to the point. 'But, really, it is hardly worth while,' he said.

'O papa!' said Elfride, with much disappointment. 'You said you would, and now you won't. That is not fair!'

'But how can we send it if we don't know whom to send it to?'

'If you really want to send such a thing it can easily be done,' said Mrs Swancourt, coming to her stepdaughter's rescue. 'An envelope addressed, "To the Critic of *The Court of King Arthur's Castle*, care of the Editor of *The Present*," would find him.'

'Yes, I suppose it would.'

'Why not write your answer yourself, Elfride?' Mrs Swancourt inquired.

'I might,' she said hesitatingly; 'and send it anonymously: that would be treating him as he has treated me.'

'No use in the world!'

'But I don't like to let him know my exact name. Suppose I put my initials only? The less you are known the more you are thought of.'

'Yes; you might do that.'

Elfride set to work there and then. Her one desire for the last fortnight seemed likely to be realized. As happens with sensitive and secluded minds, a continual dwelling upon the subject had magnified to colossal proportions the space she assumed herself to occupy or to have occupied in the occult critic's mind. At noon and at night she had been pestering herself with endeavours to perceive more distinctly his conception of her as a woman apart from an author: whether he really despised her; whether he thought more or less of her than of ordinary young women who never ventured into the fire of criticism at all. Now she would have the satisfaction of feeling that at any rate he knew her true intent in crossing his path, and annoying him so by her performance, and be taught perhaps to despise it a little less.

Four days later an envelope, directed to Miss Swancourt in a strange hand, made its appearance from the post-bag.

'O!' said Elfride, her heart sinking within her. 'Can it be from that man – a lecture for impertinence? And actually one for Mrs Swancourt in the same handwriting!' She feared to open hers. 'Yet how can he know my name? No; it is somebody else.'

'Nonsense!' said her father grimly. 'You sent your initials, and the Directory* was available. Though he wouldn't have taken the trouble to look there unless he had been thoroughly savage with you. I thought you wrote with rather more asperity than simple literary discussion required.' This timely clause was introduced to save the character of the rector's judgment under any issue of affairs.

'Well, here I go,' said Elfride, desperately tearing open the seal.

'To be sure, of course,' exclaimed Mrs Swancourt; and looking up from her own letter. 'Christopher, I quite forgot to tell you, when I mentioned that I had seen my distant relative, Harry Knight, that I invited him here for whatever length of time he could spare. And now he says he can come any day in August.'

'Write, and say the first of the month,' replied the indiscriminate rector.

She read on. 'Goodness me – and that isn't all. He is actually the reviewer of Elfride's book. How absurd, to be sure! I had no idea he reviewed novels or had anything to do with *The Present*. He is a barrister – and I thought he only wrote in the Quarterlies. Why, Elfride, you have brought about an odd entanglement! What does he say to you?'

Elfride had put down her letter with a dissatisfied flush on her face. 'I don't know. The idea of his knowing my name and all about me! ... Why, he says nothing particular, only this –

'MY DEAR MADAM, – Though I am sorry that my remarks should have seemed harsh to you, it is a pleasure to find that they have been the means of bringing forth such an ingeniously argued reply. Unfortunately, it is so long since I wrote my review, that my memory does not serve me sufficiently to say a single word in my defence, even supposing there remains one to be said, which is doubtful. You will find from a letter I have written to Mrs Swancourt that we are not such strangers to each other as we have been imagining. Possibly I may have the pleasure of seeing you soon, when any argument you choose to advance shall receive all the attention it deserves.

'That is dim sarcasm – I know it is.'

'O no, Elfride.'

'And then, his remarks didn't seem harsh – I mean I did not say so.'

'He thinks you are in a frightful temper,' chuckled Mr Swancourt in undertones.

'And he will come and see me, and find the authoress as contemptible in speech as she has been impertinent in manner. I do heartily wish I had never written a word to him!'

'Never mind,' said Mrs Swancourt, also laughing in low quiet jerks; 'it will make the meeting such a comical affair, and afford splendid by-play for your father and myself. The idea of our running our heads against Harry Knight all the time! I cannot get over that.'

The rector had immediately remembered the name to be that of Stephen Smith's preceptor and friend; but having ceased to concern himself in the matter he made no remark to that effect, consistently forbearing to allude to anything which could restore recollection of the (to him) disagreeable mistake with regard to poor Stephen's lineage and position. Elfride had of course perceived the same thing, which added to the complication of relationship a mesh that her stepmother knew nothing of.

The identification scarcely heightened Knight's attractions now, though a twelvemonth ago she would only have cared to see him for the interest he possessed as Stephen's friend. Fortunately for Knight's advent, such a reason for welcome had only begun to be awkward to her at a time when the interest he had acquired on his own account made it no longer necessary.

These coincidences, in common with all relating to him, tended to keep Elfride's mind upon the stretch concerning Knight. As was her custom when upon the horns of a dilemma, she walked off by herself among the laurel bushes, and there, standing still and splitting up a leaf without removing it from its stalk, fetched back recollections of Stephen's frequent words in praise of his friend, and wished she had listened more attentively. Then, still pulling the leaf, she would blush at some fancied mortification that would accrue to her from his words when they met, in consequence of her intrusiveness, as she now considered it, in writing to him.

The next development of her meditations was the subject of what this man's personal appearance might be – was he tall or short, dark or fair, gay or grim? She would have asked Mrs Swancourt but for the risk she might thereby incur of some teasing remark being returned. Ultimately Elfride would say, 'O, what a plague that reviewer is to me!' and turn her face to where she imagined India lay, and murmur to herself, 'Ah, my little husband, what are you doing now? Let me see, where are you – south, east, where? Behind that hill, ever so far behind!'

CHAPTER SEVENTEEN

'Her welcome, spoke in faltering phrase'*

'THERE is Henry Knight, I declare!' said Mrs Swancourt one day.

They were gazing from the jutting angle of a wild enclosure not far from The Crags, which almost overhung the valley already described as leading up from the sea and little port of Castle Boterel. The stony escarpment upon which they stood had the contour of a man's face, and it was covered with furze as with a beard. People in the field above were preserved from an accidental roll down these prominences and hollows by a hedge on the very crest, which was doing that kindly service for Elfride and her mother now.

Scrambling higher into the hedge and stretching her neck further over the furze, Elfride beheld the individual signified. He was walking leisurely along the little green path at the bottom, beside the stream, a satchel slung upon his left hip, a stout walking-stick in his hand, and a brown-holland* sun-hat upon his head. The satchel was worn and old, and the outer polished surface of the leather was cracked and peeling off.

Knight having arrived over the hills to Castle Boterel upon the top of a crazy omnibus, preferred to walk the remaining two miles up the valley, leaving his luggage to be brought on.

Behind him wandered helter-skelter a boy of whom Knight had briefly inquired the way to Endelstow; and by that natural law of physics which causes lesser bodies to gravitate towards the greater, this boy had kept near to Knight, and trotted like a little dog close at his heels, whistling as he went, with his eyes fixed upon Knight's boots as they rose and fell.

When they had reached a point precisely opposite that in which Mrs and Miss Swancourt lay in ambush, Knight stopped and turned round.

'Look here, my boy,' he said.

The boy parted his lips, opened his eyes, and answered nothing.

'Here's sixpence for you, on condition that you don't again come within twenty yards of my heels, all the way up the valley.'

The boy, who apparently had not known he had been looking at Knight's heels at all, took the sixpence mechanically, and Knight went on again, wrapt in meditation.

'A nice voice,' Elfride thought; 'but what a singular temper!'

'Now we must get indoors before he ascends the slope,' said Mrs Swancourt softly. And they went across by a short cut over a stile, entering the lawn by a side door, and so on to the house.

Mr Swancourt had gone into the village with the curate, and Elfride felt too nervous to await their visitor's arrival in the drawing-room with Mrs Swancourt. So that when the elder lady entered, Elfride made some pretence of perceiving a new variety of crimson geranium, and lingered behind among the flower beds.

There was nothing gained by this, after all, she thought; and a few minutes after boldly came into the house by the glass side-door. She walked along the corridor, and entered the drawing-room. Nobody was there.

A window at the angle of the room opened directly into an octagonal conservatory, enclosing the corner of the building. From the conservatory came voices in conversation – Mrs Swancourt's and the stranger's.

She had expected him to talk brilliantly. To her surprise he was asking questions in quite a learner's manner, on subjects connected with the flowers and shrubs that she had known for years. When after the lapse of a few minutes he spoke at some length, she considered there was a hard square decisiveness in the shape of his sentences, as if, unlike her own and Stephen's, they were not there and then newly constructed, but were drawn forth from a large store ready-made. They were now approaching the window to come in again.

'That is a flesh-coloured variety,' said Mrs Swancourt. 'But oleanders, though they are such bulky shrubs, are so very easily wounded as to be unprunable – giants with the sensitiveness of young ladies. O, here is Elfride!'

Elfride looked as guilty and crestfallen as Lady Teazle at the dropping of the screen.* Mrs Swancourt presented him half comically, and Knight in a minute or two placed himself beside the young lady.

A complexity of instincts checked Elfride's conventional smiles of complaisance and hospitality; and, to make her still less comfortable, Mrs Swancourt immediately afterwards left them together to seek her husband. Mr Knight, however, did not seem at all incommoded by his feelings, and he said with light easefulness:

'So, Miss Swancourt, I have met you at last. You escaped me by a few minutes only when we were in London.'

'Yes. I found that you had seen Mrs Swancourt.'

'And now reviewer and reviewed are face to face,' he added unconcernedly.

'Yes: though the fact of your being a relation of Mrs Swancourt's takes off the edge of it. It was strange that you should be one of her family all the time.' Elfride began to recover herself now, and to look into Knight's face. 'I was merely anxious to let you know my *real* meaning in writing the book – extremely anxious.'

'I can quite understand the wish; and I was gratified that my remarks should have reached home. They very seldom do, I am afraid.'

Elfride drew herself in. Here he was, sticking to his opinions as firmly as if friendship and politeness did not in the least require an immediate renunciation of them.

'You made me very uneasy and sorry by writing such things!' she murmured, suddenly dropping the mere *caqueterie** of a fashionable first introduction, and speaking with some of the dudgeon of a child towards a severe schoolmaster.

'That is rather the object of honest critics in such a case. Not to cause unnecessary sorrow, but: "To make you sorry after a proper manner, that ye may receive damage by us in nothing,"* – that was what, I think, a powerful pen once wrote to the Gentiles. Are you going to write another romance?'

'Write another?' she said. 'That somebody may pen a condemnation and "nail't wi' Scripture"* again, as you do now, Mr Knight?'

'You may do better next time,' he said placidly: 'I think you will. But I would advise you to confine yourself to domestic scenes.'

'Thank you. But never again!'

'Well, you may be right. That a young woman has taken to writing is not by any means the best thing to hear about her.'

'What is the best?'

'I prefer not to say.'

'Do you know? Then, do tell me, please.'

'Well' – (Knight was evidently changing his meaning) – 'I suppose to hear that she has married.'

Elfride hesitated. 'And what when she has been married?' she said at last, partly in order to withdraw her own person from the argument.

'Then to hear no more about her. It is as Smeaton said of his lighthouse:* her greatest real praise, when the novelty of her inauguration has worn off, is that nothing happens to keep the talk of her alive.'

'Yes, I see,' said Elfride softly and thoughtfully. 'But of course it is different quite with men. Why don't you write novels, Mr Knight?'

'Because I couldn't write one that would interest anybody.'

'Why?'

'For several reasons. It requires a judicious omission of your real thoughts to make a novel popular, for one thing.'

'Is that really necessary? Well, I am sure you could learn to do that with practice,' said Elfride with an *ex-cathedrâ** air, as became a person who spoke from experience in the art. 'You would make a great name for certain,' she continued.

'So many people make a name nowadays, that it is more distinguished to remain in obscurity.'

'Tell me seriously – apart from the subject – why don't you write a volume instead of loose articles?' she insisted.

'Since you are pleased to make me talk of myself, I will tell you seriously,' said Knight, not less amused at this catechism by his young friend than he was interested in her appearance. 'As I have implied, I have not the wish. And if I had the wish, I could not now concentrate sufficiently. We all have only our one cruse* of energy given us to make the best of. And where that energy has been leaked away week by week, quarter by quarter, as mine has for the last nine or ten years, there is not enough dammed back behind the mill at any given period to supply the force a complete book on any subject requires. Then there is the self-confidence and waiting power. Where quick results have grown customary, they are fatal to a lively faith in the future.'

'Yes, I comprehend; and so you choose to write in fragments?'

'No, I don't choose to do it in the sense you mean; choosing from a whole world of professions, all possible. It was by the constraint of accident merely. Not that I object to the accident.'

'Why don't you object – I mean, why do you feel so quiet about things?' Elfride was half afraid to question him so, but her intense curiosity to see what the inside of literary Mr Knight was like, kept her going on.

Knight certainly did not mind being frank with her. Instances of this trait in men who are not without feeling, but are reticent from habit, may be recalled by all of us. When they find a listener who can by no possibility make use of them, rival them, or condemn them, reserved and even suspicious men of the world become frank, keenly enjoying the inner side of their frankness.

'Why I don't mind the accidental constraint,' he replied, 'is because, in making beginnings, a chance limitation of direction is often better than absolute freedom.'

'I see – that is, I should if I quite understood what all those generalities mean.'

'Why, this: That an arbitrary foundation for one's work, which no length of thought can alter, leaves the attention free to fix itself on the work itself, and make the best of it.'

'Lateral compression forcing altitude, as would be said in that tongue,' she rejoined mischievously. 'And I suppose where no limit exists, as in the case of a rich man with a wide taste who wants to do something, it will be better to choose a limit capriciously than to have none.'

'Yes,' he said with meditation. 'I can go as far as that.'

'Well,' resumed Elfride, 'I think it better for a man's nature if he does nothing in particular.'

'There is such a case as being obliged to.'

'Yes, yes; I was speaking of when you are not obliged for any other reason than delight in the prospect of fame. I have thought many times lately that a thin widespread happiness, commencing now, and of a piece with the days of your life, is preferable to an anticipated heap far away in the future, and none now.'

'Why, that's the very thing I said just now as being the principle of all ephemeral doers like myself.'

'O, I am sorry to have parodied you,' she said with some confusion. 'Yes, of course. That is what you meant about not trying to be famous.' And she added, with the quickness of conviction characteristic of her mind: 'There is much littleness in trying to be great. A man must think a good deal of himself, and be conceited enough to believe in himself, before he tries at all.'

'But it is soon enough to say there is harm in a man's thinking a good deal of himself when it is proved he has been thinking wrong, and too soon then sometimes. Besides, we should not conclude that a man who strives earnestly for success does so with a strong sense of his own merit. He may see how little success has to do with merit, and his motive may be his very humility.'

This manner of treating her rather provoked Elfride. No sooner did she agree with him than he ceased to seem to wish it, and took the other side. 'Ah,' she thought inwardly, 'I shall have nothing to do with a man of this kind, though he is our visitor.'

'I think you will find,' resumed Knight, pursuing the conversation more for the sake of finishing off his thoughts on the subject than for engaging her attention, 'that in actual life it is merely a matter of instinct with men – this trying to push on. They awake to a recognition that they have, without premeditation, begun to try a little, and they say to themselves, "Since I have tried thus much, I will try a little more." They go on because they have begun.'

Elfride, in her turn, was not particularly attending to his words at this moment. She had, unconsciously to herself, a way of seizing any point in the remarks of an interlocutor which interested her, and dwelling upon it, and thinking thoughts of her own thereupon, totally oblivious of all that he might say in continuation. On such occasions she artlessly surveyed the person speaking; and then there was a time for a painter. Her eyes seemed to look at you, and past you, as you were then, into your future; and past your future into your eternity – not reading it, but gazing in an unused, unconscious way – her mind still clinging to its original thought.

This is how she was looking at Knight.

Suddenly Elfride became conscious of what she was doing, and was painfully confused.

'What were you so intent upon in me?' he inquired.

'As far as I was thinking of you at all, I was thinking how clever you are,' she said, with a want of premeditation that was startling in its honesty and simplicity.

Feeling restless now that she had so unwittingly spoken, she arose and stepped to the window, having heard the voices of her father and Mrs Swancourt coming up below the terrace. 'Here they are,' she said, going out. Knight walked out upon the lawn behind her. She stood upon the edge of the terrace, close to the stone balustrade, and looked towards the sun, hanging over a glade just now fair as Tempe's vale,* up which her father was walking.

Knight could not help looking at her. The sun was within ten degrees of the horizon, and its warm light flooded her face and heightened the bright rose colour of her cheeks to a vermilion red, their moderate pink hue being only seen in its natural tone where the cheek curved round into shadow. The ends of her hanging hair softly dragged themselves backwards and forwards upon her shoulder as each faint breeze thrust against or relinquished it. Fringes and ribbons of her dress, moved by the same breeze, licked like tongues upon the parts around them, and fluttering forward from shady folds caught likewise their share of the lustrous orange glow.

Mr Swancourt shouted out a welcome to Knight from a distance of about thirty yards, and after a few preliminary words proceeded to a conversation of deep earnestness on Knight's fine old family name, and theories as to lineage and intermarriage connected therewith. Knight's portmanteau having in the meantime arrived they soon retired to prepare for dinner, which had been postponed to more than an hour later than the usual time of that meal.

An arrival was an event in the life of Elfride, now that they were again in the country, and that of Knight necessarily an engrossing one. And that evening she went to bed for the first time without thinking of Stephen at all.

CHAPTER EIGHTEEN

'He heard her musical pants.'

THE old tower of West Endelstow Church had reached the last weeks of its existence. It was to be replaced by a new one from the designs of Mr Hewby, the architect who had sent down Stephen. Planks and poles had arrived in the churchyard, iron bars had been thrust into the venerable crack extending down the belfry wall to the foundation, the bells had been taken down, the owls had forsaken this home of their forefathers, and six iconoclasts in white fustian,* to whom a cracked edifice was a species of Mumbo Jumbo,* had taken lodgings in the village previous to beginning the actual removal of the stones.

This was the day after Knight's arrival. To enjoy for the last time the prospect seaward from the summit, the rector, Mrs Swancourt, Knight, and Elfride, all ascended the winding turret – Mr Swancourt stepping forward with many loud breaths, his wife struggling along silently, but suffering none the less. They had hardly reached the top when a large lurid cloud, palpably a reservoir of rain, thunder, and lightning, was seen to be advancing overhead from the north.

The two cautious elders suggested an immediate return, and proceeded to put it in practice as regarded themselves.

'Dear me, I wish I had not come up,' exclaimed Mrs Swancourt.

'We shall be slower than you two in going down,' the rector said over his shoulder, 'and so, don't you start till we are nearly at the bottom, or you will run over us and break our necks somewhere in the darkness of the turret.'

Accordingly Elfride and Knight waited on the leads* till the staircase should be clear. Knight was not in a talkative mood that morning. Elfride was rather wilful, by reason of his inattention, which she privately set down to his thinking her not worth talking to. Whilst Knight stood watching the rise of the cloud she sauntered to the other side of the tower, and there remembered a giddy feat she had performed the year before. It was to walk round upon the parapet of the tower – which was quite without battlement or pinnacle, and presented a smooth flat surface about two feet wide, forming a pathway on all the four sides. Without reflecting in the least upon what she was doing she now stepped upon the parapet in the old way, and began walking along.

'We are down, cousin Henry,' cried Mrs Swancourt up the turret. 'Follow us when you like.'

Knight turned and saw Elfride beginning her elevated promenade. His face flushed with mingled concern and anger at her rashness.

'I certainly gave you credit for more common sense,' he said.

She reddened a little and walked on.

'Miss Swancourt, I insist upon your coming down,' he exclaimed.

'I will in a minute. I am safe enough. I have done it often.'

At that moment, by reason of a slight perturbation his words had caused in her, Elfride's foot caught itself in a little tuft of grass growing in a joint of the stonework, and she almost lost her balance. Knight sprang forward with a face of horror. By what seemed the special interposition of a considerate Providence she tottered to the inner edge of the parapet instead of to the outer, and reeled over upon the lead roof two or three feet below the wall.

Knight seized her as in a vice and said, 'That ever I should have met a woman fool enough to do a thing of that kind! Good God, you ought to be ashamed of yourself!'

The close proximity of the Shadow of Death had made her sick and pale as a corpse before he spoke. Already lowered to that state, his words completely overpowered her, and she swooned away as he held her.

Elfride's eyes were not closed for more than forty seconds. She opened them, and remembered the position instantly. His face had altered its expression from stern anger to pity. But his severe remarks had rather frightened her, and she struggled to be free.

'If you can stand, of course you may,' he said, and loosened his arms. 'I hardly know whether most to laugh at your freak or to chide you for its folly.'

She immediately sank upon the lead-work. Knight lifted her again. 'Are you hurt?' he said.

She murmured an incoherent expression, and tried to smile; saying, with a fitful aversion of her face, 'I am only frightened. Put me down, do put me down!'

'But you can't walk,' said Knight.

'You don't know that; how can you? I am only frightened, I tell you,' she answered petulantly, and raised her hand to her forehead. Knight then saw that she was bleeding from a severe cut in her wrist, apparently where it had descended upon a salient* corner of the lead-work. Elfride, too, seemed to perceive and feel this now for the first time, and for a minute nearly lost consciousness again. Knight rapidly bound his handkerchief round the place, and to add to the complication the thundercloud he had been watching began to shed some heavy drops of rain. Knight looked up and saw the rector striding towards the house, and Mrs Swancourt waddling beside him like a hard-driven duck.

'As you are so faint it will be much better to let me carry you down,' said Knight; 'or at any rate inside out of the rain.' But her objection to be lifted made it impossible for him to support her for more than five steps.

'This is folly, great folly,' he exclaimed, setting her down.

'Indeed!' she murmured, with tears in her eyes. 'I say I will not be carried, and you say this is folly!'

'So it is.'

'No, it isn't!'

'It is folly, I think. At any rate, the origin of it all is.'

'I don't agree to it. And you needn't get so angry with me; I am not worth it.'

'Indeed you are. You are worth the enmity of princes, as was said of such another. Now, then, will you clasp your hands behind my neck, that I may carry you down without hurting you?'

'No, no.'

'You had better, or I shall foreclose.'

'What's that!'

'Deprive you of your chance.'

Elfride gave a little toss.

'Now, don't writhe so when I attempt to carry you.'

'I can't help it.'

'Then submit quietly.'

'I don't care, I don't care,' she murmured in languid tones and with closed eyes.

He took her into his arms, entered the turret, and with slow and cautious steps descended round and round. Then, with the gentleness of a nursing mother, he attended to the cut on her arm. During his progress through the operations of wiping it and binding it up anew, her face changed its aspect from pained indifference to something like bashful interest, interspersed with small tremors and shudders of a trifling kind.

In the centre of each pale cheek a small red spot the size of a wafer had now made its appearance, and continued to grow larger. Elfride momentarily expected a recurrence to the lecture on her foolishness, but Knight said no more than this –

'Promise me *never* to walk on that parapet again.'

'It will be pulled down soon: so I do.' In a few minutes she continued in a lower tone, and seriously, 'You are familiar of course, as everybody is, with those strange sensations we sometimes have, that the moment has been in duplicate, or will be.'

'That we have lived through that moment before?'

'Or shall again. Well, I felt on the tower that something similar to that scene is again to be common to us both.'

'God forbid!' said Knight. 'Promise me that you will never again walk on any such place on any consideration.'

'I do.'

'That such a thing has not been before, we know. That it shall not be again, you vow. Therefore think no more of such a foolish fancy.'

There had fallen a great deal of rain, but unaccompanied by lightning. A few minutes longer, and the storm had ceased.

'Now, take my arm, please.'

'O no, it is not necessary.' This relapse into wilfulness was because he had again connected the epithet foolish with her.

'Nonsense: it is quite necessary; it will rain again directly, and you are not half recovered.' And without more ado Knight took her hand, drew it under his arm, and held it there so firmly that she could not have removed it without a struggle. Feeling like a colt in a halter for the first time at thus being led along, yet afraid to be angry, it was to her great relief that she saw the carriage coming round the corner to fetch them.

Her fall upon the roof was necessarily explained to some extent upon their entering the house; but both forbore to mention a word of what she had been doing to cause such an accident. During the remainder of the afternoon Elfride was invisible; but at dinner-time she appeared as bright as ever.

In the drawing-room, after having been exclusively engaged with Mr and Mrs Swancourt through the intervening hour, Knight again found himself thrown with Elfride. She had been looking over a chess problem in one of the illustrated periodicals.

'You like chess, Miss Swancourt?'

'Yes. It is my favourite scientific game; indeed, excludes every other. Do you play?'

'I have played; though not lately.'

'Challenge him, Elfride,' said the rector heartily. 'She plays very well for a lady, Mr Knight.'

'Shall we play?' asked Elfride tentatively.

'O, certainly. I shall be delighted.'

The game began. Mr Swancourt had forgotten a similar performance with Stephen Smith the year before. Elfride had not; but she had begun to take for her maxim the undoubted truth that the necessity of continuing faithful to Stephen, without suspicion, dictated a fickle behaviour almost as imperatively as fickleness itself; a fact, however, which would give a startling advantage to the latter quality should it ever appear.

Knight, by one of those inexcusable oversights which will sometimes afflict the best of players, placed his rook in the arms of one of her pawns. It was her first advantage. She looked triumphant – even ruthless.

'By George! what was I thinking of?' said Knight quietly; and then dismissed all concern at his accident.

'Club laws we'll have, won't we, Mr Knight?' said Elfride suasively.*

'O yes, certainly,' said Mr Knight, a thought, however, just occurring to his mind, that he had two or three times allowed her to replace a man on her religiously assuring him that such a move was an absolute blunder.

She immediately took up the unfortunate rook and the contest proceeded, Elfride having now rather the better of the game. Then he won the exchange, regained his position, and began to press her hard. Elfride grew flurried, and placed her queen on his remaining rook's file.

'There – how stupid! Upon my word, I did not see your rook. Of course nobody but a fool would have put a queen there knowingly!'

She spoke excitedly, half expecting her antagonist to give her back the move.

'Nobody, of course,' said Knight serenely, and stretched out his hand towards his royal victim.

'It is not very pleasant to have it taken advantage of, then,' she said with some vexation.

'Club laws, I think you said?' returned Knight blandly, and mercilessly appropriating the queen.

She was on the brink of pouting, but was ashamed to show it; tears almost stood in her eyes. She had been trying so hard – so very hard – thinking and thinking till her brain was in a whirl; and it seemed so heartless of him to treat her so, after all.

'I think it is—' she began.

'What?'

'– Unkind to take advantage of a pure mistake I make in that way.'

'I lost my rook by even a purer mistake,' said the enemy in an inexorable tone, without lifting his eyes.

'Yes, but—' However, as his logic was absolutely unanswerable, she merely registered a protest. 'I cannot endure those cold-blooded ways of clubs and professional players, like Staunton and Morphy.* Just as if it really mattered whether you have raised your fingers from a man or no!'

Knight smiled as pitilessly as before, and they went on in silence.

'Checkmate,' said Knight.

'Another game,' said Elfride peremptorily, and looking very warm.

'With all my heart,' said Knight.

'Checkmate,' said Knight again at the end of forty minutes.

'Another game,' she returned resolutely.

'I'll give you the odds of a bishop,' Knight said to her kindly.

'No, thank you,' Elfride replied in a tone intended for courteous indifference; but, as a fact, very cavalier indeed.

'Checkmate,' said her opponent without the least emotion.

O, the difference between Elfride's condition of mind now, and when she purposely made blunders that Stephen Smith might win!

It was bedtime. Her mind as distracted as if it would throb itself out of her head, she went off to her chamber, full of mortification at being beaten time after time when she herself was the aggressor. Having for two or three years enjoyed the reputation throughout the globe of her father's brain – which almost constituted her entire world – of being an excellent player, this fiasco was intolerable; for unfortunately the person most dogged in the belief in a false reputation is always that one, the possessor, who has the best means of knowing that it is not true.

In bed no sleep came to soothe her; that gentle thing being the very middle-of-summer friend in this respect of flying away at the merest troublous cloud. After lying awake till two o'clock an idea seemed to strike her. She softly arose, got a light, and fetched a Chess Praxis* from the library. Returning and sitting up in bed she diligently studied the volume till the clock struck five, and her eyelids felt thick and heavy. She then extinguished the light and lay down again.

'You look pale, Elfride,' said Mrs Swancourt the next morning at breakfast. 'Isn't she, cousin Harry?'

A young girl who is scarcely ill at all can hardly help becoming so when regarded as such by all eyes turning upon her at the table in obedience to some remark. Everybody looked at Elfride. She certainly was pale.

'Am I pale?' she said with a faint smile. 'I did not sleep much. I could not get rid of armies of bishops and knights, try how I would.'

'Chess is a bad thing just before bedtime; especially for excitable people like yourself, dear. Don't ever play late again.'

'I'll play early instead. Cousin Knight,' she said in imitation of Mrs Swancourt, 'will you oblige me in something?'

'Even to half my kingdom.'

'Well, it is to play one game more.'

'When?'

'Now, instantly; the moment we have breakfasted.'

'Nonsense, Elfride,' said her father. 'Making yourself a slave to the game like that.'

'But I want to, papa! Honestly, I am restless at having been so ignominiously overcome. And Mr Knight doesn't mind. So what harm can there be?'

'Let us play, by all means, if you wish it,' said Knight.

So, when breakfast was over, the combatants withdrew to the quiet of the library, and the door was closed. Elfride seemed to have an idea that her conduct was rather ill-regulated and startlingly free from conventional restraint. And worse, she fancied upon Knight's face a slightly amused look at her proceedings.

'You think me foolish, I suppose,' she said recklessly; 'but I want to do my very best just once, and see whether I can overcome you.'

'Certainly: nothing more natural. Though I am afraid it is not the plan adopted by women of the world after a defeat.'

'Why, pray?'

'Because they know that as good as overcoming is skill in effacing recollection of being overcome, and turn their attention to that entirely.'

'I am wrong again, of course.'

'Perhaps your wrong is more pleasing than their right.'

'I don't quite know whether you mean that, or whether you are laughing at me,' she said, looking doubtingly at him, yet inclining to accept the more flattering interpretation. 'I am almost sure you think it vanity in me to think I am a match for you. Well, if you do, I say that vanity is no crime in such a case.'

'Well, perhaps not. Though it is hardly a virtue.'

'O yes, in battle! Nelson's bravery lay in his vanity.'*

'Indeed! Then so did his death.'

'O no, no! For it is written in the book of the prophet Shakespeare –

> "Fear and be slain? no worse can come to fight;
> And fight and die, is death destroying death!"'*

And down they sat, and the contest began, Elfride having the first move. The game progressed. Elfride's heart beat so violently that she could not sit still. Her dread was lest he should hear it. And he did discover it at last – some flowers upon the table being set throbbing by its pulsations.

'I think we had better give over,' said Knight, looking at her gently. 'It is too much for you, I know. Let us write down the position, and finish another time.'

'No, please not,' she implored. 'I should not rest if I did not know the result at once. It is your move.'

Ten minutes passed.

She started up suddenly. 'I know what you are doing!' she cried, an angry colour upon her cheeks, and her eyes indignant. 'You were thinking of letting me win to please me!'

'I don't mind owning that I was,' Knight responded phlegmatically, and appearing all the more so by contrast with her own turmoil.

'But you must not! I won't have it.'

'Very well.'

'No, that will not do; I insist that you promise not to do any such absurd thing. It is insulting me!'

'Very well, madam. I won't do any such absurd thing. You shall not win.'

'That is to be proved!' she returned proudly; and the play went on.

Nothing is now heard but the ticking of a quaint old timepiece on the summit of a bookcase. Ten minutes pass; he captures her knight; she takes his knight, and looks a very Rhadamanthus.*

More minutes tick away; she takes his pawn and has the advantage, showing her sense of it rather prominently.

Five minutes more: he takes her bishop: she brings things even by taking his knight.

Three minutes: she looks bold, and takes his queen: he looks placid, and takes hers.

Eight or ten minutes pass: he takes a pawn; she utters a little pooh! but not the ghost of a pawn can she take in retaliation.

Ten minutes pass: he takes another pawn and says, 'Check!' She flushes, extricates herself by capturing his bishop, and looks triumphant. He immediately takes her bishop: she looks surprised.

Five minutes longer: she makes a dash and takes his only remaining bishop; he replies by taking her only remaining knight.

Two minutes: he gives check; her mind is now in a painful state of tension, and she shades her face with her hand.

Yet a few minutes more: he takes her rook and checks again. She literally trembles now lest an artful surprise she has in store for him shall be anticipated by the artful surprise he evidently has in store for her.

Five minutes: 'Checkmate in two moves!' exclaims Elfride.

'If you can,' says Knight.

'O, I have miscalculated; that is cruel!'

'Checkmate,' says Knight; and the victory is won.

Elfride arose and turned away without letting him see her face. Once in the hall she ran upstairs and into her room, and flung herself down upon her bed, weeping bitterly.

'Where is Elfride?' said her father at luncheon.

Knight listened anxiously for the answer. He had been hoping to see her again before this time.

'She isn't well, sir,' was the reply.

Mrs Swancourt rose and left the room, going upstairs to Elfride's apartment.

At the door was Unity, who occupied in the new establishment a position between young lady's maid and middle-housemaid.

'She is sound asleep, ma'am,' Unity whispered.

Mrs Swancourt opened the door. Elfride was lying full-dressed on the bed, her face hot and red, her arms thrown abroad. At intervals of a minute she tossed restlessly from side to side, and indistinctly moaned words used in the game of chess.

Mrs Swancourt had a turn for doctoring, and felt her pulse. It was twanging like a harp-string, at the rate of nearly a hundred and fifty a minute. Softly moving the sleeping girl to a little less cramped position she went downstairs again.

'She is asleep now,' said Mrs Swancourt. 'She does not seem very well. Cousin Knight, what were you thinking of? her tender brain won't bear cudgelling like your great head. You should have strictly forbidden her to play again.'

In truth, the essayist's experience of the nature of young women was far less extensive than his abstract knowledge of them led himself and others to believe. He could pack them into sentences like a workman, but practically was nowhere.

'I am indeed sorry,' said Knight, feeling even more than he expressed. 'But surely, the young lady knows best what is good for her!'

'Bless you, that's just what she doesn't know. She never thinks of such things, does she, Christopher? Her father and I have to command her and keep her in order, as you would a child. She will say things worthy of a French epigrammatist, and act like a robin in a greenhouse. But I think we will send for Dr Granson – there can be no harm.'

A man was straightway despatched on horseback to Castle Boterel, and the gentleman known as Dr Granson came in the course of the afternoon. He pronounced her nervous system to be in a decided state of disorder; forwarded some soothing draught, and gave orders that on no account whatever was she to play chess again.

The next morning Knight, much vexed with himself, waited with a curiously compounded feeling for her entry to breakfast. The women servants came in to prayers at irregular intervals, and as each entered he could not, to save his life, avoid turning his head with the hope that she might be Elfride. Mr Swancourt began reading without waiting for her. Then somebody glided in noiselessly; Knight softly glanced up: it was only the little kitchen-maid. Knight thought reading prayers a bore.

He went out alone, and for almost the first time failed to recognize that holding converse with Nature's charms was not solitude. On nearing the house again he perceived his young friend crossing a slope by a path which ran into the one he was following in the angle of the field. Here they met. Elfride was at once exultant and abashed: coming into his presence had upon her the effect of entering a cathedral.

Knight had his note-book in his hand, and had, in fact, been in the very act of writing therein when they came in view of each other. He left off in the midst of a sentence, and proceeded to inquire warmly concerning her state of health. She said she was perfectly well, and indeed had never looked better. Her health was as inconsequent as her actions. Her lips were red, *without* the polish that cherries have, and their redness margined with the white skin in a clearly defined line, which had nothing of jagged confusion in it. Altogether she stood as the last person in the world to be knocked over by a game of chess, because too ephemeral-looking to play one.

'Are you taking notes?' she inquired with an alacrity plainly arising less from interest in the subject than from a wish to divert his thoughts from herself.

'Yes; I was making an entry. And with your permission I will complete it.' Knight then stood still and wrote. Elfride remained beside him a moment, and afterwards walked on.

'I should like to see all the secrets that are in that book,' she gaily flung back to him over her shoulder.

'I don't think you would find much to interest you.'

'I know I should.'

'Then of course I have no more to say.'

'But I would ask this question first. Is it a book of mere facts concerning journeys and expenditure, and so on, or a book of thoughts?'

'Well, to tell the truth, it is not exactly either. It consists for the most part of jottings for articles and essays, disjointed and disconnected, of no possible interest to anybody but myself.'

'It contains, I suppose, your developed thoughts in embryo?'

'Yes.'

'If they are interesting when enlarged to the size of an article, what must they be in their concentrated form! Pure rectified spirit, above proof; before it is lowered to be fit for human consumption: "words that burn"* indeed.'

'Rather like a balloon before it is inflated: flabby, shapeless, dead. You could hardly read them.'

'May I try?' She coaxed by a look. 'I wrote my poor romance in that way – I mean in bits, out of doors – and I should like to see whether your way of entering things is the same as mine.'

'Really, that's rather an awkward request. I suppose I can hardly refuse now you have asked so directly; but—'

'You think me ill-mannered in asking. But does not this justify me – your writing in my presence, Mr Knight? If I had lighted upon your book by chance, it would have been different; but you stand before me, and say, "Excuse me," without caring whether I do or not, and write on, and then tell me they are not private facts but public ideas.'

'Very well, Miss Swancourt. If you really must see, the consequences be upon your own head. Remember my advice to you is to leave my book alone.'

'But with that caution I have your permission?'

'Yes.'

She hesitated a moment, looked at his hand containing the book, then laughed, and saying, 'I must see it,' withdrew it from his fingers.

Knight rambled on towards the house, leaving her standing in the path turning over the leaves. By the time he had reached the wicket-gate he saw that she had moved, and waited till she came up.

Elfride had closed the note-book, and was carrying it disdainfully by the corner between her finger and thumb; her face wore a nettled look. She silently extended the volume towards him, raising her eyes no higher than her hand was lifted.

'Take it,' said Elfride quickly. 'I don't want to read it.'

'Could you understand it?' said Knight.

'As far as I looked. But I didn't care to read much.'

'Why, Miss Swancourt?'

'Only because I didn't wish to – that's all.'

'I warned you that you might not.'

'Yes, but I never supposed you would have put *me* there.'

'Your name is not mentioned once within the four corners.'

'Not my name – I know that.'

'Nor your description, nor anything by which anybody would recognize you.'

'Except myself. For what is this?' she exclaimed, taking it from him and opening a page. 'August 7. That's the day before yesterday. But I won't read it,' Elfride said, closing the book again with pretty hauteur. 'Why should I? I had no business to ask to see your book, and it serves me right.'

Knight hardly recollected what he had written, and turned over the book to see. He came to this:

'Aug. 7. Girl gets into her teens, and her self-consciousness is born. After a certain interval passed in infantine helplessness, it begins to act. Simple, young, and inexperienced at first. Persons of observation can tell to a nicety how old this consciousness is by the skill it has acquired in the art necessary to its success – the art of hiding itself. Generally begins career by actions which are popularly termed showing-off. Method adopted depends in each case upon the disposition, rank, residence, of the young lady attempting it. Town-bred girl will utter some moral paradox on fast men, or love. Country miss adopts the more material media of taking a ghastly fence, whistling, or making your blood run cold by appearing to risk her neck. (*Mem.* On Endelstow Tower.)

'An innocent vanity is of course the origin of these displays. "Look at me," say these youthful beginners in womanly artifice, without reflecting whether or not it be to their advantage to show so very much of themselves. (Amplify and correct for paper on Artless Arts.)'

'Yes, I remember now,' said Knight. 'The notes were certainly suggested by your manœuvre on the church tower. But you must not think too much of such random observations,' he continued encouragingly, as he noticed her injured looks. 'A mere fancy passing through my head assumes a factitious importance to you, because it has been made permanent by being written down. All mankind think thoughts as bad as those of people they most love on earth, but such thoughts never getting embodied on paper, it becomes assumed that they never existed. I daresay that you yourself have thought some disagreeable thing or other of me, which would seem just as bad as this if written. I challenge you, now, to tell me.'

'The worst thing I have thought of you?'

'Yes.'

'I must not.'

'O yes.'

'I thought you were rather round-shouldered.'

Knight looked slightly redder.

'And that there was a little bald spot on the top of your head.'

'Heh-heh! Two ineradicable defects,' said Knight, there being a faint ghastliness discernible in his laugh. 'They are much worse in a lady's eye than being thought self-conscious, I suppose.'

'Ah, that's very fine,' she said, too inexperienced to perceive her hit, and hence not quite disposed to forgive his notes. 'You alluded to me in that entry as if I were such a child, too. Everybody does that. I cannot understand it. I am quite a woman, you know. How old do you think I am?'

'How old? Why, seventeen, I should say. All girls are seventeen.'

'You are wrong. I am nearly twenty. Which class of women do you like best, those who seem younger, or those who seem older than they are?'

'Off-hand I should be inclined to say those who seem older.'

So it was not Elfride's class.

'But it is well known,' she said eagerly, and there was something touching in the artless anxiety to be thought much of which she revealed by her words, 'that the slower a nature is to develop, the richer the nature. Youths and girls who are men and women before they come of age are nobodies by the time that backward people have shown their full compass.'

'Yes,' said Knight thoughtfully. 'There is really something in that remark. But at the risk of offence I must remind you that you there take it for granted that the woman behind her time at a given age has not reached the end of her tether. Her backwardness may be not because she is slow to develop, but because she soon exhausted her capacity for developing.'

Elfride looked disappointed. By this time they were indoors. Mrs Swancourt, to whom match-making by any honest means was meat and drink, had now a little scheme of that nature concerning this pair. The morning-room, in which they both expected to find her, was empty; the old lady having, for the above reason, vacated it by the second door as they entered by the first.

Knight went to the chimney-piece, and carelessly surveyed two portraits on ivory.

'Though these pink ladies had very rudimentary features, judging by what I see here,' he observed, 'they had unquestionably beautiful heads of hair.'

'Yes; and that is everything,' said Elfride, possibly conscious of her own, possibly not.

'Not everything; though a great deal, certainly.'

'Which colour do you like best?' she ventured to ask.

'More depends on its abundance than on its colour.'

'Abundances being equal, may I inquire your favourite colour?'

'Dark.'

'I mean for women,' she said, with the minutest fall of countenance, and a hope that she had been misunderstood.

'So do I,' Knight replied.

It was impossible for any man not to know the colour of Elfride's hair. In women who wear it plainly such a feature may be overlooked by men not given to ocular intentness. But hers was always in the way. You saw her hair as far as you could see her sex, and knew that it was the palest brown. She perceived that Knight, being perfectly aware of this, had an independent standard of admiration in the matter.

Elfride was thoroughly vexed. She could not but be struck with the honesty of his opinions, and the worst of it was, that the more they went against her, the more she respected them. And now, like a reckless gambler, she hazarded her last and best treasure. Her eyes: they were her all now.

'What coloured eyes do you like best, Mr Knight?' she said slowly.

'Honestly, or as a compliment?'

'Of course honestly; I don't want anybody's compliment!'

And yet Elfride knew otherwise: that a compliment or word of approval from that man then would have been like a well to a famished Arab.

'I prefer hazel,' he said serenely.

She had played and lost again.

CHAPTER NINETEEN

'Love was in the next degree.'*

KNIGHT had none of those light familiarities of speech which, by judicious touches of epigrammatic flattery, obliterate a woman's recollection of the speaker's abstract opinions. So no more was said by either on the subject of hair, eyes, or development. Elfride's mind had been impregnated with sentiments of her own smallness to an uncomfortable degree of distinctness, and her discomfort was visible in her face. The whole tendency of the conversation latterly had been to quietly but surely disparage her; and she was fain to take Stephen into favour in self-defence. He would not have been so unloving, she said, as to admire an idiosyncrasy and features different from her own. True, Stephen had declared he loved her: Mr Knight had never done anything of the sort. Somehow this did not mend matters, and the sensation of her smallness in Knight's eyes still remained. Had the position been reversed – had Stephen loved her in spite of a differing taste, and had Knight been indifferent in spite of her resemblance to his ideal, it would have engendered far happier thoughts. As matters stood, Stephen's admiration might have its root in a blindness the result of passion. Perhaps any keen man's judgment was condemnatory of her.

During the remainder of Saturday they were more or less thrown with their seniors, and no conversation arose which was exclusively their own. When Elfride was in bed that night her thoughts recurred to the same subject. At one moment she insisted that it was ill-natured of him to speak so decisively as he had done; the next, that it was sterling honesty.

'Ah, what a poor nobody I am!' she said, sighing. 'People like him, who go about the great world, don't care in the least what I am like either in mood or feature.'

Perhaps a man who has got thoroughly into a woman's mind in this manner, is half way to her heart; the distance between those two stations is proverbially short.

'And are you really going away this week?' said Mrs Swancourt to Knight on the following evening, which was Sunday.

They were all leisurely pacing the slope to the church, where a last service was now to be held at the rather exceptional time of evening instead of in the afternoon, previous to the demolition of the ruinous portions.

'I am intending to cross to Cork from Bristol,' returned Knight; 'and then I go on to Dublin.'

'Return this way, and stay a little longer with us,' said the rector. 'A week is nothing. We have hardly been able to realize your presence yet. I remember a story, but it's too—'

The rector suddenly stopped. He had forgotten it was Sunday, and would probably have gone on in his week-day mode of thought had not a turn in the breeze blown the skirt of his college gown within the range of his vision, and so reminded him. He at once diverted the current of his narrative with the dexterity the occasion demanded.

'The story of the Levite who journeyed to Bethlehem-judah,* from which I took my text the Sunday before last, is quite to the point,' he continued, with the pronunciation of a man who, far from having intended to tell a week-day story a moment earlier, had thought of nothing but Sabbath matters for several weeks. 'What did he gain after all by his restlessness? Had he remained in the city of the Jebusites, and not been so anxious for Gibeah, none of his troubles would have arisen.'

'But he had wasted five days already,' said Knight, closing his eyes to the rector's commendable diversion. 'His fault lay in beginning the tarrying system originally.'

'True, true; my illustration fails.'

'But not the hospitality which prompted the story.'

'So you are to come just the same,' urged Mrs Swancourt, for she had seen an almost imperceptible fall of countenance in her stepdaughter at Knight's announcement.

Knight half promised to call on his return journey; but the uncertainty with which he spoke was quite enough to fill Elfride with a regretful interest in all he did during the few remaining hours. The curate having already officiated twice that day in the two churches, Mr Swancourt had undertaken the whole of the evening service, and Knight read the lessons for him. The sun streamed across from the dilapidated west window, and lighted all the assembled worshippers with a golden glow, Knight as he read being illuminated by the same mellow lustre. Elfride at the organ regarded him with a throbbing sadness of mood which was fed by a sense of being far removed from his sphere. As he went deliberately through the chapter appointed – a portion of the history of Elijah* – and ascended that magnificent climax of the wind, the earthquake, the fire, and the still small voice, his deep tones echoed past with such apparent disregard of her existence, that his presence inspired her with a forlorn sense of unapproachableness, which his absence would hardly have been able to cause.

At the same time, turning her face for a moment to catch the glory of the dying sun as it fell on his form, her eyes were arrested by the shape and aspect of a woman in the west gallery. It was the bleak barren countenance of the widow Jethway, whom Elfride had not seen much of since the morning of her return with Stephen Smith. Possessing the smallest of competencies, this unhappy woman appeared to spend her life in journeyings between Endelstow Churchyard and that of a village near Southampton, where her father and mother were laid.

She had not attended the service here for a considerable time, and she now seemed to have a reason for her choice of seat. From the gallery window the tomb of her son was plainly visible – standing as the nearest object in a prospect which was closed outwardly by the changeless horizon of the sea.

The streaming rays, too, flooded her face, now bent towards Elfride with a hard and bitter expression that the solemnity of the place raised to a tragic dignity it did not intrinsically possess. The girl resumed her normal attitude with an added disquiet.

Elfride's emotion was cumulative, and after a while would assert itself on a sudden. A slight touch was enough to set it free – a poem, a sunset, a cunningly contrived chord of music, a vague imagining, being the usual accidents of its exhibition. The longing for Knight's respect, which was leading up to an incipient yearning for his love, made the present conjuncture a sufficient one. Whilst kneeling down previous to leaving, when the sunny streaks had gone upward to the roof, and the lower part of the church was in soft shadow, she could not help thinking of Coleridge's morbid poem 'The Three Graves',* and shuddering as she wondered if Mrs Jethway were cursing her she wept as if her heart would break.

They came out of church just as the sun went down, leaving the landscape like a platform from which an eloquent speaker has retired, and nothing remains for the audience to do but to rise and go home. Mr and Mrs Swancourt went off in the carriage, Knight and Elfride preferring to walk, as the skilful old matchmaker had imagined. They descended the hill together.

'I liked your reading, Mr Knight,' Elfride presently found herself saying. 'You read better than papa.'

'I will praise anybody that will praise me. You played excellently, Miss Swancourt, and very correctly.'

'Correctly – yes.'

'It must be a great pleasure to you to take an active part in the service.'

'I want to be able to play with more feeling. But I have not a good selection of music, sacred or secular. I wish I had a nice little music-library – well chosen, and that the only new pieces sent me were those of genuine merit.'

'I am glad to hear such a wish from you. It is extraordinary how many women have no honest love of music as an end and not as a means, even leaving out those who have nothing in them. They mostly like it for its accessories. I have never met a woman who loves music as do ten or a dozen men I know.'

'How would you draw the line between women with something and women with nothing in them?'

'Well,' said Knight, reflecting a moment, 'I mean by nothing in them those who don't care about anything solid. This is an instance: I knew a man who had a young friend in whom he was much interested; in fact, they were going to be married. She was seemingly poetical, and he offered her a choice of two editions of the British poets, which she pretended to want badly. He said, "Which of them would you like best for me to send?" She said, "A pair of the prettiest earrings in Bond Street, if you don't mind, would be nicer than either." Now I call her a girl with not much in her but vanity; and so do you, I daresay.'

'O yes,' replied Elfride with an effort.

Happening to catch a glimpse of her face as she was speaking, and noticing that her attempt at heartiness was a miserable failure, he appeared to have misgivings.

'You, Miss Swancourt, would not, under such circumstances, have preferred the nicknacks?'

'No, I don't think I should, indeed,' she stammered.

'I'll put it to you,' said the inflexible Knight. 'Which will you have of these two things of about equal value – the well-chosen little library of the best music you spoke of – bound in morocco, walnut case, lock and key – or a pair of the very prettiest earrings in Bond Street windows?'

'Of course the music,' Elfride replied with forced earnestness.

'You are quite certain?' he said emphatically.

'Quite,' she faltered; 'if I could for certain buy the earrings afterwards.'

Knight, somewhat blamably, keenly enjoyed sparring with the palpitating mobile creature, whose excitable nature made any such thing a species of cruelty.

He looked at her rather oddly, and said, 'Fie!'

'Forgive me,' she said, laughing a little, a little frightened, and blushing very deeply.

'Ah, Miss Elfie, why didn't you say at first, as any firm woman would have said, I am as bad as she, and shall choose the same?'

'I don't know,' said Elfride wofully, and with a distressful smile.

'I thought you were exceptionally musical?'

'So I am, I think. But the test is so severe – quite painful.'

'I don't understand.'

'Music doesn't do any real good, or rather—'

'That *is* a thing to say, Miss Swancourt! Why, what—'

'You don't understand! you don't understand!'

'Why, what conceivable use is there in jimcrack jewellery?'

'No, no, no, no!' she cried petulantly; 'I didn't mean what you think. I like the music best, only I like—'

'Earrings better – own it!' he said in a teasing tone. 'Well, I think I should have had the moral courage to own it at once, without pretending to an elevation I could not reach.'

As is said of the French soldiery, Elfride was at her worst when on the defensive. So it was almost with tears in her eyes that she answered desperately:

'My meaning is, that I like earrings best just now, because I lost one of my prettiest pair last year, and papa said he would not buy any more, or allow me to myself, because I was careless; and now I wish I had some like them – that's what my meaning is – indeed it is, Mr Knight.'

'I am afraid I have been very harsh and rude,' said Knight, in a note of regret at seeing how disturbed she was. 'But seriously, if women only knew how they ruin their good looks by such appurtenances, I am sure they would never want them.'

'They were lovely, and became me so!'

'Not if they were like the ordinary hideous things women stuff their ears with nowadays – like the governor of a steam-engine,* or a pair of scales, or gold gibbets and chains, and artists' palettes, and compensation pendulums,* and Heaven knows what besides.'

'No; they were not one of those things. So pretty – like this,' she said with eager animation. And she drew with the point of her parasol an enlarged view of one of the lamented darlings, to a scale that would have suited a giantess half-a-mile high.

'Yes, very pretty – very,' said Knight dryly. 'How did you come to lose such a precious pair of articles?'

'I only lost one – nobody ever loses both at the same time.'

She made this remark with embarrassment, and a nervous movement of the fingers. Seeing that the loss occurred whilst Stephen Smith was attempting to kiss her for the first time on the cliff, her confusion was hardly to be wondered at. The question had been awkward, and received no direct answer.

Knight seemed not to notice her manner.

'Oh, nobody ever loses both – I see. And certainly the fact that it was a case of loss takes away all odour of vanity from your choice.'

'As I never know whether you are in earnest, I don't now,' she said, looking up inquiringly at the hairy face of the oracle. And coming gallantly to her own rescue, 'If I really seem vain, it is that I am only vain in my ways – not in my heart. The worst women are those vain in their hearts, and not in their ways.'

'An adroit distinction. Well, they are certainly the more objectionable of the two,' said Knight.

'Is vanity a mortal or a venial sin? You know what life is: tell me.'

'I am very far from knowing what life is. A just conception of life is too large a thing to grasp during the short interval of passing through it.'

'Will the fact of a woman being fond of jewellery be likely to make her life, in its higher sense, a failure?'

'Nobody's life is altogether a failure.'

'Well, you know what I mean, even though my words are badly selected and commonplace,' she said impatiently. 'Because I utter commonplace words, you must not suppose I think only commonplace thoughts. My poor stock of words are like a limited number of rough moulds I have to cast all my materials in, good and bad; and the novelty or delicacy of the substance is often lost in the coarse triteness of the form.'

'Very well; I'll believe that ingenious representation. As to the subject in hand – lives which are failures – you need not trouble yourself. Anybody's life may be just as romantic and strange and interesting if he or she fails as if he or she succeed. All the difference is, that the last chapter is wanting in the story. If a man of power tries to do a great deed, and just falls short of it by an accident not his fault, up to that time his history had as much in it as that of a great man who has done his great deed. It is whimsical of the world to hold that particulars of how a lad went to school and so on should be as an interesting romance or as nothing to them, precisely in proportion to his after renown.'

They were walking between the sunset and the moonrise. With the dropping of the sun a nearly full moon had begun to raise itself. Their shadows, as cast by the western glare, showed signs of becoming obliterated in the interest of a rival pair in the opposite direction which the moon was bringing to distinctness.

'I consider my life to some extent a failure,' said Knight again after a pause, during which he had noticed the antagonistic shadows.

'You! How?'

'I don't precisely know. But in some way I have missed the mark.'

'Really? To have done it is not much to be sad about, but to feel that you have done it must be a cause of sorrow. Am I right?'

'Partly, though not quite. For a sensation of being profoundly experienced serves as a sort of consolation to people who are conscious of having taken wrong turnings. Contradictory as it seems, there is nothing truer than that the people who have always gone right don't know half as much about the nature and ways of going right as those do who have gone wrong. However, it is not desirable for me to chill your summer-time by going into this.'

'You have not told me even now if I am really vain.'

'If I say Yes, I shall offend you; if I say No, you'll think I don't mean it,' he replied, looking curiously into her face.

'Ah, well,' she replied, with a little breath of distress, '"That which is exceeding deep, who can find it out?"* I suppose I must take you as I do the Bible – find out and understand all I can; and on the strength of that, swallow the rest in a lump, by simple faith. Think me vain, if you will. Worldly greatness requires so much littleness to grow up in, that an infirmity more or less is not a matter for regret.'

'As regards women, I can't say,' answered Knight carelessly; 'but it is without doubt a misfortune for a man who has a living to get, to be born of a truly noble nature. A high soul will bring a man to the workhouse; so you may be right in sticking up for vanity.'

'No, no, I don't do that,' she said regretfully. 'Mr Knight, when you are gone, will you send me something you have written? I think I should like to see whether you write as you have lately spoken, or in your better mood. Which is your true self – the cynic you have been this evening, or the nice philosopher you were up to to-night?'

'Ah, which? You know as well as I.'

Their conversation detained them on the lawn and in the portico till the stars blinked out. Elfride flung back her head, and said idly –

'There's a bright star exactly over me.'

'Each bright star is overhead somewhere.'

'Is it? O yes, of course. Where is that one?' and she pointed with her finger.

'That is poised like a white hawk probably over one of the Cape Verde Islands* or thereabout.'

'And that?'

'Looking down upon the source of the Nile.'*

'And that lonely quiet-looking one?'

'He watches the North Pole, and has no less than the whole

equator for his horizon. And that idle one low down upon the ground, that we have almost rolled round to, is in India – over the head of a young friend of mine, who very possibly looks at the star in our zenith, as it hangs low upon his horizon, and thinks of it as marking where his true love dwells.'

Elfride glanced at Knight with misgiving. Did he mean her? She could not see his features; but his attitude seemed to show unconsciousness.

'The star is over *my* head,' she said with hesitation.

'Or anybody else's in England.'

'O yes, I see.' She breathed her relief.

'His parents, I believe, are natives of this county. I don't know them, though I have been in correspondence with him for many years till lately. Fortunately or unfortunately for him he fell in love, and then went to Bombay. Since that time I have heard very little of him.'

Knight went no further in his volunteered statement, and though Elfride at one moment was inclined to profit by the lessons in honesty he had just been giving her, the flesh was weak, and the intention dispersed into silence. There seemed a reproach in Knight's blind words, and yet she was not able to define clearly any disloyalty that she had been guilty of.

CHAPTER TWENTY

'A distant dearness in the hill'*

KNIGHT turned his back upon the parish of Endelstow, and crossed over to Cork.

One day of absence superimposed itself on another, and proportionately weighted his heart. He pushed on to the Lakes of Killarney, rambled amid their luxuriant woods, surveyed the infinite variety of island, hill, and dale there to be found, listened to the marvellous echoes of that romantic spot; but altogether missed the glory and the dream* he formerly found in such favoured regions.

The girlish presence of Elfride had not perceptibly affected him to any depth whilst he was in her company. He had not been conscious that her entry into his sphere had added anything to himself; but now that she was taken away he was conscious of a great deal abstracted. The superfluity had become a necessity, and Knight was in love.

Stephen fell in love with Elfride by looking at her: Knight by ceasing to do so. When or how the spirit entered into him he knew not: certain he was that when on the point of leaving Endelstow he had felt none of that exquisite nicety of poignant sadness natural to such severances, seeing how delightful a subject of contemplation Elfride had been ever since. Had he begun to love her when she met his eye after her mishap on the tower? He had simply thought her weak. Had he grown to love her while she stood on the lawn brightened all over by the evening sun? He had thought her complexion good: no more. Was it her conversation that had sown the seed? He had thought her words ingenious, and very creditable to a young woman, but not noteworthy. Had the chess-playing anything to do with it? Certainly not: he had thought her at that time a rather conceited child.

Knight's experience was a complete disproof of the assumption that love always comes by glances of the eye and sympathetic touches of the fingers: that, like flame, it makes itself palpable at the moment of generation. Not till they were parted, and she had become sublimated in his memory, could he be said to have even attentively regarded her.

Thus, having passively gathered up images of her which his mind did not act upon till the cause of them was no longer before him, he appeared to himself to have fallen in love with her soul, which had temporarily assumed its disembodiment to accompany him on his way.

She began to rule him so imperiously now that, accustomed to analysis, he almost trembled at the possible result of the introduction of this new force among the nicely adjusted ones of his ordinary life. He became restless: then he forgot all collateral subjects in the pleasure of thinking about her.

Yet it may be that Knight loved philosophically rather than romantically.

He thought of her manner towards him. Simplicity verges on coquetry. Was she flirting? he said to himself. No forcible translation of favour into suspicion was able to uphold such a theory. The performance had been too well done to be anything but real. It had the defects without which nothing is genuine. No actress of twenty years' standing, no bald-necked lady whose earliest season 'out'* was lost in the discreet mist of evasive talk, could have played before him the part of ingenuous girl as Elfride lived it. She had the little artful ways which partly make up ingenuousness.

There are bachelors by nature and bachelors by circumstance: spinsters there doubtless are also of both kinds, though some think only of the latter. However, Knight had been looked upon as a bachelor by nature. What was he coming to? It was very odd to himself to look at his theories on the subject of love, and reading them now by the full light of a new experience, to see how much more his sentences meant than he had felt them to mean when they were written. People often discover the real force of a trite old maxim only when it is thrust upon them by a chance adventure; but Knight had never before known the case of a man who learnt the full compass of his own epigrams by such means.

He was intensely satisfied with one aspect of the affair. Inbred in him was an invincible objection to be any but the first comer in a woman's heart. He had discovered within himself the condition that if ever he did make up his mind to marry, it must be on the certainty that no cropping out of inconvenient old letters, no bows or blushes to a mysterious stranger casually met, should be a possible source of discomposure. Knight's sentiments were only the ordinary ones of a man of his age who loves genuinely, perhaps exaggerated a little by his pursuits. When men first love as lads it is with the very centre of their hearts, nothing else being concerned in the operation. With added years, more of the faculties attempt a partnership in the passion, till at Knight's age the understanding is fain to have a hand in it. It may as well be left out. A man in love setting up his brains as a gauge of his position is as one determining a ship's longitude from a light at the mast-head.

Knight argued from Elfride's unwontedness of manner, which was matter of fact, to an unwontedness in love, which was matter of inference only. *Incrédules les plus crédules.** 'Elfride,' he said, 'had hardly looked upon a man till she saw me.'

He had never forgotten his severity to her because she preferred ornament to edification, and had since excused her a hundred times by thinking how natural to womankind was a love of adornment, and how necessary became a mild infusion of personal vanity to complete the delicate and fascinating dye of the feminine mind. So at the end of the week's absence, which had brought him from Killarney round to Dublin, he resolved to curtail his tour, return to Endelstow, and commit himself by making a reality of the hypothetical offer of that Sunday evening.

Notwithstanding that he had concocted a great deal of paper theory on social amenities and modern manners generally, the special ounce of practice was wanting, and now for his life Knight could not recollect whether it was considered correct to give a young lady personal ornaments before a regular engagement to marry had been initiated. But the day before leaving Dublin he looked around anxiously for a high-class jewellery establishment, in which he purchased what he considered would suit her best.

It was with a most awkward and unwonted feeling that after entering and closing the door of his room he sat down, opened the morocco case, and held up each of the fragile bits of gold-work before his eyes. Many things had become old to the solitary man of letters, but these were new, and he handled like a child an outcome of civilization which had never before been touched by his fingers. A sudden fastidious decision that the pattern chosen would not suit her after all caused him to rise in a flurry and tear down the street to change them for others. After a great deal of trouble in reselecting, during which his mind became so bewildered that the critical faculty on objects of art seemed to have vacated his person altogether, Knight carried off another pair of ear-rings. These remained in his possession till the afternoon, when, after contemplating them fifty times with a growing misgiving that the last choice was worse than the first, he felt that no sleep would visit his pillow till he had improved upon his previous purchases yet again. In a perfect heat of vexation with himself for such tergiversation, he went anew to the shop-door, was absolutely ashamed to enter and give further trouble, went to another shop, bought a pair at an enormously increased price, because they seemed the very thing, asked the goldsmiths if they would take the other pair in exchange, was told that they could not exchange articles bought of another maker, paid down the money, and went off with the two pairs in his possession, wondering what on earth to do with the superfluous pair. He almost wished he could lose them, or that somebody would steal them, and was burdened with an interposing sense that, as a capable man, with true ideas of economy, he must necessarily sell them somewhere, which he did at last for a mere song. Mingled with a blank feeling of a whole day being lost to him in running about the city on this new and extraordinary class of errand, and of several pounds being lost through his bungling, was a slight sense of satisfaction that he had emerged for ever from his antediluvian ignorance on the subject of ladies' jewellery, as well as secured a truly artistic production at last. During the remainder of that day he scanned the ornaments of every lady he met with the profoundly experienced eye of an appraiser.

Next morning Knight was again crossing St George's Channel – not returning to London by the Holyhead route as he had originally intended, but towards Bristol – availing himself of Mr and Mrs Swancourt's invitation to revisit them on his homeward journey.

We flit forward to Elfride.

Woman's ruling passion – to fascinate and influence those more powerful than she – though operant in Elfride, was decidedly purposeless. She had wanted her friend Knight's good opinion from the first: how much more than that elementary ingredient of friendship she now desired, her fears would hardly allow her to think. In originally wishing to please the highest class of man she had ever intimately known, there was no disloyalty to Stephen Smith. She could not – and few women can – realize the possible vastness of an issue which has only an insignificant begetting.

Her letters from Stephen were necessarily few, and her sense of fidelity clung to the last she had received as a wrecked mariner clings to flotsam. The young girl persuaded herself that she was glad Stephen had such a right to her hand as he had acquired (in her eyes) by the elopement. She beguiled herself by saying, 'Perhaps if I had not so committed myself I might fall in love with Mr Knight.'

All this made the week of Knight's absence very gloomy and distasteful to her. She retained Stephen in her prayers, and his old letters were re-read – as a medicine in reality, though she deceived herself into the belief that it was as a pleasure.

These letters had grown more and more hopeful. He told her that he finished his work every day with a pleasant consciousness of having removed one more stone from the barrier which divided them. Then he drew images of what a fine figure they two would cut some day. People would turn their heads and say, 'What a prize he has won!' She was not to be sad about that wild runaway attempt of theirs (Elfride had repeatedly said that it grieved her). Whatever any other person who knew of it might think, he knew well enough the modesty of her nature. The only reproach was a gentle one for not having written quite so devotedly during her visit to London. Her letter had seemed to have a liveliness derived from other thoughts than thoughts of him.

Knight's intention of an early return to Endelstow having originally been faint, his promise to do so had been fainter. He was a man who kept his words well to the rear of his possible actions. The rector was rather surprised to see him again so soon: Mrs Swancourt was not. Knight found on meeting them all after his arrival had been announced, that they had formed an intention to go to St Leonards for a few days at the end of the month.

No satisfactory conjuncture offered itself on this first evening of his return for presenting Elfride with what he had been at such pains to procure. He was fastidious in his reading of opportunities for such an intended act. The next morning chancing to break fine after a week of cloudy weather, it was proposed and decided that they should all drive to Barwith Strand, a local lion* which neither Mrs Swancourt nor Knight had seen. Knight scented romantic occasions from afar, and foresaw that such a one might be expected before the coming night.

The journey was along a road by neutral green hills, upon which hedgerows lay trailing like ropes on a quay. Gaps in these uplands revealed the blue sea, flecked with a few dashes of white and a solitary white sail, the whole brimming up to a keen horizon which lay like a line ruled from hillside to hillside. Then they rolled down a pass, the chocolate-toned rocks forming a wall on both sides, from one of which fell a heavy jagged shade over half the roadway. A spout of fresh water burst from an occasional crevice, and pattering down upon broad green leaves, ran along as a rivulet at the bottom. Unkempt locks of heather overhung the brow of each steep, whence at divers points a bramble swung forth into mid-air, snatching at their head-dresses like a claw.

They mounted the last crest, and the bay which was to be the end of their pilgrimage burst upon them. The ocean blueness deepened its colour as it stretched to the foot of the crags, where it terminated in a fringe of white – silent at this distance, though moving and heaving like a counterpane upon a restless sleeper. The shadowed hollows of the purple and brown rocks would have been called blue had not that tint been so entirely appropriated by the water beside them.

The carriage was put up at a little cottage with a shed attached, and an ostler and the coachman carried the hamper of provisions down to the shore.

Knight found his opportunity. 'I did not forget your wish,' he began, when they were apart from their friends.

Elfride looked as if she did not understand.

'And I have brought you these,' he continued, awkwardly pulling out the case, and opening it while holding it towards her.

'O Mr Knight!' said Elfride confusedly, and turning to a lively red; 'I didn't know you had any intention or meaning in what you said. I thought it a mere supposition. I don't want them.'

A thought which had flashed into her mind gave the reply a greater decisiveness than it might otherwise have possessed. To-morrow was the day for Stephen's letter.

'But will you not accept them?' Knight returned, feeling less her master than heretofore.

'I would rather not. They are beautiful – more beautiful than any I have ever seen,' she answered earnestly, looking half-wishfully at the temptation, as Eve may have looked at the apple. 'But I don't want to have them, if you will kindly forgive me, Mr Knight.'

'No kindness at all,' said Mr Knight, brought to a full stop at this unexpected turn of events.

A silence followed. Knight held the open case, looking rather wofully at the glittering forms he had forsaken his orbit to procure; turning it about and holding it up as if, feeling his gift to be slighted by her, he was endeavouring to admire it very much himself.

'Shut them up, and don't let me see them any longer – do!' she said laughingly, and with a quaint mixture of reluctance and entreaty.

'Why, Elfie?'

'Not Elfie to you, Mr Knight. O, because I shall want them. There, I am silly, I know, to say that! But I have a reason for not taking them – now.' She kept in the last word for a moment, intending to imply that her refusal was finite, but somehow the word slipped out, and undid all the rest.

'You will take them some day?'

'I don't want to.'

'Why don't you want to, Elfride Swancourt?'

'Because I don't. I don't like to take them.'

'I have read a fact of distressing significance in that,' said Knight. 'Since you like them, your dislike to having them must be towards me?'

'No, it isn't.'

'What, then? Do you like me?'

Elfride deepened in tint, and looked into the distance with features shaped to an expression of the nicest criticism as regarded her answer.

'I like you pretty well,' she at length murmured mildly.

'Not very much?'

'You are so sharp with me, and say hard things, and so how can I?' she replied evasively.

'You think me a fogey, I suppose?'

'No, I don't – I mean I do – I don't know what I think you, I mean. Let us go to papa,' responded Elfride, with somewhat of a flurried delivery.

'Well, I'll tell you my object in getting the present,' said Knight, with a composure intended to remove from her mind any possible impression of his being what he was – her lover. 'You see it was the very least I could do in common civility.'

Elfride felt rather blank at this lucid statement.

Knight continued, putting away the case: 'I felt as anybody naturally would have, you know, that my words on your choice the other day were invidious and unfair, and thought an apology should take a practical shape.'

'O yes.'

Elfride was sorry – she could not tell why – that he gave such a legitimate reason. It was a disappointment that he had all the time a cool motive, which might be stated to anybody without raising a smile. Had she known they were offered in that spirit, she would certainly have accepted the seductive gift. And the tantalizing feature was that perhaps he suspected her to imagine them offered as a lover's token, which was mortifying enough if they were not.

Mrs Swancourt came now to where they were sitting, to select a flat boulder for spreading their table-cloth upon, and, amid the discussion on that subject, the matter pending between Knight and Elfride was shelved for a while. He read her refusal so certainly as the bashfulness of a girl in a novel position that, upon the whole, he could tolerate such a beginning. Could Knight have been told that it was a sense of fidelity struggling against new love, whilst no less assuring as to his ultimate victory it might have entirely abstracted the wish to secure it.

At the same time a slight constraint of manner was visible between them for the remainder of the afternoon. The tide turned, and they were obliged to ascend to higher ground. The day glided on to its end with the usual quiet dreamy passivity of such occasions – when every deed done and thing thought is in endeavouring to avoid doing and thinking more. Looking idly over the verge of a crag they beheld their stone dining-table gradually being splashed upon and their crumbs and fragments all washed away by the incoming sea. The rector drew a moral lesson from the scene; Knight replied in the same satisfied strain. And then the waves rolled in furiously – the neutral green-and-blue tongues of water slid up the slopes, and were metamorphosed into foam by a careless blow, falling back white and faint, and leaving trailing followers behind.

The passing of a heavy shower was the next scene – driving them to shelter in a shallow cave – after which the horses were put in, and they started to return homeward. By the time they reached the higher levels the sky had again cleared, and the sunset rays glanced directly upon the wet uphill road they had climbed. The ruts formed by their carriage-wheels on the ascent – a pair of Liliputian canals – were as shining bars of gold, tapering to nothing in the distance. Upon this also they turned their backs, and night spread over the sea.

The evening was chilly, and there was no moon. Knight sat close to Elfride, and, when the darkness rendered the position of a person a matter of uncertainty, particularly close. Elfride edged away.

'I hope you allow me my place ungrudgingly?' he whispered.

'O yes; 'tis the least I can do in common civility,' she said, accenting the words so that he might recognize them as his own returned.

Both of them felt delicately balanced between two possibilities. Thus they reached home.

To Knight this mild experience was delightful. It was to him a gentle innocent time – a time which, though there may not be much in it, seldom repeats itself in a man's life, and has a peculiar dearness when glanced at retrospectively. He is not inconveniently deep in love, and is lulled by a peaceful sense of being able to enjoy the most trivial thing with a childlike enjoyment. The movement of a wave, the colour of a stone, anything, was enough for Knight's drowsy thoughts of that day to precipitate themselves upon. Even the sermonizing platitudes the rector had delivered himself of – chiefly because something seemed to be professionally required of him in the presence of a man of Knight's proficiencies – were swallowed whole. The presence of Elfride led him not merely to tolerate that kind of talk from the necessities of ordinary courtesy; but he listened to it – took in the ideas with an enjoyable make-believe that they were proper and necessary, and indulged in a conservative feeling that the face of things was complete.

Entering her room that evening Elfride found a packet for herself on the dressing-table. How it came there she did not know. She tremblingly undid the folds of white paper that covered it. Yes; it was the treasure of a morocco case, containing those treasures of ornament she had refused in the daytime.

Elfride held them up beside her face for a moment, looked at herself in the glass, blushed hot, and put them away. They filled her dreams all that night. Never had she seen anything so lovely, and never was it more clear that as an honest woman she was in duty bound to refuse them. Why it was not equally clear to her that duty required more vigorous co-ordinate conduct as well, let those who dissect her say.

The next morning glared in like a spectre upon her. It was Stephen's letter-day, and she was bound to meet the postman – to do stealthily a deed she had never liked, to secure an end she now had ceased to desire.

But she went.

There were two letters.

One was from the bank at St Launce's, in which she had a small private deposit; it was probably something about interest. She put that in her pocket for a moment, and going indoors and upstairs to be safer from observation, tremblingly opened Stephen's.

What was this he said to her?

She was to go to the St Launce's Bank and take a sum of money which they had received private advices to pay her.

The sum was two hundred pounds.

There was no cheque, order, or anything of the nature of guarantee. In fact the information amounted to this: the money was now in the St Launce's Bank, standing in her name.

She instantly opened the other letter. It contained a deposit-note from the bank for the sum of two hundred pounds which had that day been added to her account. Stephen's information, then, was correct, and the transfer made.

'I have saved this in one year,' Stephen's letter went on to say, 'and what so proper as well as pleasant for me to do as to hand it over to you to keep for your use? I have plenty for myself, independently of this. Should you not be disposed to let it lie idle in the bank, get your father to invest it in your name on good security. It is a little present to you from your more than betrothed. He will, I think, Elfride, feel now that my pretensions to your hand are anything but the dream of a silly boy not worth rational consideration.'

With a natural delicacy, Elfride, in mentioning her father's marriage, had refrained from all allusion to the pecuniary resources of the lady.

Leaving this matter-of-fact subject, he went on, somewhat after his boyish manner:

'Do you remember, darling, that first morning of my arrival at your house, when your father read at prayers the miracle of healing the sick of the palsy* – where he is told to take up his bed and walk? I do, and I can now so well realize the force of that passage. The smallest piece of mat is the bed of the Oriental, and yesterday I saw a native perform the very action, which reminded me to mention it. But you are better read than I, and perhaps you knew all this long ago. . . . One day I bought some small native idols to send home to you as curiosities, but afterwards finding they had been cast in England, made to look old, and shipped over, I threw them away in disgust.

'Speaking of this reminds me that we are obliged to import all our house-building ironwork from England. Never was such foresight required to be exercised in building houses as here. Before we begin, we have to order every column, lock, hinge, and screw that will be required. We cannot go into the next street, as in London, and get them cast at a minute's notice. Mr L. says somebody will have to go to England very soon and superintend the selection of a large order of this kind. I only wish I may be the man.'

There before her lay the deposit-receipt for the two hundred pounds, and beside it the elegant present of Knight. Elfride grew cold – then her cheeks felt heated by beating blood. If by destroying the piece of paper the whole transaction could have been withdrawn from her experience, she would willingly have sacrificed the money it represented. She did not know what to do in either case. She almost feared to let the two articles lie in juxtaposition: so antagonistic were the interests they represented that a miraculous repulsion of one by the other was almost to be expected.

That day she was seen little of. By the evening she had come to a resolution, and acted upon it. The packet was sealed up – with a tear of regret as she closed the case upon the pretty forms it contained – directed, and placed upon the writing-table in Knight's room. And a letter was written to Stephen, stating that as yet she hardly understood her position with regard to the money sent; but declaring that she was ready to fulfil her promise to marry him. After this letter had been written she delayed posting it – although never ceasing to feel strenuously that the deed must be done.

Several days passed. There was another Indian letter for Elfride. Coming unexpectedly, her father saw it, but made no remark – why, she could not tell. The news this time was absolutely overwhelming. Stephen, as he had wished, had been actually chosen as the most fitting to execute the iron-work commission he had alluded to as impending. This duty completed he would have three months' leave. His letter continued that he should follow it in a week, and should take the opportunity to plainly ask her father to permit the engagement. Then came a page expressive of his delight and hers at the reunion; and finally, the information that he would write to the shipping agents, asking them to telegraph and tell her when the ship bringing him home should be in sight – knowing how acceptable such information would be.

Elfride lived and moved now as in a dream. Knight had at first become almost angry at her persistent refusal of his offering – and no less with the manner than the fact of it. But he saw that she began to look worn and ill – and his vexation lessened to simple perplexity.

He ceased now to remain in the house for long hours together as before, but made it a mere centre for antiquarian and geological excursions in the neighbourhood. Throw up his cards and go away he fain would have done, but could not. And, thus, availing himself of the privileges of a relative, he went in and out the premises as fancy led him – but still lingered on.

'I don't wish to stay here another day if my presence is distasteful,' he said one afternoon. 'At first you used to imply that I was severe with you; and when I am kind you treat me unfairly.'

'No, no. Don't say so.'

The origin of their acquaintanceship had been such as to render their manner towards each other peculiar and uncommon. It was of a kind to cause them to speak out their minds on any feelings of objection and difference: to be reticent on gentler matters.

'I have a good mind to go away and never trouble you again,' continued Knight.

She said nothing, but the eloquent expression of her eyes and wan face was enough to reproach him for harshness.

'Do you like me to be here, then?' inquired Knight gently.

'Yes,' she said. Fidelity to the old love and truth to the new were ranged on opposite sides, and truth virtuelessly prevailed.

'Then I'll stay a little longer,' said Knight.

'Don't be vexed if I keep by myself a good deal, will you? Perhaps something may happen, and I may tell you something.'

'Mere coyness,' said Knight to himself; and went away with a lighter heart. The trick of reading truly the enigmatical forces at work in women at given times, which with some men is an unerring instinct, is peculiar to minds less direct and honest than Knight's.

The next evening, about five o'clock, before Knight had returned from a pilgrimage along the shore, a man walked up to the house. He was a messenger from Camelton, a town a few miles off, to which place the railway had been advanced during the summer.

'A telegram for Miss Swancourt, and three and sixpence to pay for the special messenger.'

Miss Swancourt sent out the money, signed the paper, and opened her letter with a trembling hand. She read:

'Johnson, Liverpool, to Miss Swancourt, Endelstow, near Castle Boterel.

'Amaryllis telegraphed off Holyhead, four o'clock. Expect will dock and land passengers at Canning's Basin ten o'clock to-morrow morning.'

Her father called her into the study.

'Elfride, who sent you that message?' he asked suspiciously.

'Johnson.'

'Who is Johnson, for Heaven's sake?'

'I don't know.'

'The deuce you don't! Who is to know, then?'

'I have never heard of him till now.'

'That's a singular story, isn't it?'

'I don't know.'

'Come, come, miss! What was the telegram?'

'Do you really wish to know, papa?'

'Well, I do.'

'Remember, I am a full-grown woman now.'

'Well, what then?'

'Being a woman, and not a child, I may, I think, have a secret or two.'

'You will, it seems.'

'Women have, as a rule.'

'But don't keep them. So speak out.'

'If you will not press me now, I give my word to tell you the meaning of all this before the week is past.'

'On your honour?'

'On my honour.'

'Very well. I have had a certain suspicion, you know; and I shall be glad to find it false. I don't like your manner lately.'

'At the end of the week, I said, papa.'

Her father did not reply, and Elfride left the room.

She began to look out for the postman again. Three mornings later he brought an inland letter from Stephen. It contained very little matter, having been written in haste; but the meaning was bulky enough. Stephen said that, having executed a commission in Liverpool, he should arrive at his father's house, East Endelstow, at five or six o'clock that same evening; that he would after dusk walk on to the next village and meet her, if she would, in the church porch, as in the old time. He proposed this plan because he thought it unadvisable to call formally at her house so late in the evening; yet he could not sleep without having seen her. The minutes would seem hours till he clasped her in his arms.

Elfride was still steadfast in her opinion that honour compelled her to meet him. Probably the very longing to avoid him lent additional weight to the conviction; for she was markedly one of those who sigh for the unattainable – to whom, superlatively, a hope is pleasing because not a possession. And she knew it so well that her intellect was inclined to exaggerate this defect in herself.

So during the day she looked her duty steadfastly in the face; read Wordsworth's astringent yet depressing ode to that Deity;* committed herself to Her guidance; and still felt the weight of chance desires.

But she began to take a melancholy pleasure in contemplating the sacrifice of herself to the man whom a maidenly sense of propriety compelled her to regard as her only possible husband. She would meet him, and do all that lay in her power to marry him. To guard against a relapse a note was at once despatched to his father's cottage for Stephen on his arrival, fixing an hour for the interview.

CHAPTER TWENTY-ONE

'On thy cold grey stones, O sea!'*

STEPHEN had said that he should come by way of Bristol, and thence by a steamer to Castle Boterel, in order to avoid the long journey over the hills from St Launce's. He did not know of the extension of the railway to Camelton.

During the afternoon a thought occurred to Elfride, that from any cliff along the shore it would be possible to see the steamer some hours before its arrival.

She had accumulated religious force enough to do an act of supererogation. The act was this – to go to some point of land and watch for the ship that brought her future husband home.

It was a cloudy afternoon. Elfride was often diverted from a purpose by a dull sky; and though she used to persuade herself that the weather was as fine as possible on the other side of the clouds, she could not bring about any practical result from this fancy. Now, her mood was such that the humid sky harmonized with it.

Having ascended and passed over a hill behind the house, Elfride came to a small stream. She used it as a guide to the coast. It was smaller than that in her own valley, and flowed altogether at a higher level. Bushes lined the slopes of its shallow trough; but at the bottom, where the water ran, was a soft green carpet in a strip two or three yards wide.

In winter the water flowed over the grass; in summer, as now, it trickled along a channel in the midst.

Elfride had a sensation of eyes regarding her from somewhere. She turned, and there was Mr Knight. He had dropped into the valley from the side of the hill. She felt a thrill of pleasure, and rebelliously allowed it to exist.

'What utter loneliness to find you in!'

'I am going to the shore by tracking the stream. I believe it empties itself not far off, in a silver thread of water, over a cascade of great height.'

'Why do you load yourself with that heavy telescope?'

'To look over the sea with it,' she said faintly.

'I'll carry it for you to your journey's end.' And he took the glass from her unresisting hands. 'It cannot be half a mile further. See, there is the water.' He pointed to a short fragment of level muddy-gray colour, cutting against the sky.

Elfride had already scanned the small surface of ocean visible, and had seen no ship.

They walked along in company, sometimes with the brook between them – for it was no wider than a man's stride – sometimes close together. The green carpet grew swampy, and they kept higher up.

One of the two ridges between which they walked dwindled lower and became insignificant. That on the right hand rose with their advance, and terminated in a clearly defined edge against the light, as if it were abruptly sawn off. A little further, and the bed of the rivulet ended in the same fashion.

They had come to a bank breast-high, and over it the valley was no longer to be seen. It was withdrawn cleanly and completely. In its place was sky and boundless atmosphere; and perpendicularly down beneath them – small and far off – lay the corrugated surface of the Atlantic.

The small stream here found its death. Running over the precipice it was dispersed in spray before it was half-way down, and falling like rain upon projecting ledges, made minute grassy meadows of them. At the bottom the water-drops soaked away amid the débris of the cliff. This was the inglorious end of the river.

'What are you looking for?' said Knight, following the direction of her eyes.

She was gazing hard at a black object – nearer to the shore than to the horizon – from the summit of which came a nebulous haze, stretching like gauze over the sea.

'The *Puffin*, a little summer steamboat – from Bristol to Castle Boterel,' she said. 'I think that is it – look. Will you give me the glass?'

Knight pulled open the old-fashioned but powerful telescope, and handed it to Elfride, who had looked on with heavy eyes.

'I can't keep it up now,' she said.

'Rest it on my shoulder.'

'It is too high.'

'Under my arm.'

'Too low. You may look instead,' she murmured weakly.

Knight raised the glass to his eye, and swept the sea till the *Puffin* entered its field.

'Yes, it is the *Puffin* – a tiny craft. I can see her figure-head distinctly – a bird with a beak as big as its head.'

'Can you see the deck?'

'Wait a minute; yes, pretty clearly. And I can see the black forms of the passengers against its white surface. One of them has taken something from another – a glass, I think – yes, it is – and he is levelling it in this direction. Depend upon it we are conspicuous objects against the sky to them. Now, it seems to rain upon them, and they put on overcoats and open umbrellas. They vanish and go below – all but that one who has borrowed the glass. He is a slim young fellow, and still watches us.'

Elfride grew pale, and shifted her little feet uneasily.

Knight lowered the glass.

'I think we had better return,' he said. 'That cloud which is raining on them may soon reach us. Why, you look ill. How is that?'

'Something in the air affects my face.'

'Those fair cheeks are very fastidious, I fear,' returned Knight tenderly. 'This air would make those rosy that were never so before, one would think – eh, Nature's spoilt child?'

Elfride's colour returned again.

'There is more to see alongside us, after all,' said Knight.

She turned her back upon the boat and Stephen Smith, and saw, towering still higher than themselves, the vertical face of the hill on the right, which did not project seaward so far as the bed of the valley, but formed the back of a small bay, and so was visible like a concave wall, bending round from their position towards the left.

The composition of the huge hill was revealed to its backbone and marrow here at its rent extremity. It consisted of a vast stratification of blackish-gray slate, unvaried in its whole height by a single change of shade.

It is with cliffs and mountains as with persons; they have what is called a presence, which is not necessarily proportionate to their actual bulk. A little cliff will impress you powerfully; a great one not at all. It depends, as with man, upon the countenance of the cliff.

'I cannot bear to look at that cliff,' said Elfride. 'It has a horrid personality, and makes me shudder. We will go.'

'Can you climb?' said Knight. 'If so, we will ascend by that path over the grim old fellow's brow.'

'Try me,' said Elfride disdainfully. 'I have ascended steeper slopes than that.'

From where they had been loitering, a grassy path wound along inside a bank, placed as a safeguard for unwary pedestrians, to the top of the precipice, and over it along the hill in an inland direction.

'Take my arm, Miss Swancourt,' said Knight.

'I can get on better without it, thank you.'

When they were one quarter of the way up, Elfride stopped to take breath. Knight stretched out his hand.

She took it, and they ascended the remaining slope together. Reaching the very top, they sat down to rest by mutual consent.

'Heavens, what an altitude!' said Knight, looking over the waste of waters between Cam Beak and 'grim Dundagel throned along the sea'.* The cascade appeared a mere span in height from where they were now.

Elfride was looking to the left. The steamboat was in full view again, and by reason of the vast surface of sea their higher position uncovered it seemed almost close to the shore.

'Over that edge,' said Knight, 'where nothing but vacancy appears, is a moving compact mass. The wind strikes the face of the rock, runs up it, rises like a fountain to a height far above our heads, curls over us in an arch, and disperses behind us. In fact, an inverted cascade is there – as perfect as the Niagara Falls – but rising instead of falling, and air instead of water. Now look here.'

Knight threw a scrap of shale over the bank, aiming it as if to go onward over the cliff. Reaching the verge, it towered into the air like a bird, turned back, and alighted on the ground behind them. They themselves were in a dead calm.

'A boat crosses Niagara immediately at the foot of the falls, where the water is quite still, the fallen mass curving under it. We are in precisely the same position with regard to our atmospheric cataract here. If you run back from the cliff fifty yards, you will be in a brisk wind. Now I daresay over the bank is a little backward current.'

Knight rose and leant over the bank. No sooner was his head above it than his hat appeared to be sucked from his head – slipping over his forehead in a seaward direction.

'That's the backward eddy, as I told you,' he cried, and vanished over the little bank after his hat.

Elfride waited one minute; he did not return. She waited another, and there was no sign of him.

A few drops of rain fell, then a sudden shower.

She arose, and looked over the bank. On the other side were a yard or two of level ground – then a short steep preparatory slope – then the verge of the precipice.

On the slope was Knight, his hat on his head. He was on his hands and knees, trying to climb back to the level ground. The rain had wetted the shaly surface of the incline. A slight superficial wetting of the soil hereabout made it far more slippery to stand on than the same soil thoroughly drenched. The inner substance was still hard, and was lubricated by the moistened film.

'I find a difficulty in getting back,' said Knight.

Elfride's heart fell like lead.

'But you can get back?' she wildly inquired.

Knight strove with all his might for two or three minutes, and the drops of perspiration began to bead his brow.

'No, I am unable to do it,' he answered.

Elfride, by a wrench of thought, forced away from her mind the sensation that Knight was in bodily danger. But attempt to help him she must. She ventured upon the treacherous incline, propped herself with the closed telescope, and gave him her hand before he saw her movements.

'O Elfride! why did you?' said he. 'I am afraid you have only endangered yourself.'

And as if to prove his statement, in making an endeavour by her assistance they both slipped lower, and then he was again stayed. His foot was propped by a bracket of quartz rock, standing out like a tooth from the verge of the precipice. Fixed by this, he steadied her, her head being about a foot below the beginning of the slope.

Elfride had dropped the glass; it rolled to the edge and vanished over it into a nether sky.

'Hold tightly to me,' he said.

She flung her arms round his neck with such a firm grasp that whilst he remained it was impossible for her to fall.

'Don't be flurried,' Knight continued. 'So long as we stay above this block we are perfectly safe. Wait a moment whilst I consider what we had better do.'

He turned his eyes to the dizzy depths beneath them, and surveyed the position of affairs.

Two glances told him a tale with ghastly distinctness. It was that, unless they performed their feat of getting up the slope with the precision of machines, they were over the edge and whirling in mid-air.

For this purpose it was necessary that he should recover the breath and strength which his previous efforts had cost him. So he still waited, and looked in the face of the enemy.

The crest of this terrible natural façade passed among the neighbouring inhabitants as being seven hundred feet above the water it overhung. It had been proved by actual measurement to be not a foot less than six hundred and fifty.

That is to say, it is nearly three times the height of Flamborough, half as high again as the South Foreland, a hundred feet higher than Beachy Head – the loftiest promontory on the east or south side of this island – twice the height of St Aldhelm's, thrice as high as the Lizard, and just double the height of St Bee's. One sea-board point on the western coast is known to surpass it in altitude, but only by a few feet. This is Great Orme's Head, in Caernarvonshire.

And it must be remembered that the cliff exhibits an intensifying feature which some of those are without – sheer perpendicularity from the half-tide level.

Yet this remarkable rampart forms no headland: it rather walls in an inlet – the promontory on each side being much lower. Thus, far from being salient, its horizontal section is concave. The sea, rolling direct from the shores of North America, has in fact eaten a chasm into the middle of a hill, and the giant, embayed and unobtrusive, stands in the rear of pigmy supporters. Not least singularly, neither hill, chasm, nor precipice has a name. On this account the precipice may be called the Cliff without a Name.[1]

What gave an added terror to its height was its blackness. And upon this dark face the beating of ten thousand west winds had formed a kind of bloom, which had a visual effect not unlike that of a Hambro' grape.* Moreover the bloom seemed to float off into the atmosphere, and inspire terror through the lungs.

'This piece of quartz, supporting my feet, is on the very nose of the cliff,' said Knight, breaking the silence after his rigid stoical meditation. 'Now what you are to do is this. Clamber up my body till your feet are on my shoulders: when you are there you will, I think, be able to climb on to level ground.'

'What will you do?'

'Wait whilst you run for assistance.'

'I ought to have done that in the first place, ought I not?'

'I was in the act of slipping, and should have reached no standpoint without your weight, in all probability. But don't let us talk. Be brave, Elfride, and climb.'

She prepared to ascend, saying, 'This is the moment I anticipated when on the tower. I thought it would come!'

'This is not a time for superstition,' said Knight. 'Dismiss all that.'

'I will,' she said humbly.

'Now put your foot into my hand: next the other. That's good – well done. Hold to my shoulder.'

She placed her feet upon the stirrup he made of his hand, and was high enough to get a view of the natural surface of the hill over the bank.

'Can you now climb on to level ground?'

'I am afraid not. I will try.'

'What can you see?'

'The sloping common.'

'What upon it?'

'Purple heather and some grass.'

'Nothing more – no man or human being of any kind?'

'Nobody.'

'Now try to get higher in this way. You see that tuft of sea-pink above you. Get that well into your hand, but don't trust to it

[1] See Preface.

entirely. Then step upon my shoulder, and I think you will reach the top.'

With trembling limbs she did exactly as he told her. The preternatural quiet and solemnity of his manner overspread upon herself, and gave her a courage not her own. She made a spring from the top of his shoulder, and was up.

Then she turned to look at him.

By an ill fate, the force downwards of her bound, added to his own weight, had been too much for the tooth of quartz upon which his feet depended. It was, indeed, originally an igneous protrusion into the enormous masses of black strata, which had since been worn away from the sides of the alien fragment by centuries of frost and rain, and now left it without much support.

It moved. Knight seized a tuft of sea-pink with each hand.

The quartz rock which had been his salvation was worse than useless now. It rolled over, out of sight, and away into the same nether sky that had engulfed the telescope.

One of the tufts by which he held came out at the root, and Knight began to follow the quartz. It was a terrible moment. Elfride uttered a low wild wail of agony, bowed her head, and covered her face with her hands.

Between the turf-covered slope and the gigantic perpendicular rock intervened a weather-worn series of jagged edges, forming a face yet steeper than the former slope. As he slowly slid inch by inch upon these, Knight made a last desperate dash at the lowest tuft of vegetation – the last outlying knot of starved herbage ere the rock appeared in all its bareness. It arrested his further descent. Knight was now literally suspended by his arms; but the incline of the brow being what engineers would call about a third in one, it was sufficient to relieve his arms of a portion of his weight, but was very far from offering an adequately flat face to support him.

In spite of this dreadful tension of body and mind, Knight found time for a moment of thankfulness. Elfride was safe.

She lay on her side above him – her fingers clasped. Seeing him again steady she jumped upon her feet.

'Now, if I can only save you by running for help!' she cried. 'O, I would have died instead! Why did you try so hard to deliver me?' And she turned away wildly to run for assistance.

'Elfride, how long will it take you to run to Endelstow and back?'

'Three-quarters of an hour.'

'That won't do; my hands will not hold out ten minutes. And is there nobody nearer?'

'No; unless a chance passer may happen to be.'

'He would have nothing with him that could save me. Is there a pole or stick of any kind on the common?'

She gazed around. The common was bare of everything but heather and grass.

A minute – perhaps more time – was passed in mute thought by both. On a sudden the blank and helpless agony left her face. She vanished over the bank from his sight.

Knight felt himself in the presence of a personalized loneliness.

CHAPTER TWENTY-TWO

'A woman's way'

HAGGARD cliffs, of every ugly altitude, are as common as sea-fowl along the line of coast between Exmoor and Land's End; but this outflanked and encompassed specimen was the ugliest of them all. Their summits are not safe places for scientific experiment on the principles of air-currents, as Knight had now found, to his dismay.

He still clutched the face of the escarpment – not with the frenzied hold of despair, but with a dogged determination to make the most of his every jot of endurance, and so give the longest possible scope to Elfride's intentions, whatever they might be.

He reclined hand in hand with the world in its infancy. Not a blade, not an insect, which spoke of the present, was between him and the past. The inveterate antagonism of these black precipices to all strugglers for life is in no way more forcibly suggested than by the paucity of tufts of grass, lichens, or confervæ* on their outermost ledges.

Knight pondered on the meaning of Elfride's hasty disappearance, but could not avoid an instinctive conclusion that there existed but a doubtful hope for him. As far as he could judge, his sole chance of deliverance lay in the possibility of a rope or pole being brought; and this possibility was remote indeed. The soil upon these high downs was left so untended that they were unenclosed for miles, except by a casual bank or dry wall, and were rarely visited but for the purpose of collecting or counting the flock which found a scanty means of subsistence thereon.

At first, when death appeared improbable because it had never visited him before, Knight could think of no future, nor of anything connected with his past. He could only look sternly at Nature's treacherous attempt to put an end to him, and strive to thwart her.

From the fact that the cliff formed the inner face of the segment of a hollow cylinder, having the sky for a top and the sea for a bottom, which enclosed the bay to the extent of nearly a semicircle, he could see the vertical face curving round on each side of him. He looked far down the façade, and realized more thoroughly how it threatened him. Grimness was in every feature, and to its very bowels the inimical shape was desolation.

By one of those familiar conjunctions of things wherewith the inanimate world baits the mind of man when he pauses in moments of suspense, opposite Knight's eyes was an imbedded fossil, standing forth in low relief from the rock. It was a creature with eyes. The eyes, dead and turned to stone, were even now regarding him. It was one of the early crustaceans called Trilobites.* Separated by millions of years in their lives, Knight and this underling seemed to have met in their place of death. It was the single instance within reach of his vision of anything that had ever been alive and had had a body to save, as he himself had now.

The creature represented but a low type of animal existence, for never in their vernal years had the plains indicated by those numberless slaty layers been traversed by an intelligence worthy of the name. Zoophytes, mollusca, shell-fish, were the highest developments of those ancient dates. The immense lapses of time each formation represented had known nothing of the dignity of man. They were grand times, but they were mean times too, and mean were their relics. He was to be with the small in his death.

Knight was a fair geologist; and such is the supremacy of habit over occasion, as a pioneer of the thoughts of men, that at this dreadful juncture his mind found time to take in, by a momentary sweep, the varied scenes that had had their day between this creature's epoch and his own. There is no place like a cleft landscape for bringing home such imaginings as these.

Time closed up like a fan before him. He saw himself at one extremity of the years, face to face with the beginning and all the intermediate centuries simultaneously. Fierce men, clothed in the hides of beasts, and carrying, for defence and attack, huge clubs and pointed spears, rose from the rock, like the phantoms before the doomed Macbeth.* They lived in hollows, woods, and mud huts – perhaps in caves of the neighbouring rocks. Behind them stood an earlier band. No man was there. Huge elephantine forms, the mastodon,* the hippopotamus, the tapir, antelopes of monstrous size, the megatherium,* and the myledon* – all, for the moment, in juxtaposition. Further back, and overlapped by these, were perched huge-billed birds and swinish creatures as large as horses. Still more shadowy were the sinister crocodilian outlines – alligators and other uncouth shapes, culminating in the colossal lizard, the iguanodon.* Folded behind were dragon forms and clouds of flying reptiles: still underneath were fishy beings of lower development; and so on, till the lifetime scenes of the fossil confronting him were a present and modern condition of things. These images passed before Knight's inner eye in less than half a minute, and he was again considering the actual present. Was he to die? The mental picture of Elfride in the world, without himself to cherish her, smote his heart like a whip. He had hoped for deliverance, but what could a girl do? He dared not move an inch. Was Death really stretching out his hand? The previous sensation, that it was improbable he would die, was fainter now.

However, Knight still clung to the cliff.

To those musing weather-beaten West-country folk who pass the greater part of their days and nights out of doors, Nature seems to have moods in other than a poetical sense: predilections for certain deeds at certain times, without any apparent law to govern or season to account for them. She is read as a person with a curious temper; as one who does not scatter kindnesses and cruelties alternately, impartially, and in order, but heartless severities or overwhelming generosities in lawless caprice. Man's case is always that of the prodigal's favourite or the miser's pensioner. In her unfriendly moments there seems a feline fun in her tricks, begotten by a foretaste of her pleasure in swallowing the victim.

Such a way of thinking had been absurd to Knight, but he began to adopt it now. He was first spitted on to a rock. New tortures followed. The rain increased, and persecuted him with an exceptional persistency which he was moved to believe owed its cause to the fact that he was in such a wretched state already. An entirely new order of things could be observed in this introduction of rain upon the scene. It rained upwards instead of down. The strong ascending air carried the rain-drops with it in its race up the escarpment, coming to him with such velocity that they stuck into his flesh like cold needles. Each drop was virtually a shaft, and it pierced him to his skin. The water-shafts seemed to lift him on their points: no downward rain ever had such a torturing effect. In a brief space he was drenched, except in two places. These were on the top of his shoulders and on the crown of his hat.

The wind, though not intense in other situations, was strong here. It tugged at his coat and lifted it. We are mostly accustomed to look upon all opposition which is not animate as that of the stolid, inexorable hand of indifference, which wears out the patience more than the strength. Here, at any rate, hostility did not assume that slow and sickening form. It was a cosmic agency, active, lashing, eager for conquest: determination; not an insensate standing in the way.

Knight had over-estimated the strength of his hands. They were getting weak already. 'She will never come again; she has been gone ten minutes,' he said to himself.

This mistake arose from the unusual compression of his experiences just now: she had really been gone but three.

'As many more minutes will be my end,' he thought.

Next came another instance of the incapacity of the mind to make comparisons at such times.

'This is a summer afternoon,' he said, 'and there can never have been such a heavy and cold rain on a summer day in my life before.'

He was again mistaken. The rain was quite ordinary in quantity; the air in temperature. It was, as is usual, the menacing attitude in which they approached him that magnified their powers.

He again looked straight downwards, the wind and the water-dashes lifting his moustache, scudding up his cheeks, under his eyelids, and into his eyes. This is what he saw down there: the surface of the sea – visually just past his toes, and under his feet; actually one-eighth of a mile, or more than two hundred yards, below them. We colour according to our moods the objects we survey. The sea would have been a deep neutral blue had happier auspices attended the gazer: it was now no otherwise than distinctly black to his vision. That narrow white border was foam, he knew well; but its boisterous tosses were so distant as to appear a pulsation only, and its plashing was barely audible. A white border to a black sea – his funeral pall and its edging.

The world was to some extent turned upside down for him. Rain ascended from below. Beneath his feet was aërial space and the unknown; above him was the firm, familiar ground, and upon it all that he loved best.

Pitiless nature had then two voices, and two only. The nearer was the voice of the wind in his ears rising and falling as it mauled and thrust him hard or softly. The second and distant one was the moan of that unplummetted ocean below and afar – rubbing its restless flank against the Cliff without a Name.

Knight perseveringly held fast. Had he any faith in Elfride? Perhaps. Love is faith, and faith, like a gathered flower, will rootlessly live on.

Nobody would have expected the sun to shine on such an evening as this. Yet it appeared, low down upon the sea. Not with its natural golden fringe, sweeping the furthest ends of the landscape, not with the strange glare of whiteness which it sometimes puts on as an alternative to colour, but as a splotch of vermilion red upon a leaden ground – a red face looking on with a drunken leer.

Most men who have brains know it, and few are so foolish as to disguise this fact from themselves or others, even though an ostentatious display may be called self-conceit. Knight, without showing it much, knew that his intellect was above the average. And he thought – he could not help thinking – that his death would be a deliberate loss to earth of good material; that such an experiment in killing might have been practised upon some less developed life.

A fancy some people hold, when in a bitter mood, is that inexorable circumstance only tries to prevent what intelligence attempts. Renounce a desire for a long-contested position, and go on another tack, and after a while the prize is thrown at you, seemingly in disappointment that no more tantalizing is possible.

Knight gave up thoughts of life utterly and entirely, and turned to contemplate the Dark Valley* and the unknown future beyond. Into the shadowy depths of these speculations we will not follow him. Let it suffice to state what ensued.

At that moment of taking no more thought for this life, something disturbed the outline of the bank above him. A spot appeared. It was the head of Elfride.

Knight immediately prepared to welcome life again.

The expression of a face consigned to utter loneliness, when a friend first looks in upon it, is moving in its pathos. In rowing seaward to a light-ship or sea-girt lighthouse, where, without any immediate terror of death, the inmates experience the gloom of monotonous seclusion, the grateful eloquence of their countenances at the greeting, expressive of thankfulness for the visit, is enough to stir the emotions of the most careless observer.

Knight's upward look at Elfride was of a nature with, but far transcending, such an instance as this. The lines of his face had deepened to furrows, and every one of them thanked her visibly. His lips moved to the word 'Elfride', though the emotion evolved no sound. His eyes passed all description in their combination of the whole diapason* of eloquence, from lover's deep love to fellow-man's gratitude for a token of remembrance from one of his kind.

Elfride had come back. What she had come to do he did not know. She could only look on at his death, perhaps. Still, she had come back, and not deserted him utterly, and it was much.

It was a novelty in the extreme to see Henry Knight, to whom Elfride was but a child, who had swayed her as a tree sways a bird's nest, who mastered her and made her weep most bitterly at her own insignificance, thus thankful for a sight of her face. She looked down upon him, her face glistening with rain and tears. He smiled faintly.

'How calm he is!' she thought. 'How great and noble he is to be so calm!' She would have died ten times for him then.

The gliding form of the steamboat caught her eye: she heeded it no more.

'How much longer can you wait?' came from her pale lips and along the wind to his position.

'Four minutes,' said Knight in a weaker voice than her own.

'But with a good hope of being saved?'

'Seven or eight.'

He now noticed that in her arms she bore a bundle of white linen, and that her form was singularly attenuated. So preternaturally thin and flexible was Elfride at this moment, that she appeared to bend under the light blows of the rain-shafts, as they struck into her sides and bosom, and splintered into spray on her face. There is nothing like a thorough drenching for reducing the protuberances of clothes, but Elfride's seemed to cling to her like a glove.

Without heeding the attack of the clouds further than by raising her hand and wiping away the spirts of rain when they went more particularly into her eyes, she sat down and hurriedly began rending the linen into strips. These she knotted end to end, and afterwards twisted them like the strands of a cord. In a short space of time she had formed a perfect rope by this means, six or seven yards long.

'Can you wait while I bind it?' she said, anxiously extending her gaze down to him.

'Yes, if not very long. Hope has given me a wonderful instalment of strength.'

Elfride dropped her eyes again, tore the remaining material into narrow tape-like ligaments, knotted each to each as before, but on a smaller scale, and wound the lengthy string she had thus formed round and round the linen rope, which, without this binding, had a tendency to spread abroad.

'Now,' said Knight, who, watching the proceedings intently, had by this time not only grasped her scheme, but reasoned further on, 'I can hold three minutes longer yet. And do you use the time in testing the strength of the knots, one by one.'

She at once obeyed, tested each singly by putting her foot on the rope between each knot, and pulling with her hands. One of the knots slipped.

'O, think! It would have broken but for your forethought,' Elfride exclaimed apprehensively.

She retied the two ends. The rope was now firm in every part.

'When you have let it down,' said Knight, already resuming his position of ruling power, 'go back from the edge of the slope, and over the bank as far as the rope will allow you. Then lean down, and hold the end with both hands.'

He had first thought of a safer plan for his own deliverance, but it involved the disadvantage of possibly endangering her life.

'I have tied it round my waist,' she cried, 'and I will lean directly upon the bank, holding with my hands as well.'

It was the arrangement he had thought of, but would not suggest.

'I will raise and drop it three times when I am behind the bank,' she continued, 'to signify that I am ready. Take care, O, take the greatest care, I beg you!'

She dropped the rope over him, to learn how much of its length it would be necessary to expend on that side of the bank, went back, and disappeared as she had done before.

The rope was trailing by Knight's shoulders. In a few moments it twitched three times.

He waited yet a second or two, then laid hold.

The incline of this upper portion of the precipice, to the length only of a few feet, useless to a climber empty-handed, was invaluable now. Not more than half his weight depended entirely on the linen rope. Half a dozen extensions of the arms, alternating with half a dozen seizures of the rope with his feet, brought him up to the level of the soil.

He was saved, and by Elfride.

He extended his cramped limbs like an awakened sleeper, and sprang over the bank.

At sight of him she leapt to her feet with almost a shriek of joy. Knight's eyes met hers, and with supreme eloquence the glance of each told a long-concealed tale of emotion in that short half-moment. Moved by an impulse neither could resist they ran together and into each other's arms.

At the moment of embracing, Elfride's eyes involuntarily flashed towards the *Puffin* steamboat. It had doubled the point, and was no longer to be seen.

An overwhelming rush of exultation at having delivered the man she revered from one of the most terrible forms of death, shook the gentle girl to the centre of her soul. It merged in a defiance of duty to Stephen, and a total recklessness as to plighted faith. Every nerve of her will was now in entire subjection to her feeling – volition as a guiding power had forsaken her. To remain passive, as she remained now, encircled by his arms, was a sufficiently complete result – a glorious crown to all the years of her life. Perhaps he was only grateful, and did not love her. No matter: it was infinitely more to be even the slave of the greater than the queen of the less. Some such sensation as this, though it was not recognized as a finished thought, raced along the impressionable soul of Elfride.

Regarding their attitude, it was impossible for two persons to go nearer to a kiss than went Knight and Elfride during those minutes of impulsive embrace in the pelting rain. Yet they did not kiss. Knight's peculiarity of nature was such that it would not allow him to take advantage of the unguarded and passionate avowal she had tacitly made.

Elfride recovered herself, and gently struggled to be free.

He reluctantly relinquished her, and then surveyed her from crown to toe. She seemed as small as an infant. He perceived whence she had obtained the rope.

'Elfride, my Elfride!' he exclaimed in gratified amazement.

'I – think I – must leave you now,' she said, her face doubling its red, with an expression between gladness and shame. 'You follow me, but at some distance.'

'The rain and wind pierce you through; the chill will kill you. God bless you for such devotion! Take my coat and put it on.'

'No; I shall get warm running.'

Elfride had absolutely nothing between her and the weather but her diaphanous exterior robe or 'costume'. The door had been made upon a woman's wit, and it had found its way out. Behind the bank, whilst Knight reclined upon the dizzy slope waiting for death, she had taken off her whole clothing, and replaced only her outer bodice and skirt. Every thread of the remainder lay upon the ground in the form of a woollen and cotton rope.

'I am used to being wet through,' she added. 'I have been drenched on Pansy dozens of times. Good-bye till we meet, clothed and in our right minds, by the fireside at home!'

She then ran off from him through the pelting rain like a hare; or more like a pheasant when, scampering away with a lowered tail, it has a mind to fly, but does not. Elfride was soon out of sight.

Knight felt uncomfortably wet and chilled, but glowing with fervour nevertheless. He fully appreciated Elfride's girlish delicacy in refusing his escort in the meagre habiliments she wore, yet felt that necessary abstraction of herself for a short half-hour as a most grievous loss to him.

He gathered up her knotted and twisted plumage of linen, lace, and embroidery work, and laid it across his arm. He noticed on the ground an envelope, limp and wet. In endeavouring to restore this to its proper shape, he loosened from the envelope a piece of paper it had contained, which was seized by the wind in falling from Knight's hand. It was blown to the right, blown to the left – it floated to the edge of the cliff and over the sea, where it was hurled aloft. It twirled in the air, and then flew back over his head.

Knight followed the paper, and secured it. Having done so he looked to discover if it had been worth securing.

The troublesome sheet was a banker's receipt for two hundred pounds, placed to the credit of Miss Swancourt, which the impractical girl had totally forgotten she carried with her.

Knight folded it as carefully as its moist condition would allow, put it in his pocket, and followed Elfride.

CHAPTER TWENTY-THREE

'Should auld acquaintance be forgot?'*

BY this time Stephen Smith had stepped out upon the quay at Castle Boterel, and breathed his native air.

A darker skin, a more pronounced moustache, and an incipient beard, were the chief additions and changes noticeable in his appearance.

In spite of the falling rain, which had somewhat lessened, he took a small valise in his hand and, leaving the remainder of his luggage at the inn, ascended the hills towards East Endelstow. This place lay in a vale of its own, further inland than the west village, and though so near it, had little of physical feature in common with the latter. East Endelstow was more wooded and fertile: it boasted of Lord Luxellian's mansion and park, and was free from those bleak open uplands which lent such an air of desolation to the vicinage* of the coast – always excepting the small valley in which stood the rectory and Mrs Swancourt's old house, The Crags.

Stephen had arrived nearly at the summit of the ridge when the rain again increased its volume, and, looking about for temporary shelter, he ascended a steep path which penetrated dense hazel bushes in the lower part of its course. Further up it emerged upon a ledge immediately over the turnpike-road, and sheltered by an overhanging face of rubble rock, with bushes above. For a reason of his own he made this spot his refuge from the storm, and turning his face to the left, conned the landscape as a book.

He was overlooking the valley containing Elfride's residence.

From this point of observation the prospect exhibited the peculiarity of being either brilliant foreground or the subdued tone of distance, a sudden dip in the surface of the country lowering out of sight all the intermediate prospect. In apparent contact with the trees and bushes growing close beside him appeared the distant tract, terminated suddenly by the brink of the series of cliffs which culminated in the tall giant without a name – small and unimportant as here beheld. A leaf on a bough at Stephen's elbow blotted out a whole hill in the contrasting district far away; a green bunch of nuts covered a complete upland there, and the great cliff itself was outvied by a pigmy crag in the bank hard by him. Stephen had looked upon these things hundreds of times before to-day, but he had never viewed them with such tenderness as now.

Stepping forward in this direction yet a little further, he could see the tower of West Endelstow Church, beneath which he was to meet his Elfride that night. And at the same time he noticed, coming over the hill from the cliffs, a white speck in motion. It seemed first to be a sea-gull flying low, but ultimately proved to be a human figure, running with great rapidity. The form flitted on, heedless of the rain which had caused Stephen's halt in this place, dropped down the heathery hill, entered the vale, and was out of sight.

Whilst he meditated upon the meaning of this phenomenon he was surprised to see swim into his ken from the same point of departure another moving speck, as different from the first as well could be, insomuch that it was perceptible only by its blackness. Slowly and regularly it took the same course, and there was not much doubt that this was the form of a man. He, too, gradually descended from the upper levels, and was lost in the valley below.

The rain had by this time again abated, and Stephen returned to the road. Looking ahead he saw two men and a cart. They were soon obscured by the intervention of a high hedge. Just before they emerged again he heard voices in conversation.

''A must soon be in the neighbourhood, too, if so be he's a-coming,' said a tenor tongue, which Stephen instantly recognized as Martin Cannister's.

''A must 'a b'lieve,' said another voice – that of Stephen's father.

Stephen stepped forward, and came before them face to face. His father and Martin were walking, dressed in their second best suits, and beside them rambled along a grizzel horse* and brightly painted spring-cart.*

'All right, Mr Cannister; here's the lost man!' exclaimed young Smith, entering at once upon the old style of greeting. 'Father, here I am.'

'All right, my sonny; and glad I be for't!' returned John Smith, overjoyed to see the young man. 'How be ye? Well, come along home, and don't let's bide out here in the damp. Such weather must be terrible bad for a young chap just come from a fiery nation like Indy; hey, neighbour Cannister?'

'Trew, trew. And about getting home his traps?* Boxes, monstrous bales, and noble packages of foreign description, I make no doubt?'

'Hardly all that,' said Stephen, laughing.

'We brought the cart, meaning to go right on to Castle Boterel before ye landed,' said his father. '"Put in the horse," says Martin. "Ay," says I, "so we will"; and did it straightway. Now, maybe, Martin had better go on wi' the cart for the things, and you and I walk home-along.'

'And I shall be back a'most as soon as you. Peggy is a pretty step still, though time begins to tell upon her as upon the rest o' us.'

Stephen told Martin where to find his baggage, and then continued his journey homeward in the company of his father.

'Owing to your coming a day sooner than we first expected,' said John, 'you'll find us in a turk of a mess,* sir – "sir," says I to my own son! but ye've gone up so, Stephen. We've killed the pig this morning for 'ee, thinking you'd be hungry, and glad of a morsel of fresh meat. And 'a won't be cut up till to-night. However, we can make 'ee a good supper of fry, which will chaw up* well wi' a dab o' mustard and a few nice new taters, and a drop of shilling ale* to wash it down. Your mother has had the house scrubbed through because you were coming, and dusted all the chimmer* furniture, and bought a new basin and jug of a travelling crockery-woman that came to our door, and scoured the candle-sticks, and cleaned the winders! Ay, I don't know what 'a ha'n't a done. Never were such a steer,* 'a b'lieve.'

Conversation of this kind and inquiries of Stephen for his mother's wellbeing occupied them for the remainder of the journey. When they drew near the river, and the cottage behind it, they could hear the master-mason's clock striking off the bygone hours of the day at intervals of a quarter of a minute, during which intervals Stephen's imagination readily pictured his mother's forefinger wandering round the dial in company with the minute-hand.

'The clock stopped this morning, and your mother is putting it right seemingly,' said his father; and they went up the garden to the door.

When they had entered, and Stephen had dutifully and warmly greeted his mother – who appeared in a cotton dress of a dark-blue ground, covered broadcast with a multitude of new and full moons, stars, and planets, with an occasional dash of a comet-like aspect to diversify the scene – the crackle of cart-wheels was heard outside, and Martin Cannister stamped in at the doorway, in the form of a pair of legs beneath a great box, his body being barely visible. When the luggage had been all taken down, and Stephen had gone upstairs to change his clothes, Mrs Smith's mind seemed to recover a lost thread.

'Really our clock is not worth a penny,' she said, turning to it and attempting to start the pendulum.

'Stopped again?' inquired Martin with commiseration.

'Yes, sure,' replied Mrs Smith; and continued after the manner of certain matrons, to whose tongues the harmony of a subject with a casual mood is a greater recommendation than its pertinence to the occasion, 'John would spend pounds a year upon the jimcrack old thing, if he might, in having it cleaned, when at the same time you may doctor it yourself as well. "The clock's stopped again, John," I say to him. "Better have 'n cleaned," says he. There's five shillings. "That clock grinds again," I say to him. "Better have 'n cleaned," 'a says again. "That clock strikes wrong, John," says I. "Better have 'n cleaned," he goes on. The wheels would have been polished to skeletons by this time if I had listened to him, and I assure you we could have bought a china-faced beauty wi' the good money we've flung away these last ten years upon this old green-faced thing. And, Martin, you must be wet. My son is gone up to change. John is damper than I should like to be, but 'a calls it nothing. Some of Mrs Swancourt's servants have been here – they ran in out of the rain when going for a walk – and I assure you the state of their bonnets was frightful.'

'How's the folks? We've been over to Castle Boterel, and what wi' running and stopping out of the storms, my poor head is beyond everything! fizz, fizz, fizz; 'tis frying o' fish from morning to night,' said a cracked voice in the doorway at this instant.

'Lord, who's that?' said Mrs Smith, in a private exclamation, and turning round saw William Worm, endeavouring to make himself look passing civil and friendly by overspreading his face with a large smile that seemed to have no connection with the humour he was in. Behind him stood a woman about twice his size, with a large umbrella over her head. This was Mrs Worm, William's wife.

'Come in, William,' said John Smith. 'We don't kill a pig every day. And you, likewise, Mrs Worm. I make ye welcome. Since ye left Parson Swancourt, William, I don't see much of 'ee.'

'No, for to tell the truth, since I took to the turnpike-gate line, I've been out but little, coming to church o' Sundays not being my duty now, as 'twas in a parson's family, you see. However, our boy is able to mind the gate now, and I said, says I, "Barbara, let's call and see John Smith."'

'I am sorry to hear your poor head is so bad still.'

'Ay, I assure you that frying o' fish is going on for nights and days. And, you know, sometimes 'tisn't only fish, but rashers o' bacon and inions.* Ay, I can hear the fat pop and fizz as nateral as life; can't I, Barbara?'

Mrs Worm, who had been all this time engaged in closing her umbrella, corroborated this statement, and now, coming indoors, showed herself to be a wide-faced, comfortable-looking woman, with a wart upon her cheek, bearing a small tuft of hair in its centre.

'Have ye ever tried anything to cure yer noise, Maister Worm?' inquired Martin Cannister.

'O ay; bless 'ee, I've tried everything. Providence means merciful, I reckon, and I have hoped he'd have found it out by this time, living so many years in a parson's family, too, but 'a don't seem to relieve me. Ay, I be a poor wambling man, and life's a mint o' trouble!'

'True; mournful true. The world wants looking to, or 'tis all sixes and sevens wi' us.'

'Take your things off, Mrs Worm,' said Mrs Smith. 'We are rather in a muddle, to tell the truth, for my son is just dropped in from Indy a day sooner than we expected, and the pig-killer* is coming presently to cut up.'

Mrs Barbara Worm, not wishing to take any mean advantage of persons in a muddle by observing them, removed her bonnet and mantle with eyes fixed upon the flowers in the plot outside the door.

'What beautiful tiger-lilies!' said Mrs Worm.

'Yes, they are very well, but such a trouble to me on account of the children that come here. They will go eating the berries on the stem, and call 'em currants. Taste wi' juvinals* is quite fancy, really.'

'And your snapdragons look as fierce as ever.'

'Well, really,' answered Mrs Smith, entering didactically into the subject, 'they are more like Christians than flowers. But they make up well enough wi' the rest, and don't require much tending. And the same can be said o' these miller's wheels. 'Tis a flower I like very much, though so simple. John says he never cares about the flowers of 'em, but men have no eye for anything neat. He says his favourite flower is a cauliflower. And I assure you I tremble in the springtime, for 'tis perfect murder.'

'You don't say it, Mrs Smith!'

'John digs round the roots, you know. In goes his blundering spade, through roots, bulbs, everything that hasn't got a good show above ground, turning 'em up cut all to slices. Only the very last fall I went to move some tulips, when I found every bulb upside down, and the stems crooked round. He had turned 'em over in the spring, and the cunning creatures had soon found that heaven was not where it used to be.'

'What's that long-favoured flower under the hedge?'

'They? O, they are the horrid Jacob's ladders!* Instead of praising 'em, I am mad wi' 'em for being so ready to grow where they are not wanted. They are very well in their way, but I do not care for things that neglect won't kill. Do what I will, dig, drag, scrap, pull, I get too many of 'em. I chop the roots: up they'll come, treble strong. Throw 'em over hedge; there they'll grow, staring me in the face like a hungry dog driven away, and creep back again in a week or two the same as before. 'Tis Jacob's ladder here, Jacob's ladder there, and plant them where nothing in the world will grow, you get crowds of 'em in a month or two. John made a new manure mixen* last summer, and he said, "Maria,* now if you've got any flowers or such like that you don't want, you may plant them round my mixen so as to hide it a bit, though 'tis not likely anything of much value will grow there." I thought, "There's the Jacob's ladders; I'll put them there, since they can't do harm in such a place"; and I planted the Jacob's ladders sure enough. They grew, and they grew, in the mixen and out of the mixen, all over the litter, covering it quite up. When John wanted to use it about the garden, he said, "Nation seize them Jacob's ladders of yours, Maria! They've eat the goodness out of every morsel of my manure, so that 'tis no better than sand itself!" Sure enough the hungry mortals had. 'Tis my belief that in the secret souls of 'em, Jacob's ladders are weeds, and not flowers at all, if the truth was known.'

Robert Lickpan, pig-killer and carrier, arrived at this moment. The fatted animal hanging in the back kitchen was cleft down the middle of its backbone, Mrs Smith being meanwhile engaged in cooking supper.

Between the cutting and chopping, ale was handed round, and Worm and the pig-killer listened to John Smith's description of the meeting with Stephen, with eyes blankly fixed upon the table-cloth, in order that nothing in the external world should interrupt their efforts to conjure up the scene correctly.

Stephen came downstairs in the middle of the story, and after the little interruption occasioned by his entrance and welcome, the narrative was again continued, precisely as if he had not been there at all, and was told inclusively to him, as to somebody who knew nothing about the matter.

'"Ay," I said, as I catched sight of him through the brambles, "that's the lad, for I know him by his grandfather's walk"; for 'a stepped out like poor father for all the world. Still there was a touch o' the frisky that set me wondering. 'A got closer, and I said, "That's the lad, for I know him by his carrying a black case like a travelling man." Still, a road is common to all the world, and there be more travelling men than one. But I kept my eye cocked, and I said to Martin, "'Tis the boy, now, for I know him by the old twirl o' the stick and the family step." Then 'a come closer, and 'a said, "All right." I could swear to him then.'

Stephen's personal appearance was next criticized.

'He looks a deal thinner in face, surely, than when I seed him at the parson's, and never knowed him, if ye'll believe me,' said Martin.

Said another, without removing his eyes from Stephen's face, 'I should ha' knowed him anywhere. 'Tis his father's nose to a T.'

'It has been often remarked,' said Stephen modestly.

'And he's certainly taller,' said Martin, letting his glance run over Stephen's form from bottom to top.

'I was thinking 'a was exactly the same height,' Worm replied.

'Bless thy soul, that's because he's bigger round likewise.' And the united eyes all moved to Stephen's waist.

'I be a poor wambling man, but I can make allowances,' said William Worm. 'Ah, sure, and how he came as a stranger and pilgrim to Parson Swancourt's that time, not a soul knowing him after so many years! Ay, life's a strange picter, Stephen: but I suppose I must say Sir to 'ee?'

'O, it is not necessary,' Stephen replied, though mentally resolving to avoid the vicinity of that familiar friend as soon as he had made pretensions to the hand of Elfride.

'Ah, well,' said Worm musingly, 'some would have looked for no less than a Sir. There's a sight of difference in people.'

'And in pigs likewise,' observed John Smith, looking at the halved carcass of his own.

Robert Lickpan, the pig-killer, here seemed called upon to enter the lists of conversation.

'Yes, they've got their particular naters good-now,' he remarked initially. 'Many's the rum-tempered pig I've knowed.'

'I don't doubt it, Master Lickpan.' Martin's answer expressed that his convictions, no less than good manners, demanded the reply.

'Yes,' continued the pig-killer, as one accustomed to be heard. 'One that I knowed was deaf and dumb, and we couldn't make out what was the matter wi' the pig. 'A would eat well enough when 'a seed the trough, but when his back was turned, you might a-rattled the bucket all day, the poor soul never heard 'ee. Ye could play tricks upon him behind his back, and 'a wouldn't find it out no quicker than poor deaf Grammer Bates. But 'a fatted well, and I never seed a pig open better when 'a was killed, and 'a was very tender eating, very; as pretty a bit of meat as ever you see; you could suck that meat through a quill.

'And another I knowed,' resumed the killer, after quietly letting a pint of ale run down his throat of its own accord, and setting down the cup with mathematical exactness upon the spot from which he had raised it – 'another went out of his mind.'

'How very mournful!' murmured Mrs Worm.

'Ay, poor thing, 'a did! As clean out of his mind as the cleverest Christian could go. In early life 'a was very melancholy, and never seemed a hopeful pig by no means. 'Twas Andrew Stainer's pig – that's whose pig 'twas.'

'I can mind the pig well enough,' attested John Smith.

'And a pretty little porker 'a was. And you all know Farmer Buckle's sort? Every jack o' em suffer from the rheumatism to this day, owing to a damp sty they lived in when they were striplings, as 'twere.'

'Well, now we'll weigh,' said John.

'If so be he were not so fine, we'd weigh 'n whole: but as he is, we'll take a side at a time. John, you can mind my old joke, ey?'

'I do so; though 'twas a good few years ago I first heard it.'

'Yes,' said Lickpan, 'that there old familiar joke have been in our family for generations, I may say. My father used that joke regular at pig-killings for more than five and forty years – the time he followed the calling. And 'a told me that 'a had it from his father when he was quite a chiel, who made use o't just the same at every killing more or less; and pig-killings were pig-killings in those days.'

'Truly they were.'

'I've never heard the joke,' said Mrs Smith tentatively.

'Nor I,' chimed in Mrs Worm, who, being the only other lady in the room, felt bound by the laws of courtesy to feel like Mrs Smith in everything.

'Surely, surely you have,' said the killer, looking sceptically at the benighted matrons. 'However, 'tisn't much – I don't wish to say it is. It commences like this: "Bob will tell the weight of your pig, 'a b'lieve," says I. The congregation of neighbours think I mean my son Bob, naturally; but the secret is that I mean the bob o' the steelyard. Ha, ha, ha!'

'Haw, haw, haw!' laughed Martin Cannister, who had heard the explanation of this striking story for the hundredth time.

'Huh, huh, huh!' laughed John Smith, who had heard it for the thousandth.

'Hee, hee, hee!' laughed William Worm, who had never heard it at all, but was afraid to say so.

'Thy grandfather, Robert, must have been a wide-awake chap to make that story,' said Martin Cannister, subsiding to a placid aspect of delighted criticism.

'He had a head, by all account. And, you see, as the first-born of the Lickpans have all been Roberts, they've all been Bobs, so the story was handed down to the present day.'

'Poor Joseph, your second boy, will never be able to bring it out in company, which is rather unfortunate,' said Mrs Worm thoughtfully.

''A won't. Yes, grandfer was a clever chap, as ye say; but I knowed a cleverer. 'Twas my uncle Levi. Uncle Levi made a snuff-box that should be a puzzle to his friends to open. He used to hand it round at wedding parties, christenings, funerals, and in other jolly company, and let 'em try their skill. This extraordinary snuff-box had a spring behind that would push in and out – a hinge where seemed to be the cover; a slide at the end, a screw in front, and knobs and queer notches everywhere. One man would try the spring, another would try the screw, another would try the slide; but try as they would, the box wouldn't open. And they couldn't open it, and they didn't open it. Now what might you think was the secret of that box?'

All put on an expression that their united thoughts were inadequate to the occasion.

'Why the box wouldn't open at all. 'A were made not to open, and ye might have tried till the end of Revelations,* 'twould have been as naught, for the box was glued all round.'

'A very deep man to have made such a box.'

'Yes. Like uncle Levi all over.'

''Twas. I can mind the man very well. Tallest man ever I seed.'

''A was so. He never slept upon a bedstead after he growed up a hard boy-chap – never could get one long enough. When 'a lived in that little small house by the pond, he used to have to leave open his chamber door every night at going to his bed, and let his feet poke out upon the landing.'

'He's dead and gone now, like worse ones, poor man,' observed Worm, to fill the pause which followed the conclusion of Robert Lickpan's speech.

The weighing and cutting up was pursued amid an animated discourse on Stephen's travels; and at the finish the first-fruits of the day's slaughter, fried in onions, were then served up, each piece steaming and hissing till it reached their very mouths.

It must be owned that the gentlemanly son of the house looked rather out of place in the course of these operations. Nor was his mind quite philosophic enough to allow him to be comfortable with the old-established persons his father's friends. He had never lived long at home – scarcely at all since his childhood. The presence of William Worm was the most awkward feature of the case, for, though Worm had left the house of Mr Swancourt, the being hand-in-glove with a *ci-devant** servitor reminded Stephen too forcibly of the rector's classification of himself before he went from England. Mrs Smith was conscious of the defect in her arrangements which had brought about the undesired conjunction. She spoke to Stephen privately.

'I am above having such people here, Stephen; but what could I do? And your father is so rough in his nature that he's more mixed up with them than need be.'

'Never mind, mother,' said Stephen; 'I'll put up with it now.'

'When we leave my lord's service, and get further up the country – as I hope we shall soon – it will be different. We shall be among fresh people, and in a larger house, and shall keep ourselves up a bit, I hope.'

'Is Miss Swancourt at home, do you know?' Stephen inquired.

'Yes, your father saw her this morning.'

'Do you often see her?'

'Scarcely ever. Mr Glim, the curate, calls occasionally, but the Swancourts don't come into the village now any more than to drive through it. They dine at my lord's oftener than they used. Ah, here's a note was brought this morning for you by a boy.'

Stephen eagerly took the note and opened it, his mother watching him. He read what Elfride had written and sent before she started for the cliff that afternoon:

'Yes; I will meet you in the church at nine to-night. – E.S.'

'I don't know, Stephen,' his mother said meaningly, 'whe'r you still think about Miss Elfride, but if I were you I wouldn't concern about her. They say that none of old Mrs Swancourt's money will come to her step-daughter.'

'I see the evening has turned out fine; I am going out for a little while to look round the place,' he said, evading the direct query. 'Probably by the time I return our visitors will be gone, and we can have a more confidential talk.'

CHAPTER TWENTY-FOUR

'Breeze, bird, and flower confess the hour.'*

THE rain had ceased since the sunset, but it was a cloudy night; and the light of the moon, softened and dispersed by its misty veil, was distributed over the land in pale gray.

A dark figure stepped from the doorway of John Smith's riverside cottage, and strode rapidly towards West Endelstow with a light footstep. Soon ascending from the lower levels he turned a corner, followed a cart-track, and saw the tower of the church he was in quest of distinctly shaped forth against the sky. In less than half an hour from the time of starting he swung himself over the churchyard stile.

The wild irregular enclosure was as much as ever an integral part of the old hill. The grass was still long, the graves were shaped precisely as passing years chose to alter them from their orthodox form as laid down by Martin Cannister, and by Stephen's own grandfather before him.

A sound sped into the air from the direction in which Castle Boterel lay. It was the striking of the town church-clock, distinct in the still atmosphere as if it had come from the tower hard by, which, wrapt in its solitary silentness, gave out no such sounds of life.

'One, two, three, four, five, six, seven, eight, nine.' Stephen carefully counted the strokes, though he well knew their number beforehand. Nine o'clock. It was the hour Elfride had herself named as the most convenient for meeting him.

Stephen stood at the door of the porch and listened. He could have heard the softest breathing of any person within the porch; nobody was there. He went inside the doorway, sat down upon the stone bench, and waited with a beating heart.

The faint sounds heard only accentuated the silence. The rising and falling of the sea, far away along the coast, was the most important. A minor sound was the scurr of a distant night-hawk.* Among the minutest where all were minute were the light settlement of gossamer fragments floating in the air, a toad humbly labouring along through the grass near the entrance, the crackle of a dead leaf which a worm was endeavouring to pull into the earth, a waft of air, getting nearer and nearer, and expiring at his feet under the burden of a winged seed.

With all these soft sounds there came not the only soft sound he cared to hear – the footfall of Elfride.

For a whole quarter of an hour Stephen sat thus intent, without moving a muscle. At the end of that time he walked to the west front of the church. Turning the corner of the tower, a white form stared him in the face. He started back, and recovered himself. It was the tomb of young farmer Jethway, looking still as fresh and as new as when it was first erected, the pale stone in which it was hewn having a singular weirdness amid the dark blue slabs from local quarries, of which the whole remaining gravestones were formed.

He thought of the night when he had sat thereon with Elfride as his companion, and well remembered his regret that she had received, even unwillingly, earlier homage than his own. But his present tangible anxiety reduced such a feeling to sentimental nonsense in comparison; and he strolled on over the graves to the border of the churchyard, whence in the daytime could be clearly seen the rectory and the present residence of the Swancourts. No footstep was discernible upon the path across there, but a light was shining from a window in the last-named house.

Stephen knew there could be no mistake about the time or place, and no difficulty about keeping the engagement. He waited yet longer, passing from impatience into a mood which failed to take any account of the lapse of time. He was awakened from his reverie by Castle Boterel clock.

One, two, three, four, five, six, seven, eight, nine, TEN.

One little fall of the hammer in addition to the number it had been sharp pleasure to hear, and what a difference to him!

He left the churchyard on the side opposite to his point of entrance, and went into the lane. Slowly he drew near the gate of her house. This he softly opened, and walked up the gravel drive to the door. Here he paused for several minutes.

At the expiration of that time the murmured speech of a manly voice came out to his ears through an open window behind the corner of the house. This was responded to by a clear soft laugh. It was the laugh of Elfride.

Stephen was conscious of a gnawing pain at his heart. He retreated as he had come. There are disappointments which wring us, and there are those which inflict a wound whose mark we bear to our graves. Such are so keen that no future gratification of the same desire can ever obliterate them: they become registered as a permanent loss of happiness. Of this sort was Stephen's now: the crowning aureola of the dream had been the meeting by stealth; and if Elfride had come to him only ten minutes after he had turned away, the disappointment would have been recognizable still.

When the young man reached home he found there a letter which had arrived in his absence. Believing it to contain some reason for her non-appearance, yet unable to imagine one that could justify her, he hastily tore open the envelope.

The paper contained not a word from Elfride. It was the deposit-note for his two hundred pounds. On the back was the form of a cheque, and this she had filled up with the same sum, payable to the bearer.

Stephen was confounded. He attempted to divine her motive. Considering how limited was his knowledge of her later actions, he guessed rather shrewdly that, between the time of her sending the note in the morning and the evening's silent refusal of his gift, something had occurred which had caused a total change in her attitude towards him.

He knew not what to do. It seemed absurd now to go to her father next morning, as he had purposed, and ask for an engagement with her, a possibility impending all the while that Elfride herself would not be on his side. Only one course recommended itself as wise. To wait and see what the days would bring forth; to go and execute his commissions in Birmingham; then to return, learn if anything had happened, and try what a meeting might do; perhaps her surprise at his backwardness would bring her forward to show latent warmth as decidedly as in old times.

This act of patience was in keeping only with the nature of a man precisely of Stephen's constitution. Nine men out of ten would perhaps have rushed off, got into her presence, by fair means or foul, and provoked a catastrophe of some sort. Possibly for the better, probably for the worse.

He started for Birmingham the next morning. A day's delay would have made no difference; but he could not rest until he had begun and ended the programme proposed to himself. Bodily activity will sometimes take the sting out of anxiety as completely as assurance itself.

CHAPTER TWENTY-FIVE

'Mine own familiar friend'*

DURING these days of absence Stephen lived under alternate conditions. Whenever his emotions were active, he was in agony. Whenever he was not in agony, the business in hand had driven out of his mind by sheer force all deep reflection on the subject of Elfride and love.

By the time he took his return journey at the week's end, Stephen had very nearly worked himself up to an intention to call and see her face to face. On this occasion also he adopted his favourite route – by the little summer steamer from Bristol to Castle Boterel; the time saved by speed on the railway being wasted at junctions, and in following a devious course.

It was a bright silent evening at the beginning of September when Smith again set foot in the little town. He felt inclined to linger awhile upon the quay before ascending the hills, having formed a romantic intention to go home by way of her house, yet not wishing to wander in its neighbourhood till the evening shades should sufficiently screen him from observation.

And thus waiting for night's nearer approach, he watched the placid scene, over which the pale luminosity of the west cast a sorrowful monochrome, that became slowly embrowned by the dusk. A star appeared, and another, and another. They sparkled amid the yards and rigging of the two coal brigs lying alongside, as if they had been tiny lamps suspended in the ropes. The masts rocked sleepily to the infinitesimal flux of the tide, which clucked and gurgled with idle regularity in nooks and holes of the harbour wall.

The twilight was now quite pronounced enough for his purpose; and as, sadly sick at heart, he was about to move on, a little boat containing two persons glided up the middle of the harbour with the lightness of a shadow. The boat came opposite him, passed on, and touched the landing-steps at the further end. One of its occupants was a man, as Stephen had known by the easy stroke of the oars. When the pair ascended the steps and came into greater prominence, he was enabled to discern that the second personage was a woman; also that she wore a white decoration – apparently a feather – in her hat or bonnet, which spot of white was the only distinctly visible portion of her clothing.

Stephen remained a moment in their rear and they passed on, when he pursued his way also, and soon forgot the circumstance. Having crossed a bridge, forsaken the high road, and entered the footpath which led up the vale to West Endelstow, he heard a little wicket click softly together some yards ahead. By the time that Stephen had reached the wicket and passed it, he heard another click of precisely the same nature from another gate yet further on. Clearly some person or persons were preceding him along the path, their footsteps being rendered noiseless by the soft carpet of turf. Stephen now walked a little more quickly, and perceived two forms. One of them bore aloft the white feather he had noticed in the woman's hat on the quay: they were the couple he had seen in the boat. Stephen dropped a little further to the rear.

From the bottom of the valley along which the path had hitherto lain, beside the margin of the trickling streamlet, another path now diverged, and ascended the slope of the left-hand hill. This footway led only to the residence of Mrs Swancourt and a cottage or two in its vicinity. No grass covered this diverging path in portions of its length, and Stephen was reminded that the pair in front of him had taken this route by the occasional rattle of loose stones under their feet. Stephen climbed in the same direction, but for some undefined reason he trod more softly than did those preceding him. His mind was unconsciously in exercise upon whom the woman might be – whether a visitor to The Crags, a servant, or Elfride. He put it to himself yet more forcibly; could the lady be Elfride? A possible reason for her unaccountable failure to keep the appointment with him returned with painful force.

They entered the grounds of the house by the side wicket, whence the path, now wide and well trimmed, wound fantastically through the shrubbery to an octagonal pavilion called the Belvedere,* by reason of the comprehensive view over the adjacent district that its green seats afforded. The path passed this erection and went on to the house as well as to the gardener's cottage on the other side, straggling thence to East Endelstow; so that Stephen felt no hesitation in following through the wicket and entering a promenade which could scarcely be called private.

He fancied that he heard the gate again open and swing together behind him. Turning, he saw nobody.

The people of the boat preceded him to the summer-house. One of them spoke.

'I am afraid we shall get a scolding for being so late.'

Stephen instantly recognized the familiar voice, richer and fuller now than it used to be. 'Elfride!' he whispered to himself, and held fast by a sapling, to steady himself under the agitation her presence caused him. His heart swerved from its beat; he shunned receiving the meaning he sought.

'A breeze is rising again; how the ash tree rustles!' said Elfride. 'Don't you hear it? I wonder what the time is.'

Stephen relinquished the sapling.

'I will get a light and tell you. Step into the summer-house; the air is quiet there.'

The cadence of that voice – its peculiarity – seemed to come home to him like that of some notes of the northern birds on his return to his native clime, as an old natural thing renewed, yet not particularly noticed as natural before that renewal.

They entered the Belvedere. In the lower part it was formed of close woodwork nailed crosswise, and had openings in the upper by way of windows.

The scratch of a striking light was heard, and a glow radiated from the interior of the building. The light gave birth to dancing leaf-shadows, stem-shadows, lustrous streaks, dots, sparkles, and threads of silver sheen of all imaginable variety and transience. It awakened gnats, which flew towards it, revealed shiny gossamer threads, disturbed earthworms. Stephen gave but little attention to these phenomena, and less time. He saw in the summer-house a strongly illuminated picture.

First, the face of his friend and preceptor Henry Knight, between whom and himself an estrangement had arisen, not from any definite causes beyond those of absence, increasing age, and diverging sympathies.

Next, his bright particular star, Elfride. The face of Elfride was more womanly than when she had called herself his, but as clear and healthy as ever. Her plenteous twines of beautiful hair were looking much as usual, with the exception of a slight modification in their arrangement in deference to the changes of fashion.

Their two foreheads were close together, almost touching, and both were looking down. Elfride was holding her watch, Knight was holding the light with one hand, his left arm being round her waist. Part of the scene reached Stephen's eyes through the horizontal bars of woodwork, which crossed their forms like the ribs of a skeleton.

Knight's arm stole still further round the waist of Elfride.

'It is half-past eight,' she said in a low voice, which had a peculiar music in it, seemingly born of a thrill of pleasure at the new proof that she was beloved.

The flame dwindled down, died away, and all was wrapped in a darkness to which the gloom before the illumination bore no comparison in apparent density. Stephen, shattered in spirit and sick to his heart's centre, turned away. In turning, he saw a shadowy outline behind the summer-house on the other side. His eyes grew accustomed to the darkness. Was the form a human form, or was it an opaque bush of juniper?

The lovers arose, brushed against the laurestines, and pursued their way to the house. The indistinct figure had moved, and now passed across Smith's front. So completely enveloped was the person that it was impossible to discern him or her any more than as a shape. The shape glided noiselessly on.

Stephen stepped forward, fearing any mischief was intended to the other two. 'Who are you?' he said.

'Never mind who I am,' answered a weak whisper from the enveloping folds. '*What* I am, may she be! Perhaps I knew well – ah, so well! – a youth whose place you took, as he there now takes yours. Will you let her break your heart, and bring you to an untimely grave, as she did the one before you?'

'You are Mrs Jethway, I think. What do you do here? And why do you talk so wildly?'

'Because my heart is desolate, and nobody cares about it. May hers be so that brought trouble upon me!'

'Silence!' said Stephen, staunch to Elfride in spite of himself. 'She would harm nobody wilfully, never would she! How do you come here?'

'I saw the two coming up the path, and wanted to learn if she were not one of them. Can I help disliking her if I think of the past? Can I help watching her if I remember my boy? Can I help ill-wishing her if I well-wish him?'

The bowed form went on, passed through the wicket, and was enveloped by the shadows of the field.

Stephen had heard that Mrs Jethway, since the death of her son, had become a crazed, forlorn woman; and bestowing a pitying thought upon her he dismissed her fancied wrongs from his mind, but not her condemnation of Elfride's faithlessness. That entered into and mingled with the sensations his new experience had begotten. The tale told by the little scene he had witnessed ran parallel with the unhappy woman's opinion, which, however baseless it might have been antecedently, had become true enough as regarded himself.

A slow weight of despair, as distinct from a violent paroxysm as starvation from a mortal shot, filled him and wrung him body and soul. The discovery had not been altogether unexpected, for throughout his anxiety of the last few days since the night in the churchyard, he had been inclined to construe the uncertainty unfavourably for himself. His hopes for the best had been but periodic interruptions to a chronic fear of the worst.

A strange concomitant of his misery was the singularity of its form. That his rival should be Knight, whom once upon a time he had adored as a man is very rarely adored by another in modern times, and whom he loved now, added deprecation to sorrow, and cynicism to both. Henry Knight, whose praises he had so frequently trumpeted in her ears, of whom she had actually been jealous, lest she herself should be lessened in Stephen's love on account of him, had probably won her the more easily by reason of those very praises which he had only ceased to utter by her command. She had ruled him like a queen in that matter, as in all others. Stephen could tell by her manner, brief as had been his observation of it, and by her words, few as they were, that her position was far different with Knight. That she looked up at and adored her new lover from below his pedestal, was even more perceptible than that she had smiled down upon Stephen from a height above him.

The suddenness of Elfride's renunciation of himself was food for more torture. To an unimpassioned outsider it admitted of at least two interpretations – it might either have proceeded from an endeavour to be faithful to her first choice till the lover seen absolutely overpowered the lover remembered, or from a wish not to lose his love till sure of the love of another. But to Stephen Smith the motive involved in the latter alternative made it untenable where Elfride was the actor.

He mused on her letters to him, in which she had never mentioned a syllable concerning Knight. It is desirable, however, to observe that only in two letters could she possibly have done so. One was written about a week before Knight's arrival, when, though she did not mention his promised coming to Stephen, she had hardly a definite reason in her mind for neglecting to do it. In the next she did casually allude to Knight. But Stephen had left Bombay long before that letter arrived.

Stephen looked at the black form of the adjacent house, where it cut a dark polygonal notch out of the sky, and felt that he hated the spot. He did not know many facts of the case, but could not help instinctively associating Elfride's fickleness with the marriage of her father, and their introduction to London society. He closed the iron gate bounding the shrubbery as noiselessly as he had opened it, and went into the grassy field. Here he could see the old vicarage, the house alone that was associated with the sweet pleasant time of his incipient love for Elfride. Turning sadly from the place that was no longer a nook in which his thoughts might nestle when he was far away, he wandered in the direction of the east village, to reach his father's house before they retired to rest.

The nearest way to the cottage was by crossing the park. He did not hurry. Happiness frequently has reason for haste, but it is seldom that desolation need scramble or strain. Sometimes he paused under the low-hanging arms of the trees, looking vacantly on the ground.

Stephen was standing thus, scarcely less crippled in thought than he was blank in vision, when a clear sound permeated the quiet air about him, and spread on far beyond. The sound was the stroke of a bell from the tower of East Endelstow Church, which stood in a dell not forty yards from Lord Luxellian's mansion, and within the park enclosure. Another stroke greeted his ear, and gave character to both: then came a slow succession of them.

'Somebody is dead,' he said aloud.

The death-knell of an inhabitant of the eastern parish was being tolled.

An unusual feature in the tolling was that it had not been begun according to the custom in Endelstow and other parishes in the neighbourhood. At every death the sex and age of the deceased were announced by a system of changes. Three times three strokes signified that the departed one was a man; three times two, a woman; twice three, a boy; twice two, a girl. The regular continuity of the tolling suggested that it was the resumption rather than the beginning of a knell – the opening portion of which Stephen had not been near enough to hear.

The momentary anxiety he had felt with regard to his parents passed away. He had left them in perfect health, and had any serious illness seized either, a communication would have reached him ere this. At the same time, since his way homeward lay under the churchyard yews, he resolved to look into the belfry in passing by, and speak a word to Martin Cannister, who would be there.

Stephen reached the brow of the hill, and felt inclined to renounce his idea. His mood was such that talking to any person to whom he could not unburden himself would be wearisome. However, before he could put any inclination into effect, the young man saw from amid the trees a bright light shining, the rays from which radiated like needles through the sad plumy foliage of the yews. Its direction was from the centre of the churchyard.

Stephen mechanically went forward. Never could there be a greater contrast between two places of like purpose than between this graveyard and that of the further village. Here the grass was carefully tended, and formed virtually a part of the manor-house lawn; flowers and shrubs being planted indiscriminately over both, whilst the few graves visible were mathematically exact in shape and smoothness, appearing in the day-time like chins newly shaven. There was no wall, the division between God's Acre* and Lord Luxellian's being marked only by a few square stones set at equidistant points. Among those persons who have romantic sentiments on the subject of their last dwelling-place, probably the greater number would have chosen such a spot as this in preference to any other: a few would have fancied a constraint in its trim neatness, and would have preferred the wild hill-top of the neighbouring site, with Nature in her most negligent attire.

The light in the churchyard he next discovered to have its source in a point very near the ground, and Stephen imagined it might come from a lantern in the interior of a partly-dug grave. But a nearer approach showed him that its position was immediately under the wall of the aisle, and within the mouth of an archway. He could now hear voices, and the truth of the whole matter began to dawn upon him. Walking on towards the opening Smith discerned on his left hand a heap of earth, and before him a flight of stone steps which the removed earth had uncovered, leading down under the edifice. It was the entrance to a large family vault, extending under the north aisle.

Stephen had never before seen it open, and descending one or two steps stooped to look under the arch. The vault appeared to be crowded with coffins, with the exception of an open central space, which had been necessarily kept free for ingress and access to the sides, round three of which the coffins were stacked in stone bins or niches.

The place was well lighted with candles stuck in slips of wood that were fastened to the wall. On making the descent of another step the living inhabitants of the vault were recognizable. They were his father the master-mason, an under-mason, Martin Cannister, and two or three young and old labouring-men. Crowbars and workmen's hammers were scattered about. The whole company, sitting round on coffins which had been removed from their places, apparently for some alteration or enlargement of the vault, were eating bread and cheese, and drinking ale from a cup with two handles, passed round from each to each.

'Who is dead?' Stephen inquired, stepping down.

CHAPTER TWENTY-SIX

'To that last nothing under earth'*

ALL eyes were turned to the entrance as Stephen spoke, and the ancient-mannered conclave scrutinized him inquiringly.

'Why, 'tis our Stephen!' said his father, rising from his seat; and, still retaining the frothy mug in his left hand, he swung forward his right for a grasp. 'Your mother is expecting 'ee – thought you would have come before dark. But you'll wait and go home with me? I have all but done for the day, and was going directly.'

'Yes, 'tis Master Stephy, sure enough. Glad to see you so soon again, Master Smith,' said Martin Cannister, chastening the gladness expressed in his words by a neutrality of countenance, in order to harmonize the feeling as much as possible with the solemnity of a family vault.

'The same to you, Martin; and you, William,' said Stephen, nodding around to the rest, who, having their mouths full of bread and cheese, were of necessity compelled to reply merely by compressing their eyes to friendly lines and wrinkles.

'And who is dead?' Stephen repeated.

'Lady Luxellian, poor gentlewoman, as we all shall,' said the under-mason. 'Ay; we be going to enlarge the vault to make room for her.'

'When did she die?'

'Early this morning,' his father replied, with an appearance of recurring to a chronic thought. 'Martin has been tolling ever since, almost. There, 'twas expected. She was very limber.'*

'Ay, poor soul, this morning,' resumed the under-mason, a marvellously old man, whose skin seemed so much too large for his body that it would not stay in position. 'She must know by this time whether she's to go up or down, poor woman.'

'What was her age?'

'Not more than seven or eight and twenty by candle-light. But, Lord! by day 'a was forty if 'a were an hour.'

'Ay, night-time or day-time makes a difference of twenty years to rich females,' observed Martin.

'She was one and thirty really,' said John Smith. 'I had it from them that know.'

'Not more than that!'

''A looked very bad, poor lady. In faith, ye might say she was dead for years afore 'a would own it.'

'As my old father used to say, "dead, but wouldn't drop down".'

'I seed her, poor soul,' said a labourer from behind some removed coffins, 'only but last Valentine's-day* of all the world. 'A was arm in crook wi' my lord. I says to myself, "You be ticketed Churchyard, my noble lady, although you don't dream on't."'

'I suppose my lord will write to all the other lords anointed in the nation, to let 'em know that she that was is now no more?'

''Tis done and past. I see a bundle of letters go off an hour after the death. Sich wonderful black rims as they letters had – half-an-inch wide, at the very least.'

'Too much,' observed Martin. 'In short, 'tis out of the question that a human being can be so mournful as black edges half-an-inch wide. I'm sure people don't feel more than a very narrow border when they feels most of all.'

'And there are two little girls, are there not?' said Stephen.

'Nice clane little faces! – left motherless now.'

'They used to come to Parson Swancourt's to play with Miss Elfride when I were there,' said William Worm. 'Ah, they did so's!' The latter sentence was introduced to add the necessary melancholy to a remark which, intrinsically, could hardly be made to possess enough for the occasion. 'Yes,' continued Worm, 'they'd run upstairs, they'd run down; flitting about with her everywhere. Very fond of her, they were. Ah, well!'

'Fonder than ever they were of their mother, so 'tis said here and there,' added a labourer.

'Well, you see, 'tis natural. Lady Luxellian stood aloof from 'em so – was so drowsy-like, that they couldn't love her in the jolly-companion way children want to like folks. Only last winter I seed Miss Elfride talking to my lady and the two children, and Miss Elfride wiped their noses for 'em – my lady never once seeing that it wanted doing; and, naturally, children take to people that's their best friend.'

'Be as 'twill, the woman is dead and gone, and we must make a place for her,' said John. 'Come, lads, drink up your ale, and we'll just rid this corner, so as to have all clear for beginning at the wall, as soon as 'tis light to-morrow.'

Stephen then asked where Lady Luxellian was to lie.

'Here,' said his father. 'We are going to set back this wall and make a recess; and 'tis enough for us to do before the funeral. When my lord's mother died, she said, "John, the place must be enlarged before another can be put in." But 'a never expected 'twould be wanted so soon. Better move Lord George first, I suppose, Simeon?'

He pointed with his foot to a heavy coffin, covered with what had originally been red velvet, the colour of which could only just be distinguished now.

'Just as ye think best, Master John,' replied the shrivelled mason. 'Ah, poor Lord George!' he continued, looking contemplatively at the huge coffin; 'he and I were as bitter enemies once as any could be when one is a lord and t'other only a creeping man. Poor fellow! He'd clap his hand upon my shoulder and cuss me as familiar and neighbourly as if he'd been a common chap. Ay, 'a cussed me up hill and 'a cussed me down; and then 'a would rave out again, and the goold* clamps of his fine new teeth would glisten in the sun like fetters of brass, while I, being a small man and poor, was fain to say nothing at all. Such a strappen fine gentleman as he was too! Yes, I rather liked en sometimes. But once now and then, when I looked at his towering height, I'd think in my inside, "What a weight you'll be, my lord, for our arms to lower under the aisle of Endelstow Church some day!"'

'And was he?' inquired a young labourer.

'He was. He was five hundredweight if 'a were a pound. What with his lead, and his oak, and his handles, and his one thing and t'other' – here the ancient man slapped his hand upon the cover with a force that caused a rattle among the bones inside – 'he half broke my back when I took his feet to lower him down the steps there. "Ah," saith I to John there – didn't I, John? – "that ever one man's glory should be such a weight upon another man!" But there, I liked my lord George sometimes.'

''Tis a strange thought,' said another, 'that while they be all here under one roof, a snug united family o' Luxellians, they be really scattered miles away from one another in the form of good sheep and wicked goats, isn't it?'

'True; 'tis a thought to look at.'

'And that one, if he's gone upward, don't know what his wife is doing no more than the man in the moon if she's gone downward. And that some unfortunate one in the hot place is a-hollering across to a lucky one up in the clouds, and quite forgetting their bodies be boxed close together all the time.'

'Ay, 'tis a thought to look at, too, that I can say "Hullo!" close to fiery Lord George, and 'a can't hear me.'

'And that I be eating my onion close to dainty Lady Jane's nose, and she can't smell me.'

'What do 'em put all their heads one way for?' inquired a young man.

'Because 'tis churchyard law, you simple. The law of the living is, that a man shall be upright and downright; and the law of the dead is, that a man shall be east and west. Every state of society have its laws.'

'We must break the law wi' a few of the poor souls however. Come, buckle to,' said the master-mason.

And they set to work anew.

The order of interment could be distinctly traced by observing the appearance of the coffins as they lay piled around. On those which had been standing there but a generation or two the trappings still remained. Those of an earlier period showed bare wood, with a few tattered rags dangling therefrom. Earlier still, the wood lay in fragments on the floor of the niche, and the coffin consisted of naked lead alone; whilst in the case of the very oldest, even the lead was bulging and cracking in pieces, revealing to the curious eye a heap of dust within. The shields upon many were quite loose, and removable by the hand, their lustreless surfaces still indistinctly exhibiting the name and title of the deceased.

Overhead the groins and concavities of the arches curved in all directions, dropping low towards the walls, where the height was no more than sufficient to enable a person to stand upright.

The body of the fourteenth and latest baron, together with two or three others, all of more recent date than the great bulk of coffins piled there, had, for want of room, been placed at the end of the vault on tressels, and not in niches like the others. These it was necessary to remove, to form behind them the chamber in which they were ultimately to be deposited. Stephen, finding the place and proceedings in keeping with the sombre colours of his mind, waited there still.

'Simeon, I suppose you can mind poor Lady Elfride, and how she ran away with the singer?' said John Smith, after awhile. 'I think it fell upon the time my father was sexton here. Let us see – where is she?'

'Here somewhere,' returned Simeon, looking round him.

'Why, I've got my arms round the very gentlewoman at this moment.' He lowered the end of the coffin he was holding, wiped his face, and throwing a morsel of rotten wood upon another as an indicator, continued: 'That's her husband there. They was as fair a couple as you should see anywhere round about; and a good-hearted pair likewise. Ay, I can mind it, though I was but a chiel at the time. She fell in love with this young man of hers, and their banns were asked in some church in London; and the old lord her father actually heard 'em asked the three times, and didn't notice her name, being gabbled on wi' a host of others. When she had married she told her father, and 'a fleed* into a monstrous rage, and said she shouldn' hae a farthing. Lady Elfride said she didn't think of wishing it; if he'd forgie her 'twas all she asked, and as for a living, she was content to sing songs with her husband. This frightened the old lord, and 'a gie'd 'em a house to live in, and a great garden, and a little field or two, and a carriage, and a good few guineas. Well, the poor thing died at her first groaning, and her husband – who was as tender-hearted a man as ever eat meat, and would have died for her – went wild in his mind, and broke his heart (so 'twas said). Anyhow, they were buried the same day – father and mother – but the baby lived. Ay, my lord's family made much of that man then, and put him here with his wife, and there in the corner the man is now. The Sunday after there was a funeral sermon: the text was, "Or ever the silver cord be loosed, or the golden bowl be broken";* and when 'twas preaching the men drew their hands across their eyes several times, and every woman cried out loud.'

'And what became of the baby?' said Stephen, who had frequently heard portions of the story.

'She was brought up by her grandmother, and a pretty maid she were. And she must needs run away with the curate – Parson Swancourt that is now. Then her grandmother died, and the title and everything went away to another branch of the family altogether. Parson Swancourt wasted a good deal of his wife's money, and she left him Miss Elfride. That trick of running away seems to be handed down in families, like craziness or gout. And they two women be alike as peas.'

'Which two?'

'Lady Elfride and young Miss that's alive now. The same hair and eyes: but Miss Elfride's mother was darker a good deal.'

'Life's a strange bubble,' said William Worm musingly. 'For if the Lord's anointment had descended upon women instead of men, Miss Elfride would be Lord Luxellian – Lady, I mean. But as it is, the blood is run out, and she's nothing to the Luxellian family by law, whatever she may be by gospel.'

'I used to fancy,' said Simeon, 'when I seed Miss Elfride hugging the little ladyships, that there was a likeness; but I suppose 'twas only my dream, for years must have altered the old family shape.'

'And now we'll move these two, and home-along,' interposed John Smith, reviving, as became a master, the spirit of labour, which had showed unmistakable signs of being nearly vanquished by the spirit of talk. 'The flagon of ale we don't want we'll led bide here till to-morrow; none of the folk here will touch it 'a b'lieve.'

So the evening's work was concluded, and the party drew from the abode of the quiet dead, closing the old iron door, and shooting the lock loudly into the huge copper staple – an incongruous act of imprisonment towards those who had no dreams of escape.

CHAPTER TWENTY-SEVEN

'How should I greet thee?'*

LOVE frequently dies of time alone – much more frequently of displacement. With Elfride Swancourt a powerful reason why the displacement should be successful was that the new-comer was a greater man than the first. By the side of the instructive and piquant snubbings she received from Knight, Stephen's general agreeableness seemed watery; by the side of Knight's spare love-making, Stephen's continual outflow seemed lackadaisical. She had begun to sigh for somebody further on in manhood. Stephen was hardly enough of a man.

Perhaps there was a proneness to inconstancy in her nature – a nature, to those who contemplate it from a standpoint beyond the influence of that inconstancy, the most exquisite of all in its plasticity and ready sympathies. Partly, too, Stephen's failure to make his hold on her heart a permanent one was his too timid habit of dispraising himself to her – a peculiarity which, exercised towards sensible men, stirs a kindly chord of attachment that a marked assertiveness would leave untouched, but inevitably leads the most sensible woman in the world to undervalue him who practises it. Directly domineering ceases in the man, snubbing begins in the woman; the trite but no less unfortunate fact being that the gentler creature rarely has the capacity to appreciate fair treatment from her natural complement. The abiding perception of the position of Stephen's parents had, of course, a little to do with Elfride's renunciation. To such girls poverty may not be, as to the more worldly masses of humanity, a sin in itself; but it is a sin because graceful and dainty manners seldom exist in such an atmosphere. Few women of old family can be thoroughly taught that a fine soul may wear a smock-frock, and an admittedly common man in one is but a worm in their eyes. John Smith's rough hands and clothes, his wife's speeches, the necessary narrowness of their ways, being constantly under Elfride's notice, were not without their deflecting influence.

On reaching home after the perilous adventure by the sea-shore Knight had felt unwell, and retired almost immediately. The young lady who had so materially assisted him had done the same, but she reappeared, properly clothed, about five o'clock. She wandered restlessly about the house, but not on account of their joint narrow escape from death. The storm which had torn the tree had merely bowed the reed, and with the deliverance of Knight all deep thought of the accident had left her. The mutual avowal which it had been the means of precipitating occupied a far longer length of her meditations.

Elfride's disquiet now was on account of that miserable promise to meet Stephen, which returned like a spectre again and again. The perception of his littleness beside Knight grew upon her alarmingly. She now thought how sound had been her father's advice to her to give him up, and was as passionately desirous of following it as she had hitherto been averse. Perhaps there is nothing more hardening to the tone of young minds than thus to discover how their dearest and strongest wishes become gradually attuned by Time the Cynic to the very note of some selfish policy which in earlier days they despised.

The hour of appointment came, and with it a crisis; and with the crisis a collapse.

'God forgive me – I can't meet Stephen!' she exclaimed to herself. 'I don't love him less, but I love Mr Knight more!'

Yes: she would save herself from a man not fit for her – in spite of vows. She would obey her father, and have no more to do with Stephen Smith. Thus the fickle resolve showed signs of assuming the complexion of a virtue.

The following days were passed without any definite avowal from Knight's lips. Such solitary walks and scenes as that witnessed by Smith in the summer-house were frequent, but he courted her so intangibly that to any but such a delicate perception as Elfride's it would have appeared no courtship at all. The time now really began to be sweet with her. She dismissed the sense of sin in her past actions, and was automatic in the intoxication of the moment. The fact that Knight made no actual declaration was no drawback. Knowing since the betrayal of his sentiments that love for her really existed, she preferred it for the present in its form of essence, and was willing to avoid for awhile the grosser medium of words. Their feelings having been forced to a rather premature demonstration, a reaction was indulged in by both.

But no sooner had she got rid of her troubled conscience on the matter of faithlessness than a new anxiety confronted her. It was lest Knight should accidentally meet Stephen in the parish, and that herself should be the subject of discourse.

Elfride, learning Knight more thoroughly, perceived that, far from having a notion of Stephen's precedence, he had no idea that she had ever been wooed before by anybody. On ordinary occasions she had a tongue so frank as to show her whole mind, and a mind so straightforward as to reveal her heart to its innermost shrine. But the time for a change had come. She never alluded to even a knowledge of Knight's friend. When women are secret they are secret indeed; and more often than not they only begin to be secret with the advent of a second lover.

The elopement was now a spectre worse than the first, and, like the Spirit in Glenfinlas,* it waxed taller with every attempt to lay it. Her natural honesty invited her to confide in Knight, and trust to his generosity for forgiveness: she knew also that as mere policy it would be better to tell him early if he was to be told at all. The longer her concealment the more difficult would be the revelation. But she put it off. The intense fear which accompanies intense love in young women was too strong to allow the exercise of a moral quality antagonistic to itself:

> 'Where love is great, the littlest doubts are fear;
> Where little fears grow great, great love grows there.'*

The match was looked upon as made by her father and mother. The rector remembered her promise to reveal the meaning of the telegram she had received, and two days after the scene in the summer-house asked her pointedly. She was frank with him now.

'I had been corresponding with Stephen Smith ever since he left England, till lately,' she calmly said.

'What!' cried the rector aghast; 'under the eyes of Mr Knight, too?'

'No; when I found I cared most for Mr Knight, I obeyed you.'

'You were very kind, I'm sure. When did you begin to like Mr Knight?'

'I don't see that that is a pertinent question, papa; the telegram was from the shipping agent, and was not sent at my request. It announced the arrival of the vessel bringing him home.'

'Home! What, is he here?'

'Yes; in the village, I believe.'

'Has he tried to see you?'

'Only by fair means. But don't, papa, question me so! It is torture.'

'I will only say one word more,' he replied. 'Have you met him?'

'I have not. I can assure you that at the present moment there is no more of an understanding between me and the young man you so much disliked than between him and you. You told me to forget him; and I have forgotten him.'

'Oh, well; though you did not obey me in the beginning, you are a good girl, Elfride, in obeying me at last.'

'Don't call me "good", papa,' she said bitterly; 'you don't know – and the less said about some things the better. Remember, Mr Knight knows nothing about the other. O, how wrong it all is! I don't know what I am coming to.'

'As matters stand, I should be inclined to tell him; or, at any rate, I should not alarm myself about his knowing. He found out the other day that this was the parish young Smith's father lives in – what puts you in such a flurry?'

'I can't say; but promise – pray don't let him know! It would be my ruin!'

'Pooh, child. Knight is a good fellow and a clever man; but at the same time it does not escape my perceptions that he is no great catch for you. Men of his turn of mind are nothing so wonderful in the way of husbands. If you had chosen to wait you might have mated with a much wealthier man. But remember, I have not a word to say against your having him, if you like him. Charlotte is delighted, as you know.'

'Well, papa,' she said, smiling hopefully through a sigh, 'it is nice to feel that in giving way to – to caring for him, I have pleased my family. But I am not good; O no, I am very far from that!'

'None of us are good, I am sorry to say,' said her father blandly; 'but girls have a chartered right to change their minds, you know. It has been recognized by poets from time immemorial. Catullus says, "Mulier cupido quod dicit amanti, in vento—"* What a memory mine is! However, the passage is, that a woman's words to a lover are as a matter of course written only on wind and water. Now don't be troubled about that, Elfride.'

'Ah, you don't know!'

They had been standing on the lawn, and Knight was seen lingering some way down a winding walk. When Elfride met him it was with a much greater lightness of heart; things were more straightforward now. The responsibility of her fickleness seemed partly shifted from her own shoulders to her father's. Still, there were shadows.

'Ah, could he have known how far I went with Stephen, and yet have said the same, how much happier I should be!' That was her prevailing thought.

In the afternoon the lovers went out together on horseback for an hour or two; and though not wishing to be observed, by reason of the late death of Lady Luxellian, whose funeral had taken place very privately on the previous day, they yet found it necessary to pass East Endelstow Church.

The steps to the vault, as has been stated, were on the outside of the building, immediately under the aisle wall. Being on horseback both Knight and Elfride could overlook the shrubs which screened the churchyard.

'Look, the vault seems still to be open,' said Knight.

'Yes, it is open,' she answered.

'Who is that man close by it? The mason, I suppose?'

'Yes.'

'I wonder if it is John Smith, Stephen's father?'

'I believe it is,' said Elfride.

'Ah, and can it be? I should like to inquire how his son, my truant protégé, is going on. And from your father's description of the vault, the interior must be interesting. Suppose we go in.'

'Had we better, do you think? May not Lord Luxellian be there?'

'It is not at all likely.'

Elfride then assented, since she could do nothing else. Her heart, which at first had quailed in consternation, recovered itself when she considered the character of John Smith. A quiet unassuming man, he would be sure to act towards her as before those love passages with his son, which might have given a more pretentious mechanic airs. So without much alarm she took Knight's arm after dismounting, and went with him between and over the graves. The master-mason recognized her as she approached, and, as usual, lifted his hat respectfully.

'I know you to be Mr Smith, my former friend Stephen's father,' said Knight, directly he had scanned the embrowned and ruddy features of John.

'Yes, sir, I b'lieve I be.'

'How is your son now? I have only once heard from him since he went to India. I daresay you have heard him speak of me – Mr Knight, who became acquainted with him some years ago in Exonbury.'

'Ay, that I have. Stephen is very well, thank you, and he's in England; in fact, he's at home. In short, sir, he's down in the vault there, looking at the departed nobles.'

Elfride's heart fluttered like a butterfly.

Knight looked amazed. 'Well, that is extraordinary,' he murmured. 'Did he know I was in the parish?'

'I really can't say, sir,' said John, wishing himself out of the entanglement he rather suspected than thoroughly understood.

'Would it be considered an intrusion by the family if we went into the vault?'

'O, bless you, no, sir; scores of folk have been stepping down. 'Tis left open a-purpose.'

'We will go down, Elfride.'

'I am afraid the air is close,' she said appealingly.

'O no, ma'am,' said John. ''Twas smelly at first; but we white-limed the walls and arches the day 'twas opened, as we always do, and again on the morning of the funeral; the place is as sweet as a granary.'

'Then I should like you to accompany me, Elfie; having originally sprung from the family too.'

'I don't like going where death is so emphatically present. I'll stay by the horses whilst you go in; they may get loose.'

'What nonsense! I had no idea your sentiments were so flimsy as to be perturbed by a few remnants of mortality; but stay out, if you are so afraid, by all means.'

'O no, I am not afraid; don't say that.'

She held miserably to his arm, thinking that, perhaps, the revelation might as well come at once as ten minutes later, for Stephen would be sure to accompany his friend to his horse.

At first, the gloom of the vault, which was lighted only by a couple of candles, was too great to admit of their seeing anything distinctly; but with a further advance Knight discerned, in front of the black masses lining the walls, a young man standing, and writing in a pocket-book.

Knight said one word: 'Stephen!'

Stephen Smith, not being in such absolute ignorance of Knight's whereabouts as Knight had been of Smith's, instantly recognized his friend, and knew by rote the outlines of the fair woman standing behind him.

Stephen came forward and shook him by the hand, without speaking.

'Why have you not written, my boy?' said Knight, without in any way signifying Elfride's presence to Stephen. To the essayist, Smith was still the country lad whom he had patronized and tended; one to whom the formal presentation of a lady betrothed to himself would have seemed incongruous and absurd.

'Why haven't you written to me?' said Stephen.

'Ah, yes. Why haven't I? why haven't we? That's always the query which we cannot clearly answer without an unsatisfactory sense of our inadequacies. However, I have not forgotten you, Smith. And now we have met; and we must meet again, and have a longer chat than this can conveniently be. I must know all you have been doing. That you have thriven, I know, and you must teach me the way.'

Elfride stood in the background. Stephen had read the position at a glance, and immediately guessed that she had never mentioned his name to Knight. His tact in avoiding catastrophes was the chief quality which made him intellectually respectable, in which quality he far transcended Knight; and he decided that a tranquil issue out of the encounter, without any harrowing of the feelings of either

Knight or Elfride, was to be attempted if possible. His old sense of indebtedness to Knight had never wholly forsaken him; his love for Elfride was generous now.

As far as he dared look at her movements he saw that her bearing towards him would be dictated by his own towards her; and if he acted as a stranger she would do likewise as a means of deliverance. Circumstances favouring this course, it was desirable also to be rather reserved towards Knight, to shorten the meeting as much as possible.

'I am afraid that my time is almost too short to allow even of such a pleasure,' he said. 'I leave here to-morrow. And until I start for the Continent and India, which will be in a fortnight, I shall have hardly a moment to spare.'

Knight's disappointment and dissatisfied looks at this reply sent a pang through Stephen as great as any he had felt at the sight of Elfride. The words about shortness of time were literally true, but their tone was far from being so. He would have been gratified to talk with Knight as in past times, and saw as a dead loss to himself that, to save the woman who cared nothing for him, he was deliberately throwing away his friend.

'Oh, I am sorry to hear that,' said Knight, in a changed tone. 'But of course, if you have weighty concerns to attend to they must not be neglected. And if this is to be our first and last meeting, let me say that I wish you success with all my heart!' Knight's warmth revived towards the end; the solemn impressions he was beginning to receive from the scene around them abstracting from his heart as a puerility any momentary vexation at words. 'It is a strange place for us to meet in,' he continued, looking round the vault.

Stephen briefly assented, and there was a silence. The blackened coffins were now revealed more clearly than at first, the whitened walls and arches throwing them forward in strong relief. It was a scene which was remembered by all three as an indelible mark in their history. Knight, with an abstracted face, was standing between his companions, though a little in advance of them, Elfride being on his right hand, and Stephen Smith on his left. The white daylight on his right side gleamed faintly in, and was toned to a blueness by contrast with the yellow rays from the candle against the wall.

Elfride, timidly shrinking back, and nearest the entrance, received most of the light therefrom, whilst Stephen was entirely in candle-light, and to him the spot of outer sky visible above the steps was as a steely blue patch, and nothing more.

'I have been here two or three times since it was opened,' said Stephen. 'My father was engaged in the work, you know.'

'Yes. What are you doing?' Knight inquired, looking at the note-book and pencil Stephen held in his hand.

'I have been sketching a few details in the church, and since then I have been copying the names from some of the coffins here. Before I left England I used to do a good deal of this sort of thing.'

'Yes; of course. Ah, that's poor Lady Luxellian, I suppose.' Knight pointed to a coffin of light satinwood, which stood on the stone sleepers in the new niche. 'And the remainder of the family are on this side. Who are those two, so snug and close together?'

Stephen's voice altered slightly as he replied: 'That's Lady Elfride Kingsmore – born Luxellian, and that is Arthur, her husband. I have heard my father say that they – he – ran away with her, and married her against the wish of her parents.'

'Then I imagine this to be where you got your Christian name, Miss Swancourt?' said Knight, turning to her. 'I think you told me it was three or four generations ago that your family branched off from the Luxellians?'

'She was my grandmother,' said Elfride, vainly endeavouring to moisten her dry lips before she spoke. Elfride had then the conscience-stricken look of Guido's Magdalen,* rendered upon a more childlike form. She kept her face partially away from Knight and Stephen, and set her eyes upon the sky visible outside, as if her salvation depended upon quickly reaching it. Her left hand rested lightly within Knight's arm, half withdrawn, from a sense of shame at claiming him before her old lover, yet unwilling to renounce him; so that her glove merely touched his sleeve. '"Can one be pardoned, and retain the offence?"'* quoted Elfride's heart then.

Conversation seemed to have no self-sustaining power, and went on in the shape of disjointed remarks. 'One's mind gets thronged with thoughts while standing so solemnly here,' Knight said, in a measured quiet voice. 'How much has been said on death from time to time! how much we ourselves can think upon it! We may fancy each of these who lie here saying:

'For Thou, to make my fall more great,
Didst lift me up on high.'*

What comes next, Elfride? It is the Hundred-and-second Psalm I am thinking of.'

'Yes, I know it,' she murmured, and went on in a still lower voice, seemingly afraid for any words from the emotional side of her nature to reach Stephen:

'"My days, just hastening to their end,
Are like an evening shade;
My beauty doth, like wither'd grass,
With waning lustre fade."'

'Well,' said Knight musingly, 'let us leave them. Such occasions as these seem to compel us to roam outside ourselves, far away from the fragile frame we live in, and to expand till our perception grows so vast that our physical reality bears no sort of proportion to it. We look back upon the weak and minute stem on which this luxuriant growth depends, and ask, Can it be possible that such a capacity has a foundation so small? Must I again return to my daily walk in that narrow cell, a human body, where worldly thoughts can torture me? Do we not?'

'Yes,' said Stephen and Elfride.

'One has a sense of wrong, too, that such an appreciative breadth as a sentient being possesses should be committed to the frail casket of a body. What weakens one's intentions regarding the future like the thought of this? . . . However, let us tune ourselves to a more cheerful chord, for there's a great deal to be done yet by us all.'

As Knight meditatively addressed his juniors thus, unconscious of the deception practised, for different reasons, by the severed hearts at his side, and of the scenes that had in earlier days united them, each one felt that he and she did not gain by contrast with their musing mentor. Physically not so handsome as either the youthful architect or the rector's daughter, the thoroughness and integrity of Knight illuminated his features with a dignity not even incipient in the other two. It is difficult to frame rules which shall apply to both sexes, and Elfride, an undeveloped girl, must, perhaps, hardly be laden with the moral responsibilities which attach to a man in like circumstances. The charm of woman, too, lies partly in her subtleness in matters of love. But if honesty is a virtue in itself, Elfride, having none of it now, seemed, being for being, scarcely good enough for Knight. Stephen, though deceptive for no unworthy purpose, was deceptive after all; and whatever high results grace such strategy if it succeed, it seldom draws admiration, especially when it fails.

On an ordinary occasion, had Knight been even quite alone with Stephen, he would hardly have alluded to his possible relationship to Elfride. But moved by attendant circumstances Knight was impelled to be confiding.

'Stephen,' he said, 'this lady is Miss Swancourt. I am staying at her father's house, as you probably know.' He stepped a few paces nearer to Smith, and said in a lower tone: 'I may as well tell you that we are engaged to be married.'

Low as the words had been spoken, Elfride had heard them, and awaited Stephen's reply in breathless silence, if that could be called silence where Elfride's dress, at each throb of her heart, shook and indicated it like a pulse-glass,* rustling also against the wall in reply to the same throbbing. The ray of daylight which reached her face lent it a blue pallor in comparison with those of the other two.

'I congratulate you,' Stephen whispered; and said aloud, 'I know Miss Swancourt – a little. You must remember that my father is a parishioner of Mr Swancourt's.'

'I thought you might possibly not have lived at home since they have been here.'

'I have never lived at home, certainly, since that time.'

'I have seen Mr Smith,' faltered Elfride.

'Well, there is no excuse for me. As strangers to each other I ought, I suppose, to have introduced you: as acquaintances, I should not have stood so persistently between you. But the fact is, Smith, you seem a boy to me, even now.'

Stephen appeared to have a more than previous consciousness of the intense cruelty of his fate at the present moment. He could not repress the words, uttered with a dim bitterness:

'You should have said that I seemed still the rural builder's son I am, and hence an unfit subject for the ceremony of introductions.'

'O no, no! I won't have that.' Knight endeavoured to give his reply a laughing tone in Elfride's ears, and an earnestness in Stephen's: in both which efforts he signally failed, and produced a forced speech pleasant to neither. 'Well, let us go into the open air again; Miss Swancourt, you are particularly silent. You mustn't mind Smith. I have known him for years, as I have told you.'

'Yes, you have,' she said.

'To think she has never mentioned her knowledge of me!' Smith murmured, and thought with some remorse how much her conduct resembled his own on his first arrival at her house as a stranger to the place.

They ascended to the daylight, Knight taking no further notice of Elfride's manner, which, as usual, he attributed to the natural shyness of a young woman at being discovered walking with him on terms which left not much doubt of their meaning. Elfride stepped a little in advance, and passed through the churchyard.

'You are changed very considerably, Smith,' said Knight, 'and I suppose it is no more than was to be expected. However, don't imagine that I shall feel any the less interest in you and your fortunes whenever you care to confide them to me. I have not forgotten the attachment you spoke of as your reason for going away to India. A London young lady, was it not? I hope all is prosperous?'

'No: the match is broken off.'

It being always difficult to know whether to express sorrow or gladness under such circumstances – all depending upon the character of the match – Knight took shelter in the safe words: 'I trust it was for the best.'

'I hope it was. But I beg that you will not press me further: no, you have not pressed me – I don't mean that – but I would rather not speak upon the subject.'

Stephen's words were hurried.

Knight said no more, and they followed in the footsteps of Elfride, who still kept some paces in advance, and had not heard Knight's unconscious allusion to her. Stephen bade him adieu at the churchyard-gate without going outside, and watched whilst he and his sweetheart mounted their horses.

'Good heavens, Elfride,' Knight exclaimed, 'how pale you are! I suppose I ought not to have taken you into that close vault. What is the matter?'

'Nothing,' said Elfride faintly. 'I shall be myself in a moment. All was so strange and unexpected down there, that it made me unwell.'

'I thought you said very little. Shall I get some water?'

'No, no.'

'Do you think it is safe for you to mount?'

'Quite – indeed it is,' she said, with a look of appeal.

'Now then – up she goes!' whispered Knight, and lifted her tenderly into the saddle.

Her old lover still looked on at the performance as he leant over the gate a dozen yards off. Once in the saddle, and having a firm grip of the reins, she turned her head as if by a resistless fascination, and for the first time since that memorable parting on the moor outside St Launce's after the passionate attempt at marriage with him, Elfride looked in the face of the young man she first had loved. He was the youth who had called her his inseparable wife many a time, and whom she had even addressed as her husband. Their eyes met. Measurement of life should be proportioned rather to the intensity of the experience than to its actual length. Their glance, but a moment chronologically, was a season in their history. To Elfride the intense agony of reproach in Stephen's eye was a nail piercing her heart with a deadliness no words can describe. With a spasmodic effort she withdrew her eyes, urged on the horse, and in the chaos of perturbed memories was oblivious of any presence beside her. The deed of deception was complete.

Gaining a knoll on which the park transformed itself into wood and copse, Knight came still closer to her side, and said, 'Are you better now, dearest?'

'O yes.' She pressed a hand to her eyes, as if to blot out the image of Stephen. A vivid scarlet spot now shone with preternatural brightness in the centre of each cheek, leaving the remainder of her face lily-white as before.

'Elfride,' said Knight, rather in his old tone of mentor, 'you know I don't for a moment chide you, but is there not a great deal of unwomanly weakness in your allowing yourself to be so overwhelmed by the sight of what, after all, is no novelty? Every woman worthy of the name should, I think, be able to look upon death with something like composure. Surely you think so too?'

'Yes; I own it.'

His obtuseness to the cause of her indisposition, by evidencing his entire freedom from the suspicion of anything behind the scenes, showed how incapable Knight was of deception himself, rather than any inherent dulness in him regarding human nature. This, clearly perceived by Elfride, added poignancy to her self-reproach, and she idolized him the more because of their difference. Even the recent sight of Stephen's face and the sound of his voice, which for a moment had stirred a chord or two of ancient kindness, were unable to keep down the adoration re-existent now that he was again out of view.

She had replied to Knight's question hastily, and immediately went on to speak of indifferent subjects. After they had reached home she was apart from him till dinner-time. When dinner was over, and they were watching the dusk in the drawing-room, Knight stepped out upon the terrace. Elfride went after him very decisively, on the spur of a virtuous intention.

'Mr Knight, I want to tell you something,' she said, with quiet firmness.

'And what is it about?' gaily returned her lover. 'Happiness, I hope. Do not let anything keep you so sad as you seem to have been to-day.'

'I cannot mention the matter until I tell you the whole substance of it,' she said. 'And that I will do to-morrow. I have been reminded of it to-day. It is about something I once did, and don't think I ought to have done.'

This, it must be said, was rather a mild way of referring to a frantic passion and flight which, much or little in itself, only accident had saved from being a scandal in the public eye.

Knight thought the matter some trifle, and said pleasantly:

'Then I am not to hear the dreadful confession now?'

'No, not now. I did not mean to-night,' Elfride responded, with a slight decline in the firmness of her voice. 'It is not light as you think it – it troubles me a great deal.' Fearing now the effect of her own earnestness, she added forcedly, 'Though, perhaps, you may think it light after all.'

'But you have not said when it is to be?'

'To-morrow morning. Name a time, will you, and bind me to it? I want you to fix an hour, because I am weak, and may otherwise try to get out of it.' She added a little artificial laugh, which showed how timorous her resolution was still.

'Well, say after breakfast – at eleven o'clock.'

'Yes, eleven o'clock. I promise you. Bind me strictly to my word.'

CHAPTER TWENTY-EIGHT

'I lull a fancy, trouble-tost.'*

'MISS SWANCOURT, it is eleven o'clock.'

She was looking out of her dressing-room window on the first floor, and Knight was regarding her from the terrace balustrade, upon which he had been idly sitting for some time – dividing the glances of his eye between the pages of a book in his hand, the brilliant hues of the geraniums and calceolarias, and the open window above-mentioned.

'Yes, it is, I know. I am coming.'

He drew closer, and under the window.

'How are you this morning, Elfride? You look no better for your long night's rest.'

She appeared at the door shortly after, took his offered arm, and together they walked slowly down the gravel path leading to the river and away under the trees.

Her resolution, sustained during the last fifteen hours, had been to tell the whole truth, and now the moment had come.

Step by step they advanced, and still she did not speak. They were nearly at the end of the walk, when Knight broke the silence.

'Well, what is the confession, Elfride?'

She paused a moment, drew a long breath; and this is what she said:

'I told you one day – or rather I gave you to understand – what was not true. I fancy you thought me to mean I was twenty my next birthday, but it was my last I was twenty.'

The moment had been too much for her. Now that the crisis had come, no qualms of conscience, no love of honesty, no yearning to make a confidence and obtain forgiveness with a kiss, could string Elfride up to the venture. Her dread lest he should be unforgiving was heightened by the thought of yesterday's artifice, which might possibly add disgust to his disappointment. The certainty of one more day's affection, which she gained by silence, outvalued the hope of a perpetuity combined with the risk of all.

The trepidation caused by these thoughts on what she had intended to say shook so naturally the words she did say, that Knight never for a moment suspected them to be a last moment's substitution. He smiled and pressed her hand warmly.

'My dear Elfie – yes, you are now – no protestation – what a winning little woman you are, to be so absurdly scrupulous about a mere iota! Really, I never once have thought whether your twentieth year was the last or the present. And, by George, well I may not; for it would never do for a staid fogey a dozen years older to stand upon such a trifle as that.'

'Don't praise me – don't praise me! Though I prize it from your lips, I don't deserve it now.'

But Knight, being in an exceptionally genial mood, merely saw this distressful exclamation as modesty. 'Well,' he added, after a minute, 'I like you all the better, you know, for such moral precision, although I called it absurd.' He went on with tender earnestness: 'For, Elfride, there is one thing I do love to see in a woman – that is, a soul truthful and clear as heaven's light. I could put up with anything if I had that – forgive nothing if I had it not. Elfride, you have such a soul, if ever woman had; and having it, retain it, and don't ever listen to the fashionable theories of the day about a woman's privileges and natural right to practise wiles. Depend upon it, my dear girl, that a noble woman must be as honest as a noble man. I specially mean by honesty, fairness not only in matters of business and social detail, but in all the delicate dealings of love, to which the licence given to your sex particularly refers.'

Elfride looked troublously at the trees.

'Now let us go on to the river, Elfie.'

'I would if I had a hat on,' she said with a shade of suppressed woe.

'I will get it for you,' said Knight, very willing to purchase her companionship at so cheap a price. 'You sit down there a minute.' And he turned and walked rapidly back to the house for the article in question.

Elfride sat down upon one of the rustic benches which adorned this portion of the grounds, and remained with her eyes upon the grass. She was induced to lift them by hearing the brush of light and irregular footsteps hard by. Passing along the path which intersected the one she was in and traversed the outer shrubberies, Elfride beheld the farmer's widow, Mrs Jethway. Before she noticed Elfride she paused to look at the house, portions of which were visible through the bushes. Elfride, shrinking back, hoped the unpleasant woman might go on without seeing her. But Mrs Jethway, silently apostrophizing the house, with actions which seemed dictated by a half-overturned reason, had discerned the girl, and immediately came up and stood in front of her.

'Ah, Miss Swancourt! Why did you disturb me? Mustn't I trespass here?'

'You may walk here if you like, Mrs Jethway. I do not disturb you.'

'You disturb my mind, and my mind is my whole life; for my boy is there still, and he is gone from my body.'

'Yes, poor young man. I was sorry when he died.'

'Do you know what he died of?'

'Consumption.'

'O no, no!' said the widow. 'That word "consumption" covers a good deal. He died because you were his own well-agreed sweetheart, and then proved false – and it killed him. Yes, Miss Swancourt,' she said in an excited whisper, 'you killed my son!'

'How can you be so wicked and foolish!' replied Elfride, rising indignantly. But indignation was not natural to her, and having been so worn and harrowed by late events, she lost any powers of defence that mood might have lent her. 'I could not help his loving me, Mrs Jethway!'

'That's just what you could have helped. You know how it began, Miss Elfride. Yes: you said you liked the name of Felix better than any other name in the parish, and you knew it was his name, and that those you said it to would report it to him.'

'I knew it was his name – of course I did; but I am sure, Mrs Jethway, I did not intend anybody to tell him.'

'But you knew they would.'

'No, I didn't.'

'And then, after that, when you were riding on Revels-day* by our house, and the lads were gathered there, and you wanted to dismount, when Jim Drake and George Upway and three or four more ran forward to hold your pony, and Felix stood back timid, why did you beckon to him, and say you would rather he held it?'

'O Mrs Jethway, you do think so mistakenly! I liked him best – that's why I wanted him to do it. He was gentle and nice – I always thought him so – and I liked him.'

'Then why did you let him kiss you?'

'It is a falsehood; O it is, it is!' said Elfride, weeping with desperation. 'He came behind me, and attempted to kiss me; and that was why I told him never to let me see him again.'

'But you did not tell your father or anybody, as you would have if you had looked upon it then as the insult you now pretend it was.'

'He begged me not to tell, and foolishly enough I did not. And I wish I had now. I little expected to be scourged with my own kindness. Pray leave me, Mrs Jethway.' The girl only expostulated now.

'Well, you harshly dismissed him, and he died. And before his body was cold you took another to your heart. Then as carelessly sent him about his business, and took a third. And if you consider that nothing, Miss Swancourt,' she continued, drawing closer; 'it led on to what was very serious indeed. Have you forgotten the would-be runaway marriage? The journey to London, and the return the next day without being married, and that there's enough disgrace in that to ruin a woman's good name far less light than yours? You may have: I have not. Fickleness towards a lover is bad, but fickleness after playing the wife is wantonness.'

'O, it's a wicked cruel lie! Do not say it; O, do not!'

'Does your new man know of it? I think not, or he would be no man of yours! As much of the story as was known is creeping about the neighbourhood even now; but I know more than any of them, and why should I respect your love?'

'I defy you!' cried Elfride tempestuously. 'Do and say all you can to ruin me; try; put your tongue at work; I invite it! I defy you as a slanderous woman! Look, there he comes.' And her voice trembled greatly as she saw through the leaves the beloved form of Knight coming from the door with her hat in his hand. 'Tell him at once; I can bear it.'

'Not now,' said the woman, and disappeared down the path.

The excitement of her latter words had restored colour to

Elfride's cheeks; and hastily wiping her eyes she walked further on, so that by the time her lover had overtaken her the traces of emotion had nearly disappeared from her face. Knight put the hat upon her head, took her hand, and drew it within his arm.

It was the last day but one previous to their departure for St Leonards; and Knight seemed to have a purpose in being much in her company that day. They rambled along the valley. The season was that period in the autumn when the foliage alone of an ordinary plantation is rich enough in hues to exhaust the chromatic combinations of an artist's palette. Most lustrous of all are the beeches, graduating from bright rusty red at the extremity of the boughs to a bright yellow at their inner parts; young oaks are still of a neutral green; Scotch firs and hollies are nearly blue; whilst occasional dottings of other varieties give maroons and purples of every tinge.

The river – such as it was – here pursued its course amid flagstones as level as a pavement, but divided by crevices of irregular width. With the summer drought the torrent had narrowed till it was now but a thread of crystal clearness, meandering along a central channel in the rocky bed of the winter current. Knight scrambled through the bushes which at this point nearly covered the brook from sight, and leapt down upon the dry portion of the river bottom.

'Elfride, I never saw such a sight!' he exclaimed. 'The hazels overhang the river's course in a perfect arch, and the floor is beautifully paved. The place reminds one of the passages of a cloister. Let me help you down.'

He assisted her through the marginal underwood and down to the stones. They walked on together to a tiny cascade about a foot wide and high, and sat down beside it on the flags that for nine months in the year were submerged beneath a gushing bourne. From their feet trickled the attenuated thread of water which alone remained to tell the intent and reason of this leaf-covered aisle, and journeyed on in a zigzag line till lost in the shade.

Knight, leaning on his elbow, after contemplating all this, looked critically at Elfride.

'Does not such a luxuriant head of hair exhaust itself and get thin as the years go on from eighteen to eight-and-twenty?' he asked at length.

'O no!' she said quickly, with a visible disinclination to harbour such a thought, which came upon her with an unpleasantness whose force it would be difficult for men to understand. She added afterwards, with smouldering uneasiness, 'Do you really think that a great abundance of hair is more likely to get thin than a moderate quantity?'

'Yes, I really do. I believe – am almost sure, in fact – that if statistics could be obtained on the subject, you would find the persons with thin hair were those who had a superabundance originally, and that those who start with a moderate quantity retain it without much loss.'

Elfride's troubles sat upon her face as well as in her heart. Perhaps to a woman it is almost as dreadful to think of losing her beauty as of losing her reputation. At any rate, she looked quite as gloomy as she had looked at any minute that day.

'You shouldn't be so troubled about a mere personal adornment,' said Knight, with some of the severity of tone that had been customary before she had beguiled him into softness.

'I think it is a woman's duty to be as beautiful as she can. If I were a scholar, I would give you chapter and verse for it from one of your own Latin authors. I know there is such a passage, for papa has alluded to it.'

'"Munditiæ, et ornatus, et cultus," &c.* – is that it? A passage in Livy which is no defence at all.'

'No, it is not that.'

'Never mind, then; for I have a reason for not taking up my old cudgels against you, Elfie. Can you guess what the reason is?'

'No; but I am glad to hear it,' she said thankfully. 'For it is dreadful when you talk so. For whatever dreadful name the weakness may deserve, I must candidly own that I am terrified to think my hair may ever get thin.'

'Of course; a sensible woman would rather lose her wits than her beauty.'

'I don't care if you do say satire and judge me cruelly. I know my hair is beautiful; everybody says so.'

'Why, my dear girl,' he tenderly replied, 'I have not said anything against it. But you know what is said about handsome being and handsome doing.'

'Poor Miss Handsome-does cuts but a sorry figure beside Miss Handsome-is in every man's eyes, your own not excepted, Mr Knight, though it pleases you to throw off so,' said Elfride saucily. And lowering her voice: 'You ought not to have taken so much trouble to save me from falling over the cliff, for you don't think mine a life worth much trouble evidently.'

'Perhaps you think mine was not worth yours.'

'It was worth anybody's!'

Her hand was plashing in the little waterfall, and her eyes were bent the same way.

'You talk about my severity with you, Elfride. You are unkind to me, you know.'

'How?' she asked, looking up from her idle occupation.

'After my taking trouble to get jewellery to please you, you wouldn't accept it.'

'Perhaps I would now; perhaps I want to.'

'Do!' said Knight.

And the packet was withdrawn from his pocket and presented the third time. Elfride took it with delight. The obstacle was rent in twain, and the significant gift was hers.

'I'll take out these ugly ones at once,' she exclaimed, 'and I'll wear yours – shall I?'

'I should be gratified.'

Now, though it may seem unlikely, considering how far the two had gone in converse, Knight had never yet ventured to kiss Elfride. Far slower was he than Stephen Smith in matters like that. The utmost advance he had made in such demonstrations had been to the degree witnessed by Stephen in the summer-house. So Elfride's cheek being still forbidden fruit to him he said impulsively:

'Elfie, I should like to touch that seductive ear of yours. Those are my gifts; so let me dress you in them.'

She hesitated with a stimulating hesitation.

'Let me put just one in its place, then?'

Her face grew much warmer.

'I don't think it would be quite the usual or proper course,' she said, suddenly turning and resuming her operation of plashing in the miniature cataract.

The stillness of things was disturbed by a bird coming to the streamlet to drink. After watching him dip his bill, sprinkle himself, and fly into a tree, Knight replied, with the courteous brusqueness she so much liked to hear –

'Elfride, now you may as well be fair. You would mind my doing it but little, I think; so give me leave, do.'

'I will be fair, then,' she said confidingly, and looking him full in the face. It was a particular pleasure to her to be able to do a little honesty without fear. 'I should not mind your doing so – I should like such an attention. My thought was, would it be right to let you?'

'Then I will!' he rejoined, with that singular earnestness about a small matter – in the eyes of a ladies' man but a peg for momentary flirtation or jest – which is only found in deep natures who have been wholly unused to toying with womankind, and which, from its unwontedness, is in itself a tribute the most precious that can be rendered, and homage the most exquisite to be received.

'And you shall,' she whispered, without reserve, and no longer mistress of the ceremonies. And then Elfride inclined herself towards him, thrust back her hair, and poised her head sideways. In doing this her arm and shoulder necessarily rested against his breast.

At the touch, the sensation of both seemed to be concentrated at the point of contact. All the time he was performing the delicate manœuvre Knight trembled like a young surgeon in his first operation.

'Now the other,' said Knight in a whisper.

'No, no.'

'Why not?'

'I don't know exactly.'

'You must know.'

'It agitates me so. Let us go home.'

'Don't say that, Elfride. What is it, after all? A mere nothing. Now turn round, dearest.'

She was powerless to disobey, and turned forthwith; and then, without any defined intention in either's mind, his face and hers drew closer together; and he supported her there, and kissed her.

Knight was at once the most ardent and the coolest man alive.

When his emotions slumbered he appeared almost phlegmatic; when they were moved he was no less than passionate. And now, without having quite intended an early marriage, he put the question plainly. It came with all the ardour which was the accumulation of long years behind a natural reserve.

'Elfride, when shall we be married?'

The words were sweet to her; but there was a bitter in the sweet. These newly-overt acts of his, which had culminated in this plain question, coming on the very day of Mrs Jethway's blasting reproaches, painted distinctly her fickleness as an enormity. Loving him in secret had not seemed such thoroughgoing inconstancy as the same love recognized and acted upon in the face of threats. Her distraction was interpreted by him at her side as the outward signs of an unwonted experience.

'I don't press you for an answer now, darling,' he said, seeing she was not likely to give a lucid reply. 'Take your time.'

Knight was as honourable a man as was ever loved and deluded by woman. It may be said that his blindness in love proved the point, for shrewdness in love usually goes with meanness in general. Once the passion had mastered him, insight began to be blurred. Knight as a lover was far simpler than his friend Stephen, who in other capacities was shallow beside him.

Without saying more on the subject of their marriage Knight held her at arm's length, as if she had been a large bouquet, and looked at her with critical affection.

'Does your pretty gift become me?' she inquired, with tears of excitement on the fringes of her eyes.

'Undoubtedly, perfectly!' said her lover, adopting a lighter tone to put her at her ease. 'Ah, you should see them; you look shinier than ever. Fancy that I have been able to improve you!'

'Am I really so nice? I am glad for your sake. I wish I could see myself.'

'You can't. You must wait till we get home.'

'I shall never be able,' she said, laughing. 'Look: here's a way.'

'So there is. Well done, woman's wit!'

'Hold me steady!'

'O yes.'

'And don't let me fall, will you?'

'By no means.'

Below their seat the thread of water paused to spread out into a smooth small pool. Knight supported her whilst she knelt down and leant over it.

'I can see myself. Really, try as religiously as I will, I cannot help admiring my appearance in them.'

'Doubtless. How can you be so fond of finery? I believe you are corrupting me into a taste for it. I used to hate every such thing before I knew you.'

'I like ornaments, because I want people to admire what you possess, and envy you, and say, "I wish I was he."'

'I suppose I ought not to object after that. And how much longer are you going to look in there at yourself?'

'Until you are tired of holding me? O, I want to ask you something.' And she turned round. 'Now tell truly, won't you? What colour of hair do you like best now?'

Knight did not answer at the moment.

'Say light, do!' she whispered coaxingly. 'Don't say dark, as you did that time.'

'Light-brown, then. Exactly the colour of my lady's.'

'Really?' said Elfride, enjoying as truth what she knew to be flattery.

'Yes.'

'And blue eyes, too, not hazel? Say yes, say yes!'

'One recantation is enough for to-day.'

'No, no.'

'Very well, blue eyes.' And Knight laughed, and drew her close and kissed her the second time, which operations he performed with the carefulness of a fruiterer touching a bunch of grapes so as not to disturb their bloom.

Elfride objected to a second, and flung away her face, the movement causing a slight disarrangement of hat and hair. Hardly thinking what she said in the trepidation of the moment, she exclaimed, clapping her hand to her ear –

'Ah, we must be careful! I lost the other earring doing like this.'

No sooner did she realize the significant words than a troubled look passed across her face, and she shut her lips as if to keep them back.

'Doing like what?' said Knight, perplexed.

'Oh, sitting down out of doors,' she replied hastily.

CHAPTER TWENTY-NINE

'Care, thou canker'*

IT is an evening at the beginning of October, and the mellowest of autumn sunsets irradiates London, even to its uttermost eastern end. Between the eye and the flaming West, columns of smoke stand up in the still air like tall trees. Everything in the shade is rich and misty blue.

Mr and Mrs Swancourt and Elfride are looking at these lustrous and lurid contrasts from the window of a large hotel near Blackfriars Bridge. The visit to their friends at St Leonards is over, and they are staying a day or two in the metropolis on their way home.

Knight spent the same interval of time in crossing over to Brittany by way of Jersey and St Malo. He then passed through Normandy, and returned to London also, his arrival there having been two days later than that of Elfride and her parents.

So the evening of this October day saw them all meeting at the above-mentioned hotel, where they had previously engaged apartments. During the afternoon Knight had been to his lodgings at Richmond to make a little change in the nature of his baggage; and on coming up again there was never ushered by a bland waiter into a comfortable room a happier man than Knight when shown to where Elfride and her stepmother were sitting after a fatiguing day of shopping.

Elfride looked none the better for her change: Knight was as brown as a nut. They were soon engaged by themselves in a corner of the room. Now that the precious words of promise had been spoken, the young girl had no idea of keeping up her price by the system of reserve which other more accomplished maidens use. Her lover was with her again, and it was enough: she made her heart over to him entirely.

Dinner was soon despatched. And when a preliminary round of conversation concerning their doings since the last parting had been concluded, they reverted to the subject of to-morrow's journey home.

'That enervating ride through the myrtle climate of South Devon – how I dread it to-morrow!' Mrs Swancourt was saying. 'I had hoped the weather would have been cooler by this time.'

'Did you ever go by water?'* said Knight.

'Never – by never, I mean not since the time of railways.'

'Then if you can afford an additional day, I propose that we do it,' said Knight. 'The Channel is like a lake just now. We should reach Plymouth in about forty hours, I think, and the boats start from just below London Bridge here' (pointing over his shoulder eastward).

'Hear, hear!' said the rector.

'It's an idea, certainly,' said his wife.

'Of course these coasters are rather tubby,' said Knight. 'But you wouldn't mind that?'

'No: we wouldn't mind.'

'And the saloon is a place like the fishmarket of a ninth-rate country town, but that wouldn't matter?'

'O dear, no. If we had only thought of it soon enough we might have had the use of Lord Luxellian's yacht. But never mind, we'll go. We shall escape the worrying rattle through the whole length of London to-morrow morning – not to mention the risk of being killed by excursion trains, which is not a little one at this time of the year, if the papers are true.'

Elfride, too, thought the arrangement delightful; and accordingly, ten o'clock the following morning saw two cabs crawling round by the Mint, and between the preternaturally high walls of Nightingale Lane towards the river side.

The first vehicle was occupied by the travellers in person, and the second brought up the luggage, under the supervision of Mrs Snewson, Mrs Swancourt's maid – and for the last fortnight Elfride's also; for although the younger lady had never been accustomed to any such attendant at robing times, her stepmother forced her into a semblance of familiarity with one when they were away from home.

Presently waggons, bales, and smells of all descriptions increased to such an extent that the advance of the cabs was at the slowest possible rate. At intervals it was necessary to halt entirely, that the heavy vehicles unloading in front might be moved aside, a feat which was not accomplished without a deal of swearing and noise. The rector put his head out of the window.

'Surely there must be some mistake in the way,' he said with great concern, drawing in his head again. 'There's not a respectable conveyance to be seen here except ours. I've heard that there are strange dens in this part of London, into which people have been entrapped and murdered – surely there is no conspiracy on the part of the cabman?'

'O no, no. It is all right,' said Mr Knight, who was as placid as dewy eve by the side of Elfride.

'But what I argue from,' said the rector, with a greater emphasis of uneasiness, 'are plain appearances. This can't be the highway from London to Plymouth by water, because it is no way at all to any place. We shall miss our steamer and our train too – that's what I think.'

'Depend upon it we are right. In fact, here we are.'

'Trimmer's Wharf,'* said the cabman, opening the door.

No sooner had they alighted than they perceived a tussle going on between the hindmost cabman and a crowd of light porters who had charged him in column, to obtain possession of the bags and boxes, Mrs Snewson's hands being seen stretched towards heaven in the midst of the mêlée. Knight advanced gallantly, and after a hard struggle reduced the crowd to two, upon whose shoulders and trucks the goods vanished away in the direction of the water's edge with startling rapidity.

Then more of the same tribe, who had run on ahead, were heard shouting to boatmen, three of whom pulled alongside, and two being vanquished, the luggage went tumbling into the remaining one.

'Never saw such a dreadful scene in my life – never!' said Mr Swancourt, floundering into the boat. 'Worse than Famine and Sword* upon one. I thought such customs were confined to continental ports. Aren't you astonished, Elfride?'

'O no,' said Elfride, appearing amid the dingy scene like a rainbow in a murky sky. 'It is a pleasant novelty, I think.'

'Where in the wide ocean is our steamer?' the rector inquired. 'I can see nothing but old hulks,* for the life of me.'

'Just behind that one,' said Knight; 'we shall soon be round under her.'

The object of their search was soon after disclosed to view – a great lumbering form of inky blackness, which looked as if it had never known the touch of a paint-brush for fifty years. It was lying beside just such another, and the way on board was down a narrow lane of water between the two, about a yard and a half wide at one end, and gradually converging to a point. At the moment of their entry into this narrow passage a brilliantly painted rival paddled down the river like a trotting steed, creating such a series of waves and splashes that their frail wherry was tossed like a teacup, and the rector and his wife slanted this way and that, inclining their heads into contact with a Punch-and-Judy air and countenance, the wavelets striking the sides of the two hulls, and flapping back into their laps.

'Dreadful! horrible!' Mr Swancourt murmured privately; and said aloud, 'I thought we walked on board. I don't think really I should have come, if I had known this trouble was attached to it.'

'If they must splash, I wish they would splash us with clean water,' said the elder lady, wiping her dress with her handkerchief.

'I hope it is perfectly safe,' continued the rector.

'O papa! you are not very brave,' cried Elfride merrily.

'Bravery is only obtuseness to the perception of contingencies,' Mr Swancourt severely answered.

Mrs Swancourt laughed, and Elfride laughed, and Knight laughed, in the midst of which pleasantness a man shouted to them from some position between their heads and the sky, and they found they were close to the *Juliet*, into which they quiveringly ascended.

It having been found that the lowness of the tide would prevent their getting off for an hour, the Swancourts, having nothing else to do, allowed their eyes to idle upon men in blue jerseys performing mysterious mending operations with tar-twine;* they turned to look at the dashes of lurid sunlight, like burnished copper stars afloat on the ripples, which danced into and tantalized their vision; or listened to the loud music of a steam-crane at work close by; or to sighing sounds from the funnels of passing steamers, getting dead as they grew more distant; or to shouts from the decks of different craft in their vicinity, all of them assuming the form of 'Ah-he-hay!'

Half-past ten: not yet off. Mr Swancourt breathed a breath of weariness, and looked at his fellow-travellers in general. Their faces were certainly not worth looking at. The expression 'Waiting' was written upon them so absolutely that nothing more could be discerned there. All animation was suspended till Providence should raise the water and let them go.

'I have been thinking,' said Knight, 'that we have come amongst the rarest class of people in the kingdom. Of all human characteristics, a low opinion of the value of his own time by an individual must be among the strangest to find. Here we see numbers of that patient and happy species. Rovers, as distinct from travellers.'

'But they are pleasure-seekers, to whom time is of no importance.'

'O no. The pleasure-seekers we meet on the grand routes are more anxious than commercial travellers to rush on. And added to the loss of time in getting to their journey's end, these exceptional people take their chance of sea-sickness by coming this way.'

'Can it be?' inquired the rector with apprehension. 'Surely not, Mr Knight, just here in our English Channel – close at our doors, as I may say.'

'Entrance passages are very draughty places, and the Channel is like the rest. It ruins the temper of sailors. It has been calculated by philosophers that more damns go up to heaven from the Channel, in the course of a year, than from all the five oceans put together.'

They really start now, and the dead looks of all the throng come to life immediately. The man who has been frantically hauling in a rope that bade fair to have no end ceases his labours, and they glide down the serpentine bends of the Thames.

Anything anywhere was a mine of interest to Elfride, and so was this.

'It is well enough now,' said Mrs Swancourt, after they had passed the Nore, 'but I can't say I have cared for my voyage hitherto.' For being now in the open sea a slight breeze had sprung up, which cheered her as well as her two younger companions. But unfortunately it had a reverse effect upon the rector, who, after turning a sort of putty colour, interspersed with dashes of purple, pleaded indisposition, and vanished from their sight.

The afternoon wore on. Mrs Swancourt kindly sat apart by herself reading, and the betrothed pair were left to themselves. Elfride clung trustingly to Knight's arm, and proud was she to walk with him up and down the deck, or to go forward, and leaning with him against the forecastle rails, watch the setting sun gradually withdrawing itself over their stern into a huge bank of livid cloud with golden edges that rose to meet it.

She was childishly full of life and spirits, though in pacing up and down with him before the other passengers, and getting noticed by them, she was at starting rather confused, it being the first time she had shown herself so openly under that kind of protection. 'I expect they are envious and saying things about us, don't you?' she would whisper to Knight with a stealthy smile.

'O no,' he would answer unconcernedly. 'Why should they envy us, and what can they say?'

'Not any harm, of course,' Elfride replied, 'except such as this: "How happy those two are! she is proud enough now." What makes it worse,' she continued in the extremity of confidence, 'I heard those two cricketing men say just now, "She's the nobbiest* girl on the boat." But I don't mind it, you know, Harry.'

'I should hardly have supposed you did, even if you had not told me,' said Knight with great blandness.

She was never tired of asking her lover questions and admiring his answers, good, bad, or indifferent as they might be. The evening grew dark and night came on, and lights shone upon them from the horizon and from the sky.

'Now look there ahead of us, at that halo in the air, of silvery brightness. Watch it, and you will see what it comes to.'

She watched for a few minutes, when two white lights emerged from the side of a hill, and showed themselves to be the origin of the halo.

'What a dazzling brilliance! What do they mark?'

'The South Foreland: they were previously covered by the cliff.'

'What is that level line of little sparkles – a town, I suppose?'

'That's Dover.'

All this time, and later, soft sheet lightning expanded from a cloud in their path, enkindling their faces as they paced up and down, shining over the water, and, for a moment, showing the horizon as a keen line.

Elfride slept soundly that night. Her first thought the next morning was the thrilling one that Knight was as close at hand as when they were at home at Endelstow, and her first sight, on looking out of the cabin window, was the perpendicular face of Beachy Head, gleaming white in a brilliant six-o'clock-in-the-morning sun. This fair daybreak, however, soon changed its aspect. A cold wind and a pale mist descended upon the sea, and seemed to threaten a dreary day.

When they were nearing Southampton Mrs Swancourt came to say that her husband was so ill that he wished to be put on shore here, and left to do the remainder of the journey by land. 'He will be perfectly well directly he treads firm ground again. Which shall we do – go with him, or finish our voyage as we intended?'

Elfride was comfortably housed under an umbrella which Knight was holding over her to keep off the wind. 'O, don't let us go on shore!' she said with dismay. 'It would be such a pity!'

'That's very fine,' said Mrs Swancourt archly, as to a child. 'See, the wind has increased her colour, the sea her appetite and spirits, and somebody her happiness. Yes, it would be a pity, certainly.'

''Tis my misfortune to be always spoken to from a pedestal,' sighed Elfride.

'Well, we will do as you like, Mrs Swancourt,' said Knight, 'but—'

'I myself would rather remain on board,' interrupted the elder lady. 'And Mr Swancourt particularly wishes to go by himself. So that shall settle the matter.'

The rector, now a drab colour, was put ashore, and became as well as ever forthwith.

Elfride, sitting alone in a retired part of the vessel, saw a veiled woman walk aboard among the very latest arrivals at this port. She was clothed in black silk, and carried a dark shawl upon her arm. The woman, without looking around her, turned to the quarter allotted to the second-cabin* passengers. All the carnation Mrs Swancourt had complimented her stepdaughter upon possessing left Elfride's cheeks, and she trembled visibly.

She ran to the other side of the boat, where Mrs Swancourt was standing.

'Let us go home by railway with papa, after all,' she pleaded earnestly. 'I would rather go with him – shall we?'

Mrs Swancourt looked around for a moment, as if unable to decide. 'Ah,' she exclaimed, 'it is too late now. Why did not you say so before, when we had plenty of time?'

The *Juliet* had at that minute let go, the engines had started, and they were gliding slowly away from the quay. There was no help for it but to remain, unless the *Juliet* could be made to put back, and that would create a great disturbance. Elfride gave up the idea and submitted quietly. Her happiness was sadly mutilated now.

The woman whose presence had so disturbed her was much like Mrs Jethway. She seemed to haunt Elfride like a shadow. After several minutes' vain endeavour to account for any design Mrs Jethway could have in watching her, Elfride decided to think that, if it were the widow, the encounter was accidental. She remembered that the widow in her restlessness was often visiting the village near Southampton which was her original home, and it was possible that she chose water-transit with the idea of saving expense.

'What is the matter, Elfride?' Knight inquired, standing before her.

'Nothing more than that I am rather depressed.'

'I don't much wonder at it; that wharf was depressing. We seemed underneath and inferior to everything around us. But we shall be in the sea breeze again soon, and that will freshen you, dear.'

The evening closed in and dusk increased as they made way down Southampton Water and through the Solent. Elfride's disturbance of mind was such that her light spirits of the foregoing four and twenty hours had entirely deserted her. The weather too had grown more gloomy, for though the showers of the morning had ceased, the sky was covered more closely than ever with dense leaden clouds. How beautiful was the sunset when they rounded the North Foreland the previous evening! now it was impossible to tell within half an hour the time of the luminary's going down. Knight led her about, and, being by this time accustomed to her sudden changes of mood, overlooked the necessity of a cause in regarding the conditions – impressionableness and elasticity.

Elfride glanced stealthily to the other end of the vessel. Mrs

Jethway, or her double, was sitting at the stern – her eye steadily regarding Elfride.

'Let us go to the forepart,' she said quickly to Knight. 'See there – the man is fixing the lights for the night.'

Knight assented, and after watching the operation of hanging the red and the green lights on the port and starboard bows, and the hoisting of the white light to the masthead, he walked up and down with her till the increase of wind rendered promenading difficult. Elfride's eyes were occasionally to be found furtively gazing abaft, to learn if her enemy were really there. Nobody was visible now.

'Shall we go below?' said Knight, seeing that the deck was nearly deserted.

'No,' she said. 'If you will kindly get me a rug from Mrs Swancourt I should like, if you don't mind, to stay here.' She had recently fancied the assumed Mrs Jethway might be a first-class passenger, and dreaded meeting her by accident.

Knight appeared with the rug, and they sat down behind a weather-cloth on the windward side, just as the two red eyes of the Needles glared upon them from the gloom, their pointed summits rising like shadowy phantom figures against the sky. It became necessary to go below to an eight-o'clock meal of nondescript kind, and Elfride was immensely relieved at finding no sign of Mrs Jethway there. They again ascended, and remained above till Mrs Snewson staggered up to them with the message that Mrs Swancourt thought it was time for Elfride to come below. Knight accompanied her down, and returned again to pass a little more time on deck.

Elfride partly undressed herself and lay down, and soon became unconscious, though her sleep was light. How long she had lain, she knew not, when by slow degrees she seemed to have a sense of a whispering in her ear.

'You are well on with him, I can see. Well, provoke me now, but I shall win, you will find.' That seemed to be the utterance, or words to that effect.

Elfride became broad awake and terrified. She knew the words, if real, could be only those of one person, and that person the widow Jethway. But she might have been dreaming only.

The lamp had gone out and the place was in darkness. In the next berth she could hear her stepmother breathing heavily, further on Snewson breathing more heavily still. These were the only other legitimate occupants of the cabin, and Mrs Jethway might have stealthily come in by some means and retreated again, or else have entered an empty berth next Snewson's. The fear that this was the case increased Elfride's perturbation, till it assumed the dimensions of a certainty, for how could a stranger from the other end of the ship possibly contrive to get in? Could it have been a dream?

Elfride raised herself higher and looked out of the window. There was the sea, floundering and rushing against the ship's side just by her head, and thence stretching away, dim and moaning, into an expanse of indistinctness; and far beyond all this two placid lights like rayless stars. Now almost fearing to turn her face inwards again, lest Mrs Jethway should appear at her elbow, Elfride meditated upon whether to call Snewson to keep her company. 'Four bells'* sounded, and she heard voices, which gave her a little courage. It was not worth while to call Snewson.

At any rate Elfride could not stay there panting longer, at the risk of being again disturbed by that dreadful whispering. So wrapping herself up hurriedly she emerged into the passage, and by the aid of a faint light burning at the entrance to the saloon found the foot of the stairs, and ascended to the deck. Dreary the place was in the extreme. It seemed a new spot altogether in contrast with its day-time self. She could see the glowworm light from the binnacle,* and the dim outline of the man at the wheel; also a form at the bows. Not another soul was apparent from stem to stern.

Yes, there were two more – by the bulwarks. One proved to be her Harry, the other the mate. She was glad indeed, and on drawing closer found they were holding a low slow chat about nautical affairs. She ran up and slipped her hand through Knight's arm, partly for love, partly for stability.

'Elfie! not asleep?' said Knight, after moving a few steps aside with her.

'No: I cannot sleep. May I stay here? It is so dismal down there, and – and I was afraid. Where are we now?'

'Due south of Portland Bill. Those are the lights abeam* of us: look. A terrible spot, that, on a stormy night. And do you see a very small light that dips and rises to the right? That's a light-ship on the dangerous shoal called the Shambles, where many a good vessel has gone to pieces. Between it and ourselves is the Race – a place where antagonistic currents meet and form whirlpools – a spot which is rough in the smoothest weather, and terrific in a wind. That dark, dreary horizon we just discern to the left is the West Bay, terminated landwards by the Chesil Beach.'

'What time is it, Harry?'

'Just past two.'

'Are you going below?'

'O no; not to-night. I prefer pure air.'

She fancied he might be displeased with her for coming to him at this unearthly hour. 'I should like to stay here too, if you will allow me,' she said timidly. 'I want to ask you things.'

'Allow you, Elfie!' said Knight, putting his arm round her and drawing her closer. 'I am twice as happy with you by my side. Yes: we will stay, and watch the approach of day.'

So they again sought out the sheltered nook, and sitting down wrapped themselves in the rug as before.

'What were you going to ask me?' he inquired, as they undulated up and down.

'O, it was not much – perhaps a thing I ought not to ask,' she said hesitatingly. Her sudden wish had really been to discover at once whether he had ever before been engaged to be married. If he had, she would make that a ground for telling him a little of her conduct with Stephen. Mrs Jethway's seeming words had so depressed the girl that she herself now painted her flight in the darkest colours, and longed to ease her burdened mind by an instant confession. If Knight had ever been imprudent himself, he might, she hoped, forgive all.

'I wanted to ask you,' she went on, 'if – you had ever been engaged before.' She added tremulously, 'I hope you have – I mean, I don't mind at all if you have.'

'No, I never was,' Knight instantly and heartily replied. 'Elfride' – and there was a certain happy pride in his tone – 'I am twelve years older than you, and I have been about the world, and, in a way, into society, and you have not. And yet I am not so unfit for you as strict-thinking people might imagine, who would assume the difference in age to signify most surely an equal addition to my practice in love-making.'

Elfride shivered.

'You are cold – is the wind too much for you?'

'No,' she said gloomily. The belief which had been her sheet-anchor in hoping for forgiveness had proved false. This account of the exceptional nature of his experience, a matter which would have set her rejoicing two years ago, chilled her now like a frost.

'You don't mind my asking you?' she continued.

'O no – not at all.'

'And have you never kissed many ladies?' she whispered, hoping he would say a hundred at the least.

The time, the circumstances, and the scene were such as to draw confidences from the most reserved. 'Elfride,' whispered Knight in reply, 'it is strange you should have asked that question. But I'll answer it, though I have never told such a thing before. I have been rather absurd in my avoidance of women. I have never given a woman a kiss in my life, except yourself and my mother.' The man of two and thirty with the experienced mind warmed all over with a boy's ingenuous shame as he made the confession.

'What, not one?' she faltered.

'No; not one.'

'How very strange!'

'Yes, the reverse experience may be commoner. And yet, to those who have observed their own sex, as I have, my case is not remarkable. Men about town are women's favourites – that's the postulate – and superficial people don't think far enough to see that there may be reserved, lonely exceptions.'

'Are you proud of it, Harry?'

'No, indeed. Of late years I have wished I had gone my ways and trod out my measure like lighter-hearted men. I have thought of how many happy experiences I may have lost through never going to woo.'

'Then why did you hold aloof?'

'I cannot say. I don't think it was my nature to: circumstance hindered me, perhaps. I have regretted it for another reason. This great remissness of mine has had its effect upon me. The older I have grown, the more distinctly have I perceived that it was absolutely preventing me from liking any woman who was not as unpractised as I; and I gave up the expectation of finding a nineteenth-century young lady in my own raw state. Then I found you, Elfride, and I felt for the first time that my fastidiousness was a blessing. And it helped to make me worthy of you. I felt at once that, differing as we did in other experiences, in this matter I resembled you. Well, aren't you glad to hear it, Elfride?'

'Yes, I am,' she answered in a forced voice. 'But I always had thought that men made lots of engagements before they married – especially if they don't marry very young.'

'So all women think, I suppose – and rightly, indeed, of the majority of bachelors, as I said before. But an appreciable minority of slow-coach men do not – and it makes them very awkward when they do come to the point. However, it didn't matter in my case.'

'Why?' she asked uneasily.

'Because you know even less of love-making and matrimonial prearrangement than I, and so you can't draw invidious comparisons if I do my engaging improperly.'

'I think you do it beautifully!'

'Thank you, dear. But,' continued Knight laughingly, 'your opinion is not that of an expert, which alone is of value.'

Had she answered 'Yes, it is' half as strongly as she felt it, Knight might have been a little astonished.

'If you had ever been engaged to be married before,' he went on, 'I expect your opinion of my addresses would be different. But then, I should not—'

'Should not what, Harry?'

'O, I was merely going to say that in that case I should never have given myself the pleasure of proposing to you, since your freedom from that experience was your attraction, darling.'

'You are severe on women, are you not?'

'No, I think not. I had a right to please my taste, and that was for untried lips. Other men than those of my sort acquire the taste as they get older – but don't find an Elfride—'

'What horrid sound is that we hear when we pitch forward?'

'Only the screw – don't find an Elfride as I did. To think that I should have discovered such an unseen flower down there in the West – to whom a man is as much as a multitude to some women, and a trip down the English Channel like a voyage round the world!'

'And would you,' she said, and her voice was tremulous, 'have given up a lady – if you had become engaged to her – and then found she had had *one* kiss before yours – and would you have – gone away and left her?'

'One kiss, – no, hardly for that.'

'Two?'

'Well – I could hardly say inventorially like that. Too much of that sort of thing certainly would make me dislike a woman. But let us confine our attention to ourselves, not go thinking of might have beens.'

So Elfride had allowed her thoughts to 'dally with false surmise',* and every one of Knight's words fell upon her like a weight. After this they were silent for a long time, gazing upon the black mysterious sea, and hearing the strange voice of the restless wind. A rocking to and fro on the waves, when the breeze is not too violent and cold, produces a soothing effect even upon the most highly-wrought mind. Elfride slowly sank against Knight, and looking down, he found by her soft regular breathing that she had fallen asleep. Not wishing to disturb her he continued still, and took an intense pleasure in supporting her warm young form as it rose and fell with her every breath.

Knight fell to dreaming too, though he continued wide awake. It was pleasant to realize the implicit trust she placed in him, and to think of the charming innocence of one who could sink to sleep in so simple and unceremonious a manner. More than all, the musing unpractical student felt the immense responsibility he was taking upon himself by becoming the protector and guide of such a trusting creature. The quiet slumber of her soul lent a quietness to his own. Then she moaned and turned herself restlessly. Presently her mutterings became distinct:

'Don't tell him – he will not love me. . . . I did not mean any disgrace – indeed I did not, so don't tell him. We were going to be married – that was why I ran away. . . . And he says he will not have a kissed woman. . . . And if you tell him he will go away, and I shall die. I pray have mercy – O!'

Elfride started up wildly.

The previous moment a musical ding-dong had spread into the air from their right hand, and awakened her.

'What is it?' she exclaimed in terror.

'Only "eight bells",'* said Knight soothingly. 'Don't be frightened, little bird, you are safe. What have you been dreaming about?'

'I can't tell, I can't tell!' she said with a shudder. 'O, I don't know what to do!'

'Stay quietly with me. We shall soon see the dawn now. Look, the morning star is lovely over there. The clouds have completely cleared off whilst you have been sleeping. What have you been dreaming of?'

'A woman in our parish.'

'Don't you like her?'

'I don't. She doesn't like me. Where are we?'

'About south of the Exe.'

Knight said no more on the words of her dream. They watched the sky till Elfride grew calm, and the dawn appeared. It was mere wan lightness first. Then the wind blew in a changed spirit, and died away to a zephyr. The star dissolved into the day.

'That's how I should like to die,' said Elfride, rising from her seat and leaning over the bulwark to watch the star's last expiring gleam.

'As the lines say,' Knight replied –

> '"To set as sets the morning star, which goes
> Not down behind the darken'd west, nor hides
> Obscured among the tempests of the sky,
> But melts away into the light of heaven."'*

'O, other people have thought the same thing, have they? That's always the case with my originalities – they are original to nobody but myself.'

'Not only the case with yours. When I was a young hand at reviewing I used to find that a frightful pitfall – dilating upon subjects I met with, which were novelties to me, and finding afterwards they had been exhausted by the thinking world when I was in pinafores.'

'That is delightful. Whenever I find you have done a foolish thing I am glad, because it seems to bring you a little nearer to me, who have done many.' And Elfride thought again of her enemy, possibly asleep under the deck they trod.

All up the coast, prominences singled themselves out from

recesses. Then a rosy sky spread over the eastern sea and behind the low line of land, flinging its livery in dashes upon the thin airy clouds in that direction. Every projection on the land seemed now so many fingers anxious to catch a little of the liquid light thrown so prodigally over the sky, and after a fantastic time of lustrous yellows in the east, the higher elevations along the shore were flooded with the same hues. The bluff and bare contours of Start Point caught the brightest, earliest glow of all, and so also did the sides of its white lighthouse, perched upon a shelf in its precipitous front like a mediæval saint in a niche. Their lofty neighbour Bolt Head on the left remained as yet ungilded, and retained its gray.

Then up came the sun, as it were in jerks, just to seaward of the easternmost point of land, flinging out a Jacob's-ladder path of light* from itself to Elfride and Knight, and coating them with rays in a few minutes. The inferior dignitaries of the shore – Froward Point, Berry Head, and Prawle – all had acquired their share of the illumination ere this, and at length the very smallest protuberance of wave, cliff, or inlet, even to the innermost recesses of the lovely valley of the Dart, had its portion; and sunlight, now the common possession of all, ceased to be the wonderful and coveted thing it had been a short half hour before.

After breakfast, Plymouth arose into view, and grew distincter to their nearing vision, the Breakwater appearing like a streak of phosphoric light upon the surface of the sea. Elfride looked furtively around for Mrs Jethway, but could discern no shape like hers. Afterwards, in the bustle of landing, she looked again with the same result. The woman had either glided upon the quay unobserved or she had never been there at all. Expanding with a sense of relief, Elfride waited whilst Knight looked to their luggage, and then saw her father approaching through the crowd, twirling his walking-stick to catch their attention. Elbowing their way to him they all entered the town, which smiled as sunny a smile upon Elfride as it had done between one and two years earlier, when she had entered it at precisely the same hour as the bride-elect of Stephen Smith.

CHAPTER THIRTY

'Vassal unto Love'*

ELFRIDE clung more closely to Knight as day succeeded day. Whatever else might admit of question, there could be no dispute that the allegiance she bore him absorbed her whole soul and existence. A greater than Stephen had arisen, and she had left all to follow him.

The unreserved girl was never chary of letting her lover discover how much she admired him. She never once held an idea in opposition to any one of his, or insisted on any point with him, or showed any independence, or held her own on any subject. His lightest whim she respected and obeyed as law, and if, expressing her opinion on a matter, he took up the subject and differed from her, she instantly threw down her own opinion as wrong and untenable. Even her ambiguities and *espièglerie** were but media of the same manifestation; acted charades, embodying the words of her prototype, the tender and susceptible daughter-in-law of Naomi:* 'Let me find favour in thy sight, my lord; for that thou hast comforted me, and for that thou hast spoken friendly unto thine handmaid.'

She was syringing the plants one wet day in the greenhouse. Knight was sitting under a great passion-flower observing the scene. Sometimes he looked out at the rain from the sky, and then at Elfride's inner rain of larger drops, which fell from trees and shrubs, after having previously hung from the twigs like small silver fruit.

'I must give you something to make you think of me during this autumn at your chambers,' she was saying. 'What shall it be? Portraits do more harm than good, by selecting the worst expression of which your face is capable. Hair is unlucky. And you don't like jewellery.'

'Something which shall bring back to my mind the many scenes we have enacted in this conservatory. I see what I should prize very much. That dwarf myrtle* tree in the pot, which you have been so carefully tending.'

Elfride looked thoughtfully at the myrtle.

'I can carry it comfortably in my hat box,' said Knight. 'And I will put it in my window, and so, it being always before my eyes, I shall think of you continually.'

It so happened that the myrtle which Knight had singled out had a peculiar beginning and history. It had originally been a twig worn in Stephen Smith's button-hole, and he had taken it thence, stuck it into the pot, and told her that if it grew, she was to take care of it, and keep it in remembrance of him when he was far away.

She looked wistfully at the plant, and a sense of fairness to Smith's memory caused her a pang of regret that Knight should have asked for that very one. It seemed exceeding a common heartlessness to let it go.

'Is there not anything you like better?' she said sadly. 'That is only an ordinary myrtle.'

'No: I am fond of myrtle.' Seeing that she did not take kindly to the idea, he said again, 'Why do you object to my having that?'

'O no – I don't object precisely – it was a feeling. – Ah, here's another cutting lately struck, and just as small – of a better kind, and with prettier leaves – myrtus microphylla.'

'That will do nicely. Let it be put in my room, that I may not forget it. What romance attaches to the other?'

'It was a gift to me.'

The subject then dropped. Knight thought no more of the matter till, on entering his bedroom in the evening, he found the second myrtle placed upon his dressing-table as he had directed. He stood for a moment admiring the fresh appearance of the leaves by candlelight, and then he thought of the transaction of the day.

Male lovers as well as female can be spoilt by too much kindness, and Elfride's uniform submissiveness had given Knight a rather exacting manner at crises, attached to her as he was. 'Why should she have refused the one I first chose?' he now asked himself. Even such slight opposition as she had shown then was exceptional enough to make itself noticeable. He was not vexed with her in the least: the mere variation of her way to-day from her usual ways kept him musing on the subject, because it perplexed him. 'It was a gift' – those were her words. Admitting it to be a gift, he thought she could hardly value a mere friend more than she valued him as a lover, and giving the plant into his charge would have made no difference. 'Except, indeed, it was the gift of a lover,' he murmured.

'I wonder if Elfride has ever had a lover before?' he said aloud, as a new idea, quite. This and companion thoughts were enough to occupy him completely till he fell asleep – rather later than usual.

The next day, when they were again alone, he said to her rather suddenly –

'Do you love me more or less, Elfie, for what I told you on board the steamer?'

'You told me so many things,' she returned, lifting her eyes to his and smiling.

'I mean the confession you coaxed out of me – that I had never been in the position of lover before.'

'It is a satisfaction, I suppose, to be the first in your heart,' she said to him, with an attempt to continue her smiling.

'I am going to ask you a question now,' said Knight, somewhat awkwardly. 'I only ask it in a whimsical way, you know: not with great seriousness, Elfride. You may think it odd, perhaps.'

Elfride tried desperately to keep the colour in her face. She could not, though distressed to think that getting pale showed consciousness of deeper guilt than merely getting red.

'O no – I shall not think that,' she said, because obliged to say something to fill the pause which followed her questioner's remark.

'It is this: have you ever had a lover? I am almost sure you have not; but, have you?'

'Not, as it were, a lover; I mean, not worth mentioning, Harry,' she faltered.

Knight, overstrained in sentiment as he knew the feeling to be, felt some sickness of heart.

'Still he was a lover?'

'Well, a sort of lover, I suppose,' she responded tardily.

'A man, I mean, you know.'

'Yes; but only a mere person, and—'

'But truly your lover?'

'Yes; a lover certainly – he was that. Yes, he might have been called my lover.'

Knight said nothing to this for a minute or more, and kept silent time with his finger to the tick of the old library clock, in which room the colloquy was going on.

'You don't mind, Harry, do you?' she said anxiously, nestling close to him, and watching his face.

'Of course, I don't seriously mind. In reason, a man cannot object to such a trifle. I only thought you hadn't – that was all.'

However, one ray was abstracted from the glory about her head. But afterwards, when Knight was wandering by himself over the bare and breezy hills, and meditating on the subject, that ray suddenly returned. For she might have had a lover, and never have cared in the least for him. She might have used the word improperly, and meant 'admirer' all the time. Of course she had been admired; and one man might have made his admiration more prominent than that of the rest – a very natural case.

They were sitting on one of the garden seats when he found occasion to put the supposition to the test. 'Did you love that lover or admirer of yours ever so little, Elfie?'

She murmured reluctantly, 'Yes, I think I did.'

Knight felt the same faint touch of misery. 'Only a very little?' he said.

'I am not sure how much.'

'But you are sure, darling, you loved him a little?'

'I think I am sure I loved him a little.'

'And not a great deal, Elfie?'

'My love was not supported by reverence for his powers.'

'But, Elfride, did you love him deeply?' said Knight restlessly.

'I don't exactly know how deep you mean by deeply.'

'That's nonsense.'

'You misapprehend; and you have let go my hand!' she cried, her eyes filling with tears. 'Harry, don't be severe with me, and don't question me. I did not love him as I do you. And could it be deeply if I did not think him cleverer than myself? For I did not. You grieve me so much – you can't think.'

'I will not say another word about it.'

'And you will not think about it, either, will you? I know you think of weaknesses in me after I am out of your sight; and not knowing what they are, I cannot combat them. I almost wish you were of a grosser nature, Harry; in truth I do! Or rather, I wish I could have the advantages such a nature in you would afford me, and yet have you as you are.'

'What advantages would they be?'

'Less anxiety, and more security. Ordinary men are not so delicate in their tastes as you; and where the lover or husband is not fastidious, and refined, and of a deep nature, things seem to go on better, I fancy – as far as I have been able to observe the world.'

'Yes; I suppose it is right. Shallowness has this advantage, that you can't be drowned there.'

'But I think I'll have you as you are; yes, I will!' she said winsomely. 'The practical husbands and wives who take things philosophically are very humdrum, are they not? Yes, it would kill me quite. You please me best as you are.'

'Even though I wish you had never cared for one before me?'

'Yes. And you must not wish it. Don't!'

'I'll try not to, Elfride.'

So she hoped, but her heart was troubled. If he felt so deeply on this point, what would he say did he know all, and see it as Mrs Jethway saw it? He would never make her the happiest girl in the world by taking her to be his own for aye. The thought enclosed her as a tomb whenever it presented itself to her perturbed brain. She tried to believe that Mrs Jethway would never do her such a cruel wrong as to increase the bad appearance of her folly by innuendoes; and concluded that concealment, having been begun, must be persisted in, if possible. For what he might consider as bad as the fact, was her previous concealment of it by strategy.

But Elfride knew Mrs Jethway to be her enemy, and to hate her. It was possible she would do her worst. And should she do it, all might be over.

Would the woman listen to reason, and be persuaded not to ruin one who had never intentionally harmed her?

It was night in the valley between Endelstow Crags and the shore. The brook which trickled that way to the sea was distinct in its murmurs now, and over the line of its course there began to hang a white riband of fog. Against the sky, on the left hand of the vale, the black form of the church could be seen. On the other rose hazel-bushes, a few trees, and where these were absent, furze tufts – as tall as men – on stems nearly as stout as timber. The shriek of some bird was occasionally heard, as it flew terror-stricken from its first roost to seek a new sleeping-place where it might pass the night unmolested.

In the evening shade, some way down the valley, and under a row of scrubby oaks, a cottage could still be discerned. It stood absolutely alone. The house was rather large, and the windows of some of the rooms were nailed up with boards on the outside, which gave a particularly deserted appearance to the whole erection. From the front door an irregular series of rough and misshapen steps, cut in the solid rock, led down to the edge of the streamlet, which, at their extremity, was hollowed into a basin the water trickled through. This was evidently the means of water supply to the dweller or dwellers in the cottage.

A light footstep was heard descending from the higher slopes of the hillside. Indistinct in the pathway appeared a moving female shape, who advanced and knocked timidly at the door. No answer being returned the knock was repeated, with the same result, and it was then repeated a third time. This also was unsuccessful.

From one of the only two windows on the ground floor which were not boarded up came rays of light, no shutter or curtain obscuring the room from the eyes of a passer on the outside. So few walked that way after nightfall that any such means to secure secrecy were probably deemed unnecessary.

The inequality of the rays falling upon the trees outside told that the light had its origin in a flickering fire only. The visitor, after the third knocking, stepped a little to the left in order to gain a view of the interior, and threw back the hood from her face. The dancing yellow sheen revealed the fair and anxious countenance of Elfride.

Inside the house this firelight was enough to illumine the room distinctly, and to show that the furniture of the cottage was superior to what might have been expected from so unpromising an exterior. It also showed to Elfride that the room was empty. Beyond the light quiver and flap of the flames nothing moved or was audible therein.

She turned the handle and entered, throwing off the cloak which enveloped her, under which she appeared without hat or bonnet, and in the sort of half-toilette* country people ordinarily dine in. Then advancing to the foot of the staircase she called distinctly, but somewhat fearfully, 'Mrs Jethway!'

No answer.

With a look of relief and regret combined, denoting that ease came to the heart and disappointment to the brain, Elfride paused for several minutes, as if undecided how to act. Determining to wait, she sat down on a chair. The minutes drew on, and after sitting on the thorns of impatience for half an hour, she searched her pocket, took therefrom a letter, and tore off the blank leaf. Then taking out a pencil she wrote upon the paper:

DEAR MRS JETHWAY, – I have been to visit you. I wanted much to see you, but I cannot wait any longer. I came to beg you not to execute the threats you have repeated to me. Do not, I beseech you, Mrs Jethway, let any one know what I did! It would ruin me, and break my heart. I will do anything for you, if you will be kind to me. In the name of our common womanhood, do not, I implore you, make a scandal of me. – Yours,

E. SWANCOURT

She folded the note cornerwise, directed it, and placed it on the table. Then again drawing the hood over her curly head she emerged silently as she had come.

Whilst this episode had been in action at Mrs Jethway's cottage, Knight had gone from the dining-room into the drawing-room, and found Mrs Swancourt there alone.

'Elfride has vanished upstairs or somewhere,' she said. 'And I have been reading an article in an old number of *The Present* that I lighted on by chance a short time ago; it is an article you once told us was yours. Well, Harry, with due deference to your literary powers, allow me to say that this effusion is all nonsense, in my opinion.'

'What is it about?' said Knight, taking up the paper and reading.

'There: don't get red about it. Own that experience has taught you to be more charitable. I have never read such unchivalrous sentiments in my life – from a man, I mean. There, I forgive you; it was before you knew Elfride.'

'O yes,' said Knight, looking up. 'I remember now. The text of that sermon was not my own at all, but was suggested to me by a young man named Smith – the same whom I have mentioned to you as coming from this parish. I thought the idea rather ingenious at the time, and enlarged it to the weight of a few guineas, because I had nothing else in my head.'

'Which idea do you call the text? I am curious to know that.'

'Well, this,' said Knight, somewhat unwillingly. 'That experience teaches, and your sweetheart, no less than your tailor, is necessarily very imperfect in her duties if you are her first patron: and conversely, the sweetheart who is graceful under the initial kiss must be supposed to have had some practice in the trade.'

'And do you mean to say that you wrote that upon the strength of another man's remark, without having tested it by practice?'

'Yes – indeed I do.'

'Then I think it was uncalled for and unfair. And how do you know it is true? I expect you regret it now.'

'Since you bring me into a serious mood, I will speak candidly. I do believe that remark to be perfectly true, and, having written it, I would defend it anywhere. But I do often regret having ever written it, as well as others of the sort. I have grown older since, and I find such a tone of writing is calculated to do harm in the world. Every literary Jack becomes a gentleman if he can only pen a few indifferent satires upon womankind: women themselves, too, have taken to the trick; and so, upon the whole, I begin to be rather ashamed of my companions.'

'Ah, Henry, you have fallen in love since, and it makes a difference,' said Mrs Swancourt with bantering dryness.

'That's true; but that is not my reason.'

'Having found that, in a case of your own experience, a so-called goose was a swan, it seems absurd to deny such a possibility in other men's experiences.'

'You can hit palpably, cousin Charlotte,' said Knight. 'You are like the boy who puts a stone inside his snowball, and I shall play with you no longer. Excuse me – I am going for my evening stroll.'

Though Knight had spoken jestingly, this incident and conversation had caused him a sudden depression. Coming, rather singularly, just after his discovery that Elfride had known what it was to love warmly before she had known him, his mind dwelt upon the subject, and the familiar pipe he smoked whilst pacing up and down the shrubbery-path failed to be a solace. He thought again of those idle words – hitherto quite forgotten – about the first kiss of a girl, and the theory seemed more than reasonable. Of course their sting now lay in their bearing on Elfride.

Elfride, under Knight's kiss, had certainly been a very different woman from herself under Stephen's. Whether for good or for ill, she had marvellously well learnt a betrothed lady's part; and the fascinating finish of her deportment in this second campaign did probably arise from her unreserved encouragement of Stephen. Knight, with all the rapidity of jealous sensitiveness, pounced upon some words she had inadvertently let fall about an earring, which he had only partially understood at the time. It was during that 'initial kiss' by the little waterfall:

'We must be careful. I lost the other by doing this!'

A flush which had in it as much of wounded pride as of sorrow, passed over Knight as he thought of what he had so frequently said to her in his simplicity. 'I always meant to be the first comer in a woman's heart, fresh lips or none for me.' How childishly blind he must have seemed to this mere girl! How she must have laughed at him inwardly! He absolutely writhed as he thought of the confession she had wrung from him on the boat in the darkness of night. The one conception which had sustained his dignity when drawn out of his shell on that occasion – that of her charming ignorance of all such matters – how absurd it was!

This man, whose imagination had been fed up to preternatural size by lonely study and silent observations of his kind – whose emotions had been drawn out long and delicate by his seclusion, like plants in a cellar – was now absolutely in pain. Moreover, several years of poetic study, and, if the truth must be told, poetic efforts, had tended to develop the affective side of his constitution still further, in proportion to his active faculties. It was his belief in the absolute newness of blandishment to Elfride which had constituted her primary charm. He began to think it was as hard to be earliest in a woman's heart as it was to be first in the Pool of Bethesda.*

That Knight should have been thus constituted: that Elfride's second lover should not have been one of the great mass of bustling mankind, little given to introspection, whose good-nature might have compensated for any lack of appreciativeness, was the chance of things. That her throbbing, self-confounding, indiscreet heart should have to defend itself unaided against the keen scrutiny and logical power which Knight, now that his suspicions were awakened, would sooner or later be sure to exercise against her, was her misfortune. A miserable incongruity was apparent in the circumstance of a strong mind practising its unerring archery upon a heart which the owner of that mind loved better than his own.

Elfride's docile devotion to Knight was now its own enemy. Clinging to him so dependently, she taught him in time to presume upon that devotion – a lesson men are not slow to learn. A slight rebelliousness occasionally would have done him no harm, and would have been a world of advantage to her. But she idolized him, and was proud to be his bond-servant.

CHAPTER THIRTY-ONE

'A worm i' the bud'*

ONE day the man of letters said, 'Let us go to the cliffs again, Elfride'; and, without consulting her wishes, he moved as if to start at once.

'The cliff of our dreadful adventure?' she inquired, with a shudder. 'Death stares me in the face in the person of that cliff.'

Nevertheless, so entirely had she sunk her individuality in his that the remark was not uttered as an expostulation, and she immediately prepared to accompany him.

'No, not that place,' said Knight. 'It is ghastly to me, too. That other, I mean; what is its name? – Windy Beak.'

Windy Beak was the second cliff in height along that coast, and, as is frequently the case with the natural features of the globe no less than with the intellectual features of men, it enjoyed the reputation of being the first. Moreover, it was the cliff to which Elfride had ridden with Stephen Smith, on a well-remembered morning of his summer visit.

So, though thought of the former cliff had caused her to shudder at the perils to which her lover and herself had there been exposed, by being associated with Knight only it was not so objectionable as Windy Beak. That place was worse than gloomy, it was a perpetual reproach to her.

But not liking to refuse she said, 'It is further than the other cliff.'

'Yes; but you can ride.'

'And will you too?'

'No, I'll walk.'

A duplicate of her original arrangement with Stephen. Some fatality must be hanging over her head. But she ceased objecting.

'Very well, Harry, I'll ride,' she said meekly.

A quarter of an hour later she was in the saddle. But how different the mood from that of the former time. She had, indeed, given up her position as queen of the less to be vassal of the greater.

Here was no showing off now; no scampering out of sight with Pansy, to perplex and tire her companion; no saucy remarks on *La Belle Dame sans Merci.* Elfride was burdened with the very intensity of her love.

Knight did most of the talking along the journey. Elfride silently listened, and entirely resigned herself to the motions of the ambling horse upon which she sat, alternately rising and sinking gently, like a sea bird upon a sea wave.

When they had reached the limit of a quadruped's possibilities in walking, Knight tenderly lifted her from the saddle, tied the horse, and rambled on with her to the seat in the rock. Knight sat down, and drew Elfride deftly beside him, and they looked over the sea.

Two or three degrees above that melancholy and eternally level line the ocean horizon, hung a sun of brass, with no visible rays, in a sky of ashen hue. It was a sky the sun did not illuminate or enkindle, as is usual at sunsets. This sheet of sky was met by the salt mass of gray water, flecked here and there with white. A waft of dampness occasionally rose to their faces, which was probably rarefied spray from the blows of the sea upon the foot of the cliff.

Elfride wished it could be a longer time ago that she had sat there with Stephen as her lover, and agreed to be his wife. The significant closeness of that time to the present was another item to add to the list of passionate fears which were chronic with her now.

Yet Knight was very tender this evening, and sustained her close to him as they sat.

Not a word had been uttered by either since sitting down, when Knight said musingly, looking still afar –

'I wonder if any lovers in past years ever sat here with arms locked, as we do now. Probably they have, for the place seems formed for a seat.'

Her recollection of a well-known pair who had, and the much-talked-of loss which had ensued therefrom, and how the young man had been sent back to look for the missing article, led Elfride to glance down to her side, and behind her back. Many people who lose a trinket involuntarily give a momentary look for it in passing the spot ever so long afterwards. They do not often find it. Elfride, in turning her head, saw something shine weakly from a crevice in the rocky sedile. Only for a few minutes during the day did the sun light the alcove to its innermost rifts and slits, but these were the minutes now, and its level rays did Elfride the good or evil turn of revealing the lost ornament.

Elfride's thoughts instantly reverted to the words she had unintentionally uttered upon what had been going on when the earring was lost. And she was immediately seized with a misgiving that Knight, on seeing the object, would be reminded of her words. Her instinctive act therefore was to secure it privately.

It was so deep in the crack that Elfride could not pull it out with her hand, though she made several surreptitious trials.

'What are you doing, Elfie?' said Knight, noticing her attempts and looking behind him likewise.

She had relinquished the endeavour, but too late.

Knight peered into the joint from which her hand had been withdrawn, and saw what she had seen. He instantly took a penknife from his pocket, and by dint of probing and scraping brought the earring out upon open ground.

'It is not yours, surely?' he inquired.

'Yes, it is,' she said quietly.

'Well, that is a most extraordinary thing, that we should find it like this!' Knight then remembered more circumstances; 'What, is it the one you have told me of?'

'Yes.'

The unfortunate remark of hers at the kiss came into his mind, if eyes were ever an index to be trusted. Trying to repress the words he yet spoke on the subject, more to obtain assurance that what it had seemed to imply was not true than from a wish to pry into bygones.

'Were you really engaged to be married to that lover?' he said, looking straight forward at the sea again.

'Yes – but not formally. Yet I think I was.'

'O Elfride, engaged to be married!' he murmured.

'It would have been called a – secret engagement, I suppose. But don't look so disappointed; don't blame me.'

'No, no.'

'Why do you say "No, no," in such a way? Kindly enough, but so barely?'

Knight made no direct reply to this. 'Elfride, I told you once,' he said, following out his thoughts, 'that I never kissed a woman as her lover until I kissed you. A kiss is not much, I suppose, and it happens to few young people to be able to avoid all blandishments and attentions except from the one they afterwards marry. But I have peculiar weaknesses, Elfride; and because I have led a peculiar life I must suffer for it, I suppose. I had hoped – well, what I had no right to hope in connection with you. You naturally granted your former lover the privileges you grant me.'

A 'yes' came from her like the last sad whisper of a breeze.

'And he used to kiss you – of course he did.'

'Yes.'

'And perhaps you allowed him a more free manner in his love-making than I have shown in mine.'

'No, I did not.' This was rather more alertly spoken.

'But he adopted it without being allowed?'

'Yes.'

'How much I have made of you, Elfride, and how I have kept aloof!' said Knight in hurt tones. 'So many days and hours as I have hoped in you – I have feared to kiss you more than those two times. And he made no scruples to. . . .'

She crept closer to him and trembled as if with cold. Her dread that the whole story, with random additions, would become known to him, caused her manner to be so agitated that Knight was alarmed and perplexed into stillness. The actual innocence which made her think so fearfully of what, as the world goes, was not a ruinous matter, magnified her apparent guilt. It may have said to Knight that a woman who was so flurried in the preliminaries must have a dreadful sequel to her tale.

'I know,' continued Knight, with an indescribable drag of manner and intonation, – 'I know I am absurdly scrupulous about you – that I want you too exclusively mine. In your past before you knew me – from your very cradle – I wanted to think you had been mine. I would make you mine by main force. Elfride,' he went on vehemently, 'I can't help this jealousy over you! It is my nature, and must be so, and I *hate* the fact that you have been caressed before: yes, hate it!'

She drew a long deep breath which was half a sob. Knight's face was hard, and he never looked at her at all, still fixing his gaze far out to sea, which the sun had now resigned to the shade. In high places it is not long from sunset to night, dusk being in a measure banished, and though only evening where they sat it had been twilight in the valleys for half an hour. Upon the dull expanse of sea there gradually intensified itself into existence the gleam of a distant light-ship.

'When that lover first kissed you, Elfride, was it in such a place as this?'

'Yes, it was.'

'You don't tell me anything but what I wring out of you. Why is that? Why have you suppressed all mention of this when casual confidences of mine should have suggested confidence in return? On board the *Juliet*, why were you so secret? It seems like being made a fool of, dear, to think that, when I was teaching you how desirable it was that we should have no secrets from each other, you were assenting in words, but in act contradicting me. Confidence would have been so much more promising for our happiness. If you had had confidence in me, and told me willingly, I should – be different. But you suppress everything, and I shall question you. Did you live at Endelstow at that time?'

'Yes,' she said faintly.

'Where were you when he first kissed you?'

'Sitting in this seat.'

'Ah, I thought so!' said Knight, rising and facing her.

'And that accounts for everything – the exclamation which you explained deceitfully, and all! Forgive the harsh word, Elfride – forgive it.' He smiled a surface smile as he continued: 'What a poor mortal I am to play second fiddle in everything and to be deluded by fibs!'

'O, don't say it; don't, Harry!'

'Where did he kiss you besides here?'

'Sitting on – a tomb in the – churchyard – and other places,' she answered with slow recklessness.

'Never mind, never mind,' he exclaimed, on seeing her tears and perturbation. 'I don't want to grieve you. I don't care.'

But Knight did care.

'It makes no difference, you know,' he continued, seeing she did not reply.

'I feel cold,' said Elfride. 'Shall we go home?'

'Yes; it is late in the year to sit long out of doors: we ought to be off this ledge before it gets too dark to let us see our footing. I daresay the horse is impatient.'

Knight spoke the merest commonplace to her now. He had hoped to the last moment that she would have volunteered the whole story of her first attachment. It grew more and more distasteful to him that she should have a secret of this nature. Such entire confidence as he had pictured as about to exist between himself and the innocent young wife who had known no lover's tones save his – was this its beginning? He lifted her upon the horse, and they went along constrainedly. The poison of suspicion was doing its work well.

An incident occurred on this homeward journey which was long remembered by both, as adding shade to shadow. Knight could not keep from his mind the words of Adam's reproach to Eve in *Paradise Lost*, and at last whispered them to himself –

'Fool'd and beguiled: by him thou, I by thee!'*

'What did you say?' Elfride inquired timorously.

'It was only a quotation.'

They had now dropped into a hollow, and the church tower made its appearance against the pale evening sky, its lower part being hidden by some intervening trees. Elfride, being denied an answer, was looking at the tower and trying to think of some contrasting quotation she might use to regain his tenderness. After a little thought she said in winning tones –

'"Thou hast been my hope, and a strong tower for me against the enemy."'*

They passed on. A few minutes later three or four birds were seen to fly out of the tower.

'The strong tower moves,' said Knight, with surprise.

A corner of the square mass swayed forward, sank, and vanished. A loud rumble followed, and a cloud of dust arose where all had previously been so clear.

'The church restorers have done it!' said Elfride.

At this minute Mr Swancourt was seen approaching them. He came up with a bustling demeanour, apparently much engrossed by some business in hand.

'We have got the tower down!' he exclaimed. 'It came rather quicker than we intended it should. The first idea was to take it down stone by stone, you know. In doing this the crack widened considerably, and it was not believed safe for the men to stand upon the walls any longer. Then we decided to undermine it, and three men set to work at the weakest corner this afternoon. They had left off for the evening, intending to give the final blow to-morrow morning, and had been home about half an hour, when down it came. A very successful job – a very fine job indeed. But he was a tough old fellow in spite of the crack.' Here Mr Swancourt wiped from his face the perspiration his excitement had caused him.

'Poor old tower!' said Elfride.

'Yes, I am sorry for it,' said Knight. 'It was an interesting piece of antiquity – a local record of local art.'

'Ah, but my dear sir, we shall have a new one,' expostulated Mr Swancourt; 'a splendid tower – designed by a first-rate London man – in the newest style of Gothic art, and full of Christian feeling.'

'Indeed!' said Knight.

'O yes. Not in the barbarous clumsy architecture of this neighbourhood; you see nothing so rough and pagan anywhere else in England. When the men are gone I would advise you to go and see the church before anything further is done to it. You can now sit in the chancel, and look down the nave through the west arch, and through that far out to sea. In fact,' said Mr Swancourt significantly, 'if a wedding were performed at the altar to-morrow morning, it might be witnessed from the deck of a ship on a voyage to the South Seas, with a good glass. However, after dinner, when the moon has risen, go out and see for yourselves.'

Knight assented with feverish readiness. He had decided within the last few minutes that he could not rest another night without further talk with Elfride upon the subject which now divided them: he was determined to know all, and relieve his disquiet in some way. Elfride would gladly have escaped further converse alone with him that night, but it seemed inevitable.

Just after moonrise they left the house. How little any expectation of the moonlight prospect – which was the ostensible reason of their pilgrimage – had to do with Knight's real motive in getting the gentle girl again upon his arm, Elfride no less than himself well knew.

CHAPTER THIRTY-TWO

'Had I wist before I kist.'*

It was now October, and the night air was chill. After looking to see that she was well wrapped up Knight took her along the hillside path they had ascended so many times in each other's company, when doubt was a thing unknown. On reaching the church they found that one side of the tower was, as the rector had stated, entirely removed, and lying in the shape of rubbish at their feet. The tower on its eastern side still was firm, and might have withstood the shock of storms and the siege of battering years for many a generation even now. They entered by the side-door, went eastward, and sat down by the altar-steps.

The heavy arch spanning the junction of tower and nave formed to-night a black frame to a distant misty view, stretching far westward. Just outside the arch came the heap of fallen stones, then a portion of moonlit churchyard, then the wide and convex sea behind. It was a *coup-d'œil* which had never been possible since the mediæval masons first attached the old tower to the older church it dignified, and hence must be supposed to have had an interest apart from that of simple moonlight on ancient wall and sea and shore – any mention of which has by this time, it is to be feared, become one of the cuckoo-cries which are heard but not regarded. Rays of crimson, blue, and purple shone upon the twain from the east window behind them, wherein saints and angels vied with each other in primitive surroundings of landscape and sky, and threw upon the pavement at the sitters' feet a softer reproduction of the same translucent hues, amid which the shadows of the two living heads of Knight and Elfride were opaque and prominent blots. Presently the moon became covered by a cloud, and the iridescence died away.

'There, it is gone!' said Knight. 'I've been thinking, Elfride, that this place we sit on is where we may hope to kneel together soon. But I am restless and uneasy, and you know why.'

Before she replied the moonlight returned again, irradiating that portion of churchyard within their view. It brightened the near part first, and against the background which the cloud-shadow had not yet uncovered stood, brightest of all, a white tomb – the tomb of young Jethway.

Knight, still alive on the subject of Elfride's secret, thought of her words concerning the kiss – that it once had occurred on a tomb in this churchyard.

'Dearest,' he said, with a superficial archness which did not half cover an undercurrent of reproach, 'do you know, I think you might have told me voluntarily about that past – of kisses and betrothing – without giving me so much uneasiness and trouble. Was that the tomb you alluded to as having sat on with him?'

She waited an instant. 'Yes,' she said.

The correctness of his random shot startled Knight; though, considering that almost all the other memorials in the churchyard were upright headstones upon which nobody could possibly sit, it was not so wonderful.

Elfride did not even now go on with the explanation her too exacting lover wished to have. and her reticence began to irritate him as before. He was inclined to read her a lecture.

'Why don't you tell me all?' he said somewhat indignantly. 'Elfride, there is not a single subject upon which I feel more strongly than upon this – that everything ought to be cleared up between two persons before they become husband and wife. See how desirable and wise such a course is, in order to avoid disagreeable contingencies in the form of discoveries afterwards. For, Elfride, a secret of no importance at all may be made the basis of some fatal misunderstanding only because it is discovered, and not confessed. They say there never was a couple of whom one had not some secret the other never knew or was intended to know. This may or may not be true; but if it be true, some have been happy in spite rather than in consequence of it. If a man were to see another man looking significantly at his wife, and she were blushing crimson and appearing startled, do you think he would be so well satisfied with, for instance, her truthful explanation that once, to her great annoyance, she accidentally fainted into his arms, as if she had said it voluntarily long ago, before the circumstance occurred which forced it from her? Suppose that admirer you spoke of in connection with the tomb yonder should turn up, and bother me. It would embitter our lives, if I were then half in the dark, as I am now!'

Knight spoke the latter sentences with growing force.

'It cannot be,' she said.

'Why not?' he asked sharply.

Elfride was distressed to find him in so stern a mood, and she trembled. In a confusion of ideas, probably not intending a wilful prevarication, she answered hurriedly –

'If he's dead, how can you meet him?'

'Is he dead? Oh, that's different altogether!' said Knight, immensely relieved. 'But let me see – what did you say about that tomb and him?'

'That's his tomb,' she continued faintly.

'What! was he who lies buried there the man who was your lover?' Knight asked.

'Yes; and I didn't love him or encourage him.'

'But you let him kiss you – you said so, you know, Elfride.'

She made no reply.

'Why,' said Knight, recollecting circumstances by degrees, 'you surely said you were in some degree engaged to him – and of course you were if he kissed you. And now you say you never encouraged him. And I have been fancying you said – I am almost sure you did – that you were sitting with him *on* that tomb. Good God!' he cried, suddenly starting up in anger, 'are you telling me untruths? Why should you play with me like this? I'll have the right of it. Elfride, we shall never be happy! There's a blight upon us, or me, or you, and it must be cleared off before we marry.' Knight moved away impetuously as if to leave her.

She jumped up and clutched his arm.

'Don't go, Harry – don't!'

'Tell me, then,' said Knight. 'And remember this, no more evasions, or, upon my soul, I shall be thoroughly vexed. Heavens! that I should come to this, to be made a fool of by untruths—'

'Don't, don't treat me so cruelly! O Harry, Harry, have pity, and withdraw those dreadful words! I am truthful by nature – I am – and I don't know how I came to make you misunderstand! But I was frightened!' She quivered so in her perturbation that she shook him with her.

'Did you say you were sitting on that tomb?' he asked moodily.

'Yes; and it was true.'

'Then how, in the name of Heaven, can a man sit upon his own tomb?'

'That was another man. Forgive me, Harry, won't you?'

'What, a lover in the tomb and a lover on it?'

'O – O – yes!'

'Then there were two before me?'

'I – suppose so.'

'Now, don't be a silly woman with your supposing – I hate all that,' said Knight. 'Well, we learn strange things. I don't know what I might have done – no man can say into what shape circumstances may warp him – but I hardly think I should have had the conscience to accept the favours of a new lover whilst sitting over the poor remains of the old one; upon my soul, I don't.' Knight, in moody meditation, continued looking towards the tomb, which stood staring them in the face like an avenging ghost.

'But you wrong me – O so grievously!' she cried. 'I did not meditate any such thing: believe me, Harry, I did not. It only happened so – quite of itself.'

'Well, I suppose you didn't *intend* such a thing,' he said. 'Nobody ever does,' he sadly continued.

'And him in the grave I never once loved.'

'I suppose the second lover and you, as you sat there, vowed to be faithful to each other for ever?'

Elfride only replied by quick heavy breaths, showing she was on the brink of a sob.

'You don't choose to be anything but reserved, then?'

'Of course we did,' she responded.

'"Of course!" You seem to treat the subject very lightly?'

'It is past, and is nothing to us now.'

'Elfride, it is a nothing which, though it may make a careless man laugh, cannot but make a genuine one grieve. It is a very gnawing pain. Tell me straight through – all of it.'

'Never. O Harry! how can you expect it when so little of it makes you so harsh with me?'

'Now, Elfride, listen to this. You know that what you have told only jars the subtler fancies in one, after all. The feeling I have about it would be called, and is, mere sentimentality; and I don't want you to suppose that an ordinary previous engagement of a straightforward kind would make any practical difference in my love, or my wish to make you my wife. But you seem to have more to tell, and that's where the wrong is. Is there more?'

'Not much more,' she wearily answered.

Knight preserved a grave silence for a minute. '"Not much more,"' he said at last. 'I should think not, indeed!' His voice assumed a low and steady pitch. 'Elfride, you must not mind my saying a strange-sounding thing, for say it I shall. It is this: that if there *were* much more to add to an account which already includes all the particulars that a broken marriage engagement could possibly include with propriety, it must be some exceptional thing which might make it impossible for me or any one else to love you and marry you.'

Knight's disturbed mood led him much further than he would have gone in a quieter moment. And, even as it was, had she been assertive to any degree he would not have been so peremptory; and had she been a stronger character – more practical and less imaginative – she would have made more use of her position in his heart to influence him. But the confiding tenderness which had won him is ever accompanied by a sort of self-committal to the stream of events, leading every such woman to trust more to the kindness of fate for good results than to any argument of her own.

'Well, well,' he murmured cynically; 'I won't say it is your fault: it is my ill-luck, I suppose. I had no real right to question you – everybody would say it was presuming. But when we have misunderstood, we feel injured by the subject of our misunderstanding. You never said you had had nobody else here making love to you, so why should I blame you? Elfride, I beg your pardon.'

'No, no! I would rather have your anger than that cool aggrieved politeness. Do drop that, Harry! Why should you inflict that upon me? It reduces me to the level of a mere acquaintance.'

'You do that with me. Why not confidence for confidence?'

'Yes; but I didn't ask you a single question with regard to your past: I didn't wish to know about it. All I cared for was that, wherever you came from, whatever you had done, whoever you had loved, you were mine at last. Harry, if originally you had known I had loved, would you never have cared for me?'

'I won't quite say that. Though I own that the idea of your inexperienced state had a great charm for me. But I think this: that if I had known there was any phase of your past love you would refuse to reveal if I asked to know it, I should never have loved you.'

Elfride sobbed bitterly. 'Am I such a – mere characterless toy – as to have no attrac – tion in me, apart from – freshness? Haven't I brains? You said – I was clever and ingenious in my thoughts, and – isn't that anything? Have I not some beauty? I think I have a little – and I know I have – yes, I do! You have praised my voice, and my manner, and my accomplishments. Yet all these together are so much rubbish because I – accidentally saw a man before you!'

'O come, Elfride. "Accidentally saw a man" is very cool. You loved him, remember.'

'– And loved him a little!'

'And refuse now to answer the simple question how it ended. Do you refuse still, Elfride?'

'You have no right to question me so – you said so. It is unfair. Trust me as I trust you.'

'That's not at all.'

'I shall not love you if you are so cruel. It is cruel to me to argue like this.'

'Perhaps it is. Yes, it is. I was carried away by my feeling for you. Heaven knows that I didn't mean to; but I have loved you so that I have used you badly.'

'I don't mind it, Harry!' she instantly answered, creeping up and nestling against him; 'and I will not think at all that you used me harshly if you will forgive me, and not be vexed with me any more? I do wish I had been exactly as you thought I was, but I could not help it, you know. If I had only known you had been coming, what a nunnery I would have lived in to have been good enough for you!'

'Well, never mind,' said Knight; and he turned to go. He endeavoured to speak sportively as they went on. 'Diogenes Laertius* says that philosophers used voluntarily to deprive themselves of sight to be uninterrupted in their meditations. Men, becoming lovers, ought to do the same thing.'

'Why? – but never mind – I don't want to know. Don't speak laconically to me.' She was plaintive in her deprecation.

'Why? Because they would never then be distracted by discovering their idol was second-hand.'

She looked down and sighed; and they passed out of the crumbling old place, and slowly crossed to the churchyard entrance. Knight was not himself, and he could not pretend to be. She had not told all.

He supported her lightly over the stile, and was practically as attentive as a lover could be. But there had passed away a glory, and the dream was not as it had been of yore. Perhaps Knight was not shaped by Nature for a marrying man. Perhaps his lifelong constraint towards women, which he had attributed to accident, was not chance after all, but the natural result of instinctive acts so minute as to be undiscernible even by himself. Or whether the rough dispelling of any bright illusion, however imaginative, depreciates the real and unexaggerated brightness which appertains to its basis, one cannot say. Certain it was that Knight's disappointment at finding himself second or third in the field, at Elfride's momentary equivoque, and at her reluctance to be candid, brought him to the verge of cynicism.

CHAPTER THIRTY-THREE

'O daughter of Babylon, wasted with misery'*

A HABIT of Knight's, when not immediately occupied with Elfride – to walk by himself for half an hour or so between dinner and bedtime – had become familiar to his friends at Endelstow, Elfride herself among them. When he had helped her over the stile she said gently, 'If you wish to take your usual turn on the hill, Harry, I can run down to the house alone.'

'Thank you, Elfie; then I think I will.'

Her form diminished to blackness in the moonlight, and Knight, after remaining upon the churchyard stile a few minutes longer, turned back again towards the building. His usual course was now to light a cigar or pipe, and indulge in a quiet meditation. But to-night his mind was too tense to bethink itself of such a solace. He merely walked round to the site of the fallen tower, and sat himself down upon some of the large stones which had composed it until this day, when the chain of circumstance originated by Stephen Smith, while in the employ of Mr Hewby, the London man of art, had brought about its overthrow.

Pondering on the possible episodes of Elfride's past life, and on how he had supposed her to have had no past justifying the name, he sat and regarded the white tomb of young Jethway, now close in front of him. The sea, though comparatively placid, could as usual be heard from this point along the whole distance between promontories to the right and left, floundering and entangling itself among the insulated stacks of rock which dotted the water's edge – the miserable skeletons of tortured old cliffs that would not even yet succumb to the wear and tear of the tides.

As a change from thoughts not of a very cheerful kind, Knight attempted exertion. He stood up, and prepared to ascend to the summit of the ruinous heap of stones, from which a more extended outlook was obtainable than from the ground. He stretched out his arm to seize the projecting arris* of a larger block than ordinary, and so help himself up, when his hand lighted plump upon a substance differing in the greatest possible degree from what he had expected to seize – hard stone. It was stringy and entangled, and trailed upon the stone. The deep shadow from the aisle wall prevented his seeing anything here distinctly, and he began guessing as a necessity. 'It is a tressy species of moss or lichen,' he said to himself.

But it lay loosely over the stone.

'It is a tuft of grass,' he said.

But it lacked the roughness and humidity of the finest grass.

'It is a mason's whitewash-brush.'

Such brushes, he remembered, were more bristly; and however much used in repairing a structure would not be required in pulling one down.

He said, 'It must be a thready silk fringe.'

He felt further in. It was somewhat warm. Knight instantly felt somewhat cold.

To find the coldness of inanimate matter where you expect warmth is startling enough; but a colder temperature than that of the body being rather the rule than the exception in common substances, it hardly conveys such a shock to the system as finding warmth where utter frigidity is anticipated.

'God only knows what it is,' he said.

He felt further, and in the course of a minute put his hand upon a human head. The head was warm, but motionless. The thready mass was the hair of the head – long and straggling, showing that the head was a woman's.

Knight in his perplexity stood still for a moment, and collected his thoughts. The rector's account of the fall of the tower was that the workmen had been undermining it all the day, and had left in the evening intending to give the finishing stroke the next morning. Half an hour after they had gone the undermined angle came down. The woman who was half buried must, as it seemed, have been beneath it at the moment of the fall.

Knight leapt up and began endeavouring to remove the rubbish with his hands. The heap overlying the body was for the most part fine and dusty, but in immense quantity. It would be a saving of time to run for assistance. He crossed to the churchyard wall, and hastened down the hill.

A little way on an intersecting road passed over a small ridge, which now showed up darkly against the moon, and this road here formed a kind of notch in the sky-line. At the moment that Knight arrived at the crossing he beheld a man on this eminence, coming towards him. Knight turned aside and met the stranger.

'There has been an accident at the church,' said Knight, without preface. 'The tower has fallen on somebody, who has been lying there ever since. Will you come and help?'

'That I will,' said the man.

'It is a woman,' said Knight, as they hurried back, 'and I think we two are enough to extricate her. Do you know of a shovel?'

'The grave-digging shovels are about somewhere. They used to stay in the tower.'

'And there must be some belonging to the workmen.'

They searched about, and in an angle of the porch found three carefully stowed away. Going round to the west end Knight signified the spot of the tragedy.

'We ought to have brought a lantern,' he exclaimed. 'But we may be able to do without.' He set to work removing the superincumbent* mass.

The other man, who looked on somewhat helplessly at first, now followed the example of Knight's activity, and removed the larger stones which were mingled with the rubbish. But with all their efforts it was quite ten minutes before the body of the unfortunate creature could be extricated. They lifted her as carefully as they could, breathlessly carried her to Felix Jethway's tomb, which was only a few steps westward, and laid her thereon.

'Is she dead indeed?' said the stranger.

'She appears to be,' said Knight. 'Which is the nearest house? The rectory, I suppose.'

'Yes; but since we shall have to call a surgeon from Castle Boterel, I think it would be better to carry her in that direction, instead of away from the town.'

'But is it not much further to the first house we come to going that way, than to the rectory or to The Crags?'

'Not much,' the stranger replied.

'Certainly we'll take her there, then. And I think the best way to do it would be thus, if you don't mind joining hands with me.'

'Not in the least; I am glad to assist.'

Making a kind of cradle, by clasping their hands crosswise under the inanimate woman, they lifted her, and walked on side by side down a path indicated by the stranger, who appeared to know the locality well.

'I had been sitting in the church for nearly an hour,' Knight resumed, when they were out of the churchyard. 'Afterwards I walked round to the site of the fallen tower, and so found her. It is painful to think I unconsciously wasted so much time in the very presence of a perishing, flying soul.'

'The tower fell at dusk, did it not? quite two hours ago, I think?'

'Yes. She must have been there alone. What could have been her object in visiting the churchyard then?'

'It is difficult to say.' The stranger looked inquiringly into the reclining face of the motionless form they bore. 'Would you turn her round for a moment, so that the light shines on her face?' he said.

They turned her face to the moon, and the man looked closer into her features. 'Why, I know her!' he exclaimed.

'Who is she?'

'Mrs Jethway. And the cottage we are taking her to is her own. She is a widow; and I was speaking to her only this afternoon. I was at Castle Boterel post-office, and she came there to post a letter. Poor soul! Let us hurry on.'

'Hold my wrist a little tighter. Was not that tomb we laid her on the tomb of her only son?'

'Yes, it was. Yes, I see it now. She was there to visit the tomb. Since the death of that son she has been a desolate, desponding woman, always bewailing him. She was a farmer's wife, very well educated.'

Knight's heart was moved to sympathy. His own fortunes seemed in some strange way to be interwoven with those of this Jethway family, through the influence of Elfride over himself and the unfortunate son of that house. He made no reply, and they still walked on.

'She begins to feel heavy,' said the stranger, breaking the silence.

'Yes, she does,' said Knight; and after another pause added, 'I think I have met you before, though where I cannot recollect. May I ask who you are?'

'O yes. I am Lord Luxellian. Who are you?'

'I am a visitor at The Crags – Mr Knight.'

'I have heard of you, Mr Knight.'

'And I of you, Lord Luxellian. I am glad to meet you.'

'I may say the same. I am familiar with your name in print.'

'And I with yours. Is this the house?'

'Yes.'

The door was locked. Knight, reflecting a moment, searched the pocket of the lifeless woman, and found therein a large key which, on being applied to the door, opened it easily. The fire was out, but the moonlight entered the quarried window, and made patterns upon the floor. The rays enabled them to see that the room into which they had entered was pretty well furnished, it being the same room that Elfride had visited alone two or three evenings earlier. They deposited their still burden on an old-fashioned couch which stood against the wall, and Knight searched about for a lamp or candle. He found a candle on a shelf, lighted it, and placed it on the table.

Both Knight and Lord Luxellian examined the pale countenance attentively, and both were nearly convinced that there was no hope. No marks of violence were visible in the casual examination they made.

'I think that as I know where Doctor Granson lives,' said Lord Luxellian, 'I had better run for him whilst you stay here.'

Knight agreed to this. Lord Luxellian then went off, and his hurrying footsteps died away. Knight continued bending over the body, and a few minutes longer of careful scrutiny perfectly satisfied him that the woman was far beyond the reach of the lancet and the drug. Her extremities were already beginning to get stiff and cold. Knight covered her face, and sat down.

The minutes went by. The essayist remained musing on all the occurrences of the night. His eyes were directed upon the table, and he had seen for some time that writing-materials were spread upon it. He now noticed these more particularly: there were an inkstand, pen, blotting-book, and note-paper. Several sheets of paper were thrust aside from the rest, upon which letters had been begun and relinquished, as if their form had not been satisfactory to the writer. A stick of black sealing-wax and seal were there too, as if the ordinary fastening had not been considered sufficiently secure. The abandoned sheets of paper lying as they did open upon the table, made it possible, as he sat, to read the few words written on each. One ran thus:

'SIR, – As a woman who was once blest with a dear son of her own, I implore you to accept a warning—'

Another:

'SIR, – If you will deign to receive warning from a stranger before it is too late to alter your course, listen to—'

The third:

'SIR, – With this letter I enclose to you another which, unaided by any explanation from me, tells a startling tale. I wish, however, to add a few words to make your delusion yet more clear to you—'

It was plain that, after these renounced beginnings, a fourth letter had been written and despatched, which had been deemed a proper one. Upon the table were two drops of sealing-wax, the stick from which they were taken having been laid down overhanging the edge of the table; the end of it drooped, showing that the wax was placed there whilst warm. There was the chair in which the writer had sat, the impression of the letter's address upon the blotting-paper, and the poor widow who had caused these results lying dead hard by. Knight had seen enough to lead him to the conclusion that Mrs Jethway, having matter of great importance to communicate to some friend or acquaintance, had written him a very careful letter, and gone herself to post it; that she had not returned to the house from that time of leaving it till Lord Luxellian and himself had brought her back dead.

The unutterable melancholy of the whole scene, as he waited on, silent and alone, did not altogether clash with the mood of Knight, even though he was the affianced of a fair and winning girl, and though so lately he had been in her company. While sitting on the remains of the demolished tower he had defined a new sensation; that the lengthened course of inaction he had lately been indulging in on Elfride's account might probably not be good for him as a man who had work to do. It could quickly be put an end to by hastening on his marriage with her.

Knight, in his own opinion, was one who had missed his mark by excessive aiming. Having now, to a great extent, given up ideal ambitions, he wished earnestly to direct his powers into a more practical channel, and thus correct the introspective tendencies which had never brought himself much happiness, or done his fellow-creatures any great good. To make a start in this new direction by marriage, which, since knowing Elfride, had been so entrancing an idea, was less exquisite to-night. That the curtailment of his illusion regarding her had something to do with the reaction, and with the return of his old sentiments on wasting time, is more than probable. Though Knight's heart had so greatly mastered him, the mastery was not so complete as to be easily maintained in the face of a moderate intellectual revival.

His reverie was broken by the sound of wheels, and a horse's tramp. The door opened to admit the surgeon, Lord Luxellian, and a Mr Coole, coroner for the division (who had been attending at Castle Boterel that day, and was having an after-dinner chat with the doctor when Lord Luxellian arrived); next came two female nurses and some idlers.

Mr Granson, after a cursory examination, pronounced the woman dead from suffocation, induced by intense pressure on the respiratory organs; and arrangements were made that the inquiry should take place on the following morning, before the return of the coroner to St Launce's.

Shortly afterwards the house of the widow was deserted by all its living occupants, and she abode in death, as she had in her life during the past two years, entirely alone.

CHAPTER THIRTY-FOUR

'Yea, happy shall he be that rewardeth thee as thou hast served us.'*

SIXTEEN hours had passed. Knight was entering the ladies' boudoir at The Crags, upon his return from attending the inquest touching the death of Mrs Jethway. Elfride was not in the apartment.

Mrs Swancourt made a few inquiries concerning the verdict and collateral circumstances. Then she said –

'The postman came this morning the minute after you left the house. There was only one letter for you, and I have it here.'

She took a letter from the lid of her workbox, and handed it to him. Knight took the missive abstractedly, but struck by its appearance murmured a few words and left the room.

The letter was fastened with a black seal, and the handwriting in which it was addressed had lain under his eyes, long and prominently, only the evening before.

Knight was greatly agitated, and looked about for a spot where he might be secure from interruption. It was the season of heavy dews, which lay on the herbage in shady places all the day long; nevertheless, he entered a small patch of neglected grass-plat enclosed by the shrubbery, and there perused the letter, which he had opened on his way thither.

The handwriting, the seal, the paper, the introductory words, all had told on the instant that the letter had come to him from the hands of the widow Jethway, now dead and cold. He had instantly understood that the unfinished notes which caught his eye yesternight were intended for nobody but himself. He had remembered some of the words of Elfride in her sleep on the steamer, that somebody was not to tell him of something, or it would be her ruin – a circumstance hitherto deemed so trivial and meaningless that he had well-nigh forgotten it. All these things infused into him an emotion intense in power and supremely distressing in quality. The paper in his hand quivered as he read

'The Valley, Endelstow

'Sir, – A woman who has not much in the world to lose by any censure this act may bring upon her, wishes to give you some hints concerning a lady you love. If you will deign to accept a warning before it is too late, you will notice what your correspondent has to say.

'You are deceived. Can such a woman as this be worthy?

'One who encouraged an honest youth to love her, then slighted him, so that he died.

'One who next took a man of no birth as a lover, who was forbidden the house by her father.

'One who secretly left her home to be married to that man, met him, and went with him to London.

'One who, for some reason or other, returned again unmarried.

'One who, in her after-correspondence with him, went so far as to address him as her husband.

'One who wrote the enclosed letter to ask me, who better than anybody else knows the story, to keep the scandal a secret.

'I hope soon to be beyond the reach of either blame or praise. But before removing me God has put it in my power to avenge the death of my son.

'Gertrude Jethway'

The letter enclosed was the note in pencil that Elfride had written in Mrs Jethway's cottage:

'Dear Mrs Jethway, – I have been to visit you. I wanted much to see you, but I cannot wait any longer. I came to beg you not to execute the threats you have repeated to me. Do not, I beseech you, Mrs Jethway, let any one know what I did! It would ruin me, and break my heart. I will do anything for you, if you will be kind to me. In the name of our common womanhood, do not, I implore you, make a scandal of me. – Yours,

'E. Swancourt'

Knight turned his face wearily towards the house. The ground rose from the walls to the shrubbery in which he stood, raising it almost to a level with the first floor of The Crags. Elfride's dressing-room lay in the salient angle in this direction, and it was lighted by two windows in such a position that, from Knight's standing-place, his sight passed through both windows, and raked the room. Elfride was there; she was pausing between the two windows, looking at her figure in the cheval-glass. She regarded herself long and attentively in front; turned, flung back her head, and observed the reflection over her shoulder.

Nobody can predicate as to her object or fancy; she may have done the deed in the very abstraction of deep sadness. She may have been moaning from the bottom of her heart, 'How unhappy am I!' But the impression produced on Knight was not a good one. He dropped his eyes moodily. The dead woman's letter had a virtue in the accident of its juncture far beyond any it intrinsically exhibited. Circumstance lent to evil words a ring of pitiless justice echoing from the grave. Knight could not endure their possession. He tore the letter into fragments.

He heard a brushing among the bushes behind, and turning his head he saw Elfride following him. The fair girl looked in his face with a wistful smile of hope, too forcedly hopeful to displace the firmly established dread beneath it. His severe words of the previous night still sat heavy upon her.

'I saw you from my window, Harry,' she said timidly.

'The dew will make your feet wet,' he observed, as one deaf.

'I don't mind it.'

'There is danger in getting wet feet.'

'Yes. . . . Harry, what is the matter?'

'O, nothing. Shall I resume the serious conversation I had with you last night? No, perhaps not; perhaps I had better not.'

'I cannot tell! How wretched it all is! Ah, I wish you were your own dear self again, and had kissed me when I came up! Why didn't you ask me for one? why don't you now?'

'Too free in manner by half,' he heard murmur the voice within him.

'It was that hateful conversation last night,' she went on. 'O, those words! Last night was a black night for me.'

'Kiss! – I hate that word! Don't talk of kissing, for God's sake! I should think you might with advantage have shown tact enough to keep back that word "kiss", considering those you have accepted.'

She became very pale, and a rigid and desolate charactery took possession of her face. That face was so delicate and tender in appearance now, that one could fancy the pressure of a finger upon it would cause a livid spot.

Knight walked on, and Elfride with him, silent and unopposing.

He opened a gate, and they entered a path across a stubble-field.

'Perhaps I intrude upon you?' she said as he closed the gate. 'Shall I go away?'

'No. Listen to me, Elfride.' Knight's voice was low and unequal. 'I have been honest with you: will you be so with me? If any – strange – connection has existed between yourself and a predecessor of mine, tell it now. It is better that I know it now, even though the knowledge should part us, than that I should discover it in time to come. And suspicions have been awakened in me. I think I will not say how, because I despise the means. A discovery of any mystery of your past would embitter our lives.'

Knight waited with a slow manner of calmness. His eyes were sad and imperative. They went further along the path.

'Will you forgive me if I tell you all?' she exclaimed entreatingly.

'I can't promise; so much depends upon what you have to tell.'

Elfride could not endure the silence which followed.

'Are you not going to love me?' she burst out. 'Harry, Harry, love me, and speak as usual! Do; I beseech you, Harry!'

'Are you going to act fairly by me?' said Knight; 'or are you not? What have I done to you that I should be put off like this? Be caught like a bird in a springe;* everything intended to be hidden from me! Why is it, Elfride? That's what I ask you.'

In their agitation they had left the path, and were wandering among the wet and obstructive stubble, without knowing or heeding it.

'What have *I* done?' she faltered.

'What? How can you ask what, when you know so well? You *know* that I have designedly been kept in ignorance of something attaching to you, which, had I known of it, might have altered all my conduct; and yet you say, what?'

She drooped visibly, and made no answer.

'Not that I believe in malicious letter-writers and whisperers; not I. I don't know whether I do or don't: upon my soul, I can't tell. I know this: a religion was building itself upon you in my heart. I looked into your eyes, and thought I saw there truth and innocence as pure and perfect as ever embodied by God in the flesh of woman. Perfect truth is too much to expect, but ordinary truth I *will have* or nothing at all. Just say, then; is the matter you keep back of the gravest importance, or is it not?'

'I don't understand all your meaning. If I have hidden anything from you, it has been because I loved you so, and I feared – feared – to lose you.'

'Since you are not given to confidence, I want to ask you some plain questions. Have I your permission?'

'Yes,' she said, and there came over her face a weary resignation. 'Say the harshest words you can; I will bear them!'

'There is a scandal in the air concerning you, Elfride; and I cannot even combat it without knowing definitely what it is. It may not refer to you entirely, or even at all.' Knight trifled in the very bitterness of his feeling. 'In the time of the French Revolution, Pariseau, a ballet-master, was beheaded by mistake for Parisot, a captain of the King's Guard. I wish there was another "E. Swancourt" in the neighbourhood. Look at this.'

He handed her the letter she had written and left on the table at Mrs Jethway's. She looked over it vacantly.

'It is not so much as it seems!' she pleaded. 'It seems wickedly deceptive to look at now, but it had a much more natural origin than you think. My sole wish was not to endanger our love. O Harry! that was all my idea. It was not much harm.'

'Yes, yes; but independently of the poor miserable creature's remarks, it seems to imply – something wrong.'

'What remarks?'

'Those she wrote me – now torn to pieces. Elfride, *did* you run away with a man you loved? – that was the damnable statement. Has such an accusation life in it – really, truly, Elfride?'

'Yes,' she whispered.

Knight's countenance sank. 'To be married to him?' came huskily from his lips.

'Yes. O, forgive me! I had never seen you, Harry.'

'To London?'

'Yes; but I—'

'Answer my questions; say nothing else, Elfride. Did you ever deliberately try to marry him in secret?'

'No; not deliberately.'

'But did you do it?'

A feeble red passed over her face.

'Yes,' she said.

'And after that – did you – write to him as your husband; and did he address you as his wife?'

'Listen, listen! It was—'

'Do answer me; only answer me!'

'Then, yes, we did.' Her lips shook; but it was with some little dignity that she continued: 'I would gladly have told you; for I knew and know I had done wrong. But I dared not; I loved you too well. O, so well! You have been everything in the world to me – and you are now. Will you not forgive me?'

It is a melancholy thought that men who at first will not allow the verdict of perfection they pronounce upon their sweethearts or wives to be disturbed by God's own testimony to the contrary, will, once suspecting their purity, morally hang them upon evidence they would be ashamed to admit in judging a dog.

The reluctance to tell, which arose from Elfride's simplicity in thinking herself so much more culpable than she really was, had been doing fatal work in Knight's mind. The man of many ideas, now that his first dream of impossible things was over, vibrated too far in the contrary direction; and her every movement of feature – every tremor – every confused word – was taken as so much proof of her unworthiness.

'Elfride, we must bid good-bye to compliment,' said Knight: 'we must do without politeness now. Look in my face, and as you believe in God above, tell me truly one thing more. Were you away alone with him?'

'Yes.'

'Did you return home the same day on which you left it?'

'No.'

The word fell like a bolt, and the very land and sky seemed to suffer. Knight turned aside. Meantime Elfride's countenance wore a look indicating utter despair of being able to explain* matters so that they would seem no more than they really were, – a despair which not only relinquishes the hope of direct explanation, but wearily gives up all collateral chances of extenuation.

The scene was engraved for years on the retina of Knight's eye: the dead and brown stubble, the weeds among it, the distant belt of beeches shutting out the view of the house, the leaves of which were now red and sick to death.

'You must forget me,' he said. 'We shall not marry, Elfride.'

How much anguish passed into her soul at those words from him was told by the look of supreme torture she wore.

'What meaning have you, Harry? You only say so, do you?'

She looked doubtingly up at him, and tried to laugh, as if the unreality of his words must be unquestionable.

'You are not in earnest, I know – I hope you are not? Surely I belong to you, and you are going to keep me for yours?'

'Elfride, I have been speaking too roughly to you; I have said what I ought only to have thought. I like you; and let me give you a word of advice. Marry your man as soon as you can. However weary of each other you may feel, you belong to each other, and I am not going to step between you. Do you think I would – do you think I could for a moment? If you cannot marry him now, and another makes you his wife, do not reveal this secret to him after marriage, if you do not before. Honesty would be damnation then.'

Bewildered by his expressions, she exclaimed –

'No, no; I will not be a wife unless I am yours; and I must be yours!'

'If we had married—'

'But you don't *mean* – that – that – you will go away and leave me, and not be anything more to me – O, you don't!'

Convulsive sobs took all nerve out of her utterance. She checked them, and continued to look in his face for the ray of hope that was not to be found there.

'I am going indoors,' said Knight. 'You will not follow me, Elfride; I wish you not to.'

'O no; indeed, I will not.'

'And then I am going to Castle Boterel. Good-bye.'

He spoke the farewell as if it were but for the day – lightly, as he had spoken such temporary farewells many times before – and she seemed to understand it as such. Knight had not the power to tell her plainly that he was going for ever; he hardly knew for certain that he was: whether he should rush back again upon the current of an irresistible emotion, or whether he could sufficiently conquer himself, and her in him, to establish that parting as a supreme farewell, and present himself to the world again as no woman's.

Ten minutes later he had left the house, leaving directions that if he did not return in the evening his luggage was to be sent to his chambers in London, whence he intended to write to Mr Swancourt as to the reasons of his sudden departure. He descended the valley, and could not forbear turning his head. He saw the stubble-field, and a slight girlish figure in the midst of it – up against the sky. Elfride, docile as ever, had hardly moved a step, for he had said, Remain. He looked and saw her again – he saw her for weeks and months. He withdrew his eyes from the scene, swept his hand across them, as if to brush away the sight, breathed a low groan, and went on.

CHAPTER THIRTY-FIVE

'And wilt thou leave me thus? – say nay – say nay!'*

THE scene shifts to Knight's chambers in Bede's Inn. It was late in the evening of the day following his departure from Endelstow. A drizzling rain descended upon London, forming a humid and dreary halo over every well-lighted street. The rain had not yet been prevalent long enough to give to rapid vehicles that clear and distinct rattle which follows the thorough washing of the stones by a drenching rain, but was just sufficient to make footway and roadway slippery, adhesive, and clogging to both feet and wheels.

Knight was standing by the fire, looking into its expiring embers previously to emerging from his door for a dreary journey home to Richmond. His hat was on, and the gas turned off. The blind of the window overlooking the alley was not drawn down; and with the light from beneath, which shone over the ceiling of the room, came, in place of the usual babble, only the reduced clatter and quick speech which were the result of necessity rather than choice.

Whilst he thus stood, waiting for the expiration of the few minutes that were wanting to the time for his catching the train, a light tapping upon the door mingled with the other sounds that reached his ears. It was so faint at first that the outer noises were almost sufficient to drown it. Finding it repeated Knight crossed the lobby crowded with books and rubbish, and opened the door.

A woman, closely muffled up, but visibly of fragile build, was standing on the landing under the gaslight. She sprang forward, flung her arms round Knight's neck, and uttered a low cry –

'O Harry, Harry, you are killing me! I could not help coming. Don't send me away – don't! Forgive your Elfride for coming – I love you so!'

Knight's agitation and astonishment mastered him for a few moments.

'Elfride!' he cried, 'what does this mean? What have you done?'

'Do not hurt me and punish me – O do not! I couldn't help

coming; it was killing me. Last night, when you did not come back, I could not bear it – I could not! Only let me be with you, and see your face, Harry; I don't ask for more.'

Her eyelids were hot, heavy, and thick with excessive weeping, and the delicate rose-red of her cheeks was disfigured and inflamed by the constant chafing of the handkerchief in wiping her many tears.

'Who is with you? Have you come alone?' he hurriedly inquired.

'Yes. When you did not come last night I sat up hoping you would come – and the night was all agony – and I waited on and on, and you did not come! Then when it was morning, and your letter said you were gone, I could not endure it; and I ran away from them to St Launce's, and came by the train. And I have been all day travelling to you, and you won't make me go away again, will you, Harry, because I shall always love you till I die?'

'Yet it is wrong for you to stay. O Elfride! what have you committed yourself to? It is ruin to your good name to run to me like this! Has not your first experience been sufficient to keep you from these things?'

'My name! Harry, I shall soon die, and what good will my name be to me then? O, could *I* but be the man and *you* the woman, I would not leave you for such a little fault as mine! Do not think it was so vile a thing in me to run away with him. Ah, how I wish you could have run away with twenty women before you knew me, that I might show you I would think it no fault, but be glad to get you after them all, so that I had you! If you only knew me through and through, how true I am, Harry. Cannot I be yours? Say you love me just the same, and don't let me be separated from you again, will you? I cannot bear it – all the long hours and days and nights going on, and you not there, but away because you hate me!'

'Not hate you, Elfride,' he said gently, and supported her with his arm. 'But you cannot stay here now – just at present, I mean.'

'I suppose I must not – I wish I might. I am afraid that if – you lose sight of me – something dark will happen, and we shall not meet again. Harry, if I am not good enough to be your wife, I wish I could be your servant and live with you, and not be sent away never to see you again. I don't mind what it is except that!'

'No, I cannot send you away: I cannot. God knows what dark future may arise out of this evening's work; but I cannot send you away! You must sit down, and I will endeavour to collect my thoughts and see what had better be done.'

At that moment a loud knocking at the house door was heard by both, accompanied by a hurried ringing of the bell that echoed from attic to basement. The door was quickly opened, and after a few hasty words of converse in the hall, heavy footsteps ascended the stairs.

The face of Mr Swancourt, flushed, grieved, and stern, appeared round the landing of the staircase. He came higher up, and stood beside them. Glancing over and past Knight with silent indignation, he turned to the trembling girl.

'O Elfride! and have I found you at last? Are these your tricks, madam? When will you get rid of your idiocies, and conduct yourself like a decent woman? Is my family name and house to be disgraced by acts that would be a scandal to a washerwoman's daughter? Come along, madam; come!'

'She is so weary!' said Knight, in a voice of intensest anguish. 'Mr Swancourt, don't be harsh with her – let me beg of you to be tender with her, and love her!'

'To you, sir,' said Mr Swancourt, turning to him as if by the sheer pressure of circumstances, 'I have little to say. I can only remark, that the sooner I can retire from your presence the better I shall be pleased. Why you could not conduct your courtship of my daughter like an honest man, I do not know. Why she – a foolish inexperienced girl – should have been tempted to this piece of folly, I do not know. Even if she had not known better than to leave her home, you might have, I should think.'

'It is not his fault: he did not tempt me, papa! I came.'

'If you wished the marriage broken off, why didn't you say so plainly? If you never intended to marry, why could you not leave her alone? Upon my soul, it grates me to the heart to be obliged to think so ill of a man I thought my friend!'

Knight, soul-sick and weary of his life, did not arouse himself to utter a word in reply. How should he defend himself when his defence was the accusation of Elfride? On that account he felt a miserable satisfaction in letting her father go on thinking and speaking wrongfully. It was a faint ray of pleasure straying into the great gloominess of his brain to think that the rector might never know but that he, as her lover, tempted her away, which seemed to be the form Mr Swancourt's misapprehension had taken.

'Now, are you coming?' said Mr Swancourt to her again. He took her unresisting hand, drew it within his arm, and led her down the stairs. Knight's eyes followed her, the last moment begetting in him a frantic hope that she would turn her head. She passed on, and never looked back.

He heard the door open – close again. The wheels of a cab grazed the kerbstone, a murmured direction followed. The door was slammed together, the wheels moved, and they rolled away.

From that hour of her reappearance a dreadful conflict raged within the breast of Henry Knight. His instinct, emotion, affectiveness – or whatever it may be called – urged him to stand forward, seize upon Elfride, and be her cherisher and protector through life. Then came the devastating thought that Elfride's childlike, unreasoning, and indiscreet act in flying to him only proved that the proprieties must be a dead letter with her; that the unreserve, which was really artlessness without ballast, meant indifference to decorum; and what so likely as that such a woman had been deceived in the past? He said to himself, in a mood of the bitterest cynicism: 'The suspicious discreet woman who imagines dark and evil things of all her fellow-creatures is far too shrewd to be deluded by man: trusting beings like Elfride are the women who fall.'

Hours and days went by, and Knight remained inactive. Lengthening time, which made fainter the heart-awakening power of her presence, strengthened the mental ability to reason her down. Elfride loved him, he knew, and he could not leave off loving her; but marry her he would not. If she could but be again his own Elfride – the woman she had seemed to be – but that woman was dead and buried, and he knew her no more! And how could he marry this Elfride, one who, if he had originally seen her as she was, would have been barely an interesting pitiable acquaintance in his eyes – no more?

It cankered his heart to think he was confronted by the closest instance of a worse state of things than any he had assumed in the pleasant social philosophy and satire of his essays.

The moral rightness of this man's life was worthy of all praise;

but in spite of some intellectual acumen, Knight had in him a modicum of that wrongheadedness which is mostly found in scrupulously honest people. With him, truth seemed too clean and pure an abstraction to be so hopelessly churned in with error as practical persons find it. Having now seen himself mistaken in supposing Elfride to be peerless, nothing on earth could make him believe she was not so very bad after all.

He lingered in town a fortnight, doing little else than vibrate between passion and opinions. One idea remained intact – that it was better Elfride and himself should not meet.

When he surveyed the volumes on his shelves – few of which had been opened since Elfride first took possession of his heart – their untouched and orderly arrangement reproached him as an apostate from the old faith of his youth and early manhood. He had deserted those never-failing friends, so they seemed to say, for an unstable delight in a ductile woman, which had ended all in bitterness. The spirit of self-denial, verging on asceticism, which had ever animated Knight in old times, announced itself as having departed with the birth of love, with it having gone the self-respect which had compensated for the lack of self-gratification. Poor little Elfride, instead of holding, as formerly, a place in his religion, began to assume the hue of a temptation. Perhaps it was human and correctly natural that Knight never once thought whether he did not owe her a little sacrifice for her unchary devotion in saving his life.

With a consciousness of having thus, like Antony, kissed away kingdoms and provinces,* he next considered how he had revealed his higher secrets and intentions to her, an unreserve he would never have allowed himself with any man living. How was it that he had not been able to refrain from telling her of adumbrations heretofore locked in the closest strongholds of his mind?

Knight's was a robust intellect, which could escape outside the atmosphere of heart, and perceive that his own love, as well as other people's, could be reduced by change of scene and circumstances. At the same time the perception was a superimposed sorrow:

> 'O last regret, regret can die!'*

But being convinced that the death of this regret was the best thing for him, he did not long shrink from attempting it. He closed his chambers, suspended his connection with editors, and left London for the Continent. Here we will leave him to wander without purpose, beyond the nominal one of encouraging obliviousness of Elfride.

CHAPTER THIRTY-SIX

'The pennie's the jewel that beautifies a'.'*

'I CAN'T think what's coming to these St Launce's people at all at all.'

'With their "How-d'ye-do's", do you mean?'

'Ay, with their "How-d'ye-do's", and shaking of hands, asking me in, and tender inquiries for you, John.'

These words formed part of a conversation between John Smith and his wife on a Saturday evening in the spring which followed Knight's departure from England. Stephen had long since returned to India; and the persevering couple themselves had migrated from Lord Luxellian's park at Endelstow to a comfortable roadside dwelling about a mile out of St Launce's, where John had opened a small stone and slate yard in his own name.

'When we came here six months ago,' continued Mrs Smith, 'though I had paid ready money so many years in the town, my friskier shopkeepers would only speak over the counter. Meet them in the street half-an-hour after, and they'd treat me with staring ignorance of my face.'

'Look through ye as through a glass window?'

'Yes, the brazen ones would. The quiet and cool ones would glance over the top of my head, past my side, over my shoulder, but never meet my eye. The gentle-modest would turn their faces south if I were coming east, flit down a passage if I were about to halve the pavement with them. There was the spruce young bookseller would play the same tricks; the butcher's daughters; the upholsterer's young men. Hand in glove when doing business out of sight with you; but caring nothing for an old woman when playing the genteel away from all signs of their trade.'

'True enough, Maria.'

'Well, to-day 'tis all different. I'd no sooner got to market than Mrs Joakes rushed up to me in the eyes of the town and said, "My dear Mrs Smith, now you must be tired with your walk! Come in and have some lunch! I insist upon it; knowing you so many years as I have! Don't you remember when we used to go looking for owls' feathers together in the Castle ruins?" There's no knowing what you may need, so I answered the woman civilly. I hadn't got to the corner before that thriving young lawyer, Sweet, who's quite the dandy, ran after me out of breath. "Mrs Smith," he says, "excuse my rudeness, but there's a bramble on the tail of your dress, which you've dragged in from the country; allow me to pull it off for you." If you'll believe me, this was in the very front of the Town Hall. What's the meaning of such sudden love for an old woman?'

'Can't say; unless 'tis repentance.'

'Repentance! was there ever such a fool as you, John? Did anybody ever repent with money in's pocket and fifty years to live?'

'Now, I've been thinking too,' said John, passing over the query as hardly pertinent, 'that I've had more loving-kindness from folks to-day than I ever have before since we moved here. Why, old Alderman Tope walked out to the middle of the street where I was, to shake hands with me – so 'a did. Having on my working clothes, I thought 'twas odd. Ay, and there was young Werrington.'

'Who's he?'

'Why, the man in Hill Street, who plays and sells flutes, and fiddles, and grand pianners. He was talking to Egloskerry, that very small bachelor-man with money in the funds.* I was going by, I'm sure, without thinking or expecting a nod from men of that glib kidney when in my working clothes—'

'You always will go poking into town in your working clothes. Beg you to change how I will, 'tis no use.'

'Well, however, I was in my working clothes. Werrington saw me. "Ah, Mr Smith! a fine morning; excellent weather for building," says he, out as loud and friendly as if I'd met him in some deep hollow, where he could get nobody else to speak to at all. 'Twas odd: for Werrington is one of the very ringleaders of the fast class.'

At that moment a tap came to the door. The door was immediately opened by Mrs Smith in person.

'You'll excuse us, I'm sure, Mrs Smith, but this beautiful spring weather was too much for us. Yes, and we could stay in no longer; and I took Mrs Trewen upon my arm directly we'd had a cup of tea, and out we came. And seeing your beautiful crocuses in such a bloom, we've taken the liberty to enter. We'll step round the garden, if you don't mind.'

'Not at all,' said Mrs Smith; and they walked round the garden. She lifted her hands in amazement directly their backs were turned. 'Goodness send us grace!'

'Who be they?' said her husband.

'Actually Mr Trewen, the bank-manager, and his wife.'

John Smith, staggered in mind, went out of doors and looked over the garden gate, to collect his ideas. He had not been there two minutes when wheels were heard, and a carriage and pair rolled along the road. A distinguished-looking lady, with the demeanour of a duchess, reclined within. When opposite Smith's gate she turned her head, and instantly commanded the coachman to stop.

'Ah, Mr Smith, I am glad to see you looking so well. I could not help stopping a moment to congratulate you and Mrs Smith upon the happiness you must enjoy. Joseph, you may drive on.'

And the carriage rolled away towards St Launce's.

Out rushed Mrs Smith from behind a laurel-bush, where she had stood pondering.

'Just going to raise my hat to her,' said John; 'just for all the world as I would have to poor Lady Luxellian years ago.'

'Lord! who is she?'

'The public-house woman – what's her name? Mrs – Mrs – at the Falcon.'

'Public-house woman. The clumsiness of the Smith family! You *might* say the landlady of the Falcon Hotel, since we are in for politeness. The people are ridiculous enough, but give them their due.'

The possibility is that Mrs Smith was getting mollified, in spite of herself, by these remarkably friendly phenomena among the people of St Launce's. And in justice to them it was quite desirable that she should do so. The interest which the unpractised ones of this town expressed so grotesquely was genuine of its kind, and equal in intrinsic worth to the more polished smiles of larger communities.

By this time Mr and Mrs Trewen were returning from the garden.

'I'll ask 'em flat,' whispered John to his wife. 'I'll say, "We are in a fog – you'll excuse my asking a question, Mr and Mrs Trewen. How is it you all be so friendly to-day?" Hey? 'Twould sound right and sensible, wouldn't it?'

'Not a word! Good mercy, when ever will you have manners!'

'It must be a proud moment for you, I am sure, Mr and Mrs Smith, to have a son so celebrated,' said the bank-manager advancing.

'Ah, 'tis Stephen – I knew it!' said Mrs Smith triumphantly to herself.

'We don't know particulars,' said John.

'Not know!'

'No.'

'Why, 'tis all over town. Our worthy Mayor alluded to it in a speech at the dinner last night of the Every-Man-his-own-Maker Club.'

'And what about Stephen?' urged Mrs Smith.

'Why, your son has been fêted by deputy-governors and Parsee princes and nobody-knows-who in India; is hand in glove with nabobs, and is to design a large palace, and cathedral, and hospitals, colleges, halls, and fortifications, by the general consent of the ruling powers, Christian and Pagan alike.'

''Twas sure to come to the boy,' said Mr Smith unassumingly.

''Tis in yesterday's *St Launce's Gazette*; and our worthy Mayor in the chair introduced the subject into his speech last night in a masterly manner.'

''Twas very good of the worthy Mayor in the chair, I'm sure,' said Stephen's mother. 'I hope the boy will have the sense to keep what he's got; but he may go the way of all his sex. Some woman will hook him.'

'Well, Mr and Mrs Smith, the evening closes in, and we must be going; and remember this, that every Saturday when you come in to market, you are to make our house as your own. There will be always a tea-cup and saucer for you, as you know there has been for months, though you may have forgotten it. I'm a plain-speaking woman, and what I say I mean.'

When the visitors were gone, and the sun had set, and the moon's rays were just beginning to assert themselves upon the walls of the dwelling, John Smith and his wife sat down to the newspaper they had hastily procured from the town. And when the reading was done, they considered how best to meet the new social requirements settling upon them, which Mrs Smith considered could be done by new furniture and house enlargement alone.

'And, John, mind one thing,' she said in conclusion. 'In writing to Stephen, never by any means mention the name of Elfride Swancourt again. We've left the place, and know no more about her except by hearsay. He seems to be getting free of her, and glad am I for it. It was a cloudy hour for him when he first set eyes upon the girl. That family's been no good to him, first or last; so let them keep their blood to themselves if they want to. He thinks of her, I know, but not so hopelessly. So don't try to know anything about her, and we can't answer his questions. She may die out of his mind then.'

'That shall be it,' said John.

CHAPTER THIRTY-SEVEN

'After many days'*

KNIGHT roamed south, under colour of studying Continental antiquities.

He paced the lofty aisles of Amiens, loitered by Ardennes Abbey, climbed into the strange towers of Laon, analyzed Noyon and Rheims. Then he went to Chartres, and examined its scaly spires and quaint carving: then he idled about Coutances. He rowed beneath the base of Mont St Michel, and caught the varied skyline of the crumbling edifices encrusting it. St Ouen's, Rouen, knew him for days; so did Vezelay, Sens, and many a hallowed monument besides. Abandoning the inspection of early French art with the same purposeless haste as he had shown in undertaking it, he went further, and lingered about Ferrara, Padua, and Pisa. Satiated with mediævalism, he tried the Roman Forum. Next he observed moonlight and starlight effects by the bay of Naples. He turned to Austria, became enervated and depressed on Hungarian and Bohemian plains, and was refreshed again by breezes on the declivities of the Carpathians.

Then he found himself in Greece. He visited the plain of Marathon,* and strove to imagine the Persian defeat; to Mars Hill, to picture St Paul addressing the ancient Athenians;* to Thermopylæ and Salamis, to run through the facts and traditions of the Second Invasion* – the result of his endeavours being more or less chaotic. Knight grew as weary of these places as of all others. Then he felt the shock of an earthquake in the Ionian Islands, and went to Venice. Here he shot in gondolas up and down the winding thoroughfare of the Grand Canal, and loitered on calle* and piazza at night, when the lagunes* were undisturbed by a ripple, and no sound was to be heard but the stroke of the midnight clock. Afterwards he remained for weeks in the museums, galleries, and libraries of Vienna, Berlin, and Paris; and thence came home.

Time thus rolls us on to a February afternoon, divided by fifteen months from the parting of Elfride and her lover in the brown stubble field towards the sea.

Two men obviously not Londoners, and with a touch of foreignness in their guise, met by accident on one of the gravel walks leading across Hyde Park. The younger, more given to looking about him than his fellow, saw and noticed the approach of his senior some time before the latter had raised his eyes from the ground, upon which they were bent in an abstracted gaze that seemed habitual with him.

'Mr Knight – indeed it is!' exclaimed the younger man.

'Ah, Stephen Smith!' said Knight.

Simultaneous operations might now have been observed progressing in both, the result being that an expression less frank and impulsive than the first took possession of their features. It was manifest that the next words uttered were a superficial covering to constraint on both sides.

'Have you been in England long?' said Knight.

'Only two days,' said Smith.

'India ever since?'

'Nearly ever since.'

'They were making a fuss about you at St Launce's last year. I fancy I saw something of the sort in the papers.'

'Yes; I believe something was said about me.'

'I must congratulate you on your achievements.'

'Thanks, but they are nothing very extraordinary. A natural professional progress where there was no opposition.'

There followed that want of words which will always assert itself between nominal friends who find they have ceased to be real ones, and have not yet sunk to the level of mere acquaintance. Each looked up and down the Park. Knight may possibly have borne in mind during the intervening months Stephen's manner towards him the last time they had met, and may have encouraged his former interest in Stephen's welfare to die out of him as misplaced. Stephen certainly was full of the feelings begotten by the belief that Knight had taken away the woman he loved so well.

Stephen Smith then asked a question, adopting a certain recklessness of manner and tone to hide, if possible, the fact that the subject was a much greater one to him than his friend had ever supposed.

'Are you married?'

'I am not.'

Knight spoke in an indescribable tone of bitterness that was almost moroseness.

'And I never shall be,' he added decisively. 'Are you?'

'No,' said Stephen, sadly and quietly, like a man in a sick-room. Totally ignorant whether or not Knight knew of his own previous claims upon Elfride, he yet resolved to hazard a few more words upon the topic which had an aching fascination for him even now.

'Then your engagement to Miss Swancourt came to nothing,' he said. 'You remember I met you with her once?'

Stephen's voice gave way a little here, in defiance of his firmest will to the contrary. Indian affairs had not yet lowered those emotions down to the point of control.

'It was broken off,' came quickly from Knight. 'Engagements to marry often end like that – for better or for worse.'

'Yes; so they do. And what have you been doing lately?'

'Doing? Nothing.'

'Where have you been?'

'I can hardly tell you. In the main, going about Europe; and it may perhaps interest you to know that I have been attempting the serious study of Continental art of the Middle Ages. My notes on each example I visited are at your service. They are of no use to me.'

'I shall be glad with them.... Oh, travelling far and near!'

'Not far,' said Knight, with moody carelessness. 'You know, I daresay, that sheep occasionally become giddy – hydatids in the head 'tis called, in which their brains become eaten up, and the animal exhibits the strange peculiarity of walking round and round in a circle continually. I have travelled just in the same way – round and round like a giddy ram.'

The reckless, bitter, and rambling style in which Knight talked, as if rather to vent his images than to convey any ideas to Stephen, struck the young man painfully. His former friend's days had become cankered in some way: Knight was a changed man. He himself had changed much, but not as Knight had changed.

'Yesterday I came home,' continued Knight, 'without having, to the best of my belief, imbibed half-a-dozen ideas worth retaining.'

'You out-Hamlet Hamlet* in morbidness of mood,' said Stephen, with regretful frankness.

Knight made no reply.

'Do you know,' Stephen continued, 'I could almost have sworn that you would be married before this time, from what I saw?'

Knight's face grew harder. 'Could you?' he said.

Stephen was powerless to forsake the depressing, luring subject.

'Yes; and I simply wonder at it.'

'Whom did you expect me to marry?'

'Her I saw you with.'

'Thank you for that wonder.'

'Did she jilt you?'

'Smith, now one word to you,' Knight returned steadily. 'Don't you ever question me on that subject. I have a reason for making this request, mind. And if you do question me, you will not get an answer.'

'Oh, I don't for a moment wish to ask what is unpleasant to you – not I. I had a momentary feeling that I should like to explain something on my side, and hear a similar explanation on yours. But let it go, let it go, by all means.'

'What would you explain?'

'I lost the woman I was going to marry: you have not married as you intended. We might have compared notes.'

'I have never asked you a word about your case.'

'I know that.'

'And the inference is obvious.'

'Quite so.'

'The truth is, Stephen, I have doggedly resolved never to allude to the matter – for which I have a very good reason.'

'Doubtless. As good a reason as you had for not marrying her.'

'You talk insidiously. I had a good one – a miserably good one!'

Smith's anxiety urged him to venture one more question.

'Did she not love you enough?' He drew his breath in a slow and attenuated stream, as he waited in timorous hope for the answer.

'Stephen, you rather strain ordinary courtesy in pressing questions of that kind after what I have said. I cannot understand you at all. I must go on now.'

'Why, good God!' exclaimed Stephen passionately, 'you talk as if you hadn't at all taken her away from anybody who had better claims to her than you!'

'What do you mean by that?' said Knight, with a puzzled air. 'What have you heard?'

'Nothing. I too must go on. Good-day.'

'If you will go,' said Knight, reluctantly now, 'you must, I suppose. I am sure I cannot understand why you behave so.'

'Nor I why you do. I have always been grateful to you, and as far as I am concerned we need never have become so estranged as we have.'

'And have I ever been anything but well-disposed towards you, Stephen? Surely you know that I have not! The system of reserve began with you: you know that.'

'No, no! You altogether mistake our position. You were always from the first reserved to me, though I was confidential to you. That was, I suppose, the natural issue of our differing positions in life. And when I, the pupil, became reserved like you, the master, you did not like it. However, I was going to ask you to come round and see me.'

'Where are you staying?'

'At the Grosvenor Hotel, Pimlico.'

'So am I.'

'That's convenient, not to say odd. Well, I am detained in London for a day or two; then I am going down to see my father and mother, who live at St Launce's now. Will you see me this evening?'

'I may; but I will not promise. I was wishing to be alone for an hour or two; but I shall know where to find you, at any rate. Good-bye.'

CHAPTER THIRTY-EIGHT

'Jealousy is cruel as the grave.'*

STEPHEN pondered not a little on this meeting with his old friend and once-beloved exemplar. He was grieved, for amid all the distractions of his latter years a still small voice of fidelity to Knight had lingered on in him. Perhaps this staunchness was because Knight ever treated him as a mere disciple – even to snubbing him sometimes; and had at last, though unwittingly, inflicted upon him the greatest snub of all, that of taking away his sweetheart. The emotional side of his constitution was built rather after a feminine than a male model; and that tremendous wound from Knight's hand may have tended to keep alive a warmth which solicitousness would have extinguished altogether.

Knight, on his part, was vexed, after they had parted, that he had not taken Stephen in hand a little after the old manner. Those words which Smith had let fall concerning somebody having a prior claim to Elfride, would, if uttered when the man was younger, have provoked such a query as, 'Come, tell me all about it, my lad,' from Knight, and Stephen would straightway have delivered himself of all he knew on the subject.

Stephen the ingenuous boy, though now obliterated externally by Stephen the contriving man, returned to Knight's memory vividly that afternoon. He was at present but a sojourner in London; and after attending to the two or three matters of business which remained to be done that day, he walked abstractedly into the gloomy corridors of the British Museum for the half-hour previous to their closing. That meeting with Smith had reunited the present with the past, closing up the chasm of his absence from England as if it had never existed, until the final circumstances of his previous time of residence in London formed but a yesterday to the circumstances now. The conflict that then had raged in him concerning Elfride Swancourt revived, strengthened by its sleep. Indeed, in those many months of absence, though quelling the intention to make her his wife, he had never forgotten that she was the type of woman adapted to his nature; and instead of trying to obliterate thoughts of her altogether, he had grown to regard them as an infirmity it was necessary to tolerate.

Knight returned to his hotel much earlier in the evening than he would have done in the ordinary course of things. He did not care to think whether this arose from a friendly wish to close the gap that had slowly been widening between himself and his earliest acquaintance, or from a hankering desire to hear the meaning of the dark oracles Stephen had hastily pronounced, betokening that he knew something more of Elfride than Knight had supposed.

He made a hasty dinner, inquired for Smith, and soon was ushered into the young man's presence, whom he found sitting in front of a comfortable fire, beside a table spread with a few scientific periodicals and art reviews.

'I have come to you, after all,' said Knight. 'My manner was odd this morning, and it seemed desirable to call; but that you had too much sense to notice, Stephen, I know. Put it down to my wanderings in France and Italy.'

'Don't say another word, but sit down. I am only too glad to see you again.'

Stephen would hardly have cared to tell Knight just then that the minute before Knight was announced he had been reading over some old letters of Elfride's. They were not many; and until to-night had been sealed up, and stowed away in a corner of his leather trunk, with a few other mementoes and relics which had accompanied him in his travels. The familiar sights and sounds of London, the meeting with his friend, had with him also revived that sense of abiding continuity with regard to Elfride and love which his absence at the other side of the world had to some extent suspended, though never ruptured. He at first intended only to look over these letters on the outside; then he read one; then another; until the whole was thus re-used as a stimulus to sad memories. He folded them away again, placed them in his pocket and, instead of going on with an examination into the state of the artistic world, had remained musing on the strange circumstance that he had returned to find Knight not the husband of Elfride after all.

The possibility of any given gratification begets a cumulative sense of its necessity. Stephen gave the rein to his imagination, and felt more intensely than he had felt for many months that, without Elfride, his life would never be any great pleasure to himself, or honour to his Maker.

They sat by the fire, chatting on external and random subjects, neither caring to be the first to approach the matter each most longed to discuss. On the table with the periodicals lay two or three pocketbooks, one of them being open. Knight seeing from the exposed page that the contents were sketches only, began turning the leaves over carelessly with his finger. When, some time later, Stephen was out of the room, Knight proceeded to pass the interval by looking at the sketches more carefully.

The first crude ideas, pertaining to dwellings of all kinds, were roughly outlined on the different pages. Antiquities had been copied; fragments of Indian columns, colossal statues, and outlandish ornament from the temples of Elephanta and Kenneri, were carelessly intruded upon by outlines of modern doors, windows, roofs, cooking-stoves, and household furniture; everything, in short, which comes within the range of a practising architect's experience, who travels with his eyes open. Among these occasionally appeared rough delineations of mediæval subjects for carving or illumination – heads of Virgins, Saints, and Prophets.

Stephen was not professedly a free-hand draughtsman, but he drew the human figure with correctness and skill. In its numerous repetitions on the sides and edges of the leaves, Knight began to notice a peculiarity. All the feminine saints had one type of feature. There were large nimbi* and small nimbi about their drooping heads, but the face was always the same. That profile – how well Knight knew that profile!

Had there been but one specimen of the familiar countenance, he might have passed over the resemblance as accidental; but a repetition meant more. Knight thought anew of Smith's hasty words earlier in the day, and looked at the sketches again and again.

On the young man's entry, Knight said with palpable agitation –

'Stephen, who are those intended for?'

Stephen looked over the book with utter unconcern: 'Saints and angels, done in my leisure moments. They were intended as designs for the stained glass of an English church.'

'But whom do you idealize by that type of woman you always adopt for the Virgin?'

'Nobody.'

And then a thought raced along Stephen's mind, and he looked up at his friend.

The truth is, Stephen's introduction of Elfride's lineaments had been so unconscious that he had not at first understood his companion's drift. The hand, like the tongue, easily acquires the trick of repetition by rote, without calling in the mind to assist at all; and this had been the case here. Young men who cannot write verses about their Loves generally take to portraying them, and in the early days of his attachment Smith had never been weary of outlining Elfride. The lay-figure of Stephen's sketches now initiated an adjustment of many things. Knight had recognized her. The opportunity of comparing notes had come unsought.

'Elfride Swancourt, to whom I was engaged,' he said quietly.

'Stephen!'

'I know what you mean by speaking like that.'

'Was it Elfride? *You* the man, Stephen?'

'Yes; and you are thinking why did I conceal the fact from you that time at Endelstow, are you not?'

'Yes, and more – more.'

'I did it for the best; blame me if you will; I did it for the best. And now say how could I be with you afterwards as I had been before?'

'I don't know at all; I can't say.'

Knight remained fixed in thought, and once he murmured –

'I had a suspicion this afternoon that there might be some such meaning in your words about my taking her away. But I dismissed it. How came you to know her?' he presently asked, in almost a peremptory tone.

'I went down about the church; years ago now.'

'When you were with Hewby, of course, of course. Well, I can't understand it.' His tones rose. 'I don't know what to say, your hoodwinking me like this for so long!'

'I don't see that I have hoodwinked you at all.'

'Yes, yes, but—'

Knight arose from his seat, and began pacing up and down the room. His face was markedly pale, and his voice perturbed, as he said –

'You did not act as I should have acted towards you in those circumstances. I feel it deeply; and I tell you plainly, I shall never forget it!'

'What?'

'Your behaviour at that meeting in the family vault, when I told you we were going to be married. Deception, dishonesty, everywhere; all the world's of a piece!'

Stephen did not much like this misconstruction of his motives, even though it was but the hasty conclusion of a friend disturbed by emotion.

'I could do no otherwise than I did, with due regard to her,' he said stiffly.

'Indeed!' said Knight, in the bitterest tone of reproach. 'Nor could you with due regard to her have married her, I suppose! I have hoped – longed – that *he*, who turns out to be *you*, would ultimately have done that.'

'I am much obliged to you for that hope. But you talk very mysteriously. I think I had about the best reason anybody could have had for not doing that.'

'Oh, what reason was it?'

'That I could not.'

'You ought to have made an opportunity; you ought to do so now, in bare justice to her, Stephen!' cried Knight, carried beyond himself. 'That you know very well, and it hurts and wounds me more than you dream to find you never have tried to make any reparation to a woman of that kind – so trusting, so apt to be run away with by her feelings – poor little fool, so much the worse for her!'

'Why, you talk like a madman! You took her away from me, did you not?'

'Picking up what another throws down can scarcely be called "taking away". However, we shall not agree too well upon that subject, so we had better part.'

'But I am quite certain you misapprehend something most

grievously,' said Stephen, shaken to the bottom of his heart. 'What have I done; tell me? I have lost Elfride, but is that such a sin?'

'Was it her doing, or yours?'

'Was what?'

'That you parted.'

'I will tell you honestly. It was hers entirely, entirely.'

'What was her reason?'

'I can hardly say. But I'll tell the story without reserve.'

Stephen until to-day had unhesitatingly held that she grew tired of him and turned to Knight; but he did not like to advance the statement now, or even to think the thought. To fancy otherwise accorded better with the hope to which Knight's estrangement had given birth: that love for his friend was not the direct cause, but a result of her suspension of love for himself.

'Such a matter must not be allowed to breed discord between us,' Knight returned, relapsing into a manner which concealed all his true feeling, as if confidence now was intolerable. 'I do see that your reticence towards me in the vault may have been dictated by prudential considerations.' He concluded artificially, 'It was a strange thing altogether; but not of much importance, I suppose, at this distance of time; and it does not concern me now, though I don't mind hearing your story.'

These words from Knight, uttered with such an air of renunciation and apparent indifference, prompted Smith to speak on – perhaps with a little complacency – of his old secret engagement to Elfride. He told the details of its origin, and the peremptory words and actions of her father to extinguish their love.

Knight persevered in the tone and manner of a disinterested outsider. It had become more than ever imperative to screen his emotions from Stephen's eye; the young man would otherwise be less frank, and their meeting would be again embittered. What was the use of untoward candour?

Stephen had now arrived at the point in his ingenuous narrative where he left the rectory because of her father's manner. Knight's interest increased. Their love seemed so innocent and childlike thus far.

'It is a nice point in casuistry,' he observed, 'to decide whether you were culpable or not in not telling Swancourt that your friends were parishioners of his. It was only human nature to hold your tongue in the circumstances. Well, what was the result of your dismissal by him?'

'That we agreed to be secretly faithful. And to insure this we thought we would marry.'

Knight's suspense and agitation rose higher when Stephen entered upon this phase of the subject.

'Do you mind telling on?' he said.

'O, not at all.'

Then Stephen gave in full the particulars of the meeting with Elfride at the railway station; the necessity they were under of going to London, unless the ceremony were to be postponed. The long journey of the afternoon and evening; her timidity and revulsion of feeling; its culmination on reaching London; the crossing over to the down-platform and their immediate departure again, solely in obedience to her wish; the journey all night; their anxious watching for the dawn; their arrival at St Launce's at last – were detailed. And he told how a village woman named Jethway was the only person who recognized them, either going or coming; and how dreadfully this terrified Elfride. He told how he waited in the fields whilst this then reproachful sweetheart went for her pony, and how the last kiss he ever gave her was given a mile out of the town, on the way to Endelstow.

These things Stephen related with a will. He believed that in doing so he established word by word the reasonableness of his claim to Elfride.

'Curse her! curse that woman! – that miserable woman who parted us! O God!'

Knight began pacing the room again, and uttered this at further end.

'What did you say?' said Stephen, turning round.

'Say? Did I say anything? Oh, I was merely thinking about your story, and the oddness of my having a fancy for the same woman afterwards. And that now I – I have forgotten her almost; and neither of us care about her, except just as a friend, you know, eh?'

Knight still continued at the further end of the room, somewhat in shadow.

'Exactly,' said Stephen, inwardly exultant, for he was really deceived by Knight's off-hand manner.

Yet he was deceived less by the completeness of Knight's disguise than by the persuasive power which lay in the fact that Knight had never before deceived him in anything. So this supposition that his companion had ceased to love Elfride was an enormous lightening of the weight which had turned the scale against him.

'Admitting that Elfride *could* love another man after you,' said the elder, under the same varnish of careless criticism, 'she was none the worse for that experience.'

'The worse? Of course she was none the worse.'

'Did you ever think it a wild and thoughtless thing for her to do?'

'Indeed, I never did,' said Stephen. 'I persuaded her. She saw no harm in it until she decided to return, nor did I; nor was there, except to the extent of indiscretion.'

'Directly she thought it was wrong she would go no further?'

'That was it. I had just begun to think it wrong too.'

'Such a childish escapade might have been misrepresented by any evil-disposed person, might it not?'

'It might; but I never heard that it was. Nobody who really knew all the circumstances would have done otherwise than smile. If all the world had known it, Elfride would still have remained the only one who thought her action a sin. Poor child, she always persisted in thinking so, and was frightened more than enough.'

'Stephen, do you love her now?'

'Well, I like her; I always shall, you know,' he said evasively, and with all the strategy love suggested. 'But I have not seen her for so long that I can hardly be expected to love her. Do you love her still?'

'How shall I answer without being ashamed? What fickle beings we men are, Stephen! Men may love strongest for a while, but women love longest. I used to love her – in my way, you know.'

'Yes, I understand. Ah, and I used to love her in my way. In fact, I loved her a good deal at one time; but travel has a tendency to obliterate early fancies.'

'It has – it has, truly.'

Perhaps the most extraordinary feature in this conversation was the circumstance that, though each interlocutor had at first his suspicions of the other's abiding passion awakened by several little acts, neither would allow himself to see that his friend might now be speaking deceitfully as well as he.

'Stephen,' resumed Knight, 'now that matters are smooth between us, I think I must leave you. You won't mind my hurrying off to my quarters?'

'You'll stay to some sort of supper surely? Why didn't you come to dinner!'

'You must really excuse me this once.'

'Then you'll drop in to breakfast to-morrow.'

'I shall be rather pressed for time.'

'An early breakfast, which shall interfere with nothing?'

'I'll come,' said Knight, with as much readiness as it was possible to graft upon a huge stock of reluctance. 'Yes, early; eight o'clock say, as we are under the same roof.'

'Any time you like. Eight it shall be.'

And Knight left him. To wear a mask, to dissemble his feelings as he had done in their late miserable conversation, was such torture that he could support it no longer. It was the first time in Knight's life that he had ever been so entirely the player of a part. And the man he had thus deceived was Stephen, who had docilely looked up to him from youth as a superior of unblemished integrity.

He went to bed, and allowed the fever of his excitement to rage uncontrolled. Stephen – it was only he who was the rival – only Stephen! There was an anti-climax of absurdity which Knight, wretched and conscience-stricken as he was, could not help recognizing. Stephen was but a boy to him. Where the great grief lay was in perceiving that the very innocence of Elfride in reading her little fault as one so grave was what had fatally misled him. Had Elfride, with any degree of coolness, asserted that she had done no harm, the poisonous breath of the dead Mrs Jethway would have been inoperative. Why did he not make his little docile girl tell more? If on that subject he had only exercised the imperativeness customary with him on others, all might have been revealed. It smote his heart like a switch when he remembered how gently she had borne his scourging speeches, never answering him with a single reproach, only assuring him of her unbounded love.

Knight blessed Elfride for her sweetness, and forgot her fault. He pictured with a vivid fancy those fair summer scenes with her. He again saw her as at their first meeting, timid at speaking, yet in her eagerness to be explanatory borne forward almost against her will. How she would wait for him in green places, without showing any of the ordinary womanly affectations of indifference! How proud she was to be seen walking with him, bearing legibly in her eyes the thought that he was the greatest genius in the world!

He formed a resolution; and after that could make pretence of slumber no longer. Rising and dressing himself, he sat down and waited for day.

That night Stephen was restless too. Not because of the unwontedness of a return to English scenery; not because he was about to meet his parents, and settle down for awhile to English cottage life. He was indulging in dreams, and for the nonce the warehouses of Bombay and the plains and forts of Poonah were but a shadow's shadow. His dream was based on this one atom of fact: Elfride and Knight had become separated, and their engagement was as if it had never been. Their rupture must have occurred soon after Stephen's discovery of the fact of their union; and, Stephen went on to think, what so probable as that a return of her errant affection to himself was the cause?

Stephen's opinions in this matter were those of a lover, and not the balanced judgment of an unbiassed spectator. His naturally sanguine spirit built hope upon hope, till scarcely a doubt remained in his mind that her lingering tenderness for him had in some way been perceived by Knight, and had provoked their parting.

To go and see Elfride was the suggestion of impulses it was impossible to withstand. At any rate, to run down from St Launce's to Castle Boterel, a distance of less than twenty miles, and glide like a ghost about their old haunts, making stealthy inquiries about her, would be a fascinating way of passing the first spare hours after reaching home on the day after the morrow.

He was now a richer man than heretofore, standing on his own bottom; and the definite position in which he had rooted himself nullified old local distinctions. He had become illustrious, even *sanguine clarus*,* judging from the tone of the worthy Mayor of St Launce's.

CHAPTER THIRTY-NINE

'Each to the loved one's side'*

THE friends and rivals breakfasted together the next morning. Not a word was said on either side upon the matter discussed the previous evening so glibly and so hollowly. Stephen was absorbed the greater part of the time in wishing he were not forced to stay in town yet another day.

'I don't intend to leave for St Launce's till to-morrow, as you know,' he said to Knight at the end of the meal. 'What are you going to do with yourself to-day?'

'I have an engagement just before ten,' said Knight deliberately; 'and after that time I must call upon two or three people.'

'I'll look for you this evening,' said Stephen.

'Yes, do. You may as well come and dine with me; that is, if we can meet. I may not sleep in London to-night; in fact, I am absolutely unsettled as to my movements yet. However, the first thing I am going to do is to get my luggage shifted from this place to Bede's Inn. Good-bye for the present. I'll write, you know, if I can't meet you.'

It now wanted a quarter to nine o'clock. When Knight was gone, Stephen felt yet more impatient of the circumstance that another day would have to drag itself away wearily before he could set out for that spot of earth whereon a soft thought of him might perhaps be nourished still. On a sudden he admitted to his mind the possibility that the engagement he was waiting in town to keep might be postponed without much harm.

It was no sooner perceived than attempted. Looking at his watch he found it wanted forty minutes to the departure of the ten o'clock train from Paddington, which left him a surplus quarter of an hour before it would be necessary to start for the station.

Scribbling a hasty note or two – one putting off the business meeting, another to Knight apologizing for not being able to see him in the evening – paying his bill, and leaving his heavier luggage to follow him by goods-train, he jumped into a cab and rattled off to the Great Western Station.*

Shortly afterwards he took his seat in the railway carriage.

The guard paused on his whistle to let into the next compartment to Smith's a man of whom Stephen had caught but a hasty glimpse as he ran across the platform at the last moment.

Smith sank back into the carriage, stilled by perplexity. The man was like Knight – astonishingly like him. Was it possible it could be he? To have got there he must have driven like the wind to Bede's Inn, and hardly have alighted before starting again. No, it could not be he; that was not his way of doing things.

During the early part of the journey Stephen Smith's thoughts busied themselves till his brain seemed swollen. One subject was concerning his own approaching actions. He was a day earlier than his letter to his parents had stated, and his arrangement with them had been that they should meet him at Plymouth; a plan which pleased the worthy couple beyond expression. Once before the same engagement had been made, which he had then quashed by antedating his arrival. This time he would go right on to Castle Boterel; ramble in that well-known neighbourhood during the evening and next morning, making inquiries; and return to Plymouth to meet them as arranged – a contrivance which would leave their cherished project undisturbed, relieving his own impatience also.

At Chippenham there was a little waiting, and some loosening and attaching of carriages.

Stephen looked out. At the same moment another man's head emerged from the adjoining window. Each looked in the other's face.

Knight and Stephen confronted one another.

'You here!' said the younger man.

'Yes. It seems that you are too,' said Knight, strangely.

'Yes.'

The selfishness of love and the cruelty of jealousy were fairly exemplified at this moment. Each of the two men looked at his friend as he had never looked at him before. Each was *troubled* at the other's presence.

'I thought you said you were not coming till to-morrow,' remarked Knight.

'I did. It was an afterthought to come to-day. This journey was your engagement, then?'

'No, it was not. This is an afterthought of mine too. I left a note to explain it, and account for my not being able to meet you this evening as we arranged.'

'So did I for you.'

'You don't look well: you did not this morning.'

'I have a headache. You are paler to-day than you were.'

'I, too, have been suffering from headache. We have to wait here a few minutes, I think.'

They walked up and down the platform, each one more and more embarrassingly concerned with the awkwardness of his friend's presence. They reached the end of the footway, and paused in sheer absentmindedness. Stephen's vacant eyes rested upon the operations of some porters, who were shifting a dark and curious-looking van from the rear of the train, to shunt another which was between it and the fore part of the train. This operation having been concluded, the two friends returned to the side of their carriage.

'Will you come in here?' said Knight, not very warmly.

'I have my rug and portmanteau and umbrella with me: it is rather bothering to move now,' said Stephen reluctantly. 'Why not you come here?'

'I have my traps too. It is hardly worth while to shift them, for I shall see you again, you know.'

'O yes.'

And each got into his own place. Just at starting, a man on the platform held up his hands and stopped the train.

Stephen looked out to see what was the matter.

One of the officials was exclaiming to another, 'That carriage should have been attached again. Can't you see it is for the main line? Quick! What fools there are in the world!'

'What a confounded nuisance these stoppages are!' exclaimed Knight impatiently, looking out from his compartment. 'What is it?'

'That singular carriage we saw has been unfastened from our train by mistake, it seems,' said Stephen.

He was watching the process of attaching it. The van or carriage, which he now recognized as having seen at Paddington before they started, was rich and solemn rather than gloomy in aspect. It seemed to be quite new, and of modern design, and its impressive personality attracted the notice of others beside himself. He beheld it gradually wheeled forward by two men on each side: slower and more sadly it seemed to approach: then a slight concussion, and they were connected with it, and off again.

Stephen sat all the afternoon pondering upon the reason of Knight's unexpected reappearance. Was he going as far as Castle Boterel? If so, he could only have one object in view – a visit to Elfride. And what an idea it seemed!

At Plymouth Smith got himself something to eat, and then went round to the side from which the train started for Camelton, the new station near Castle Boterel and Endelstow.

Knight was already there.

Stephen walked up and stood beside him without speaking. Two men at this moment crept out from among the wheels of the waiting train.

'The carriage is light enough,' said one in a grim tone. 'Light as vanity; full o' nothing.'

'Nothing in size, but a good deal in signification,' said the other, a man of brighter mind and manners.

Smith then perceived that to their train was attached that same carriage of grand and dark aspect which had haunted them all the way from London.

'You are going on, I suppose?' said Knight, turning to Stephen, after idly looking at the same object.

'Yes.'

'We may as well travel together for the remaining distance, may we not?'

'Certainly we will'; and they both entered the same door.

Evening drew on apace. It chanced to be the eve of St Valentine's – that bishop of blessed memory to youthful lovers – and the sun shone low under the rim of a thick hard cloud, decorating the eminences of the landscape with crowns of orange fire. As the train changed its direction on a curve, the same rays stretched in through the window, and coaxed open Knight's half-closed eyes.

'You will get out at St Launce's, I suppose?' he murmured.

'No,' said Stephen, 'I am not expected till to-morrow.' Knight was silent.

'And you – are you going to Endelstow?' said the younger man pointedly.

'Since you ask, I can do no less than say I am, Stephen,' continued Knight slowly, and with more resolution of manner than he had shown all the day. 'I am going to Endelstow to see if Elfride Swancourt is still free; and if so, to ask her to be my wife.'

'So am I,' said Stephen Smith.

'I think you'll lose your labour,' Knight returned with decision.

'Naturally you do.' There was a strong accent of bitterness in Stephen's voice. 'You might have said *hope* instead of *think*,' he added.

'I might have done no such thing. I gave you my opinion. Elfride Swancourt may have loved you once, no doubt, but it was when she was so young that she hardly knew her own mind.'

'Thank you,' said Stephen laconically. 'She knew her mind as well as I did. We are the same age. If you hadn't interfered—'

'Don't say that – don't say it, Stephen! How can you make out that I interfered? Be just, please!'

'Well,' said his friend, 'she was mine before she was yours – you know that! And it seemed a hard thing to find you had got her, and that if it had not been for you, all might have turned out well for me.' Stephen spoke with a swelling heart, and looked out of the window to hide the emotion that would make itself visible upon his face.

'It is absurd,' said Knight in a kinder tone, 'for you to look at the matter in that light. What I tell you is for your good. You naturally do not like to realize the truth – that her liking for you was only a girl's first fancy, which has no root ever.'

'It is not true!' said Stephen passionately. 'It was you put me out. And now you'll be pushing in again between us, and depriving me of my chance again! My right, that's what it is! How ungenerous of you to come anew and try to take her away from me! When you had won her, I did not interfere; and you might, I think, Mr Knight, do by me as I did by you!'

'Don't "Mr" me; you are as well in the world as I am now, and better.'

'First love is deepest; and that was mine.'

'Who told you that?' said Knight superciliously.

'I had her first love. And it was through me that you and she parted. I can guess that well enough.'

'It was. And if I were to explain to you in what way that operated in parting us, I should convince you that you do quite wrong in intruding upon her – that, as I said at first, your labour will be lost. I don't choose to explain, because the particulars are painful. But if you won't listen to me, go on, for Heaven's sake. I don't care what you do, my boy.'

'You have no right to domineer over me as you do. Just because, when I was a lad, I was accustomed to look up to you as a master, and you helped me a little, for which I was grateful to you and have loved you, you assume too much now, and step in before me. It is cruel – it is unjust – of you to injure me so!'

Knight showed himself keenly hurt at this. 'Stephen, those words are untrue and unworthy of any man, and they are unworthy of you. You know you wrong me. If you have ever profited by any instruction of mine, I am only too glad to know it. You know it was given ungrudgingly, and that I have never once looked upon it as making you in any way a debtor to me.'

Stephen's naturally gentle nature was touched, and it was in a troubled voice that he said, 'Yes, yes. I am unjust in that – I own it.'

'This is St Launce's Station, I think. Are you going to get out?'

Knight's manner of returning to the matter in hand drew Stephen again into himself. 'No; I told you I was going to Endelstow,' he resolutely replied.

Knight's features became impassive, and he said no more. The train continued rattling on, and Stephen leant back in his corner and closed his eyes. The yellows of evening had turned to browns, the dusky shades thickened, and a flying cloud of dust occasionally stroked the window – borne upon a chilling breeze which blew from the north-east. The previously gilded but now dreary hills began to lose their daylight aspects of rotundity, and to become black discs vandyked* against the sky, all nature wearing the cloak that six o'clock casts over the landscape at this time of the year.

Stephen started up in bewilderment after a long stillness, and it was some time before he recollected himself.

'Well, how real, how real!' he exclaimed, brushing his hand across his eyes.

'What is?' said Knight.

'That dream. I fell asleep for a few minutes, and have had a dream – the most vivid I ever remember.'

He wearily looked out into the gloom. They were now drawing near to Camelton. The lighting of the lamps was perceptible through the veil of evening – each flame starting into existence at intervals, and blinking weakly against the gusts of wind.

'What did you dream?' said Knight moodily.

'O, nothing to be told. 'Twas a sort of incubus. There is never anything in dreams.'

'I hardly supposed there was.'

'I know that. However, what I so vividly dreamt was this, since you would like to hear. It was the brightest of bright mornings at East Endelstow Church, and you and I stood by the font. Far away in the chancel Lord Luxellian was standing alone, cold and impassive, and utterly unlike his usual self: but I knew it was he. Inside the altar rail stood a strange clergyman with his book open. He looked up and said to Lord Luxellian, "Where's the bride?" Lord Luxellian said, "There's no bride." At that moment somebody came in at the door, and I knew her to be Lady Luxellian who died. He turned and said to her, "I thought you were in the vault below us; but that could have only been a dream of mine. Come on." Then she came on. And in brushing between us she chilled me so with cold that I exclaimed, "The life is gone out of me!" and, in the way of dreams, I awoke. But here we are at Camelton.'

They were slowly entering the station.

'What are you going to do?' said Knight. 'Do you really intend to call on the Swancourts?'

'By no means. I am going to make inquiries first. I shall stay at the Luxellian Arms to-night. You will go right on to Endelstow, I suppose, at once?'

'I can hardly do that at this time of the day. Perhaps you are not aware that the family – her father, at any rate – is at variance with me as much as with you.'

'I didn't know it.'

'And that I cannot rush into the house as an old friend any more than you can. Certainly I have the privileges of a distant relationship, whatever they may be.'

Knight let down the window, and looked ahead. 'There are a great many people at the station,' he said. 'They seem all to be on the look-out for us.'

When the train stopped the half-estranged friends could perceive by the lamplight that the assemblage of idlers enclosed as a kernel a group of men in black cloaks. A side gate in the platform railing was open, and outside this stood a dark vehicle, which they could not at first characterize. Then Knight saw on its upper part forms against the sky like cedars by night, and knew the vehicle to be a hearse. Few people were at the carriage doors to meet the passengers – the majority had congregated at this upper end. Knight and Stephen alighted, and turned for a moment in the same direction.

The sombre van, which had accompanied them all day from London, now began to reveal that their destination was also its own. It had been drawn up exactly opposite the open gate. The bystanders all fell back, forming a clear lane from the gateway to the van, and the men in cloaks entered the latter conveyance.

'They are labourers, I fancy,' said Stephen. 'Ah, it is strange; but I recognize three of them as Endelstow men. Rather remarkable this.'

Presently they began to come out, two and two; and under the rays of the lamp they were seen to bear between them a light-coloured coffin of satin-wood, brightly polished, and without a nail. The eight men took the burden upon their shoulders, and slowly crossed with it over to the gate.

Knight and Stephen went outside, and came close to the procession as it moved off. A carriage belonging to the cortège turned round close to a lamp. The rays shone in upon the face of the rector of Endelstow, Mr Swancourt – looking many years older than when they had last seen him. Knight and Stephen involuntarily drew back.

Knight spoke to a bystander. 'What has Mr Swancourt to do with that funeral?'

'He is the lady's father,' said the bystander.

'What lady's father?' said Knight, in a voice so hollow that the man stared at him.

'The father of the lady in the coffin. She died in London, you know, and has been brought here by this train. She is to be taken home to-night, and buried to-morrow.'

Knight stood staring blindly at where the hearse had been; as if he saw it, or some one, there. Then he turned, and beheld the lithe form of Stephen bowed down like that of an old man. He took his young friend's arm, and led him away from the light.

CHAPTER FORTY

'Welcome, proud lady.'*

HALF an hour has passed. Two miserable men are wandering in the darkness up the miles of road from Camelton to Endelstow.

'Has she broken her heart?' said Henry Knight. 'Can it be that I have killed her? I was bitter with her, Stephen, and she has died! And may God have *no* mercy upon me!'

'How can you have killed her more than I?'

'Why, I went away from her – stole away almost – and didn't tell her I should not come again; and at that last meeting I did not kiss her once, but let her miserably go. I have been a fool – a fool! I wish the most abject confession of it before crowds of my countrymen could in any way make amends to my darling for the intense cruelty I have shown her!'

'*Your* darling!' said Stephen, with a sort of laugh. 'Any man can say that, I suppose; any man can. I know this, she was *my* darling before she was yours; and after too. If anybody has a right to call her his own, it is I.'

'You talk like a man in the dark; which is what you are. Did she ever do anything for you? Risk her name, for instance, for you?'

'Yes, she did,' said Stephen emphatically.

'Not entirely. Did she ever live for you – prove she could not live without you – laugh and weep for you?'

'Yes.'

'Never! Did she ever risk her life for you – no! My darling did for me.'

'Then it was in kindness only. When did she risk her life for you?'

'To save mine on the cliff yonder. The poor child was with me looking at the approach of the *Puffin* steamboat, and I slipped down. We both had a narrow escape. I wish we had died there!'

'Ah, but wait,' Stephen pleaded with wet eyes. 'She went on that cliff to see me arrive home: she had promised it. She told me she would months before. And would she have gone there if she had not cared for me at all?'

'You have an idea that Elfride died for you, no doubt,' said Knight, with a mournful sarcasm too nerveless to support itself.

'Never mind. If we find that – that she died yours, I'll say no more ever.'

'And if we find she died yours, I'll say no more.'

'Very well – so it shall be.'

The dark clouds into which the sun had sunk had begun to drop rain in an increasing volume.

'Can we wait somewhere here till this shower is over?' said Stephen desultorily.

'As you will. But it is not worth while. We'll hear the particulars, and return. Don't let people know who we are. I am not much now.'

They had reached a point at which the road branched into two – just outside the west village, one fork of the diverging routes passing into the latter place, the other stretching on to East Endelstow. Having come some of the distance by the footpath, they now found that the hearse was only a little in advance of them.

'I fancy it has turned off to East Endelstow. Can you see?'

'I cannot. You must be mistaken.'

Knight and Stephen entered the village. A bar of fiery light lay across the road, proceeding from the half-open door of a smithy, in which bellows were heard blowing and a hammer ringing. The rain had increased, and they mechanically turned for shelter towards the warm and cosy scene.

Close at their heels came another man, without overcoat or umbrella, and with a parcel under his arm.

'A wet evening,' he said to the two friends, and passed by them. They stood in the outer penthouse, but the man went in to the fire.

The smith ceased his blowing, and began talking to the man who had entered.

'I have walked all the way from Camelton,' said the latter. 'Was obliged to come to-night, you know.'

He held the parcel, which was a flat one, towards the firelight, to learn if the rain had penetrated it. Resting it edgewise on the forge, he supported it perpendicularly with one hand, wiping his face with the handkerchief he held in the other.

'I suppose you know what I've got here?' he observed to the smith.

'No, I don't,' said the smith, pausing again on his bellows.

'As the rain's not over, I'll show you,' said the bearer.

He laid the thin and broad package, which had acute angles in different directions, flat upon the anvil, and the smith blew up the fire to give him more light. First, after untying the package, a sheet of brown paper was removed: this was laid flat. Then he unfolded a piece of baize: this also he spread flat on the paper. The third covering was a wrapper of tissue paper, which was spread out in its turn. The enclosure was revealed, and he held it up for the smith's inspection.

'O – I see!' said the smith, kindling with a chastened interest, and drawing close. 'Poor young lady – ah, terrible melancholy thing – so soon too!'

Knight and Stephen turned their heads and looked.

'And what's that?' continued the smith.

'That's the coronet – beautifully finished, isn't it? Ah, that cost some money!'

''Tis as fine a bit of metal work as ever I see – that 'tis.'

'It came from the same people as the coffin, you know, but was not ready soon enough to be sent round to the house in London yesterday. I've got to fix it on this very night.'

The carefully-packed articles were a coffin-plate and coronet.

Knight and Stephen came forward. The undertaker's man, on seeing them look for the inscription, civilly turned it round towards them, and each read, almost at one moment, by the ruddy light of the coals:

ELFRIDE,

Wife of Spenser Hugo Luxellian,

Fifteenth Baron Luxellian:

Died February 10, 18—.

They read it, and read it, and read it again – Stephen and Knight – as if animated by one soul. Then Stephen put his hand upon Knight's arm, and they retired from the yellow glow, further, further, till the chill darkness enclosed them round, and the quiet sky asserted its presence overhead as a dim gray sheet of blank monotony.

'Where shall we go?' said Stephen.

'I don't know.'

A long silence ensued.... 'Elfride married!' said Stephen then in a thin whisper, as if he feared to let the assertion loose on the world.

'False,' whispered Knight.

'And dead. Denied us both. I hate "false" – I hate it!'

Knight made no answer.

Nothing was heard by them now save the slow measurement of time by their beating pulses, the soft touch of the dribbling rain upon their clothes, and the low purr of the blacksmith's bellows hard by.

'Shall we follow Elfie any further?' Stephen said.

'No: let us leave her alone. She is beyond our love, and let her be beyond our reproach. Since we don't know half the reasons that made her do as she did, Stephen, how can we say, even now, that she was not pure and true in heart?' Knight's voice had become mild and gentle as a child's. He went on: 'Can we call her ambitious? No. Circumstance has, as usual, overpowered her purposes – fragile and delicate as she – liable to be overthrown in a moment by the coarse elements of accident. I know that's it, – don't you?'

'It may be – it must be. Let us go on.'

They began to bend their steps towards Castle Boterel, whither they had sent their bags from Camelton. They wandered on in silence for many minutes. Stephen then paused, and lightly put his hand within Knight's arm.

'I wonder how she came to die,' he said in a broken whisper. 'Shall we return and learn a little more?'

They turned back again, and entering Endelstow a second time, came to a door which was standing open. It was that of an inn called the Welcome Home, and the house appeared to have been recently repaired and entirely modernized. The name too was not that of the same landlord as formerly, but Martin Cannister's.

Knight and Smith entered. The inn was quite silent, and they followed the passage till they reached the kitchen, where a huge fire was burning, which roared up the chimney, and sent over the floor, ceiling, and newly-whitened walls a glare so intense as to make the candle quite a secondary light. A woman in a white apron and black gown was standing there alone behind a cleanly-scrubbed deal table. Stephen first, and Knight afterwards, recognized her as Unity, who had been parlour-maid at the rectory and young lady's-maid at The Crags.

'Unity,' said Stephen softly, 'don't you know me?'

She looked inquiringly a moment, and her face cleared up.

'Mr Smith – ay, that it is!' she said. 'And that's Mr Knight. I beg you to sit down. Perhaps you know that since I saw you last I have married Martin Cannister.'

'How long have you been married?'

'About five months. We were married the same day that my dear Miss Elfie became Lady Luxellian.' Tears appeared in Unity's eyes, and filled them, and fell down her cheek, in spite of efforts to the contrary.

The pain of the two men in resolutely controlling themselves when thus exampled to admit relief of the same kind was distressing. They both turned their backs and walked a few steps away.

Then Unity said, 'Will you go into the parlour, gentlemen?'

'Let us stay here with her,' Knight whispered, and turning said, 'No; we will sit here. We want to rest and dry ourselves here for a time, if you please.'

That evening the sorrowing friends sat with their hostess beside the large fire, Knight in the recess formed by the chimney breast, where he was in shade. And by showing a little confidence they won hers, and she told them what they had stayed to hear – the latter history of Elfride.

'One day – just after you, Mr Knight, left us for the last time – she was missed from The Crags, and her father went after her, and brought her home ill. Where she went to, I never knew – but she was very unwell for weeks afterwards. And she said to me that she didn't care what became of her, and she wished she could die. When she was better, I said she would live to be married yet, and she said then, "Yes; I'll do anything for the benefit of my family, so as to turn my useless life to some practical account." Well, it began like this about Lord Luxellian courting her. The first Lady Luxellian had died, and he was in great trouble because the little girls were left motherless. After a while they used to come and see her in their little black frocks, for they liked her as well or better than their own mother – that's true. They used to call her "little mamma". These children made her a shade livelier, but she was not the girl she had been – I could see that – and she grew thinner a good deal. Well, my lord got to ask the Swancourts oftener and oftener to dinner – nobody else of his acquaintance – and at last the rector's family were backwards and forwards at all hours of the day. Well, people say that the little girls asked their father to let Miss Elfride come and live with them, and that he said perhaps he would if they were good children. However, the time went on, and one day I said "Miss Elfride, you don't look so well as you used to; and though nobody else seems to notice it I do." She laughed a little, and said, "I shall live to be married yet, as you told me."

'"Shall you, miss? I am glad to hear that," I said.

'"Whom do you think I am going to be married to?" she said again.

'"Mr Knight, I suppose," said I.

'"O!" she cried, and turned off so white, and afore I could get to her she had sunk down like a heap of clothes, and fainted away. Well, then, she came to herself after a time, and said, "Unity, now we'll go on with our conversation."

'"Better not to-day, miss," I said.

'"Yes, we will," she said. "Whom do you think I am going to be married to?"

'"I don't know," I said this time.

'"Guess," she said.

'"'Tisn't my lord, is it?" says I.

'"Yes, 'tis," says she, in a sick wild way.

'"But he don't come courting much," I said.

'"Ah! you don't know," she said, and told me 'twas going to be in October. After that she freshened up a bit – whether 'twas with the thought of getting away from home or not, I don't know. For, perhaps, I may as well speak plainly, and tell you that her home was no home to her now. Her father was bitter to her and harsh upon her; and though Mrs Swancourt was well enough in her way, 'twas a sort of cold politeness that was not worth much, and the little thing had a worrying time of it altogether. About a month before the wedding, she and my lord and the two children used to ride about together upon horseback, and a very pretty sight they were; and if you'll believe me, I never saw him once with her unless the children were with her too – which made the courting so strange-looking.

Ay, and my lord is so handsome, you know, so that at last I think she rather liked him; and I have seen her smile and blush a bit at things he said. He wanted her the more because the children did, for everybody could see that she would be a most tender mother to them, and friend and playmate too. And my lord is not only handsome, but a splendid courter, and up to all the ways o't. So he made her the beautifullest presents; ah, one I can mind – a lovely bracelet, with diamonds and emeralds. O, how red her face came when she saw it! The old roses came back to her cheeks for a minute or two then. I helped dress her the day we both were married – it was the last service I did her, poor child! When she was ready, I ran upstairs and slipped on my own wedding gown, and away they went, and away went Martin and I; and no sooner had my lord and my lady been married than the parson married us. It was a very quiet pair of weddings – hardly anybody knew it. Well, hope will hold its own in a young heart, if so be it can; and my lady freshened up a bit, for my lord was *so* handsome and kind.'

'How came she to die – and away from home?' murmured Knight.

'Don't you see, sir, she fell off again afore they'd been married long, and my lord took her abroad for change of scene. They were coming home, and had got as far as London, when she was taken very ill with a miscarriage, and couldn't be moved, and there she died.'

'Was he very fond of her?'

'What, my lord? O he was!'

'*Very* fond of her?'

'*Very*, beyond everything. Not suddenly, but by slow degrees. 'Twas her nature to win people more when they knew her well. He'd have died for her, I believe. Poor my lord, he's heart-broken now!'

'The funeral is to-morrow?'

'Yes; my husband is now at the vault with the masons, opening the steps and cleaning down the walls.'

The next day two men walked up the familiar valley from Castle Boterel to East Endelstow Church. And when the funeral was over, and every one had left the lawn-like churchyard, the pair went softly down the steps of the Luxellian vault, and under the low-groined arches they had beheld once before, lit up then as now. In the new niche of the crypt lay a rather new coffin, which had lost some of its lustre, and a newer coffin still, bright and untarnished in the slightest degree.

Beside the latter was the dark form of a man, kneeling on the damp floor, his body flung across the coffin, his hands clasped, and his whole frame seemingly given up in utter abandonment to grief. He was still young – younger, perhaps, than Knight – and even now showed how graceful was his figure and symmetrical his build. He murmured a prayer half aloud, and was quite unconscious that two others were standing within a few yards of him.

Knight and Stephen had advanced to where they once stood beside Elfride on the day all three had met there, before she had herself gone down into silence like her ancestors, and shut her bright blue eyes for ever. Not until then did they see the kneeling figure in the dim light. Knight instantly recognized the mourner as Lord Luxellian, the bereaved husband of Elfride.

They felt themselves to be intruders. Knight pressed Stephen back, and they silently withdrew as they had entered.

'Come away,' he said, in a broken voice. 'We have no right to be there. Another stands before us – nearer to her than we!'

And side by side they retraced their steps down the grey still valley to Castle Boterel.

Notes

Title-page. *'A violet . . . No more.'* From Shakespeare's *Hamlet*, Act I, sc. III.

35 *craze for indiscriminate church-restoration.* See F. E. Hardy, *The Life of Thomas Hardy, 1840–1928* (1962) p. 79:

> It was at this time [1870], too, that he saw the last of St Juliot Church in its original condition of picturesque neglect, the local builder laying hands on it shortly after, and razing to the ground the tower and the north aisle (which had hitherto been the nave), and the transept. Hardy much regretted the obliteration in this manner of the church's history, and, too, that he should be instrumental in such obliteration, the building as he had first set eyes on it having been so associated with what was romantic in his life.

36 *idea . . . later book.* i.e., *Tess of the d'Urbervilles.*

37 *Off-Wessex, or Lyonnesse.* Hardy had not begun to use the term 'Wessex' when he wrote *A Pair of Blue Eyes.* (It made its first appearance in ch. 50 of *Far from the Madding Crowd* in an instalment published in the *Cornhill Magazine* in November 1874.) Thus it does not appear in the first edition; nor does the term 'Lyonnesse', a name associated with Arthurian legend and the north coast of Cornwall and popularised by Tennyson in *Idylls of the King.* Hardy at one time thought of calling *A Pair of Blue Eyes* 'Elfride of Lyonnesse', but hesitated to do so because it might embarrass the Rector of St Juliot and his family.

39 *'A fair vestal, throned in the west'.* From Shakespeare's *A Midsummer Night's Dream,* Act II, sc. I.

39 *monstrari digito.* (Latin) literally, 'being pointed at with the finger'; i.e., receiving notice, attention.

39 *Madonna della Sedia.* Celebrated painting by Raphael in Pitti Palace in Florence.

40 *Correggio.* Antonio da Correggio, Italian painter (*c.* 1494–1534). The many references to painters in this and other works by Hardy reflect the intense interest he took in painting in his early twenties, when he visited the National Gallery 'on every day it was open', studying a single picture each time (*Life*, p. 52).

40 *thoughts that lie too deep for tears.* An allusion to William Wordsworth's ode 'Intimations of Immortality':

> To me the meanest flower that blows can give
> Thoughts that do often lie too deep for tears.

40 *a Miranda-like curiosity.* Curiosity like that of Miranda in Shakespeare's *The Tempest*, who had never seen a human being other than her father.

40 *genial-faced, handsome man of fifty.* The 1st ed. reads: 'fine, red-faced, handsome man of forty'.

41 *High tea.* A substantial early-evening meal, usually replacing dinner.
41 *Od.* A minced form of 'God'.
43 *dog-cart.* An open vehicle with two transverse seats back to back.
43 *Lord Luxellian's.* The village of Luxulian, named after a Cornish saint, is near Lostwithiel.
44 *smock-frock.* A term in use from 1800 to describe a coarse linen garment which farm labourers wore over the rest of their clothes (*OED*).
44 *prented.* (Dial.) printed.
45 *glebe.* Land belonging to a church as its dowry, from which a rector draws part of the income.
46 *figged keakes.* (Dial.) fig cakes.
46 *horn lantern.* A case made of transparent horn to contain a light.
46 *the Turk.* The strongest or toughest man, as in 'My master comes like any Turk, and bangs me most severely' (John Gay, 'Sally in Our Alley').
46 *wambling.* (Dial.) shaky or unsteady.
47 *flank movement.* Side movement.
47 *in demi-toilette.* In informal indoor dress.
47 *prelusively.* As a prelude.
47 *'the weariness, the fever, and the fret'.* From John Keats's 'Ode to a Nightingale', st. 3.
47 *Babylon the Second.* 'London is a modern Babylon' (Benjamin Disraeli, *Tancred*, 1847).
50 *'Melodious birds sing madrigals.'* From Christopher Marlowe's 'The Passionate Shepherd to His Love'.
50 *refection.* Refreshment.
51 *Sweet-and-Twenty.* 'Then come kiss me, sweet and twenty', from the song 'O mistress mine' in Shakespeare's *Twelfth Night*, Act III, sc. III.
52 *"Landed Gentry".* John Burke's directory, *Landed Gentry*, first published in three volumes in 1833–5.
52 *cut his joke.* Indulge his weakness for jokes.
53 *Canto coram latrone.* From Juvenal's tenth Satire, l. 22: 'cantabit vacuus coram latrone viator' ('the empty-handed traveller will whistle in the robber's face').
53 *canterbury.* A music and magazine rack (*OED*).
53 *'Should he upbraid'.* A well-known song by Sir H. R. Bishop (1786–1855), from his operatic arrangement of Shakespeare's *The Two Gentlemen of Verona*.
54 *de Leyre.* Alexandre Deleyre (1726–97). Some of his songs were set to music by Jean-Jacques Rousseau.
54 *"When the lamp is shattered".* First line of Shelley's 'The Flight of Love'.
54 *aureola.* The golden glory around the head of a saint.
54 *diminuendo.* Musical term for a gradual decrease in loudness.
54 *'O Love ... bier!'* From Shelley's 'The Flight of Love'.
56 *had fired a small Troy.* Had caused a conflagration in Stephen's heart like that which burned Troy.
57 *'Where heaves ... heap.'* From Thomas Gray's 'Elegy Written in a Country Churchyard'.

57 *William Pitt.* (1759–1806). He became Prime Minister at the age of twenty-five.
57 *Nollekens.* Joseph Nollekens, sculptor (1737–1823).
58 *cock-watching.* Getting up early to see the cock crow.
59 *ensemble.* (French) general appearance.
59 *lych-gate.* The covered gate of a churchyard where the coffin rested until the priest arrived. (From *lich,* Old English word for 'corpse'.)
59 *fly-wheel.* Regulator. (A fly-wheel is a wheel attached to the driving-shaft of an engine to equalise its motion.)
60 *naterel.* (Dial.) natural.
60 *dissenters.* Nonconformists, probably Methodists in Mr Swancourt's country.
62 *'the purple light'.* Translation of the Virgilian phrase *lumen purpureum,* signifying the light of love.
62 *to be a preacher.* The first edition has this interjection by Hardy, subsequently omitted: 'Has the reader ever seen a winsome girl in a pulpit? Perhaps not. The writer knows somebody who has, and who can never forget that sight.'
62 *game of forfeits.* A game in which the loser has to pay a penalty in the shape of such things as 'Bow to the prettiest, kneel to the biggest, and kiss the hand of the one you love best.' Many 'forfeits' are designed to humiliate and to provide mirth to the onlookers.
63 *hoiden.* Hoyden, rough girl.
64 *Mighty I!* (Dial.) God Almighty!
67 *'Bosom'd high in tufted trees'.* From John Milton's 'L'Allegro'.
68 *en l'air.* (French) disconcerted, confused.
69 *ultima Thule.* Farthest Thule, the extreme limit of travel and discovery, which the ancients supposed to be the most northerly region of the world; the name was also applied to the Shetlands and Orkneys.
69 *patron of this living.* One who holds the right to present a benefice to a priest. It becomes the priest's livelihood or 'living'.
71 *turnpike road.* Main road with toll-gates at intervals, where fees were collected to pay for road-making and maintenance.
71 *Dahl.* Michael Dahl (1656–1743), portrait painter.
72 *high-shouldered Tudor arch.* The flattened arch of the last, or 'Perpendicular', style of Gothic architecture.
72 *licence to crenellate mansum infra manerium suum.* Nobles and knights, etc., wishing to fortify their houses by building battlements could only do so by licence from the king. 'Crenellate' (from the French *cren,* a dent or cranny) means construct a dented wall for the use of archers. The Latin words mean 'the dwelling-house within a manorial property'.
72 *chivaler.* Knight.
72 *dormer lights.* Windows which project from the roof of a house.
72 *apex stones.* The pointed stones at the top of the windows.
72 *rampant, passant, and couchant.* Heraldic terms for beasts rearing, walking with one paw raised, and lying down.
72 *oriel.* A projecting upper-storey window.
72 *Pilasters.* Rectangular columns used for ornamental purposes.
73 *quarries.* Diamond-shaped panes of stained glass.

73 *Holbein, Kneller, and Lely.* Hans Holbein the Younger (1497–1543), Sir Godfrey Kneller (1646–1723), Sir Peter Lely (1618–80) – all portrait painters.

76 *'Fare thee weel awhile!'* From Robert Burns's 'O, my luve's like a red, red rose':

> And fare thee weel, my only luve,
> And fare thee weel awhile!
> And I will come again, my luve,
> Tho' it were ten thousand mile.

76 *parterre.* Formal flower-beds.

76 *petits soins.* (French) little attentions.

77 *rencounter.* (Archaic) encounter.

77 *Castilian gallantry.* Spanish gallantry; fine manners.

82 *'No more of me you knew, my love!'* From Sir Walter Scott's 'The Rover's Adieu'.

82 *Six-and-thirty old seat-ends.* Hardy's own drawings of the destroyed medieval bench-ends of St Juliot can be seen in the church there. In July 1906 he published an essay entitled 'Memories of Church Restoration' in the *Cornhill* (reprinted in *Thomas Hardy's Personal Writings*, ed. Harold Orel (Macmillan, 1967) p. 203).

83 *'"Quæ finis ... pœnas luam."'* Horace, *Epodes*, no. XVII, ll. 36–7. See the comment on p. 84.

85 *the Muzio gambit.* The gambit, named after the seventeenth-century chess master, Muzio, is seldom played today. It is a subdivision of the King's Gambit, in which a pawn is sacrificed in the second move: on the fifth move it allows the pawn-sacrifice to be converted into the sacrifice of a knight.

87 *leg-wood.* Large branches cut from trees.

87 *pony-shay.* Pony-chaise, a light open carriage.

87 *parish pay.* Parish 'relief' or the workhouse.

89 *La Belle Dame sans merci.* The enchantress in the Keats poem of that name.

91 *freak.* (Playing a) game or trick.

91 *beetling.* Overhanging.

92 *legerdemain.* Sleight of hand, conjuring.

93 *"upping-stock".* A mounting-block to assist a rider.

94 *like little mice.* An allusion to Sir John Suckling's 'Ballade upon a Wedding': 'Her feet beneath her petticoat / Like little mice, stole in and out.'

96 *hob and nob.* Hobnob; be on familiar terms.

98 *wicket-gates.* Small gates such as are found in walls or fences.

100 *'Allen-a-Dale is no baron or lord.'* From Scott's *Rokeby*, canto III, st. XXX.

102 *wych-elm. Ulmus montana*, having broader leaves and more spread than the ordinary elm.

104 *dame school.* Small school for young children run by an old lady in her own house.

104 *national school.* A school set up by the National Society for Promoting the Education of the Poor in the Principles of the Established Church, the largest single provider of elementary schools in early Victorian England.

107 *premium.* Fee paid by an apprentice for his training.

107 *improver.* Someone who works for a low wage to improve his skill.
110 *'Her father did fume.'* From Scott's *Marmion*, canto V, sect. XII.
111 *pile.* Stake.
111 *beetle.* Heavy mallet.
111 *pummy.* Pulp. 'Pummy' or pomace is the pulp of apples as used in cider-making.
111 *the 'Battle of Prague'.* A highly popular piece for piano, violin, cello and drum (1788), by F. Kocžwara (d. 1791), a forerunner of Beethoven's 'Wellington's Victory, or the Battle of Vittoria' (1813).
113 *Greuze attitude.* Jean-Baptiste Greuze (1725–1805), French portrait-painter somewhat sentimental in style.
115 *Euryalus.* A brave young Trojan who dared to enter the enemy camp.
116 *"Let a beast . . . king's mess."* From Shakespeare's *Hamlet*, Act V, sc. II.
116 *hobbledehoy.* A clumsy or awkward lad.
117 *cloven foot.* A cloven foot was the sign of the Devil.
117 *'40 Martinez.* The firm of Martinez was an exporter of port from 1797, becoming Martinez, Jones, Gassiat & Co. in 1834.
119 *'Beneath the shelter of an aged tree'.* From Robert Burns's 'The Cotter's Saturday Night' (1785).
120 *clumsy pin-maker.* In his *The Wealth of Nations* (1776), bk I, ch. 1, Adam Smith cites pin-making, which entails eighteen distinct operations, as an example of the economic advantages of the division of labour.
120 *Coryphæus.* The leading speaker of the chorus in Greek drama.
122 *dand.* (Dial.) Dandy.
122 *out-step.* Out of the way.
123 *case-clock.* A clock enclosed in a glass-fronted case which hangs on the wall.
124 *I'd have trod clay for bricks.* i.e., I'd have done anything, however lowly.
124 *or there's no bread in nine loaves.* Or there's nothing in what I perfectly well know to be true.
124 *carrier.* Professional carrier of goods by cart or wagon.
131 *'Journeys end in lovers meeting.'* From the song 'O mistress mine' in Shakespeare's *Twelfth Night*, Act II, sc. III.
131 *Great Bear.* The constellation Ursa Major, otherwise known as The Plough.
131 *Jael's tent-nail.* Jael murdered Sisera in his sleep with a tent-peg. (See Judges, IV 21.)
132 *watering-place.* Seaside resort.
133 *tilt.* Awning or cover.
133 *metamorphic rock.* Rock which has undergone change due to heat, pressure, etc.
133 *Ida.* A mountain range near Troy, the source of many beautiful rivers.
133 *Bedford Street.* One of the principal streets in the centre of Plymouth which were destroyed by bombing during the Second World War.
133 *St Andrew's church.* The mother church of Plymouth.
134 *coup d'œil.* (French) view.
135 *Fifteen days . . . marriage law.* There are two normal procedures for a Church of England marriage. Either the banns are called on three successive Sundays (i.e., over a period of fifteen days) in the church of the parish in which the parties to be married dwell; or the marriage is by a

licence, from the appropriate ecclesiastical authority, for it to take place in a parish in which one of the parties shall have resided for fifteen days beforehand.

135 *Visitation.* Official inspection of a parish.

136 *ex post facto.* (Latin) retrospective.

138 *Thou wilt not . . . gentle Elfride.* Adapted from Shakespeare's *1 Henry IV*, Act II, sc. III.

139 *gentleman from Scotland-yard.* A detective. The headquarters of the Metropolitan Police were for long situated in Great Scotland Yard, off Whitehall.

141 *Genoese filigree.* Hardy is possibly thinking not of filigree proper – i.e., fine jewel-work made of interlaced metal thread – but of Genoese lace.

142 *the steed of Adonis.* An allusion to Shakespeare's *Venus and Adonis*, l. 277: 'Sometimes he trots, as if he told the steps.'

143 *In three minutes the train had moved off.* The railway plays an immense part in Hardy's poems and stories. In *A Pair of Blue Eyes* it gradually but remorselessly pushes its way into village isolation even as the novel unfolds. Hardy himself made his first train journey, from London to Dorchester, when he was nine. Talking to a friend towards the end of his life, he said that he always saw time like a long blue railway line, with the past disappearing on the left and the future over the crossing on the right.

144 *'Adieu! . . . lily hand.'* The last line of John Gay's 'Sweet William's Farewell to Black-eyed Susan'.

144 *Crusoe's first shot.* The first use of a gun on the island – destruction of its innocence. An allusion to Daniel Defoe's *Robinson Crusoe* (1719).

148 *an old Tudor bridge.* Over the River Tamar near Launceston.

149 *why, the orange-tree must save me.* The orange was symbolic of the feminine principle and it often appears in paintings of the Madonna. A bride's orange-blossom – the custom of wearing it was brought from the Middle East to Europe by the Crusaders – means purity, chastity and eternal love.

152 *the devise of this estate.* The bequest and ordering of the estate.

152 *dower.* The provision or income for a dowager or widow.

153 *'And was this . . . referred to?'* See p. 83.

154 *signis auroque rigentes.* 'Stiff with rings and gold.' (From the description of Helen of Troy's robe in Virgil's *Aeneid*, bk I, l. 648.)

155 *toadstone.* 'Stone, sometimes precious, supposed to resemble or to have been formed in the body of a toad, formerly used as an amulet etc.' (*OED*).

157 *the most unequivocal Fabian success.* Fabius Cunctator, or 'Delayer', was a cautious Roman general who won his victories gradually, wearing down the enemy in a series of skirmishes rather than a pitched battle.

158 *'He set in order many proverbs.'* 'He gave good heed, and sought out, and set in order many proverbs' (Ecclesiastes, XII 9).

158 *Bede's Inn.* Clement's Inn. Knight's chambers were based upon the offices of Mr Raphael Brandon, an architect for whom Hardy worked in 1870 (*Life*, p. 77).

158 *postern.* Back or private door.

159 *penetralia.* Innermost depths or holy of holies.

159 *sicklied o'er by the unmistakable pale cast.* See Shakespeare's *Hamlet*, Act III, sc. I: 'And thus the native hue of resolution / Is sicklied o'er with the pale cast of thought.'

160 *parallelepipedon.* 'A geometrical term for a solid figure contained by six parallelograms, of which every two opposite ones are parallel' (*OED*).

160 *zoophytes.* 'Creatures in an intermediate category between plants and animals, sea-anemones, coral, etc.' (*OED*).

162 *alter ego.* (Latin) other self.

164 *Turner's later pictures.* J. M. W. Turner (1775–1851), whose third period (1835–45) included the brilliant atmospheric studies 'The Snow Storm' and 'Rain, Steam and Speed' which Hardy loved.

165 *novelette.* Emma, Hardy's first wife, wrote a novel called 'The Maid on the Shore', which has certain similarities to *A Pair of Blue Eyes*. It is about a girl called Rosabelle who lives in Tintagel and who has two lovers, one of whom she jilts. In 1892 Hardy confessed to having used an incident from this novel for a scene in *Tess of the d'Urbervilles* (see Edmund Blunden, *Thomas Hardy* (1942) p. 69). It is probable but not certain that Emma wrote this novel at Swanage in 1875 (see her *Some Recollections*, ed. E. Hardy and R. Gittings, 1961).

Like Elfride, Emma was very interested in the romance of the local countryside:

> Sometimes I visited a favourite in the scattered parish – an amusing woman, pleasant-mannered and lively – who told me fine old tales and strange bye-gone experiences of her own young life and hardships endured in service, which I took down afterwards in my pocket-book for matter with which to begin writing country stories, having come to the conclusion that I was hearing from one [and] other of these country-folk a good deal that was fresh, peculiar, and not yet written about. [*Some Recollections*, pp. 51–2]

There is in the tragedy of Emma Hardy an element of thwarted literary talent. Whilst she was copying out parts of *A Pair of Blue Eyes* for her fiancé she could not but have been aware of her subtle presence in the book and that of much which belonged to her own Plymouth–Bodmin–St Juliot background. (Interestingly it was Knight's edition of Shakespeare which, she says, 'formed an integral part of my education at home'. Charles Knight was a publisher and popular educator of the time.)

Some years before Hardy had invented Henry Knight and before he himself had visited north Cornwall, Emma had noted 'a great and important visitor in the village'; i.e., John Cook, editor of the *Saturday Review*. Horace Moule, Hardy's great friend and teacher, was writing reviews for Cook at this period (see *Some Recollections*, p. 41). Elfride's novelette thus touches upon an intriguing range of literary matters which gave birth to those of 'Endelstow'. Her attempts at writing came to nothing, but Emma Hardy's modest autobiography, discovered by her husband after her death, was the chief influence on the wonderful love-poems contained in his *Satires of Circumstance*, published in 1914.

166 *'We frolic while 'tis May.'* From Thomas Gray's 'Ode on the Spring'.

167 *the Drive and Row.* When Alexander Macmillan rejected Hardy's first attempt

at novel-writing, 'The Poor Man and the Lady', he praised 'the scene in Rotten Row' as being 'full of real power and insight'. Hardy, a very unwasteful writer, had drawn on this rejected manuscript for material for *Under the Greenwood Tree*, and it is almost certain that the much-praised Rotten Row scene was transferred to *A Pair of Blue Eyes*. In the serial version of the book, Mrs Swancourt is allowed to make a number of heavily class-conscious remarks which are omitted in later editions. Criticising the class attack in 'The Poor Man and the Lady', Macmillan told Hardy that Thackeray 'meant fun' but 'you *mean mischief*'. These raging opinions are held delicately in check in *A Pair of Blue Eyes* but, as Michael Millgate says (*Thomas Hardy: his career as a novelist*, 1971), were to return fully to the surface in the pages of *Jude the Obscure*.

167 *Æneas at Carthage*. An allusion to bk I of Virgil's *Aeneid*. Dryden's translation: '... he raised / His wondering eyes, and round the temple gazed, / Admired the fortune of the rising town....'

167 *Boulevard, Rialto, or Prado*. i.e., Paris, Venice or Madrid.

168 *phylactery*. An inscribed scroll. Originally a leather container for the Scriptures which pharisaical Jews wore ostentatiously.

168 *Mr Puff ... Lord Burleigh's nod*. Characters from R. B. Sheridan's play *The Critic* (1779). Mr Puff has taken his friends to the rehearsal of his play *The Spanish Armada*, in which Lord Burleigh gives only nods and shakes of the head, of which Mr Puff, however, gives profound interpretations.

169 *landau*. A four-wheeled carriage with a double hood or top.

170 *chariot*. A light carriage with only back seats.

171 *chiel*. (Dial.) a young man or a fellow.

173 *pur sang*. (French) 'pure blood'; i.e., by right of birth.

173 *et prœterea nihil*. (Latin) and nothing beyond.

175 *'A wandering voice'*. From Wordsworth's 'To the Cuckoo': 'O Cuckoo! shall I call thee Bird, / Or but a wandering Voice?'

176 *Mr G. P. R. James*. George Payne Rainsford James (1799–1860), writer of historical romances and one of Hardy's favourite boyhood authors. W. M. Thackeray parodied him in *Novels by Eminent Hands* (1847), where he is 'Barbazure'.

176 *Ivanhoe*. Novel by Sir Walter Scott (1819), set in the Middle Ages.

178 *'Then fancy shapes – as fancy can.'* From Tennyson's *In Memoriam*, sect. LXXX.

178 *show the white feather*. Turn coward. A white feather in a game-bird's tail indicated poor breeding. During the First World War women used to give a white feather to men of military age in civilian clothes.

180 *the Directory*. Presumably one of the many street-directories published by E. R. Kelly & Co.

183 *'Her welcome ... phrase.'* From Scott's 'The Maid of Neidpath'.

183 *brown-holland*. Of unbleached linen.

184 *Lady Teazle at the dropping of the screen*. In Sheridan's *The School for Scandal*, Lady Teazle, trapped behind a screen, hears the truth about her husband and her friends. When it falls, she says that she has 'recovered her senses'.

185 *caqueterie*. (French) cackling.

185 *"To make you ... nothing."* A slightly garbled version of II Corinthians, VII 9.
185 *"nail't wi' Scripture"*. From Burns's 'Death and Doctor Hornbook':

> Ev'n Ministers, they hae been kenn'd,
> In holy rapture,
> A rousing whid, at times, to vend,
> And nail't wi' Scripture.

186 *as Smeaton said of his lighthouse.* John Smeaton (1724–92) built the Eddystone Lighthouse in 1759.
186 *ex-cathedrâ.* (Latin) authoritative.
186 *cruse.* Vessel (i.e., store).
189 *Tempe's vale.* A beautiful valley in Thessaly, in the north of Greece. With its cool shades and its song-birds, it was thought of as a place of ideal beauty.
190 *fustian.* Coarse cloth.
190 *Mumbo Jumbo.* Heathen idol.
190 *leads.* The flat roofs of church towers, aisles, etc., were covered with strips of lead to make them waterproof.
192 *salient.* Projecting.
194 *suasively.* Persuasively.
195 *Staunton and Morphy.* Howard Staunton (1810–70), chess master, actor and scholar; and Paul Morphy (1837–84), American chess master. Morphy was world champion in 1858.
196 *Chess Praxis.* A manual of chess moves, by Howard Staunton, published in 1860.
197 *Nelson's bravery lay in his vanity.* He refused to cover or change his conspicuous uniform at Trafalgar and was thus an obvious target for the French marksmen.
197 *'Fear ... destroying death!'* From Shakespeare's *Richard II*, Act III, sc. II.
198 *Rhadamanthus.* The wise son of Zeus and Europa who, after his death, became a judge in Hades.
201 *"words that burn"*. From Thomas Gray's 'The Progress of Poesy': 'Thoughts that breathe, and words that burn.'
206 *'Love was in the next degree.'* From John Dryden's 'Alexander's Feast, or The Power of Music': 'The mighty master smiled to see / That love was in the next degree.'
207 *The story ... Bethlehem-judah.* See Judges, XIX.
208 *the history of Elijah.* See I Kings, XIX. Like Knight, Hardy read the lessons when he was visiting the Cornish parish where his sweetheart lived. He had a particular liking for the Book of Kings.
209 *Coleridge's morbid poem 'The Three Graves'.* In Coleridge's poem, which he presented as 'a fragment of a common ballad-tale', a woman watches a handsome young man woo her daughter and falls in love with him herself. She declares her love and is rejected with horror by her son-in-law to be, so she curses him and her daughter. All three characters in the poem die and are buried side by side, their tragedy being told by the sexton. Eventually Elfride, Felix and Mrs Jethway likewise lie – more or less – side by side.

211 *governor of a steam-engine.* A contrivance, employing two heavy balls at the end of arms, which ensures the even and regular motion of a machine.

211 *compensation pendulums.* 'A balance wheel in a chronometer having arrangements which neutralize the effect of the expansion or contraction of the metal under variations of temperature' (*OED*).

213 *"That which is ... find it out?"* Ecclesiastes, VII 24.

213 *Cape Verde Islands.* In the Atlantic, off the African coast.

213 *'Looking down upon the source of the Nile.'* John Speke had discovered the source of the Nile in 1858, but Livingstone did not believe this and was making his last great journey, which incorporated searching for it, at the same time that Hardy was writing *A Pair of Blue Eyes.* There was much controversy in England during this period about the source of the Nile.

215 *'A distant dearness in the hill'.* From Tennyson's *In Memoriam*, sect. LXIV: 'A distant dearness in the hill, / A secret sweetness in the stream.'

215 *the glory and the dream.* Probably an allusion to Wordsworth's ode 'Intimations of Immortality': 'The glory and the freshness of a dream'.

216 *whose earliest season 'out'.* An older woman is careful not to mention when she 'came out' (i.e., out of the schoolroom into Society) in case it gives her age away.

217 *Incrédules les plus crédules.* From the *Pensées* of Blaise Pascal (1623–62), no. 816.

220 *lion.* Usually meaning a celebrity; in this case a local sight.

225 *the miracle of healing the sick of the palsy.* See John, VIII.

229 *Wordsworth's ... ode to that Deity.* i.e., his 'Ode to Duty'.

230 *'On thy cold grey stones, O sea!'* From Tennyson's 'Break, Break, Break'.

233 *'grim Dundagel throned along the sea'.* From *The Quest of the Sangraal* by R. S. Hawker (1803–75). Hawker was the Vicar of Morwenstow, Cornwall, and knew Hardy's brother-in-law Cadell Holder, Rector of St Juliot. 'Dundagel' is Tintagel.

236 *a Hambro' grape.* Hamburgh grape; a black, hothouse grape.

239 *confervæ.* Green algae.

240 *Trilobites.* Members of a large group of extinct anthropods, found in Palaeozoic rocks.

240 *phantoms before the doomed Macbeth.* In Act IV, sc. I, of Shakespeare's play the three witches summon up a series of apparitions to foretell Macbeth's fate.

240 *mastodon.* Extinct elephant-like mammal.

240 *megatherium.* A huge, sloth-like beast, now extinct.

240 *myledon.* (Mylydon) Pleistocene giant sloth.

241 *iguanodon.* Giant lizard.

243 *Dark Valley.* 'The valley of the shadow of death' (Psalm XXIII).

244 *diapason.* Range or compass, as in music.

249 *'Should auld acquaintance be forgot?'* First line of the song 'Auld Lang Syne', the words of which are by Robert Burns.

249 *vicinage.* Neighbourhood.

250 *grizzel horse.* Or grizzle horse; grey horse.

250 *spring-cart.* A light cart fitted with springs.

251 *traps.* Belongings, luggage.

251 *a turk of a mess.* A dreadful mess.
251 *chaw up.* (Dial.) chew up.
251 *shilling ale.* The best ale.
251 *chimmer.* (Dial.) chamber (or bedroom).
251 *steer.* (Dial.) stir.
253 *inions.* (Dial.) onions.
253 *pig-killer.* Local slaughterman.
254 *juvinals.* (Dial.) juveniles.
254 *Jacob's ladders. Polemonium caerleum*: a tall, blue, wild flower usually found in northern England. Mrs Smith's strong dislike of certain plants is very typical of a country person's attitude to flowers, some of which are adored, others attacked with ferocity.
254 *Maria.* Hardy earlier calls her Jane.
254 *mixen.* Dung-heap.
258 *till the end of Revelations.* Till the end of time, or 'Till Kingdom come'.
259 *ci-devant.* Former.
261 *'Breeze, bird, and flower confess the hour.'* From Scott's 'County Guy', l. 7.
261 *night-hawk.* Nightjar, a nocturnal bird.
265 *'Mine own familiar friend'.* From Psalm XLI, 9: 'Yea, mine own familiar friend, in whom I trusted, which did eat of my bread, hath lifted up his heel against me.'
266 *Belvedere.* Raised summerhouse, etc., from which to enjoy a view.
271 *God's Acre.* The churchyard.
273 *'To that last nothing under earth'.* From Tennyson's 'The Two Voices':

> 'A life of nothings, nothing-worth,
> From that first nothing ere his birth
> To that last nothing under earth!'

273 *limber.* Supple.
274 *Valentine's-day.* 14 February, the day on which 'valentines' or anonymous love-messages are exchanged. Named after two Italian saints, Valentin and Valentinius. See p. 390.
275 *goold.* (Dial.) gold.
277 *fleed.* (Dial.) flew.
277 *"Or ever ... broken."* Ecclesiastes, XII 6.
279 *'How should I greet thee?'* From Lord Byron's 'When We Two Parted':

> If I should meet thee
> After long years,
> How should I greet thee? –
> With silence and tears.

281 *the Spirit in Glenfinlas.* See Scott's poem 'Glenfinlas, or Lord Ronald's Coronach'.
281 *'Where love ... grows there.'* From Shakespeare's *Hamlet*, Act III, sc. II.
283 *"Mulier cupido ... in vento."* From Catullus's Carmen LXII: '[Sed] mulier cupido quod dicit amanti / In vento et rapido scribere oportet aqua' ('But a woman's sayings to her lover, / Shall be in wind and running water writ').

287 *Guido's Magdalen.* Presumably the 'Magdalen' by Guido Reni (1575–1642) in the National Gallery.

287 *'"Can one ... offence?"'* See Shakespeare's *Hamlet*, Act III, sc. III: 'May one be pardon'd and retain the offence?'

288 *'For Thou ... on high.'* From the metrical version of Psalm CII by N. Brady and N. Tate (1696).

289 *pulse-glass.* Barometer. (Cf. R. S. Hawker, *Prose Works* (1893): 'Had this instrument, the pulse of the storm, been preserved, the crew would have received warning of the hurricane.')

294 *'I lull a fancy, trouble-tost.'* From Tennyson's *In Memoriam*, sect. LXV:

> I lull a fancy trouble-tost
> With 'Love's too precious to be lost,
> A little grain shall not be spilt.'

296 *Revels-day.* Village holiday, often held on the day of the saint after whom the parish church is named.

299 *"Munditæ, et ornatus, et cultus." &c.* From Livy's *History of Rome*, bk XXXIV, VII, 9: 'Elegance of appearance, adornment, apparel – these are the woman's badge of honour.'

306 *'Did you ever go by water?'* Hardy wrote the first 'chapter or two' of *A Pair of Blue Eyes* at Westbourne Park Villas, London, on 27 July 1872. On 7 August he boarded an Irish packet named *Avoca* at London Bridge and steamed to Cornwall. Elfride and Knight (and Mrs Jethway) return to Endelstow (St Juliot) on the *Juliet* amidst lively descriptions of what Hardy saw on his voyage.

307 *Nightingale Lane ... Trimmer's Wharf.* This would now be Tower Bridge Approach, the road between the Tower of London and St Katharine Docks.

307 *Famine and Sword.* See Isaiah, LI 19.

308 *hulks.* Bodies of dismantled ships.

308 *tar-twine.* Or tar-marl: tarred twine used in thatching (*OED*).

310 *nobbiest.* Slang for smartest and most elegant.

311 *second-cabin.* Second-class cabin.

314 *'Four bells'.* Ship 'watch': 2 a.m.

314 *binnacle.* Compass-box on a ship, usually kept near the helm.

314 *abeam.* At right angles to the ship's length.

318 *'dally with false surmise'.* An allusion to Milton's 'Lycidas': 'Let our frail thoughts dally with false surmise'.

319 *"eight bells".* The four-hour watch.

319 *"To set ... light of heaven."* From Robert Pollok's *The Course of Time* (1827), bk 5.

320 *Jacob's-ladder path of light.* A reference to the ladder from earth to heaven seen by Jacob in a dream (Genesis, XXVIII 12).

321 *'Vassal unto Love'.* From Tennyson's *In Memoriam*, sect. XLVIII:

> Her care is not to part and prove;
> She takes, when harsher moods remit,
> What slender shades of doubt may flit,
> And makes it vassal unto love.

321 *espièglerie.* (French) mischievousness.
321 *daughter-in-law of Naomi.* See Ruth, II 13.
321 *myrtle.* The myrtle was sacred to Venus. The botanical exchange between Elfride and Knight is full of concealed references to love and constancy. When she gives him a small variety of the plant and he says, 'Let it be put in my room, that I may not forget it,' Hardy is indicating a lover who knows little about Venus.
326 *half-toilette.* Demi-toilette; informal indoor dress.
329 *to be first in the Pool of Bethesda.* See John, V 2–13. The sick waited around the pool to see an angel 'trouble the water'. The first person to dip himself when the water moved was cured.
331 *'A worm i' the bud'.* From Shakespeare's *Twelfth Night*, Act II, sc. IV:

> She never told her love,
> But let concealment, like a worm i' the bud,
> Feed on her damask cheek.

336 *'Fool'd ... by thee!'* From Milton's *Paradise Lost*, bk X, l. 800.
336 *'"Thou hast ... enemy."'* Psalm LXI, 3 (Book of Common Prayer version).
339 *'Had I wist before I kist.'* From the anonymous poem 'O waly waly up the bank' or 'The Forsaken Bride'.
344 *Diogenes Laertius.* Author of the Greek Lives of the Philosophers. He died in A.D. 222.
346 *'O daughter ... misery.'* From Psalm CXXXVII (Book of Common Prayer version).
346 *arris.* 'The sharp edge formed by the contact of either planed or curved surfaces' (*OED*).
348 *superincumbent.* Overlying.
353 *'Yea, happy ... served us.'* From Psalm CXXXVII (Book of Common Prayer version).
356 *springe.* Snare.
358 *utter despair of being able to explain.* On 30 July 1870, just before making his second visit to Cornwall, Hardy wrote in his notebook, 'When a young woman is eager to explain her meaning to a lover who has carelessly, or purposely, misunderstood her, there is something painful to an observer who notices it, although it is evidence of deep love. It somehow bespeaks that, in spite of her orders to him to fetch and carry, of his devotion and her rule, he is in essence master.' (See *Thomas Hardy's Notebooks*, ed. E. Hardy (1955) p. 29.)
361 *'And wilt ... nay!'* From Sir Thomas Wyatt's 'The Appeal'.
365 *like Antony . . . provinces.* See Shakespeare's *Antony and Cleopatra*, Act III, sc. X.
365 *'O last regret, regret can die!'* From Tennyson's *In Memoriam*, sect. LXXVIII.
367 *'The pennie's the jewel that beautifies a'.'* From Burns's song 'There's a Youth'.
368 *the funds.* Government stock; a very respectable form of investment.
372 *'After many days'.* 'Cast thy bread upon the waters for thou shalt find it after many days' (Ecclesiastes, XI 1).
372 *Marathon.* Where the Athenians defeated the Persians in 490 B.C.
372 *Mars Hill ... Athenians.* See Acts, XVII 22: 'Then Paul stood in the midst of

Mars' Hill, and said, Ye men of Athens, I perceive that in all things ye are too superstitious.' Mars' Hill is the Areopagus, an eminence to the west of the Acropolis on which used to sit the ancient judicial council of the areopagus.

372 *Thermopylæ . . . Salamis . . . Second Invasion.* Defeated in 490 B.C., the Persians launched a second invasion of Greece in 480 B.C.: Leonidas' famous defence of the pass of Thermopylæ and the defeat of the Persians at the sea-battle of Salamis were incidents in this campaign.

372 *calle.* (Italian) street, alley.

372 *lagunes.* Lagoons.

374 *out-Hamlet Hamlet.* An allusion to Hamlet's phrase 'it out-herods Herod' in Shakespeare's *Hamlet*, Act III, sc. II.

377 *'Jealousy is cruel as the grave.'* From the Song of Solomon, VIII 6.

379 *nimbi.* The plural of 'nimbus', the stylised golden disc of glory surrounding the head of a saint in a painting.

386 *sanguine clarus.* (Latin) blue-blooded.

387 *'Each to the loved one's side'.* From Scott's 'Datur Hora Quieti'.

388 *the Great Western Station.* Paddington.

392 *vandyked.* A vandyke is one of a series of large points forming a border to a lace collar, etc., as common in the portraits of the Dutch painter Van Dyck.

396 *'Welcome, proud lady.'* Last line of Scott's 'Proud Maisie'. The poem has an obvious relevance:

Proud Maisie is in the wood,
  Walking so early;
Sweet Robin sits on the bush,
  Singing so rarely.

'Tell me, thou bonny bird,
  When shall I marry me?'
'When six braw gentlemen
  Kirkward shall carry ye.'

'Who makes the bridal bed,
  Birdie, say truly?'
'The grey-headed sexton,
  That delves the grave duly.

'The glowworm o'er grave and stone
  Shall light thee steady;
The owl from the steeple sing
  Welcome, proud lady.'

Note on the Text

A Pair of Blue Eyes was the third of Hardy's novels to be published, the first to be serialised. Hardy tells the reader of the *Life* that he had roughly noted down the opening chapters and general outlines of a new story, possibly to be called 'A Winning Tongue Had He', some time before July 1872. In that month he met Tinsley, the publisher of his two previous novels, and agreed to write a story for *Tinsley's Magazine* and to let him have the rights of the three-volume edition. The first instalment was written under great pressure as it had to appear in the September number of the magazine, which would be on sale on 15 August. According to the *Life*, the first chapter or two were written by Hardy one evening at his lodgings at Westbourne Park after he had returned from a day's architectural work. On 7 August he left for Cornwall, taking the steam-packet boat from London Bridge to Plymouth, and giving instructions to Tinsley to send the first proofs to him, care of Emma Gifford's father at Bodmin. It is a tribute to Hardy and to the postal service of that time that the proofs reached Bodmin, were corrected, and posted back to Tinsley in time for publication on the fifteenth. Subsequently Hardy went on to St Juliot, and much of the second instalment, sent to Tinsley rather belatedly on 7 September, must have been written in Cornwall. Later in September he returned to London but, finding he could not get on with his novel, went down to the 'seclusion of Dorset to set about it more thoroughly' (*Life*, p. 91). That Dorset had the required effect is shown by an entry in his diary for 30 September: 'Posted MS. of *A Pair of Blue Eyes* to Tinsley up to Page 163.' He was working on the January instalment in December but, encouraged by Leslie Stephen's commission to write a serial for the *Cornhill*, he pushed ahead with such speed that the revised and completed three-volume edition was published in the last week of May, while the eleventh and final instalment of the serial appeared in the following month. With each of the instalments there was an illustration by a little-known artist called J. A. Pasquier. In America the serial was printed in the *Semi-Weekly New York Tribune* from 26 September to 16 December 1873, the first edition having been published by Holt & Williams in the previous July. The portion of the manuscript which has survived is in the Berg Collection of the New York Public Library.

It was a sign of Hardy's growing confidence as a novelist that *A Pair of*

Blue Eyes was the first of his books to bear his name as author. Both the manuscript and the three-volume first edition reveal that the process of revision which was to continue for almost fifty years had begun. Important factors in the writing of the novel had been the speed and pressure brought about by the conditions of serial publication, the agreement with Tinsley to write twenty pages for each instalment, and the emotional tension of his relationship with Emma whom he had now known for more than two years but was not to marry until 1874. These factors resulted in the substantial use of material drawn from his own experiences in Cornwall, in the almost certain use of passages from his unpublished novel, 'The Poor Man and the Lady', and to what Carl Weber in his *Hardy of Wessex* (1965) calls 'inartistic prolixity'. This padding is most obvious at the beginning of the serial where Hardy ponderously avoids getting on with it. The opening sentence is typical:

> Concerning the beings categorised above it may be premised that of the aim and meaning of their appearance upon the earth, of what, in its highest sense, they came into the world to do – if much, if little, or whether to be only lookers-on and to do nothing at all – no analysis will be given.

After two paragraphs of this we meet Elfride, who is reading a three-volume romance and who weakly looks at the end of the story to find that it ends tragically. Hardy omits this, a full page in all, from the first edition, not without some loss. As Michael Millgate has pointed out, there is an important preparation here for Elfride's own fate. Further omissions are made in Chapter 1 of the first edition and there are a few cuts elsewhere, but Carl Weber in referring in his *Hardy of Wessex* to 'drastic deletions' has been misled by what has happened to the first chapter as the total omissions could not possibly be called drastic. There are some corrections of style, and one interesting clarification subsequently to disappear – the year of the correspondence at the end of Chapter 2 is changed from '18–' to '1864' – but the text is basically little altered from what it had been in the serial.

The original three-volume edition of 1873 was never reprinted. In America the novel was first published by Holt & Williams in July 1873, and it was reprinted in England in 1877 by Henry S. King & Co. There were further reprintings by Sampson Low, Marston & Co. and in Macmillan's Colonial Library, and in 1895 it was published as Volume IV of the 'Wessex Novels' edition by Osgood, McIlvaine & Co. In preparing this edition Hardy is again partly motivated by a desire to delete the unnecessary, and further small omissions are made throughout. He decided, for example, that the joke about Charles the Third and Fourth in Chapter 2 went on too long and deleted several lines of it. A page, too, was cut from the over-lengthy conversation about artificiality and snobbery in Chapter

14. Once again Hardy worked his way through the novel and made stylistic changes, and there are several interesting topographical changes. Unusually, Hardy had prefaced the story with a list of the 'Names of the Persons', a kind of *dramatis personae*, and at the end of this list we are told in the serial that the 'Scene' is 'Chiefly near the coast of a western county: occasionally in London'. By 1895 this has become 'Mostly on the outskirts of Lower Wessex'. This change is typical of the 'Wessexisation' of the whole novel. The 'Stranton' of the serial and first edition becomes the more easily recognisable 'Castle Boterel', 'St Kirrs' becomes 'St Launce's'. Mr Swancourt is successively the 'vicar of the Parish' in the serial, 'the vicar of a remote country parish' in the first edition, and 'the vicar of a parish on the sea-swept outskirts of Lower Wessex' in 1895.

There can be seen, too, in the textual changes Hardy's strange, almost pedantic, preoccupation with accuracy. In Chapter 2 of the serial and first edition he describes the dog-cart as having covered 'twelve of the fourteen miles'; by 1895 this has become 'fourteen of the sixteen miles'; and by the Wessex Edition of 1912 the distance has steadied at 'thirteen of the fifteen miles'. At the end of Chapter 20 'Stranton' had to be changed to 'Camelton' (Camelford) because there never had been a station at Boscastle.

For the 1912 Wessex Edition Hardy again worked his way through the novel, changing a word or a phrase here and there, but most of these changes are slight and the total revision is substantially less than that which had occurred in the earlier revisions. A typical change is from 'Worm said groaningly to Stephen' to 'Worm groaned to Stephen'. Apart from such improvements of style there is an occasional attempt to be more accurate. Thus in Chapter 21 the bracket of quartz which saved Knight from death is no longer balanced on the verge of the precipice, but stands 'out like a tooth from the verge'.

Hardy's special interest in this novel because of its close association with his Cornish romance was manifest as early as 1877 when he wrote to a publisher, 'There are circumstances in connection with *A Pair of Blue Eyes* which make me anxious to favour it, even at the expense of profit, if I can possibly do so' (*Life*, p. 113). This special interest is responsible in part for the constant revision, slight though much of it is, and for the fact that in a letter written to Macmillan on 18 June 1919 he said, 'I am sending the corrections for the Mellstock Edition, which as you will see, are almost all in *A Pair of Blue Eyes*.' Even then he was not finished, for he made yet further revisions when the Wessex Edition of the novel was reprinted in 1920. The changes made in 1919 and 1920 are slight but interesting. Quite apart from having become aware of the ambiguity of having Knight speaking 'between his pants' in Chapter 21, he again showed his passion for accuracy by changing 'vicar' and 'vicarage' to 'rector' and 'rectory' in most of the novel.[1] The reader is now told that the parish of the destination of the traveller in Chapter 2 'seemed to lie not far inshore, and somewhere between Cam Beak and Tintagel'. The Rector's age is increased to 'past fifty' – he had been forty-two in early editions, but only about forty in the Wessex Edition of 1912 – and, perhaps most interestingly of all, Hardy adds to the description of Elfride's singing to Stephen in Chapter 3, 'Next she took "Should he upbraid", which suited her exquisitely both in voice and mien.' So anxious was the eighty-year-old Hardy to insert this that he made a cut of comparable size later on the page.

Such a textual revision by an old man thinking of the past brings us face to face with Hardy's deep emotional involvement with his story. At an early stage of revision there is evidence of an attempt to conceal this. Thus in describing Elfride in the pulpit of the church Hardy wrote in the first edition, 'Has the reader ever seen a winsome girl in a pulpit? The writer knows somebody who has, and who can never forget that sight.' By 1895 this has been deleted, presumably because it was too personal, perhaps too painful. But twenty-five years later Hardy can bear to be more personal. On 4 March 1939 the Rev. J. H. Dickinson, Rector of St Juliot from 1906 to 1925, wrote to a friend,

> Mr Hardy on both his visits talked freely about his first wife and his novel *A Pair of Blue Eyes*, and told us that the heroine of that book was indeed Miss Emma Gifford. He also said that nearly all the incidents in the story were true, as inventing fiction was too much trouble.

The textual evidence seems to provide some support for this comment.

[1] Following the discovery by Mr Suleiman Ahmad in the Dorset County Museum of further corrections in Hardy's hand, inserted in a copy of the Wessex Edition, the word 'vicar' has been changed to 'rector', and a few minor alterations have been made, in the second impression of the hardback New Wessex Edition and the third impression of the paperback.

General Preface to the Wessex Edition of 1912

IN accepting a proposal for a definite edition of these productions in prose and verse I have found an opportunity of classifying the novels under heads that show approximately the author's aim, if not his achievement, in each book of the series at the date of its composition. Sometimes the aim was lower than at other times; sometimes, where the intention was primarily high, force of circumstances (among which the chief were the necessities of magazine publication) compelled a modification, great or slight, of the original plan. Of a few, however, of the longer novels, and of many of the shorter tales, it may be assumed that they stand to-day much as they would have stood if no accidents had obstructed the channel between the writer and the public. That many of them, if any, stand as they would stand if written *now* is not to be supposed.

In the classification of these fictitious chronicles – for which the name of 'The Wessex Novels' was adopted, and is still retained – the first group is called 'Novels of Character and Environment', and contains those which approach most nearly to uninfluenced works; also one or two which, whatever their quality in some few of their episodes, may claim a verisimilitude in general treatment and detail.

The second group is distinguished as 'Romances and Fantasies', a sufficiently descriptive definition. The third class – 'Novels of Ingenuity' – show a not infrequent disregard of the probable in the chain of events, and depend for their interest mainly on the incidents themselves. They might also be characterised as 'Experiments', and were written for the nonce simply; though despite the artificiality of their fable some of their scenes are not without fidelity to life.[1]

It will not be supposed that these differences are distinctly perceptible in

[1] Novels of Character and Environment: *Tess of the d'Urbervilles, Far from the Madding Crowd, Jude the Obscure, The Return of the Native, The Mayor of Casterbridge, The Woodlanders, Under the Greenwood Tree, Life's Little Ironies and A Few Crusted Characters, Wessex Tales.*

Romances and Fantasies: *A Pair of Blue Eyes, The Trumpet-Major, Two on a Tower, The Well-Beloved, A Group of Noble Dames.*

Novels of Ingenuity: *Desperate Remedies, The Hand of Ethelberta, A Laodicean.* [General Editor's note]

every page of every volume. It was inevitable that blendings and alternations should occur in all. Moreover, as it was not thought desirable in every instance to change the arrangement of the shorter stories to which readers have grown accustomed, certain of these may be found under headings to which an acute judgment might deny appropriateness.

It has sometimes been conceived of novels that evolve their action on a circumscribed scene – as do many (though not all) of these – that they cannot be so inclusive in their exhibition of human nature as novels wherein the scenes cover large extents of country, in which events figure amid towns and cities, even wander over the four quarters of the globe. I am not concerned to argue this point further than to suggest that the conception is an untrue one in respect of the elementary passions. But I would state that the geographical limits of the stage here trodden were not absolutely forced upon the writer by circumstances; he forced them upon himself from judgment. I considered that our magnificent heritage from the Greeks in dramatic literature found sufficient room for a large proportion of its action in an extent of their country not much larger than the half-dozen counties here reunited under the old name of Wessex, that the domestic emotions have throbbed in Wessex nooks with as much intensity as in the palaces of Europe, and that, anyhow, there was quite enough human nature in Wessex for one man's literary purpose. So far was I possessed by this idea that I kept within the frontiers when it would have been easier to overleap them and give more cosmopolitan features to the narrative.

Thus, though the people in most of the novels (and in much of the shorter verse) are dwellers in a province bounded on the north by the Thames, on the south by the English Channel, on the east by a line running from Hayling Island to Windsor Forest, and on the west by the Cornish coast, they were meant to be typically and essentially those of any and every place where

> Thought's the slave of life, and life time's fool

– beings in whose hearts and minds that which is apparently local should be really universal.

But whatever the success of this intention, and the value of these novels as delineations of humanity, they have at least a humble supplementary quality of which I may be justified in reminding the reader, though it is one that was quite unintentional and unforeseen. At the dates represented in the various narrations things were like that in Wessex: the inhabitants lived in certain ways, engaged in certain occupations, kept alive certain customs, just as they are shown doing in these pages. And in particularizing such I have often been reminded of Boswell's remarks on the trouble to which he was put and the pilgrimages he was obliged to make to authenticate some detail, though the labour was one which would bring him no praise. Unlike his achievement, however, on which an error would as he says have brought discredit, if these country customs and vocations, obsolete and obsolescent, had been detailed wrongly, nobody would have discovered such errors to the end of Time. Yet I have instituted inquiries to correct tricks of memory, and striven against temptations to exaggerate, in order to preserve for my own satisfaction a fairly true record of a vanishing life.

It is advisable also to state here, in response to inquiries from readers interested in landscape, prehistoric antiquities, and especially old English architecture, that the description of these backgrounds has been done from the real – that is to say, has something real for its basis, however illusively treated. Many features of the first two kinds have been given under their existing names; for instance, the Vale of Blackmoor or Blakemore, Hambledon Hill, Bulbarrow, Nettlecombe Tout, Dogbury Hill, High-Stoy, Bubb-Down Hill, The Devil's Kitchen, Cross-in-Hand, Long-Ash Lane, Benvill Lane, Giant's Hill, Crimmercrock Lane, and Stonehenge. The rivers Froom, or Frome, and Stour, are, of course, well known as such. And the further idea was that large towns and points tending to mark the outline of Wessex – such as Bath, Plymouth, The Start, Portland Bill, Southampton, etc. – should be named clearly. The scheme was not greatly elaborated, but, whatever its value, the names remain still.

In respect of places described under fictitious or ancient names in the novels – for reasons that seemed good at the time of writing them – and kept up in the poems – discerning people have affirmed in print that they clearly recognise the originals: such as Shaftesbury in 'Shaston', Sturminster Newton in 'Stourcastle', Dorchester in 'Casterbridge', Salisbury Plain in 'The Great Plain', Cranborne Chase in 'The Chase', Beaminster in 'Emminster', Bere Regis in 'Kingsbere', Woodbury Hill in 'Greenhill', Wool Bridge in 'Wellbridge', Harfoot or Harput Lane in 'Stagfoot Lane', Hazlebury in 'Nuttlebury', Bridport in 'Port Bredy', Maiden Newton in 'Chalk Newton', a farm near Nettlecombe Tout in 'Flintcomb-Ash', Sherborne in 'Sherton Abbas', Milton Abbey in 'Middleton Abbey', Cerne Abbas in 'Abbot's Cernel', Evershot in 'Evershed', Taunton in 'Toneborough', Bournemouth in 'Sandbourne', Winchester in 'Wintoncester', Oxford in 'Christminster', Reading in 'Aldbrickham', Newbury in 'Kennetbridge', Wantage in 'Alfredston', Basingstoke in 'Stoke Barehills', and so on. Subject to the qualifications above given, that no detail is guaranteed – that the portraiture of fictitiously named towns and villages was only suggested by certain real places, and wantonly wanders from inventorial descriptions of them – I do not contradict these keen hunters for the real; I am satisfied with their statements as at least an indication of their interest in the scenes.

*

Thus much for the novels. Turning now to the verse – to myself the more individual part of my literary fruitage – I would say that, unlike some of the fiction, nothing interfered with the writer's freedom in respect of its form or content. Several of the poems – indeed many – were produced before novel-writing had been thought of as a pursuit; but few saw the light till all the novels had been published. The limited stage to which the majority of the latter confine their exhibitions has not been adhered to here in the same proportion, the dramatic part especially having a very broad theatre of action. It may thus relieve the circumscribed areas treated in the prose, if such relief be needed. To be sure, one might argue that by surveying Europe from a celestial point of vision – as in *The Dynasts* – that continent becomes virtually a province – a Wessex, an Attica, even a mere garden – and hence is made to conform to the principle of the novels, however far it outmeasures their region. But that may be as it will.

The few volumes filled by the verse cover a producing period of some eighteen years first and last, while the seventeen or more volumes of novels represent correspondingly about four-and-twenty years. One is reminded by this disproportion in time and result how much more concise and quintessential expression becomes when given in rhythmic form than when shaped in the language of prose.

One word on what has been called the present writer's philosophy of life, as exhibited more particularly in this metrical section of his compositions. Positive views on the Whence and the Wherefore of things have never been advanced by this pen as a consistent philosophy. Nor is it likely, indeed, that imaginative writings extending over more than forty years would exhibit a coherent scientific theory of the universe even if it had been attempted – of that universe concerning which Spencer owns to the 'paralyzing thought' that possibly there exists no comprehension of it anywhere. But such objectless consistency never has been attempted, and the sentiments in the following pages have been stated truly to be mere impressions of the moment, and not convictions or arguments.

That these impressions have been condemned as 'pessimistic' – as if that were a very wicked adjective – shows a curious muddle-mindedness. It must be obvious that there is a higher characteristic of philosophy than pessimism, or than meliorism, or even than the optimism of these critics – which is truth. Existence is either ordered in a certain way, or it is not so ordered, and conjectures which harmonize best with experience are removed above all comparison with other conjectures which do not so harmonize. So that to say one view is worse than other views without proving it erroneous implies the possibility of a false view being better or more expedient than a true view; and no pragmatic proppings can make that *idolum specus* stand on its feet, for it postulates a prescience denied to humanity.

And there is another consideration. Differing natures find their tongue in the presence of differing spectacles. Some natures become vocal at tragedy, some are made vocal by comedy, and it seems to me that to whichever of these aspects of life a writer's instinct for expression the more readily responds, to that he should allow it to respond. That before a contrasting side of things he remains undemonstrative need not be assumed to mean that he remains unperceiving.

It was my hope to add to these volumes of verse as many more as would make a fairly comprehensive cycle of the whole. I had wished that those in dramatic, ballad, and narrative form should include most of the cardinal situations which occur in social and public life, and those in lyric form a round of emotional experiences of some completeness. But

The petty done, the undone vast!

The more written the more seems to remain to be written; and the night cometh. I realize that these hopes and plans, except possibly to the extent of a volume or two, must remain unfulfilled.

October 1911 T.H.

Glossary of Place-names

CAMELTON. Camelford.

CASTLE BOTEREL. Boscastle, once Chastelboteral.

CLIFF WITHOUT A NAME. Beeny Cliff and adjoining High Cliff on the north Cornish coast.

DUNDAGEL. Tintagel.

ENDELSTOW, EAST. According to Denys Kay-Robinson's *Hardy's Wessex Re-appraised* (1972), this is based on the tiny village of Lesnewth.

ENDELSTOW, WEST. Based on St Juliot, whose landscape, however, has been altered to make the parish open to the sea. St Juliot is about a mile to the east of Boscastle.

ENDELSTOW HOUSE. Based mainly on Lanhydroc House, near Bodmin.

EXONBURY. Exeter.

PARRETT DOWN. Tresparrett, near St Juliot.

ST CLEATHER. St Clether, Cornwall.

ST LAUNCE'S. Launceston.

STRATLEIGH. Bude, the name itself being taken from Stratton.

TARGAN BAY. Pentargon Bay.

VALLEY, THE. Vallency Valley.

WINDY BEAK. High Cliff.